FRANCO'S PIRATES

Naval Aspects of the Spanish Civil War 1936–39

By

E. R. HOOTON

CASEMATE

Pennsylvania & Yorkshire

Published in the United States of America and Great Britain in 2024 by
CASEMATE PUBLISHERS
1950 Lawrence Road, Havertown, PA 19083, USA
and
47 Church Street, Barnsley, S70 2AS, UK

Hardcover Edition: ISBN 978-1-63624-275-0
Digital Edition: ISBN 978-1-63624-276-7

A CIP record for this book is available from the British Library

Printed and bound in the United Kingdom by CPI Group (UK) Ltd, Croydon, CR0 4YY
Typeset in India by DiTech Publishing Services

For a complete list of Casemate titles, please contact:

CASEMATE PUBLISHERS (US)
Telephone (610) 853-9131
Fax (610) 853-9146
Email: casemate@casematepublishers.com
www.casematepublishers.com

CASEMATE PUBLISHERS (UK)
Telephone (0)1226 734350
Email: casemate@casemateuk.com
www.casemateuk.com

Cover image: Arxiu fotogràfic. Museu Marítim de Barcelona

Contents

List of Maps		iv
Preface		xv
Table of Comparative Naval Ranks		xix
1	The Faded Armada: The Background to September 1936	1
2	The Widening War: October 1936–July 1937	37
3	The Northern Blockade, August 1936–October 1937	77
4	They Called it Piracy! August 1937–February 1938	111
5	Bats, Boots and Hawks: March 1938–April 1939	149
6	The Flotsam of History	177
Appendix		186
Endnotes		191
Bibliography		221
Index		231

Maps

1 Spain and the Iberian Peninsula   v
2 The Strait of Gibraltar   vi
3 The Western Mediterranean   vii
4 The Bay of Biscay   viii
5 The Northern Coast   ix
6 The Central Mediterranean   x
7 The Aegean   xi
8 Situation, August 1, 1936   xii
9 Situation, March 31, 1937   xiii
10 Situation, July 25, 1938   xiv

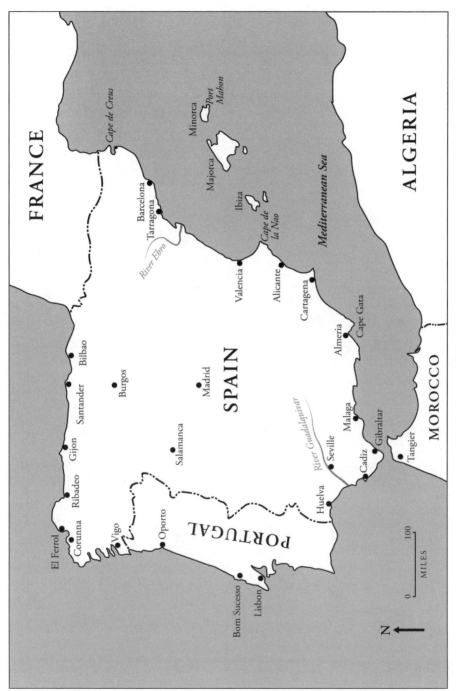

Map 1. Spain and the Iberian Peninsula

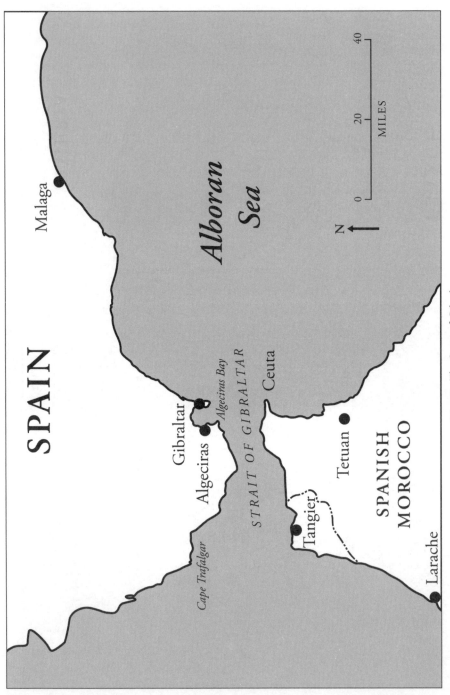

Map 2. The Strait of Gibraltar

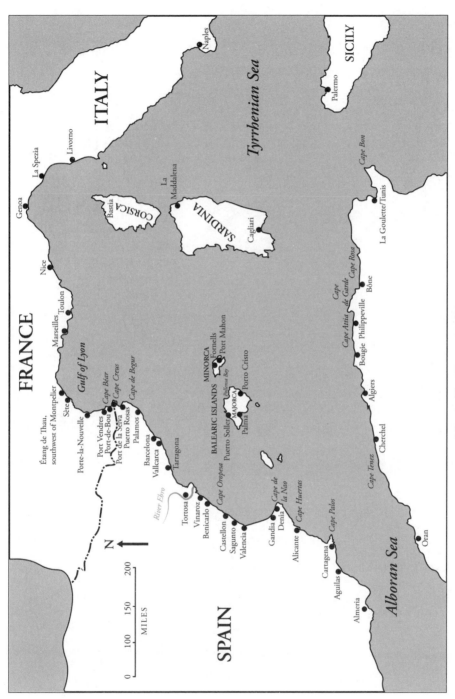

Map 3. The Western Mediterranean

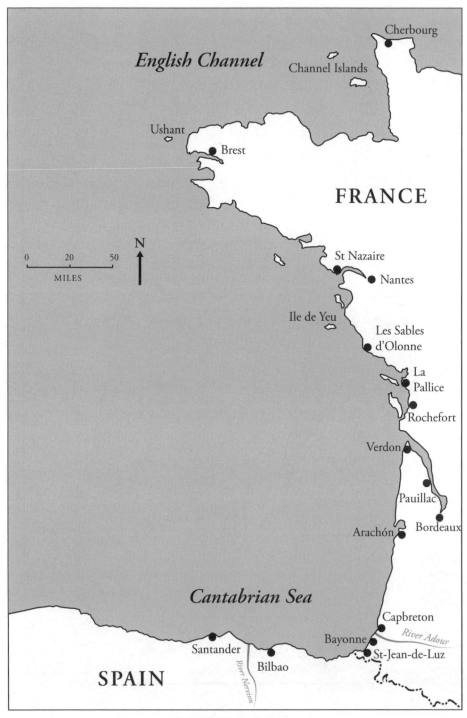

Map 4. The Bay of Biscay

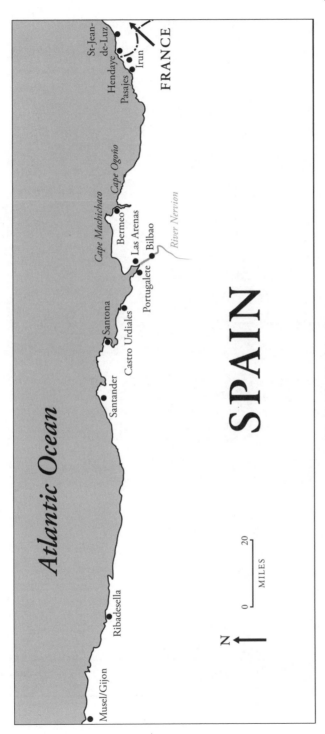

Map 5. The Northern Coast

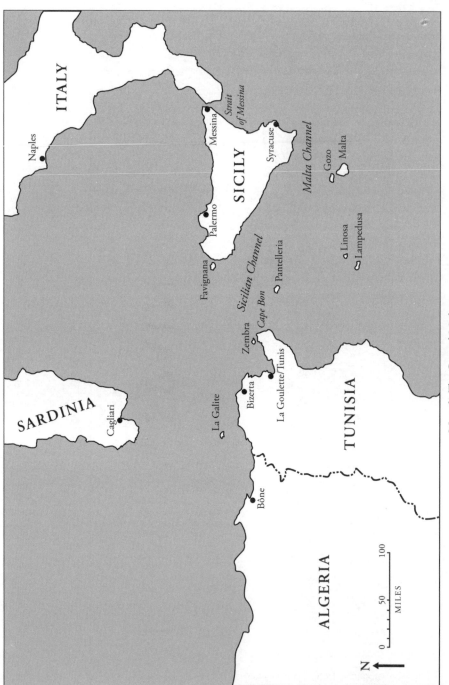

Map 6. The Central Mediterranean

Map 7. The Aegean

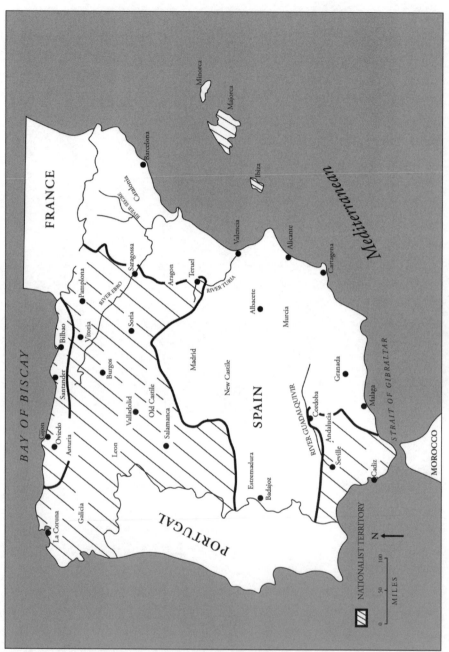

Map 8. Situation, August 1, 1936

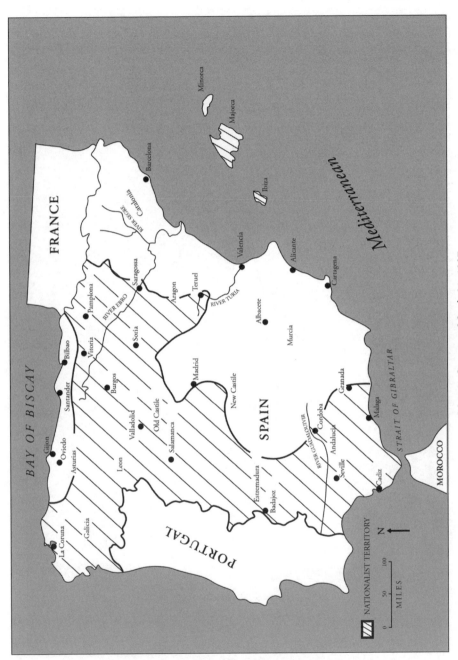

Map 9. Situation, March 31, 1937

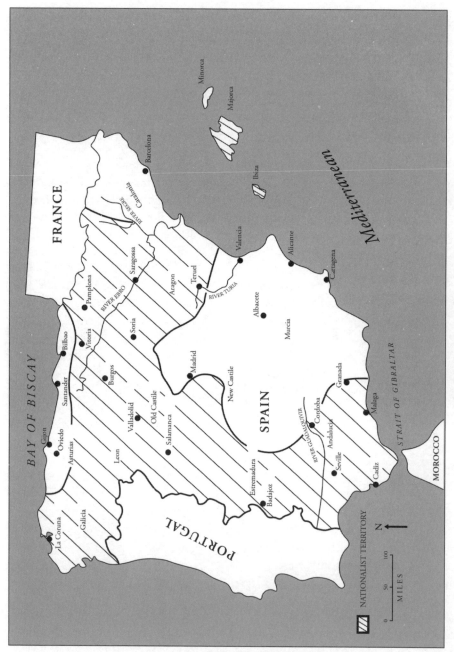

Map 10. Situation, July 25, 1938

Preface

The Spanish Civil War was won and lost at sea. This statement may spark protest from many Spaniards, who will argue that victory for the Nationalist cause was achieved on land, but if war is applied logistics, then the statement holds true.

The Nationalist cause was underpinned by a reliable flow of arms, munitions, and equipment from Germany and especially Italy, while the Republic's supply line to the Soviet Union was under constant threat; indeed, this was the reason that Moscow quickly ceased sending military aid in its own ships. Contemporary accounts of the Spanish Civil War, which became accepted historical fact until the late 1980s, held that the victory of General Francisco Franco y Bahamonde was due to a combination of foreign (largely Italian) troops and a cornucopia of Fascist arms. Franco certainly had foreign troops at his command, but, as my book *Spain in Arms* demonstrated, it was, as the song says, a case of "It ain't what you do, it's the way that you do it." Spanish troops directed by Spanish leaders were the foundation of Franco's success, the foreign forces merely a useful bonus.

The Civil War at sea was overshadowed by the land conflict, but the Spanish element was a more low-profile struggle. In part this was due to the Nationalist Navy's shortage of resources, although dynamic operations proved a valuable compensation, in marked contrast to the relatively passive strategy of the much larger Republican fleet. Admittedly, this has been exaggerated, for that fleet did conduct sweeps in an attempt to secure the Republic's communications, but it tended to restrict operations to the proximity of the Spanish coast. In part this was because its political masters were all too conscious that a clash, especially with the Italian fleet, would provide Italy's blustering leader, Benito Mussolini, with an excuse overtly to intervene in a conflict where his more limited participation was the world's worst-kept secret. Indeed, his naval and air support for Franco's maritime struggle were vital for the Nationalist success in the war.

While the operations of the opposing naval forces attracted little attention, the attacks upon foreign navies and merchant shipping led to front-page headlines. Originally made by both sides in error, for the Nationalists they became increasingly deliberate, causing the loss of many men and ships as they sought to control maritime trade to the Republic. With Italy's ill-concealed participation, and often leadership, this caused a major source of friction between London and Rome. The friction was aggravated by the Italian Navy's brutality as its destroyers openly sank ships before sailing away and abandoning men, as well as women and boys, to their fate. Little wonder it was called piracy, and for this reason—and also because of the Nationalist policy of seizing cargoes almost on a whim—I have chosen to call this book *Franco's Pirates*.

These attacks, together with those by submarines and aircraft, aroused great public indignation in Europe and especially Great Britain. Nevertheless, public opinion seemed to yearn for a return to the Victorian world of assertive and militaristic nationalism at a time when such methods seemed to be increasingly rejected in the popular postwar mood. Demands for naval action echoing the familiar Imperial cry of "send a gunboat" increased as two of the world's leading naval powers seemed to accept this piracy. The French and British navies generally succeeded in ensuring their merchantmen sailed unimpeded, especially off Spain's northern coast, and when attacked they did not hesitate to fire back. But they were also constrained by diplomacy, which limited their actions to the high seas, where their ability to intervene was hindered by international law.

For the Royal Navy especially, the British public's postwar mood was a drag anchor. Horrified by the brutality and bloodshed of the Great War of 1914–18, which seemed to dash all the values of 19th-century civilization, voters reacted with a profound repugnance against military action between "civilized" nations, underlined by the creation of the League of Nations to resolve international disputes. This in turn helped to drive naval disarmament, which severely restricted the Royal Navy's ability to react to crises even as hopes of universal peace slowly faded from the 1930s with the growing assertiveness of what were called the Fascist powers, led by Japan's actions in China. For London, these actions threatened the British Empire east of Suez. They also required a task-force-in-being based upon the Mediterranean Fleet, ready to ride to the rescue, but maintaining the necessary forces weakened the Royal Navy's worldwide presence after politicians delayed rearmament.

The problem became more acute with Germany under Adolf Hitler. He was the straw which broke the back of the Royal Navy's resolve and left it determined to avoid anything which might provoke a debilitating conflict with Italy, although the Admiralty was confident of ultimate victory against the Italian fleet. The French Navy also remained confident of success against Italy, but Paris regarded the German threat more seriously, so French politicians too were anxious to avoid a war with Italy. The political masters of both navies were also aware that Italy increasingly felt itself to be Germany's junior partner, seeking to exploit this and drive a wedge between the European Fascist powers, while Mussolini in turn tried to divide London and Paris.

Ultimately, the Anglo-French political strategy was undermined by Italy's determination to see Spain under a friendly government and its willingness to achieve this goal by using naval and air assets almost without restriction. This posed dilemmas for the British and French navies, with an extra complication being their mutual dislike for the Republican Navy, largely due to mutinies which saw so many officers—many known to their foreign colleagues—executed or murdered. Consequently, the Admiralty ignored the actions of a Spanish destroyer which aided the mined HMS *Hunter*, while the Royal Navy would aid the crews of German seaplanes hunting British merchantmen when they were forced to land.

When I came to write this book, my intention was to focus upon the struggle between the two Spanish navies, but I quickly discovered that the writings of Michael Alpert and my late friend Adrian English had pre-empted my efforts, and the multi-volume works of Admirals Fernando and Salvador Moreno de Alborán y de Reyna made such a study redundant. While highlighting key Spanish naval activities, I decided instead to focus upon the largely neglected activities of the Spanish and foreign merchant marines, which in turn meant looking at foreign naval activity. In this respect at least, I believe this is the first attempt in English at a multinational approach to this important and long-neglected aspect of the Spanish Civil War, whose land struggle I have described in my earlier work, *Spain in Arms*, also by Casemate.

While sketching out the activities of the Spanish fleets, I have tried to focus upon Nationalist decisionmaking with regard to the blockade and the activities of both sides against foreign navies and merchant marines, as well as their reactions. Reviewers of my earlier book have rightly criticized the absence of socio-economic background to the Spanish Civil War, but I would argue this is ground well-ploughed by better historians, so I have again neglected this aspect, apart from its implications upon the Spanish Navy. Similarly, I have taken a more superficial look at political and diplomatic activities, sketching out only those with a direct application to the main themes of the Civil War's impact upon foreign navies and merchant marines.

As with *Spain in Arms*, my study is based upon numerous published works, themselves the result of thousands of hours in British, French, German, Italian, Soviet, and Spanish archives, although I have used some British archive material myself, including intercepted Italian communications. Some will question this reliance upon published sources, but since they are based upon well-mined archives, the author sees no reason to reinvent the wheel, especially as many foreign writers on the subject have followed this precedent in their accounts of the conflict. I would like to pay tribute to three English-language writers. Firstly, the late American historian Professor Willard C. Franks, whose articles are a valuable insight into various naval aspects. Also British historian Admiral Sir Peter Gretton, whose book *The Forgotten Factor* pre-dates my work, yet I was able to read it in English only in manuscript form in the Caird Library, for I can find no evidence of any edition published in the United Kingdom. It is more commonly available in the Spanish version, which appears to be a slight reworking and is widely available as *El Factor Olvidado*. The third is Welsh maritime historian Paul Heaton, whose monographs on blockade runners, Welsh blockade runners, the Abbey Line, and Jack Billmeir are essential reading on the subject of the Spanish Civil War's impact upon the British merchant marine. I would also like to pay tribute to the late Spanish historian Rafael González Echegaray for his comprehensive work on the Spanish merchant marine during the Civil War. Purists may be unhappy with Spanish place names which I have Anglicized: Cataluña becomes Catalonia, Cádiz becomes Cadiz, and Mallorca becomes Majorca. However, I have tried—very hard—to provide Spanish names as they are written.

Much of my research was in libraries, and I have the great pleasure of acknowledging with great thanks the kindness and assistance of the staff of the British Library, especially during the height of the Covid pestilence, the Bodleian Library, the Caird Library at Royal Museums Greenwich, the Guildhall Library in London, and the National Aerospace Library, Farnborough. One of the joys of a preface is acknowledging the assistance I have received in writing this work, although all errors of fact and interpretation are mine alone. I would like to express my particular thanks to Tracey Mills and Ruth Sheppard from Casemate Publishers, but also the following: George Beale; Luigino Caliaro; Lieutenant Colonel Richard Cole-Mackintosh, Chief Executive Officer of The Worshipful Company of Shipwrights; Mark Cordell and Rachel Gill of the Tyne & Wear Archives; Jørgen Dieckmann Rasmussen, head of the City of Esbjerg's archives; Andres Eero (Curator-Collection Manager) and Valdur Ohmann (Chief Specialist-researcher, Office of Research and Publication) of the Estonian Maritime Museum; Ms Marja Goud, Chief Librarian, Het Scheepvaartmuseum, Amsterdam; Robert Forsyth; Will Fowler; Professor Jennifer Foray; Dr Norman Friedmann; Jordi García García Servei d'Informació del Museu Marítim de Barcelona; Marian Gray; Sara Hammond; Jannik Hartrup, Curator, Maritime Museum of Denmark; Svein Aage Knudsen; Dr Sarah Lonsdale; Craig MacLean; Gordon Martin, Regional Organizer, RMT; Bård G. Økland and Gry Bang-Andersen at Bergen Maritime Museum; Dr Matthew Potter, Curator, Limerick Museum; Nederlands Instituut voor Militaire Historie (NIMH); Jon Ruigómez Matxin, Director of the Irsas Museum, Bilbao; Captain B. J. Roberts, Chairman of the HMS Hood Association, and Mr William Sutherland; Juan Carlos Selgado Rodríguez; Dr Joshua M. Smith, Director, American Merchant Marine Museum; Brian Reynolds, Chairman of the RMT Glasgow Shipping Branch; Kaja Rosenqvist, Photo Archivist, Norwegian Maritime Museum; and Thanasis D. Sfikas.

Comparative Naval Ranks

Great Britain	France	United States	Spain	Italy	Germany	Russia
Admiral of the Fleet		Fleet Admiral	Capitán General	Grande ammiraglio*	Gross Admiral	
Admiral	Amiral	Admiral	Almirante General	Ammiraglio / Ammiraglio d'armata*	Admiral/ Generaladmiral	Flagman 1-go ranga
Vice-Admiral	Vice-Amiral/Vice-Amiral de Escadre	Vice-Admiral	Vice-Almirante	Vice-ammiraglio / Ammiraglio di Squadra*	Vize-Admiral	Flagman flota 2-go ranga
—		—	—	Ammiraglio designato d'armata*		Flagman 1-go ranga
Rear Admiral	Contre-Amiral	Rear Admiral	Contra Almirante	Contrammiraglio / Ammiraglio di Divisione*	Konter-Admiral	Flagman 2-go ranga
Commodore		—	—	Sotto Ammiraglio / Contrammiraglio*		Kapitan 1-ro Ranga
Captain	Capitaine de Vaisseau	Captain	Capitán de Navio	Capitano di Vascello	Kapitän zur See	Kapitan 2-ro Ranga
Commander	Capitaine de Frégat	Commander	Capitán de Fragata	Capitano di Fregata	Fregettankapitän	Kapitan 3-ro Ranga
Lieutenant Commander	Capitaine de Corvette	Lieutenant Commander	Capitán de Corbeta	Capitano di Corvetta	Korvettenkapitän	Kapitan-Leytenant
Lieutenant (Senior)	Lieutenant de Vaisseau	Lieutenant	Teniente de Navio	Tenente di Vascello	Kapitänleutnant	Leytenant
Lieutenant (Junior)	Enseigne	Lieutenant (Junior)			Oberleutnant zur See	
Sub-Lieutenant	Enseigne 2 Classe		Alférez de Navio	Sottotenente di Vascello	Leutnant zur See	Mladshii Leytenant
Midshipman	Aspirant			Guardamarine		

*Ranks introduced in 1938

CHAPTER ONE

The Faded Armada:
The Background to September 1936

"You may fire when you are ready, Gridley." Commodore George Dewey's famous instruction to Captain Charles V. Gridley, commander of the cruiser USS *Olympia* in Manila Bay on May 1, 1898, heralded the final humiliation of Spanish naval power and helped lay the foundations for the Spanish Civil War.

From the 16th to the 19th centuries, Spain's colonial empire in the Caribbean, Latin America, and the Philippines stimulated its navy and led to the first steam-powered warship in 1592. Even at the beginning of the 19th century, Madrid commanded the world's third-largest navy, but the Napoleonic Wars concluded with the Royal Navy supreme and shortly afterwards Spain lost its American territories. Their loss, and limited industrialization, saw the rapid decline of the Spanish Navy, underlined in 1898 when Spain clashed with the United States, a minnow compared with many European naval powers and one which 30 years earlier had a largely riverine and coastal force. Dewey easily destroyed Admiral Patricio Montojo y Pasarón's Pacific Squadron in Manila, and two months later, Admiral Pascual Cervera y Topete's Caribbean Squadron was annihilated outside Santiago de Cuba by Rear Admiral William T. Sampson and Commodore Winfield S. Schley, leading to the loss of Spain's Pacific and Caribbean colonies.[1]

Rebuilding a Navy

Only in January 1907 was the keel of a new Spanish Navy laid, but one restricted to coast defense and securing the sea-lanes to the Balearics, the Canaries, and African territories, notably Morocco.[2] It was based upon three small dreadnoughts of the España class (15,700 tonnes displacement), at a time when the Royal Navy's dreadnoughts were 20,000–27,500 tons armed with 12-inch to 15-inch guns. In displacement and main armament, the Españas were similar to the German Deutschland-class "Armoured Ships" (*Panzerschiffe*), usually called pocket battleships. The Spanish vessels reflected their limited endurance, but larger ships could not be built because financial stringency restricted the expansion of base facilities, such as dry docks, to support them.

The programs slipped by years because they depended upon foreign machinery, armor plate, and guns whose supply was disrupted by the Great War, the last *España* being completed in 1921. Naval modernization and expansion accelerated following the 1923 coup of General Miguel Primo de Rivera y Orbaneja, with authorization for Canarias-class heavy cruisers and four Júpiter-class minelayers, improvements to naval bases, and the creation of a naval aviation service. But funding prioritized the protracted Rif War in Morocco, which was not successfully concluded until 1926, leaving little money for the navy. Its most significant activity during this war was supporting the key landing at Alhucemas, near Fez, in September 1925 under General José Sanjurjo Sacanell, whose forces included a brigade under Colonel Francisco Franco y Bahamonde. The battleship *Alfonso XIII* (later the second *España*) was used as a floating command center and there was air support from the seaplane carrier *Dédalo*, while troops were landed in former British X-Lighters used at Gallipoli in 1915, now designated K-Boats or Black Beatles.[3]

By the outbreak of the Civil War in July 1936, the Spanish Navy had a pair of battleships (one decommissioned), five light cruisers (one decommissioned), and a dozen destroyers. Naval construction was the monopoly of the Sociedad Espanola de Construccion Naval (SECN), 40 percent of which was owned by the British John Brown shipyard and Vickers-Armstrong, who provided expertise with ships based upon British designs.[4] The cruisers and destroyers all had Parsons turbines, Yarrow boilers, and Vickers main armament, although some were manufactured under license, but the coastal submarines were Holland types designed by the American Electric Boat yard.[5] The Spanish Navy did consider a sea-going boat, *E-1*, designed by Ingenieurskaantor von Scheepsbouw (IvS), a Dutch front company for German designers and shipyards, but built in Cadiz. However, it proved too expensive and was sold to Turkey as the *Gür* following a favorable report by Great War U-boat ace Arnauld de la Perrière. The design would evolve into the German Type VIIA, which served during the Spanish Civil War, and the Type VIIC, which would spearhead the German operations during the Battle of the Atlantic.[6]

The Republic and the Navy

Neither Primo de Rivera nor the Republic which replaced him in 1931 could resolve the country's profound economic and social problems. The navy's woes increased because the Republic was born during the Depression and dominated by politicians who had little interest in naval matters. The Republican supporter, airman Ramón Franco Bahamonde, brother of Francisco Franco, reflected a common view among these politicians when he commented: "Our little colonies don't need a strong navy made up of large and numerous units. The policing of our harbours, the implementing of fishery laws and the prevention of smuggling are nowadays the only missions that our Navy has to do."[7] The Republic removed monarchist symbols and renamed several ships, which undermined support among officers who, like in many European navies, had strong links with the monarchy, but the Republic, like Queen Elizabeth I, had no desire to make windows into men's souls and was willing to allow monarchist officers to serve.[8]

From 1931–36, the political pendulum swung back and forth as the increasingly polarized electorate desperately sought a solution to the national ills. Liberals and the Left reduced officers' social perks, while promotion was based upon merit, rather than seniority, and conscription was reduced to a year. Sailors' conditions were improved by extending Saturday shore-leave, in an attempt to remove sources of friction and improve efficiency. Maintenance was so neglected that one of the four turrets in the *España* became unserviceable, while refits were delayed or prolonged. Although irritated, the officers were too busy to commence plotting against the government, unlike their more politicized khaki-clad colleagues, but then the army had a surplus of under-employed officers to demonstrate that the Devil makes work for idle hands.

Yet the social tensions within Spanish society were echoed within the navy. Naval college graduates have broad horizons which, for the select few, can lead to supreme command. In the Spanish Navy, these officers of the General Corps (*Cuerpo General*) were often of aristocratic or upper middle-class backgrounds. Their social lives were more glamorous than their army colleagues, for as members of yacht clubs they enjoyed a whirl of regattas, dinners, and balls, while ships held receptions for local dignitaries. In all navies, the technicians—electrical and mechanical engineers and signallers—tend to swim in a goldfish bowl, with promotion within their own specialities, but in Spain there was a further problem because most of the 680 specialists came from lower middle-class or proletarian backgrounds and were usually warrant officers denied commissions as officers. The General Corps officers had no respect for their expertise, and a senior petty officer could be beached on lower pay, or even dismissed from the service, on the word of "a beardless midshipman."[9] A commission headed by Captain Francisco Moreno Fernández vainly attempted to pull the thorn from the body naval, but despite the Republic's token gestures to improve the warrant officers' status, they still resented the General Corps who, in turn, regarded the specialists as Bolsheviks and potential mutineers. The concern was understandable, for there had been seven major mutinies world-wide during the century, but in Spanish ships there were few revolutionary cells, although warrant officers began to monitor the wardroom's loyalty and noted suspicious meetings and indiscrete talk.

By 1936, army officers led by Sanjurjo, with Brigadier Generals Emilio Mola y Vidal and Franco, finalized plans for a coup d'état following another electoral swing towards the Liberal Left. The plotters largely ignored the navy; indeed, the Naval Chief of Staff, Vice-Admiral Francisco Javier de Salas González, was apparently unaware of the plot, although its senior ranks were known to be sympathetic to the uprising's aims. While Mola had earlier specified the need "to seek the support of the navy and even its collaboration where necessary," the first contact was apparently only in March 1936 during a festival in Valencia.[10] Naval officers participating included Captain Moreno, now commanding the cruisers *Canarias* and *Baleares* fitting out in El Ferrol, and his unemployed brother, Commander Salvador Moreno Fernández, but the army plotters were interested only in securing naval bases. They sought benevolent neutrality from the fleet, and their naval colleagues assured them there would be no problem with the crews.[11]

Rising and Mutiny

On July 15, Mola sent a coded radio message calling for the uprising to begin in Morocco on July 18 and in the remainder of Spain the following day. The Moroccan and Canary Islands elements went off like clockwork, but on the mainland the uprising exploded like a string of firecrackers rather than a simultaneous explosion, allowing the rebels to be overwhelmed piecemeal after Sanjurjo died in an air crash. By July 20, the rebels under Mola had most of northern and western Spain, a coastal toehold at Seville and Cadiz, and Majorca. Meanwhile, the government nominally controlled the remainder, together with Minorca, although power quickly fell into the hands of left-wing committees, while their separatist allies held an enclave along the Biscay coast, including Gijon, Santander, and Bilbao.

Franco assumed command of the Army of Africa, after embarking his wife and daughter in the German steamer *Waldi*, which took them to Lisbon. His manifesto was broadcast on July 18, promising a new order, and was picked up by Spanish warships. Within the naval bases there was fierce fighting, especially at El Ferrol and Cadiz, where loyal crews fought from docked warships until crushed, many being executed. At Cartagena, Barcelona, and Port Mahon, however, the rebels were defeated as the Spanish Navy took center stage for the first time in decades.[12]

Warrant officers, 80 percent of whom supported the Republic, controlled the naval radio system. Their earlier warnings led the government to take precautionary measures before the uprising by dismissing some commanding officers, but at the beginning of July, the navy was still conducting routine operations. Indeed, President Manuel Azaña y Díaz was scheduled to visit Santander to inspect the battleship *Jaime I*.

Madrid now dispatched a task force consisting of the *Jaime I*, the cruisers *Libertad* and *Miguel de Cervantes*, and four destroyers into the Strait of Gibraltar (hereafter the Strait). The commanders of two destroyers sailed into Melilla to meet rebel leaders, but when they called on their crews to support the uprising, they were arrested and the ships returned to Cartagena. A third destroyer escorted two freighters with 2,685 troops from Morocco to Cadiz before the crew also arrested their officers. On July 19, the crews of the *Libertad* and *Cervantes* rose against their officers, including Admiral Miguel de Meir y del Rio, flying his flag as commander of the Heavy Squadron (*Escuadra*) in the latter vessel. Until now there had been little bloodshed at sea. On July 21, however, officers in the *Jaime I* tried to take over the ship, whose commander, Captain Joaquín García del Valle, was loyal, but the crew resisted with small arms from the armory and two officers were killed. When the crew asked what was to be done with their bodies, Madrid replied: "Lower the bodies into the sea with sober respect."

The Republic retained the bulk of the fleet, a battleship, three light cruisers, 11 destroyers (three under repair), and all the submarines, although the situation remained fluid in the weeks after the uprising. The cruiser *Méndez Núñez*, which was off West Africa when the war broke out, was ordered home on July 21 after the rebels took Equatorial Guinea, the crew ensuring this order was obeyed. When she refuelled at the French naval base of Dakar, however, two officers dived over the side.[13] The rebels, who soon called themselves Nationalists, had the remainder of the fleet—although the cruisers *Almirante Cervera* and *Républica* were in dry dock, the latter requiring a major refit—and some small surface combatants and Coast Guard cutters. Like their foes, they augmented these forces with fishing vessels equipped with a 3-inch (76mm) gun or similar caliber to create auxiliary patrol boats, which the U.S. Navy quaintly referred to as picquet boats, including eight, largely Vigo-registered, trawlers released from Algeciras Bay after mooring fees were paid.[14] The Republic could expand their fleet by completing seven destroyers and a submarine, while the rebels had valuable assets in the Canarias-class cruisers and Júpiter-class minelayers fitting out in El Ferrol. Most of the naval air force also remained in Republican hands, with a nominal 68 combat aircraft, while 15 seaplanes were in Nationalist hands.[15]

But El Ferrol was the navy's best-equipped base, including a dry dock which could accommodate the largest Spanish warships, unlike the Republican bases at Cartagena and Port Mahon in Minorca. The former's dry dock was suitable only for destroyers, the inner basin so restricted that ships were packed in like sardines, making them vulnerable to air attack, while there were no antisubmarine defenses for the outer harbor. Both navies faced manning problems, for of the 22,017 members of the pre-war Spanish Navy, more than half (12,383) were in Nationalist territory, leaving the Republic with only 9,600.

Most of the Republican vessels were under very junior officers, usually lieutenants or sub-lieutenants, with the *Jaime I* commanded by Sub-Lieutenant Carlos Esteban Hernandez. The most senior officer was Lieutenant Commander Miguel Buiza Fernández-Palacios in the cruiser *Libertad*, who commanded a tug at the time of the uprising.[16] Madrid could count on only 82 of the 694 General Corps officers, of whom 55 remained at their posts, including 40 lieutenant commanders and lieutenants, while of 621 non-commissioned officers, the Republic retained 243. One of the few professional officers to remain loyal was Lieutenant Commander Remigio Verdía Jolí, commanding the Submarine Flotilla, who did much to organize naval operations from Malaga. Chief of the Naval Staff Admiral Javier de Salas González, who had been in post for almost as long as the Republic, was jailed on July 19 and later murdered. The shortage of officers meant all the staff functions were combined into an Operations Department under submariner Lieutenant Pedro Prado Mendizábal, while on July 21 the task force was placed under distinguished naval airman Commander Fernando Navarro Capdevila.

Ships were run by crew committees (*Comités de Buque*), who combined a volatile mixture of ignorance, arrogance, and paranoia, questioning and discussing every decision and generally reluctant to take ships into harm's way. Many rebels, or those suspected of rebel sympathies, were held in two prison ships, *Sil* and *España 3*, anchored in Malaga, pending courts martial which executed 36 by mid-August and another 23 later. Courts martial at Cartagena executed many more, including Admiral de Meir. Vengeful sailors also took matters into their own hands, notably at Port Mahon on August 3, then at Malaga, with a total of 296 officers slaughtered, most of them junior officers.

The Nationalists had plenty of officers, joined by 50 cadets in a sail training ship beating its way to the Canaries in July, but there was a serious shortage of sailors and warrant officers. They were replaced by promoting experienced ratings, while volunteers, including members of the Fascist (Falange) Party, flocked to the colors and, like the pressed men in Nelson's navy, quickly formed reliable and effective crews. Surprisingly, few flag officers showed enthusiasm for the Nationalists' cause, leaving as chief of staff 66-year-old Vice-Admiral Juan Cervera Valderrama, a veteran of the 1897 Cuba campaign who had been Primo de Rivera's penultimate Naval chief of staff. Of a dozen rear admirals, only Manuel Ruiz de Atauri remained in the Nationalist Navy as commander of the Cadiz naval base, while Rear Admiral (later Vice-Admiral) Luis de Castro Arizcun was brought out of retirement to command the Ferrol naval base. Manpower shortages meant that when the cruiser *Almirante Cervera* departed Ferrol, she had only 15 officers and 280 other ranks but was supposed to have 30 and 534, respectively.

The First Clashes

There was no prospect of a decisive fleet action, leaving the Nationalists to institute a blockade, which was always porous, and begin commerce raiding, while the Republican forces became a fleet-in-being, hoping to influence events through its mere existence.[17]

Fuel problems, command inexperience, and poor morale, exacerbated by fear of air power, undermined the Republican blockade of the Strait, nominally led by Navarro. The task force sailed aimlessly, seeking sustenance for man and ship; water, for example, was only for drinking and not washing.[18] On July 20, it entered the Moroccan port of Tangier, an international zone administered by France, Great

Britain, and Spain since 1923 and home to a cosmopolitan community, including Spaniards of all political persuasions.[19] Fearing the mutinous sailors would run riot, Britain, France, Italy, and Portugal assembled in Tangiers three cruisers and four destroyers under Italy's Vice-Admiral Mario Falangola, in the light cruiser *Eugenio di Savoia*, to dissuade the Spanish from tarrying.

Commercial companies refused to supply fuel and the task force departed forlornly for Gibraltar, only to encounter the same problem when it anchored in Algeciras Bay the following evening. Doubts about payment were underlined when a Royal Navy officer rowed out to the *Jaime I* to speak to the new Fleet Commander and was met by an unkempt and sockless Navarro.[20] The naval gypsies sailed eastwards after learning an oiler had arrived in Malaga, which became their forward base, reinforced by four submarines barely able to dive and each armed with only a single torpedo.

From there they patrolled the Strait and occasionally shelled rebel-held ports, but the insurgents' aircraft, augmented by German Junkers Ju 52s and Italian Savoia-Marchetti S.81s—known as Bats (*Pipistrelli*)—began harassing them. They drove the task force from Algeciras Bay, from where some Republican air defense shells fell on Gibraltar, fortunately without causing damage or injury. Rebel and government aircraft made indiscriminate attacks upon the dozens of ships traversing the Strait every day, including British destroyers, which resembled Spanish vessels, on July 22 and August 17. To avoid attacks, neutral warships painted recognition stripes upon their turrets, while the Royal Navy replaced destroyers with cruisers to avoid confusion. Merchant ships also ran the aerial gauntlet, with bombs missing the Gibraltar-based Bland Line's *Gibel Dris* off Tangiers on July 20. The following day, an American, a Norwegian, and three British ships were attacked, while on July 22 it was the P&O cargo liner *Chitral*, the sloop HMS *Wild Swan*, then the Italian *Pellice* that were targeted. As tensions eased there were fewer air attacks in the Strait, apart from one upon a British tanker as late as September 14. However, coast-defense batteries shelled the French destroyer *Tempête* on August 25 as she escorted two submarines through the Strait, and on September 14 the guns turned their attention to Royal Fleet Auxiliary oiler *War Bahadur* as she towed a lighter.[21] Other neutral ships were attacked without damage on August 5, including the Italian cable layer *Città di Milano*, which on July 21 put a landing party into Tangier to maintain public order.[22]

On August 3, a government destroyer shelled the Oldenburg-Portugiesische Dampfschiffes Rhederei (OPDR) freighter *Sevilla* as she unloaded at the Moroccan port of Larache; her master hastily raised anchor, only to be stopped and informed he would be permitted to sail only to Tangier. The German commander of naval forces in Spain, Rear Admiral Rolf Carls, ordered the torpedo boat *Leopard* to lodge a formal protest at the Spanish consulate in Tangiers, but under an obscure clause of the Treaty of Versailles, German warships were not permitted to enter Tangiers. The *Leopard* solved this problem, without creating another international incident, by enlisting the aid of Admiral Falangola to deliver the protest to the Spanish consulate.[23]

The Nationalists established an ad hoc naval command for the Strait under Ruiz de Atauri, but he had few hulls. Meanwhile, the Republican task force's presence remained a significant obstacle to Nationalist efforts to ship troops from North Africa, which was resolved by an airlift. However, on August 5, in strong wind, heavy seas, and dense fog, a convoy consisting of three merchantmen and a tug, with two small escort vessels and 22 aircraft, carried 1,665 troops from Ceuta to Algeciras, being dubbed by the Nationalists the Victory Convoy (*El Convoy de la Victoria*). A destroyer's attempt to intercept them was held off by the gunboat *Eduardo Dato*, which also accidentally straddled HMS *Basilisk*.[24] These troops spearheaded the capture of Andalusia, aided by the German-operated airlift over the Strait in which Ju 52s carried 13,900 of the African Army's 36,000 men, with 270 tonnes of equipment, from July 28 until October 11.[25]

Republican warships occasionally harassed the aircraft with antiaircraft fire, forcing them to fly at 8,000–11,500ft (2,500–3,500 meters), but on the day of the Victory Convoy the Italians bombed the destroyer *Lepanto* as she shelled Larache. She suffered half-a-dozen casualties and sailed to Gibraltar to unload her wounded before dashing to Malaga with the destroyer *Churruca*. Harassed all the way by rebel aircraft, the ships fired-off all their air-defense ammunition, while another bomber hit the destroyer *Almirante Valdés*. The Germans attacked the Malaga base on August 12, the absence of air defenses allowing them to hit the *Jaime I* with two 250-kilogram bombs which blew a huge hole in the upper deck, killing 47 of the crew.[26] The raid was supported by meteorological and intelligence information from the German Navy, although Carls commented that the effects of these and follow-up attacks were "astonishingly small."[27]

Madrid broke its own blockade by sending the task force, including the repaired *Jaime I*, to the Cantabrian Sea in a futile political gesture which one author described as "The Cruise to the North," leaving four destroyers and a pair of submarines to maintain a symbolic blockade. The Nationalists reacted by dispatching the *Canarias* and the *Cervera* south to support the shipping of troops from Morocco.[28] On September 29, they entered the Strait, engaging two destroyers and sinking one, whose survivors were picked up by the French *Koutoubia*. While the other destroyer was badly damaged, many shells failed to detonate due to fuzing problems.

By the time the task force returned on October 13, their foes effectively controlled the Strait, forcing foreign merchantmen into Ceuta for detailed inspection of their papers and cargoes. The Nationalists were occasionally embarrassed; when the *Cervera* stopped the Soviet freighter *Dniester* on October 30, she discovered the freighter was carrying cargo loaded in Hamburg.[29] On October 23, the *Canarias* returned and was engaged by the cruiser *Libertad* and two torpedo boats, both cruisers being damaged but making port. The Republican fleet continued to use Malaga as a forward base until February 1937 but lapsed into lethargy, with even plans for an amphibious landing in North Africa fading away due to opposition from the faint hearts.

The Majorca Landing

The war's only amphibious operation in August was organized by Catalonia's recently created autonomous government, the Generalidad, to retake rebel-held islands in the Balearics, especially Majorca (Mallorca), best known for its windmills and groves of lemon trees. To lead the operation, the Generalidad selected Cuban-born air force Captain Alberto Bayo y Giróud and Valencia Civil Guard Captain Manuel Uribarri Barrutell, who embarked 2,000 militia in the Compañia Transatlántica Española (CTE) liner *Marques de Comillas* to retake Formentera on August 2 and Ibiza on August 9.[30]

On August 10, the British consul in Majorca, Lieutenant Commander Alan Hillgarth, reported the imminent Republican invasion and requested Royal Navy assistance. Hillgarth was a retired naval officer wounded at Gallipoli who became a globe-trotting adventurer after the war, writing spy novels and thrillers, but with little success. He became a close friend of James Bond creator Ian Fleming and went to Majorca in 1932 pursuing a literary muse before becoming consul, which now allowed him to pass reports of Italian activity to the Admiralty, the Foreign Office, and to Winston Churchill.[31]

For the assault on Majorca, Bayo embarked 7,000 men in a 16-vessel convoy, including the *Mar Cantabrico*, landing on August 16 with the aid of three K-Boats at Porto Cristo, then pushing inland and hunkering down in a bridgehead shielded by the destroyers' guns. Some 6,000 reinforcements arrived in the *Jaime I* and two destroyers, and they extended the bridgehead along the coast, but Bayo did not push deeper into the island.

Many foreigners now chose to be evacuated, including author Robert Graves, writer of *I, Claudius*, who reluctantly embarked in HMS *Grenville*. It would be a decade before he returned to his beloved home. The growing threat to foreigners saw British, German, and Italian warships, together with the German Neptun Line's *Hero*, arrive in Palma de Majorca on August 19 to complete the evacuation. Learning of Republican intentions to shell the harbor, the senior naval officer, Rear Admiral James Somerville in the light cruiser HMS *Galatea*—Flag Officer Destroyers in the Mediterranean Fleet since April—proposed a mass departure. Somerville was a good-humoured officer who had relieved Rear Admiral Sir Andrew Browne "ABC" Cunningham, now second-in-command of the Mediterranean Fleet.[32] In port, he would begin each day rowing around the harbor, and in a service famed for quirky signals, his could be the quirkiest, but it was his understanding of modern naval warfare which led fleet commander Admiral Sir William Fisher specifically to ask for him.[33] The warships departed, led by *Galatea* and followed by Carls in the pocket battleship *Deutschland*, the Italian Flotilla Leader *Lanzerotto Malocello*, and the British destroyer *Greyhound*, forming what the British called the "sausage-sauerkraut-macaroni squadron," but returned at dusk when nothing happened.[34]

Meanwhile, financier Juan March Ordinas decided to fund an Italian military buildup, and on August 17 the destroyer *Maestrale* sailed to Italy, secretly loaded with 604,000 gold pesetas ($82,500). Hours before the "sausage-sauerkraut-macaroni squadron" departed, three Italian flying boats landed at the Spanish seaplane base in Pollensa (or Pollencia) Bay, while the destroyer *Lanzerotto Malocello*—under Commander Carlo Margottini—arrived in Palma, remaining until November, ostensibly on humanitarian duties but acting as a command center. On August 26, a red-bearded Fascist fanatic, Major Arconovaldo Bonaccorsi, known as "Conte Aldo Rossi," arrived with three Bat bombers as the core of an ad hoc air squadron, The Dragons of Death (*Draghi della morte*). The next day, the freighter *Emilio Morandi* entered Palma, carrying six fighters together with 200 tonnes of arms and ammunition, gasoline, and air defense guns. Other freighters followed, often with Italian Navy escort, and the British and French commanders became justifiably suspicious of Margottini's activities. A detachment of the Spanish Foreign Legion was also shipped into Palma as the Italian aircraft established air superiority, on one occasion attacking the marked hospital ship *Marques de Comillas*. The Italians were not the only ones helping the defenders, for after the Porto Cristo landing, Somerville visited the landing site and passed his observations to the Nationalist authorities through Hillgarth.[35] On September 3, Italian bombers began to soften-up the bridgehead and the following day supported a counterattack which the defenders held for two days before retreating, covered by naval gunfire but leaving most of their equipment, including a dozen guns and the K-Boats, on corpse-covered beaches.

During the rest of September, Nationalists recaptured Ibiza and Formentera and life returned to a semblance of normality, with French ships calling at Palma on their normal passage to Argel. On October 31, the Italian *Le Tre Marie* inaugurated regular voyages between Majorca and Italy, with Italian ships—or Nationalist merchantmen flying the Italian ensign—arriving from the mainland via Cape Tres Forces. *Ala Littoria* flying boats also called regularly in Palma on their journeys over the western Mediterranean.[36] On December 20, the Italians told the Germans they intended to remain on Majorca until Franco's victory, and Bonaccorsi was appointed Italian proconsul on the island, proclaiming it would be forever Italian. But his overbearing personality and attempts to turn Palma into a Fascist Italian town led to clashes with the Nationalist authorities, and in February 1937 he was sent to join the Italian Army Expeditionary Corps (*Corpo Truppe Volontarie, CTV*).[37]

The Royal Navy in Crisis

The Royal Navy's response to the situation in Spain was shaped by serious dilemmas highlighted during the previous year's Abyssinia Crisis. Italy's Fascist dictator, Benito Mussolini, invaded Abyssinia, East Africa's only independent country, in October 1935, shocking a world still horrified by the experience of the Great War.[38]

All eyes turned to the League of Nations, created to prevent crises developing into conflicts, whose only option was half-hearted economic sanctions when neither London nor Paris were willing to stand up to the "Cardboard Caesar" apart from challenging his claim, through a naval buildup, that the Mediterranean was "Our Sea" (*Mare Nostrum*).

This buildup underlined the Royal Navy's postwar decline and the need for a seismic change in strategy. From a peak wartime strength of 58 capital ships, 103 cruisers, and 456 destroyers, the Royal Navy had been steadily reduced, British defense policy from August 1919 having assumed the Empire "would not be engaged in any great war during the next 10 years."[39] The naval budget was cut from £188 million in 1919/1920 to £52 million in 1923, with the 10-Year-Rule extended for financial reasons until March 1932.[40] In April 1931, the First Sea Lord and Chief of the Naval Staff, Admiral Sir Frederick Field, warned that in wartime the fleet could not protect trade due to the shortage of ships and stores, as well as the erosion of infrastructure, with the closure of many shipyards cutting capacity by a third and employees by a quarter.[41]

Yet in 1919, the only remaining major naval powers—France, Italy, Japan, and the United States—were wartime allies with whom there were no major sources of friction. This was underlined by a diplomatic stabilization of naval power, first with the 1922 Washington Naval Treaty, followed by the 1930 London Treaty. These left the Royal Navy dominant, with 15 capital ships, 45 cruisers, and 70 destroyers by 1936, while restricting cruisers to 10,000 tons displacement and defined by their armament; light cruisers having guns up to 6.1 inches (155mm) and heavy cruisers ordnance up to 8 inches (203mm). Destroyers were defined as ships under 1,850 tons with guns up to 5.1 inches (130mm), amended in 1930 to ships with a displacement up to 3,000 tons and guns up to 6.1 inches. While followed scrupulously by both the Royal Navy and the U.S. Navy, their colleagues in Rome and Tokyo regarded the definitions "flexibly," and the ending of the Anglo-Japanese naval alliance made Japan the prime postwar threat.[42]

This potential threat meant that, as in Victorian times, the Mediterranean Fleet became the prime concentration of British naval power. Acting as the keel of a task force, it would, like the U.S. Cavalry in many a Western movie, ride to the rescue in response to a Japanese threat to London's imperial possessions, leaving the rump of the Home (formerly Atlantic) Fleet to act as a deterrent.[43] In Europe, Paris and Rome tussled for regional supremacy, neither ratifying the Treaty of London. The French refused to consider parity, but political and economic turmoil polarized French society, hindering naval rearmament, which extended only to cruisers and below.[44] While the Royal Navy was confident it could defeat the Italian Navy, a conflict with Rome was never seriously considered, although from the early 1930s, Whitehall recognized Italy was becoming more assertive. This reluctance was reflected in a November 1935 comment by the Defence Requirements Committee which noted:

"Our defence requirements are so serious that it would be materially impossible … to make additional provision for a hostile Italy."[45]

While Sir Stanley Baldwin's government, and especially Chancellor of the Exchequer (Finance Minister) Neville Chamberlain, reluctantly began rearmament in 1935, they were determined the economy would not be crippled. This forced the Royal Navy to compete with the Royal Air Force (RAF), the Admiralty believing the government was dragging its heels on naval rearmament.[46] The Admiralty stubbornly supported the Far Eastern task-force concept, despite the Abyssinia Crisis highlighting the Royal Navy's problems. Indeed, by mid-1936, the service chiefs of staff feared simultaneous wars in Europe and the Far East, with only a weakened and divided France as an ally.[47] In 1935, Admiral Sir William Fisher's Mediterranean Fleet could be reinforced only by stripping the outlying stations to give it seven capital ships, two aircraft carriers, 15 cruisers, and 54 destroyers, with other warships in the Red Sea.[48] However, the fleet was a very proficient force due to continuous exercises, including night operations with destroyers, but it reflected the Royal Navy's limited air defense capability.[49]

The air threat was underestimated until April 1940, and Fisher's predecessor, now First Sea Lord Admiral Sir Ernle Chatfield, told a dinner party in 1933 the threat was "All rubbish. What we want are battleships."[50] The big gun remained not only the arbiter of naval power but also the prime means of air defense, augmented by high-speed maneuvers for all warships, including Royal Navy aircraft carriers, as Lieutenant Commander Q. P. Whitford of torpedo school HMS *Vernon* told the Southampton Master Mariners Club on February 7, 1937. Some nine months earlier, former Fleet Air Arm officer Lieutenant Commander M. H. C. Young informed members of the Royal United Services Institution that a bomber approaching a battleship had a 94 percent chance of being shot down.[51]

But in the fall of 1935, the navy was forced to face the threat head-on, for the presence of Italian air bases all around the Mediterranean underlined an acute shortage of air defense ammunition. While Fisher received 71 percent of the Royal Navy's 4-inch, 66 percent of 4.7-inch, and 96 percent of 40mm "pom-pom" ammunition, this was barely enough for a week's operations.[52] It was decided immediately to convert two Ceres-class light cruisers into air defense platforms (Antiaircraft Cruisers) and to man them from the crew of the battleship HMS *Revenge*.[53] The following year, the program was extended to more Ceres-class vessels, while V&W-class destroyers were designated as Antiaircraft Escorts with enhanced air-defense armament.[54]

Naval weakness undermined British political resolve, with the chiefs of staff concerned even a limited war with Italy would reduce the Royal Navy's capabilities, leading to a consensus within the armed forces for a negotiated solution to the crisis.[55] Chatfield was described as "the finest officer the Royal Navy produced between the wars" and was the driving force in the Admiralty, an imperialist with a global perspective but also acutely aware of Britain's naval weakness, which he sought to redress.[56] As the crisis developed, he advised the government: "Care should be taken not to precipitate the possibility of hostilities, but on the other hand every endeavour should be made to delay this possibility as long as possible."[57] This rationale continued when the Spanish Civil War added to his burdens.

From the spring of 1936, there were two significant changes which also influenced naval policy in the Spanish Civil War. In June, Sir Samuel Hoare, the Foreign Secretary (Foreign Minister) at the start of the Abyssinia Crisis, became the First Lord of the Admiralty (Navy Minister). In the Great War, he had recruited Mussolini to bolster Italian pro-war sentiments, but in December 1935 he agreed with French Premier Pierre Laval to partition Abyssinia as a solution to the crisis. The Hoare-Laval Pact was swiftly repudiated by both countries and Hoare resigned, to be replaced by Anthony Eden, but after a brief period of purdah he returned to the government.

In March, Fisher was replaced by his oldest friend in the service, his chief of staff Admiral Sir Alfred Dudley Pickman Rogers Pound, who distinguished himself in the battle of Jutland in 1916 and helped organize the 1918 Zeebrugge raid.[58] Dudley Pound, "forceful and tireless" and "a master of detail," was reluctant to delegate, and like future Premier Winston Churchill, he preferred a late start to his working day. At leisure, he enjoyed shooting, dancing, and fast cars, but not necessarily in that order. He would correspond extensively with Chatfield and his opposite number in the Atlantic Fleet, Admiral Sir Roger Backhouse, often arranging flag appointments between them.[59]

While the Admiralty's mind focused upon the Abyssinia Crisis, there was an unexpected threat. Under an increasingly assertive Fascist leader, Adolf Hitler, Germany's military and mercantile power grew, reflected in his demands to scrap the Versailles Treaty and to expand his navy, bringing the prospect of the Royal Navy facing a two-front war. The chiefs of staff warned on March 12 that the Royal Navy's Mediterranean commitments made war with Germany thoroughly dangerous, for even the small German Navy posed a threat to coastal trading. From late April, the Admiralty put pressure upon the Foreign Office to return Home Fleet vessels.[60] The Royal Navy was also disappointed at the perceived reluctance in Paris to coordinate naval operations, as chief of staff Admiral Georges Durand-Veil and planning chief Admiral Jean Ducoux both advocated lifting sanctions for fear of a two-front war against Germany and Italy.[61]

London responded with the Anglo-German Naval Agreement of June 18, 1935, the 120th anniversary of the battle of Waterloo. Germany could now expand its navy to 420,000 tons, a third of the size of the Royal Navy, the Admiralty—led by Chatfield—believing diplomacy was the only way to guarantee the Royal Navy's supremacy until the shipbuilding industry could expand. They rationalized their failure to consult Paris by blaming French "intransigence" for the collapse of later disarmament conferences, while the French naturally felt betrayed, with salt rubbed into the wound by the date of the signing. Hitler rightly regarded the treaty as a great political success, driving a wedge between the former Allies and forcing London tacitly to accept the irrelevance of the Versailles Treaty.[62] The desire to avoid an early war with Germany and Italy has led some commentators to regard the chiefs of staff as ardent appeasers.[63]

Whitehall also came to see Italy as a potential counterbalance to Germany, the mirror-image of Rome's view of London and Paris. The French recognized they needed British support to counter the growing power of Fascist Italy and Germany, especially as a third of French imports were in British hulls, while a third of French trade was with the British Empire. London in turn depended upon French land power.[64] Meanwhile, the League of Nations accepted the Abyssinia *fait accompli*, ending sanctions on July 15 and wrecking not only its own reputation but also that of Great Britain and France. Their craven attitude was underlined in March 1936 when Germany reoccupied the Rhineland in outright defiance of the Versailles Treaty, leading the Deputy Chief of the Naval Staff, Vice Admiral Sir William "Bubbles" James, to warn on April 22: "[W]e must recover our relations with Italy."[65] On July 8, Eden authorized the dispersal of the Mediterranean Fleet, which began two days later with 15 Home Fleet ships passing the Iberian coast and returning to their bases by mid-July. Some had barely arrived in Devonport when they were ordered to go to Spain.[66] In March, the government also accelerated the scale of naval rearmament with nearly £70 million ($350 million), £10 million more than the previous year, followed by a £80 million ($400 million) supplementary program in April.[67] Meanwhile, the French Naval Staff agreed with James and on July 6 sent a note to Navy Minister Alphonse Gasnier-Duparc seeking improved relations with both London and Rome, also urging a non-aggression pact for the Mediterranean powers.[68]

Saving Refugees

The initial response of governments to the Spanish uprising was to rescue their citizens, but while there were usually 91,000 foreigners in Spain during the summer, another 7,000 arrived in Barcelona in 1936 for the People's Olympiad, organized by the political left to protest the Olympics being held in Nazi Germany.[69] Many of the latter chose to remain to fight for the Republic, but others were among the 61,000 evacuated by the end of the year in 60 warships and auxiliaries, augmented by 40 chartered merchantmen. Another 14,000 were evacuated the following year.[70] Major vessels, such as the British hospital ship HMHS *Maine*, anchored in the larger ports, acting as collection points, while smaller warships visited the minor ports to round up refugees, house them in cabins or on decks, and ferry them to the larger ships.[71]

British ships evacuated 12,000 people, including English author Laurence "Laurie" Lee, future writer of *Cider with Rosie*, who departed Barcelona in HMS *Blanche*. They allowed refugees up to three suitcases per person, with pets housed in hastily constructed kennels, sometimes in seaplane hangars. Chatfield later observed:

"This was the navy's chief and happiest work."[72] All hands were especially solicitous towards children, the elderly and, in these paternalistic times, women, all of whom had priority with accommodation in wardrooms, cabins, and mess decks. The men travelled on the decks, canvas screens providing minimal shelter from the spray thrown up by the destroyer's high-speed passage, to the howls of the disgruntled canines, although the odyssey rarely lasted longer than a night. Refugees would then transfer to the relative comfort of the larger ships sailing to Marseilles or St-Jean-de-Luz, but once they disembarked, they had to make their own arrangements to reach home.

The French evacuated the largest number of refugees, some 20,000, in warships augmented by the liners *Chella* and *Djenne*, chartered from the Marseilles-based Compagnie de Navigation Paquet (CNP), although the first foreign refugees evacuated were in the Italian Tripovich Servizi Marittimi Mediterraneo freighter *Silvia Tripcovich* from Malaga on July 20. Mussolini ordered cruisers, a Società Italia Flotte Reuniti (SFIR) cargo-liner, and a hospital ship to Barcelona on July 22, and the evacuation program was later augmented by the SFIR liners *Principessa Giovanna* and *Sicilia*. Most refugees were landed in Genoa, which also received German refugees from the ports of western Spain.[73]

The German Navy reveled in its new status and its commander in chief, Admiral Erich Raeder, would deploy into Spanish waters almost all his major surface vessels—three pocket battleships and six light cruisers—during 1936, as well as half-a-dozen torpedo boats. Indeed, until 1938, up to half Berlin's surface fleet operated off the Iberian Peninsula, reflecting German self-confidence in international affairs as well as support for the Nationalists.[74] The deployment of Rear Admiral Carls's task force was hastily organized after Foreign Minister Baron Konstantin von Neurath and Raeder persuaded Hitler on July 23 that Germany needed to follow the example of other European naval powers. Many vessels departed so quickly they left crew on furlough or with laundry drying, and as they sailed south, the Navy High Command (Oberkommando der Marine, OKM) radioed: "During the execution of your duties in Spain, do not take sides." The task force, augmented by four Neptun Line freighters, evacuated 15,500 people, including German Jews, but tensions with the Republic meant ships entering Republican ports in late August manned their guns and used rebel-held ports for resupply.

Three U.S. Navy battleships on a training cruise in European waters formed the ad hoc Spanish Service Squadron, with the newly commissioned heavy cruiser USS *Quincy* on a shake-down cruise and the training cutter USCG *Cayuga*, to rescue American citizens together with Cubans, Chileans, Costa Ricans, and Puerto Ricans.[75] On September 18, a permanent U.S. Navy presence was activated in the Mediterranean as Squadron 40 (T), or European Squadron D, under Rear Admiral Arthur P. Fairfield, with a cruiser and two destroyers. Operating from French ports, Lisbon, and Gibraltar, Fairfield protected American interests, monitored the situation, and also networked with potential allies. He was relieved on December 4, 1937, by Rear Admiral Henry E. Lackey, whose relations with the pro-Republican U.S. ambassador, Claude G. Bowers, were tense.[76]

Latin American naval vessels present included the Argentine heavy cruiser ARA *Veinticinco (25) de Mayo*. An Argentinian destroyer evacuated Franco's brother-in-law, Ramón Serrano Súñer, who became the Nationalist Interior Minister, then Foreign Minister.[77] The Spanish-built Mexican "transport," or gunboat, ARM *Durango* brought refugees home in October, but her commander, Captain Manuel Zermeno Araico, purchased the *Jalisco* in Marseilles to ship arms to Spain.[78]

Warships also acted as communications centers while British and French commanders negotiated local hostage exchanges and releases or even temporary truces. Within the government-held zone there was anarchy, literally, in Catalonia and around Malaga, while within the rebel zone there appeared to be discipline and order, albeit the silence of the grave. The mutinies on Republican ships, together with their "rabble" crews and grubby warships, meant there was universal loathing of their navy, in contrast to the high regard for the discipline and smartness of the Nationalist Navy. Within the French Navy, there were half-a-dozen incidents before mid-1937 where seamen showed Republican sympathies, usually by singing the Communist anthem *The Internationale* and making left-wing clenched-fist salutes, but there were also two serious incidents.[79]

One was on the heavy cruiser *Duquesne*, flying the flag of Rear Admiral Marcel-Bruno Gensoul, Admiral Commanding the Special French Deployment in the Mediterranean (Amiral Commandant Superieur le Dispositif Spécial Francaise en Méditerranée, Alsud), commanding all French ships operating off the Iberian Penninsula. The cruiser was in Barcelona when the demoralized crew refused to collect a poorly cooked supper, the situation only easing when a gunnery officer arranged for officers to meet the crew in their messes. Gensoul, who temporarily transferred to a destroyer, agreed to return to Toulon for an inquiry. The second incident involved the submarine *Le Tonnant*, under refit in Toulon, where some of the crew spent too much time with left-wing dockyard militants. Some decided to hand over the refitted boat to the Republican Navy, but the commander nipped the plot in the bud and removed potential mutineers. Other submariners regarded her as a plague ship when she was deployed first to the Middle East and then to the Far East. The navy disciplined 54 men from both crews, either with reduced grades or short terms of imprisonment. The depth of feeling among French officers was shown when Germany's Rear Admiral Wilhelm Marschall met Captain Barberot, commander of the newly commissioned French light cruiser *Marseillaise*, in October 1937: "Barberot reported … in the event of a revolution in France, he would take his ship over to either the Germans or the Italians. His admiral indicated that in such a case he [Barberot] would only be choosing between order and chaos."[80]

While the year ended with brawls between Italian and French seamen in Tangier, the shared dangers briefly revived hopes of peaceful international cooperation.

Indeed, the French allowed a German torpedo boat to be repaired at the Toulon naval base, while foreign navies were allowed to use Gibraltar. The latter provided confirmation the Italians were ignoring the Washington Treaty when the Zara-class heavy cruiser *Goriza* suffered an explosion in the aviation gasoline tank and arrived in Gibraltar for repairs on August 25. Under the treaty, she should have been no more than 10,000 tons, but upon entering dry dock it was discovered her standard load was 11,712 tons and her full load 14,330 tons. When she departed on September 9, Whitehall sent a private, rather than public, complaint in order not to offend Mussolini.[81]

A Question of Blockade

Blockade was a significant feature in the Allies' victory in the Great War, a lesson not lost on the combatants in Spain. Nevertheless, their attempts to emulate this feat created a diplomatic dilemma over their blockade's legitimacy. One commentator noted: "The questions of where the limits of territorial waters were to be drawn, of the rights of belligerency, the transport of war material and the right to stop, search and seize neutral ships were to influence the war on maritime traffic through-out the Spanish Civil War."[82]

Under international law, only recognized belligerents may conduct a blockade, including the right to search ships for contraband on the high seas and seize them. Civil conflicts have their own issues, and during Spain's Third Carlist War (1872–76), the British Foreign Office warned Madrid it would not recognize its blockade because to do so meant acknowledging insurgents as belligerents, which in turn might encourage foreign intervention, leading to a European war. This precedent was now also influenced by the desire to maintain trade for economic recovery.[83]

From July 24 until August 13, Madrid extended nominal blockades of "War Zones" to all territories under rebel control, warning that merchant ships entered them at their own risk. The Declarations of Paris (1856) and London (1909) stated an effective blockade required "sufficient force effectively to prohibit" any access to the coast, and the Republican Navy's lack of ships made this a "paper" or unenforceable blockade.[84] On 16 August, the Admiralty issued instructions that Spanish warships outside the 3-mile limit might be allowed to inquire the destination of British ships, but if Royal Navy ships observed attempts to board them, they were to signal "stop interfering" and return fire if fired upon.

The Strait of Gibraltar was the key blockade zone, and during August and September 1936, Republican warships and submarines adopted a close blockade, one near the coast.[85] The White Ensign, symbol of the Royal Navy, protected the Red Ensign, symbol of the British Merchant Navy, but other nationalities were not so lucky. Republican destroyers arrested a Norwegian ship exporting wine from Cadiz and stopped a French Melilla-bound collier which was forced to sail into Gibraltar.

Air attacks made the close blockade unsustainable in the fall of 1936, and Madrid abandoned its blockade to avoid creating friction with the major maritime powers, especially Great Britain.[86]

Madrid's hopes of preventing military supplies reaching rebel-held ports were dashed when it learned that ship had literally sailed, for the Deutsche-Östafrika Linie (DOAL) freighter *Usamoro* arrived in Seville on August 1, the first of a trickle of German supply ships. Carls's task force shadowed her to ensure a safe arrival, the pocket battleship *Deutschland* then sailing to Ceuta, where the admiral lunched with Franco on August 3, the warship's presence also dissuading government ships from shelling the port.[87] But on August 18, the cruiser *Libertad* stopped the OPDR freighter *Kamerun* carrying aviation fuel and lubricants, ostensibly to Genoa but actually for Cadiz, and shepherded her eastwards, chaperoned by the German torpedo boat *Leopard*, all in turn being trailed by a government submarine. Carls dispatched the battleship *Admiral Scheer* to escort the freighter after intercepting a radio message from Madrid ordering a destroyer to fire upon her if she turned westwards.

The battleship arrived and, using semaphore, signaled her intentions. The destroyer duly withdrew, a wise move, for Berlin informed Madrid the commanders of the *Scheer* and light cruiser *Köln* were ordered to "respond energetically" to the use of force. However, Berlin briefly banned merchantmen from unloading at rebel-held ports.[88] Shortly afterwards, on the night of August 20/21, a submarine intercepted the freighter *Lahneck* as she tried to enter the River Guadalquivir on a commercial voyage and warned she was forbidden from entering Seville. When the *Leopard* arrived the next morning after an exchange of signals with the submarine, she escorted the freighter to Lisbon.

Despite limited resources, the Nationalists also established close blockades in the Strait and off the northern coast, with a Majorca-based distant blockade. Control of the Strait was strengthened on December 16 by establishing the Strait Flotilla (Flotilla de Estrecho) with some pre-war gunboats and a dozen mostly British-built auxiliary patrol boats, supported by three coast defense artillery batteries on the Moroccan side, because ships entering the Mediterranean use the southern sea lane through the Strait, the intercepted vessels going to Ceuta.[89] The Nationalists decided to confiscate commercial cargoes, especially fruit loaded in Republican ports, which affected 11 Belgian, Danish, and Norwegian vessels in February and March, one of the Danish vessels being the *Edith*, which would be sunk in an air attack in August. Other cargoes were also seized during the year; after capturing the Greek tanker *Ionia* in July, possibly by bribing the master, the Nationalists sold her cargo of 8,600 tonnes of fuel, although they did give both the owners and the master a percentage of the profits.[90] By the end of April, some 120 ships had been forced into Ceuta, including 74 Russian and 26 Danish, some of whom were not even bound for Spain. To add insult to injury, two Norwegian ships had their fuel bunkers drained, leaving them with only enough to reach Gibraltar. The Republicans were just as rapacious, seizing 1,500 tonnes of scrap metal for Genoa and bunker coal to heat barracks from the French *Soussien*, which put into Alicante due to storm damage in December 1936.

After the cargoes of 18 Dutch ships were seized, the Hague sent the 33-year-old coastal defense armored ship (*Pantserschip*) HrMS *Hertsog Hendrik* to the Strait on January 11 to protect vessels with the Dutch tricolor. Such shielding would continue until September 28, 1938, involving a succession of ships, including the light cruiser HrMS *Java*, the gunboat *Johann Mautits van Nassau*, four minesweepers, and four submarines. Ultimately, the Royal Netherlands Navy escorted 800 vessels, including 500 by the gunboat.[91]

Cervera claimed most of the Dutch population were Marxist sympathizers and their ships' captains were either reckless or did not understand they had to recognize the authority of his blockade, while the Royal Netherlands Navy "pretended we could not stop Dutch ships."[92] There were also endemic problems of false-flag vessels and those registered in one country when the owners were citizens of another. The Dutch reached a *modus operandi* by which their warships protected only Dutch-registered ships which were not carrying arms. Indeed, the *Java* refused to escort the Dutch-registered arms smuggler *Sarkani*, which was soon captured by the Nationalists. Scandinavian navies could not afford to deploy warships, leading seamen's unions to instruct members not to sail to Spain, with some owners retaliating by cancelling their contracts. For the owners, even short delays were costly as they had to continue to pay running costs, further reducing tight profit margins.[93]

Cervera laid down the principles of the blockade on November 5, specifying that Russian or Mexican ships were "fair game" (*presa permitida*) and should be stopped if "there are strong suspicions about their destination." The inspection of ships in Nationalist ports would be in the presence of their country's consuls, or two foreign witnesses, and war materiel would be confiscated. Ships in Spanish territorial waters, or trans-shipping cargoes on the high seas, could also be legitimately inspected, but there was no mention about ships from neutral countries, especially the British, or how they were to be treated. On December 6, the British Parliament passed the Merchant Shipping (Carriage of Munitions to Spain) Act, banning British-registered ships from carrying war materiel to Spain. The British ambassador to Spain, Sir Henry Chilton, whose embassy was over a grocer's shop in the French border town of Hendaye, informed Burgos that British vessels suspected of contravening the act would be forced to sail to Gibraltar or Malta for inspection.[94]

Chilton's assurances led Cervera to publish a "special treatment" addendum in late December which placed the onus upon London. Nationalist commanders were informed British ships were obeying the rules and should be treated with kid gloves, although warning shots might be fired to stop suspected vessels within territorial waters.[95] If suspicious British vessels were encountered within the Strait, Nationalist warships were to escort them to Gibraltar, alerting the naval base with

English-language radio messages.[96] Through misunderstanding, or constructive interpretation, Nationalist naval commanders sometimes ignored Cervera's instructions and stopped British ships, such as the *Etrib* on December 31 and the *Bramhall* on January 12, but generally the Nationalists took British claims of "fair play" seriously, and with good reason. Several challenged British vessels did sail to Gibraltar, such as the Springwell Shipping Company's new coaster *Springwear*, carrying 1,400 tons of wheat, released after an inspection on March 19, and the Westcliffe Line's *Thorpehall* on March 30.

That same month, the Stanhope Line's *Stanholm* loaded a cargo for Spain in Casablanca, the British consul confirming it contained no war materiel. Yet the Nationalists were convinced it was contraband, and forced her to put into Gibraltar, where an inspection found nothing illegal, and she was allowed to proceed. Two incidents in April, including the *Menin Ridge* on April 23, St George's Day, led Dudley Pound to protest to the Nationalist naval authorities, who quickly learned the British Lion would not roar too loudly. Nevertheless, the "failure" to find non-existent contraband, despite strident claims, fueled Nationalist officers' distrust of the Gibraltar authorities. They convinced themselves the British, and especially the French, were shielding arms shipments to the Republic despite professing neutrality. These officers believed they were fighting a crusade for civilization against Godless Communism and could not comprehend why brother officers in foreign navies supported neutrality. For their part, British and French officers had considerable sympathy for the Nationalist Navy and were willing to prevent their ships bringing in arms, but their efforts were undermined by inaccurate Nationalist naval intelligence or false information.[97] The strained relations between the three navies meant that on March 15, the *Canarias* trained her guns on the French torpedo boat *La Pomone* when they met in the Strait.[98]

In November, with the Nationalists tightening their grip on the Strait, the inevitable question arose of granting the Spanish factions belligerent rights. On November 17, Franco published a proclamation about interrupting the supply of Russian arms to eastern ports, especially Barcelona, and said his government "was resolved to prevent this traffic with every means of war at its disposal."[99] He also threatened to destroy Barcelona. While wrongly interpreted as declaring a blockade, this was a declaration of intent. The Foreign Office responded by immediately requesting the Nationalists to guarantee a safety zone in Barcelona for neutral ships, as had already been arranged at other ports.[100]

The Admiralty was worried the Royal Navy might become involved in incidents with the Nationalist Navy if they tried to protect British ships stopped while illegally carrying war materiel, and this in turn might antagonize Rome. On November 20, the Admiralty unilaterally gave both sides belligerent rights, with instructions to commanders that either side's warships might be allowed, temporarily, to stop and search British ships for arms. British ship-owners were not informed of this change in policy "to avoid giving the impression that HMG [His Majesty's Government] are not prepared to afford full support to unobjectionable activities of British ships."[101] Foreign Secretary Eden was rightly indignant, but both Hoare and the President of the Board of Trade (Trade and Industry Minister) Walter Runciman (from June 1937 Viscount Runciman, the son of a shipping magnate) backed the idea. Following an emergency Sunday meeting two days later, the Cabinet supported Eden and the Admiralty revised instructions. Spanish warships would now not be permitted to board British vessels in international waters, while the Royal Navy would continue to escort suspected vessels to a British base for inspection and would continue assisting merchantmen. The British refusal to grant belligerent rights saw a hiccup as Nationalist forces closed on Madrid and London briefly pondered recognizing the Nationalist government, following the example of Berlin and Rome on November 18. In the end, the Foreign Office's views prevailed, despite the Admiralty's frequent attempts at revision.

Spain's Merchant Marine

By ceding control of the Strait, the Republic torpedoed one of its greatest assets, its merchant marine. At the outbreak of the Civil War, Spain had 390 (1,070,839 grt) steamers and motor (diesel-powered) ships over 100 grt, including 100 ferries, together with 270 fishing vessels, the steamer fleet having expanded by 29 percent since mid-1914.

Maritime trade during the Republic was almost stagnant, with 15–17 million tons of shipping entering Spanish ports annually while 23 million tons departed. Foreign hulls were predominant, with British ships carrying a quarter of Spain's exports, including 40 percent of its oranges and minerals, and 10.4 percent of her imports in 1935. But in the early 1930s, British exports to Spain were losing out to Germany and the United States. London's decision in 1932 to foster trade with the Empire provided Spanish business opportunities for other countries such as Germany, while the Irish Free State's Limerick Steamship Company was established in 1934 to bring oranges to Ireland.[102] Yet there remained a strong "circle-of-trade" of coal from Welsh and Tyne-Tees mines to northern Spain and return journeys with iron ore, involving smaller lines such as the Llewellyn, Nailsea, and Newcastle-based Sheaf, while Constant (South Wales) was created for this trade in 1929 by transferring most of its ships from Kent.[103] General trade was conducted by larger lines calling directly or while en route to other regions, these including MacAndrews, which imported fruit from the Canary Islands, and Samuel Crawford Hogarth's Baron Line, one of the largest privately owned shipping companies in the world, whose parsimony with provisions led crew to dub the fleet "The Hungry Hogarths." The Guardian Line, formed in 1932, had the *Macgregor* heavily involved in Spanish trade, as was the Gibraltar-based Bland Line operating across the Strait and along the Iberian coast.[104]

Cash-strapped Spanish companies had difficulties competing with vessels fit only for the scrapyard, with only 6.6 percent of the Spanish merchant marine having been built since 1930 and older ships meaning increased maintenance costs. While the mid-1930s saw post-Depression world trade slowly increasing, returns remained slim and even coastal trade between the Asturian ports and Barcelona paid only a loss-making 11 pesetas (the equivalent of $1.40) a tonne. Little wonder that in 1936, 13.5 percent of the commercial fleet, or 53 ships (180,352 grt), were laid up, including 32 in Bilbao, amounting to half the tramping fleet.[105] Government attempts to improve conditions for the 44,400 seafarers were an added burden. From May Day 1936, ship's committees were established to ensure these rules were applied, sharing authority with the master and the ship-owners, who regarded them as revolutionary cells prejudicial to good order and discipline. Even the seamen's union, the CNT Marítima, noted neglect, idleness, indiscipline, and even sabotage by crew members.[106]

The fleet was scattered at the time of the uprising, with few ships in rebel ports, where they were joined by those whose masters opted to support the insurgents. Most crews were sympathetic to the Republic, partly because their families were in government-held ports, to which they sailed in defiance of their owner's wishes, while Basque-owned ships were generally loyal to the Bilbao government.[107] Many ships were in foreign ports, where some remained moored, sometimes on the owner's instructions, while others opted to carry on abroad, using their cargoes to fund the Republic. A few tried to make it home, but ran the risk of being seized by the Nationalists or even sunk (see Table 1.1).

Foreign courts became legal battlegrounds over ship ownership as the Republic tried to take control of vessels from pro-Nationalist owners, who in turn sought to regain control. The latter sometimes involved cat-and-mouse games as owners tried to find their vessels and institute legal proceedings. The Ramos Line's *Ramón Alonso Ramos* remained under the Republican ensign, but her master stayed in contact with owner Roberto Ramos and tipped him off when the ship entered Antwerp, leading to successful legal action to recover his ship. Francisco García did not regain control of the Euskalduna Line freighter *Rita Garcia* in a British court until the beginning of 1938 and after she had travelled to Narvik and Argentina on behalf of the Republic.[108]

Table 1.1. Estimated Spanish merchant fleets available for duty 1936–39 (steamers over 100 grt)

	Aug. 1, 1936	Aug. 1, 1937	Aug. 1, 1938	Jan. 1, 1939
Nationalist	65 (124,000 grt)	130 (290,00 grt)	190 (400,000 grt)	200 (435,000 grt)
Republican, Atlantic	180 (539,000 grt)	125 (360,000 grt)	20 (124,000 grt)	5 (80,000 grt)
Republican, Mediterranean	85 (318,000 grt)	80 (298,000 grt)	50 (214,000 grt)	40 (175,000 grt)

Both sides used ships to support their war efforts, one of the first being the Asturian Velasco Line's *Isleño*, requisitioned in Tenerife to carry aviation fuel to Ceuta on July 26 and then used by the Nationalist Navy for rapid military supply missions into the Balearics.[109] By the beginning of August, the first storm had blown itself out, leaving the Nationalists with 80 vessels (154,834 grt). However, only a limited number were available for trading, with 10 (27,898 grt) of the best ships converted into auxiliary warships or transports, while Germany and Italy would operate 17 (55,529 grt) captured in their ports. A further five (14,958 grt) were operated by various German lines, although doubts of the Spanish crews' reliability meant they maintained a core of armed officers and men. The poor condition of these German-operated vessels meant only the *Cabo Villano* as the *Contra* and the *Aizkarai-Mendi* as the *Blanca* were used by Henry Aschpurwis to carry military aid to the Nationalists, with five voyages between October 1936 and March 1937. They were then sold to the Sloman Line for conventional commercial activities, rejoining the Spanish register in March 1938. Most of the Italian-operated ships were controlled by the Garibaldi Line (S.A. Cooperativa de Navigazione Garibaldi) until the end of the war, many carrying war materiel, notably the Pinillos Line's *Ebro*, which became the *Aniene*. She became the prime supply vessel for Nationalist aviation, making 27 voyages from La Spezia to Seville, sometimes via Palma, with single-engined aircraft, gasoline, oil, munitions, spares, and sometimes airmen.[110]

The Nationalist blockade and commerce raiders helped recapture many Spanish ships to expand their merchant fleet, together with seized foreign vessels given the prefix *Castillo*.[111] Within a year, the fleet had nominally doubled, and by the following year it was up by two-thirds, even after eight captured vessels (33,133 grt) were transferred to Italy to support the war effort, while three (9,529 grt) became auxiliary cruisers. The figures are approximate due to limited source material. For example, on July 7, 1938, the Nationalists decided to scrap some of the vessels laid up in Bilbao, bringing the total number scrapped by the end of the war to 15 (30,965 grt).[112] What is also clear is that, whatever their political sympathies, financial necessity meant crews were willing to work ships supporting the Nationalist cause, and it is likely that these imperatives caused men from ships in foreign ports to sign on in Spain.

Chicanery also helped expand the Nationalist fleet, and the masters of two Basque-owned ships, the *El Montecillo* and *Arnabal-Mendi*, found excuses in August 1936 and January 1937 to put into Gibraltar and arrange for their ships to be captured. In February 1937, the *Nuria Ramos* docked in Oran with a crew determined to complete their voyage in a Republican port, but the pro-Nationalist master and radio operator arranged its interception by a seaplane as it approached Cartagena, giving the excuse to turn south and sail to Melilla. The same month, the *Cabo Roche* was arrested in Gibraltar with a cargo of cotton pending the outcome of an ownership claim by the Republic. She was hijacked on June 22 by men acting for her Nationalist-supporting owner and sailed to Algeciras, where

Table 1.2. Traffic in and out of Nationalist Spain

Date	Ship arrivals		Imports (t)	Exports (t)	Ship departures		Passengers disembarked
	Spanish	Foreign			Spanish	Foreign	
1936	1,517	1,811	590,112	1,283,925	2,105	21	11,096
1937	9,130	5,447	3,025,141	6,036,364	9,028	5,557	63,496
1938	14,426	5,818	4,928,515	8,910,769	14,317	6,214	100,672

Source: Francisco Moreno, 287. Spanish ships include ferries

her cargo was unloaded. In late July, the *Arichachu* departed Tyneside for Odessa, but while passing through the English Channel her master and four Nationalist supporters seized control, imprisoned the rest of the crew in the hold and then sailed to Pasajes.[113]

Ports quickly returned to normal levels of activity (see Table 1.2). From July 18, 1936 until January 1, 1939, Nationalist exports totaled 16,231,678 tonnes, while imports were 8,543,768 tonnes, with 65,391 ship movements, of which some 77 percent (50,523) were "Nationalist," a figure which includes military aid and the arrival of 316,000 men.[114] While the conflict reduced demand for consumer goods, German commercial traffic declined only slightly, with foreign lines using Nationalist ports in 1938, including Britain's MacAndrews and Hogarth, the Dutch Koninklijke Nederlandse Stoomboot-Maatschappij (KNSM), Belgium's Deppe, and Norway's Fred Olsen and the Ludwig Mowinckel freighters, en route to Latin America. The Gibraltar-based Bland Line remained very active in Spanish coastal and cross-Strait traffic.[115] The circle-of-trade to Great Britain also continued, with lines such as W. Dickinson, Ravelston, D. Alexander, and Stone & Rolfe.[116] During 1936, there was a drop in British ships visiting Nationalist ports; less than 20 foreign vessels appear to have used Nationalist-held ports in Galicia, but even here mineral exports ensured activity, with most of the 13 vessels taking iron pyrites from Huelva in 1936 being British, as until 1939 Spain was Britain's prime source of iron pyrites (Edwards, Table 9). Getting Republican-supporting stevedores to unload cargoes from Nationalist ports was sometimes difficult, and for a week in January 1937 a cargo of iron pyrites from Huelva which reached Marseilles in the German *Indra* remained in the hold, being unloaded only when the men learned it was to support rearmament against Germany and Italy.[117]

While the Republic had the lion's share of the fleet, nominally 310 vessels (910,942 grt), their crews were inefficient and poorly disciplined. The Nationalist grip on the Strait meant only a third, 107 ships (335,484 grt), were available in the Mediterranean, of which at least 13 (26,802 grt) were laid-up throughout the conflict, mostly at Port Mahon, while others would be requestioned as naval auxiliaries (see Table 1.3). In the Mediterranean, four vessels (7,087 grt) were scuttled as block ships to protect ports, while six (28,365 grt) became prison ships, although some

Table 1.3. Republican total merchant ship losses (steamers over 100 grt)

Cause	1936	1937	1938	Total
Sunk in combat	5 (14,256 grt)	24 (81,876 grt)	18 (41,555 grt)	47 (137,687 grt)
Sunk in accident	–	2 (1,756 grt)	3 (8,879 grt)	5 (10,635 grt)
Captured	11 (32,523 grt)	86 (202,930 grt)	7 (13,888 grt)	104 (249,341 grt)
Total	16 (46,779 grt)	112 (286,562 grt)	28 (64,322 grt)	156 (397,663 grt)

later reverted to the freighter role. The CTE liners *Argentina* and *Uruguay* remained floating prisons in Barcelona throughout the war.[118] The strategic lifeline to the Black Sea appears to have involved only 25 ships (111,000 grt), while another 10 (33,000 grt), together with half-a-dozen sailing vessels, brought men and supplies from France.[119] A couple of ships managed to break out of the Mediterranean and seven completed the reverse passage, but the Republican fleet was steadily eroded through blockade, enemy action, or natural hazard. Most were lost off the Iberian Peninsula or in the Mediterranean, but on October 15, 1936, the Republican steamer *Fernando Poo* was intercepted by the auxiliary cruiser *Ciudad de Mahon* off Bata in Spanish Guinea and beached, becoming a total loss.[120]

The fall of the northern enclave in October 1937 saw most of the Basque fleet opt to remain moored at neutral ports, where others gradually joined them. By the war's end, the Nationalists identified 230 merchantmen and large fishing vessels, as well as 221 smaller fishing vessels and harbor-service craft, in foreign harbors, France having 317.[121] More disturbing for the Republican cause was the seizure of the *Juan Sebastion Elcano* by the Soviet Union in January, ostensibly for errors in documentation, followed by another eight vessels, mostly in Black Sea ports. Moscow appears to have offered no explanation for these actions, which gained 47,648 grt of shipping, and there was no offer of compensation.[122] These were offset when the national oil monopoly CAMPSA (Compañia Arrendataria del Monopolio de Petróleos) acquired three tankers (8,126 grt) from the British Mid-Atlantic Shipping Company.[123] The erosion of its merchant fleet meant the Republicans grew increasingly dependent upon foreign hulls, especially British, and a Nationalist source noted that between January 1, 1937, and March 31, 1939, 2,345,833 tonnes was unloaded at Republican ports through 2,825 voyages. Of these, 2,769 could be identified by their registrations, but barely 13 percent were Spanish-registered, while 2.2 percent were Russian-registered.[124]

Under the Red Ensign

In the 1930s, the British Empire was at its zenith and in economic decline. Britain's share of world trade fell from 14.15 percent in 1913 to 10.75 percent in 1929 and 9.8 percent in 1937, making it ever-more difficult to maintain the worldwide political-economic entity which would vanish within two decades.[125] The decline was accelerated by World War I, which saw former customers seek either self-sufficiency or alternate sources, such as Japan and the United States. Yet the war and postwar demand were a catalyst upon an Edwardian industrial renaissance, and in the mid-1920s many markets were regained and new ones opened, although even within the Empire, domestic industries undermined the traditional colonial suppliers.

The Red Ensign still flew over the world's largest merchant marine at 17,183,000 grt in 1936, 27 percent of the world's steam/motor vessels, while the British Empire's dominions had another 2,990,000 grt. Yet at the beginning of the century, British ships had represented 50 percent and in 1914 41.5 percent, the postwar decline partly reflecting the losses during the U-boat holocaust of the Great War. By contrast, other fleets had expanded, the United States's sea-going fleet by 14.7 percent and Norway's by 6.3 percent, although European owners still accounted for 90 percent of the world's ships. The British fleet was also aging, with nearly 82 percent up to 20 years old and 59 percent 15 years old, compared with the world averages of 68.5 and 36 percent respectively. World-wide, the number of sea-going steamers over 4,000 grt had increased from 3,608 at the outbreak of the Great War to 6,075, plus 1,353 motor ships, including 496 (296 British), over 10,000 grt, with 265 motor ships over 8,000 grt. More than half the steam ships in the *Lloyd's Shipping Register* were 1,000 grt or smaller, and the vast majority continued to burn coal, often from South Wales.[126]

The dominance of steam and the decline of sail from the 1880s was accelerated by U-boats, for the sailing ship was a sitting duck. Indeed, Arnauld de la Perière, the most successful submarine commander of all time, sank 39 (16,139 grt) sailing vessels in a "bag" of 193 ships (453,359 grt). By 1936, they amounted to only 2 percent of the world's total tonnage, of which nearly 54 percent (570,000 grt) flew the Star-Spangled Banner. The sea is a harsh mistress, and sailing ships were more vulnerable to wind and tide than steamers. Of the 3,656 merchant vessels (4,495,532 grt) accidentally lost between 1926 and 1936, a third (1,147) were sailing ships, although they accounted for only 712,127 grt of total tonnage.[127]

From the first installation of radio transmitter/receivers (transceivers) in the Canadian Pacific Railway Company's *Lake Champlain* in 1901, steamers could also summon help, and experience with the White Star liners *Republic* and *Titanic* in 1909 and 1912, as well as in the war, led to the Merchant Shipping (Wireless Telegraphy) Act in 1919. This made it mandatory for British ships to carry both a transceiver and a trained operator, although cost-cutting often saw this task assigned to the navigator. Moreover, the law did not apply to ships under 1,600 grt, with owners operating from ports in northeastern England deliberately ordering colliers of 1,500 tons without transceivers to save money, arguing the ships were always within the sight of land.[128]

The Depression severely impacted Great Britain's merchant marine industry, with earnings from shipping dropping from £143 million in 1924 to just £68 million in 1933.[129] These services included brokerage not only for British vessels but for shipping world-wide managing business between merchants and ship-owners, and often arranging insurance through Lloyd's. Usually in London, such charters were arranged in the Baltic Exchange, standardizing types of contracts, insurance forms, and documentation which remain in use today, while ship-management companies provided ship-owners with crews and technical support. A voyage charter was the most common, with the ship-owner providing vessel and crew for a cargo to specific destinations. Time charters saw the charterer responsible for running costs, but with authority over the crew. Business within a war zone made these agreements risky, but extremely lucrative.

Crews—some 144,000 seamen in British-registered vessels—bore the brunt of postwar cost-cutting, with the pay of officers and men steadily slashed. British seamen had suffered terribly during the Great War, losing 5.5 percent of the total (15,313 dead and missing), while many more suffered crippling injuries or disabling health. The average age of British seafarers was 36, but some merchantmen sailing to Spain included boys as young as 14. The *Backworth*, challenging the Nationalist blockade of Bilbao in 1937, included two 15-year-old Whitby orphans serving as apprentices. They attended nautical training colleges or training ships before being eligible to sign on for manual work, although officer cadets did not go to sea until they were 17 or 18.

Would-be Royal Navy officers also went to sea at that age, but boys aged under 16 received at-sea training, usually in Revenge-class battleships, then joined larger Royal Navy warships, often manning the lighter guns, although they were also expected to load 37 kg 5.5-inch shells.[130] During World War II, the boys in the Royal Navy, and especially the Merchant Navy, paid a terrible price, with the latter losing more than 500 under the age of 16, some brothers being lost in the same ship. When the battleship HMS *Royal Oak* was sunk in October 1939, 134 of the 834 dead were boys. For the rest of the war, boys were not allowed to serve in warships until they reached the age of 17. It is worth noting that one of the three survivors of HMS *Hood* when she was sunk in May 1941 was 18-year-old Ted Riggs, who had joined her just before the war as a Boy Sailor.[131]

Two-thirds of seamen under the Red Ensign came from families who for generations had gone down to the sea in ships and done business in great waters. It was common for fathers and sons, brothers and cousins to serve together. The basic working week was 64 hours, compared with 45 hours ashore, usually hard manual labor, back-breaking in the case of coal-fired ships, where gangs of stokers would come off watch covered in coal dust, earning the nickname The Black Gang. In some cases, this was literally true, for some British-born crewmen were the sons of immigrants from all over the Empire. Joseph Conrad's third novel, written 40 years earlier, was about a West Indian sailor. African and West Indian men were often employed as stokers, Welsh vessels usually recruiting from Tiger Bay, Cardiff, the Principality's oldest multi-ethnic community, but they were to be found in most ports. Censuses of seamen taken by the Board of Trade (the British Department of

Commerce) between 1930 and 1935 showed that up to 30 percent of stokers and deckhands in British ships were generically referred to as *lascars* coming from British colonies in Asia, often Bengali although also including Malay and Chinese, as well as East African seamen, the latter predominantly Somali but also including Arabs.[132] British ships also used foreign seamen because they were cheaper, but between 1930 and 1935 the percentage dropped from 7.4 to 4.2.[133] There were few women in British ships, although liners had stewardesses for housekeeping duties in cabins; those found in freighters were the master's wife and the wives of his officers, who embarked at the master's discretion.

Freighters had a crew some of 20–50 men, who presented themselves to the port's Mercantile Marine Office, administering the Registrar General of Shipping and Seamen, where ships' names and destinations were chalked on blackboards.[134] The First Mate or Chief Engineer would examine the men's papers, and if they were acceptable they would "sign on" to the ship's Articles of Agreement for a voyage at agreed rates of pay. Until May 1941, this ceased if a ship was sunk, the argument being that if the owner had lost the vessel, he no longer required the crew and therefore this was "non-working time." Ships were generally divided into three departments: the deck under the First Mate, who operated the ship and dealt with cargo and apprentices; the engine-room under the First Engineer; and the chief steward, who was responsible for catering. The departments did not mix, living and eating in different parts of the ship; the boatswain (bosun) and carpenter, who also had a medical role, ate together, the former keeping discipline through forceful personality and powerful fists. The crew's quarters were cold, cramped, and damp, with the men in bunks of three or more levels, and while each man received one or two blankets, they had to supply their own straw mattress (or "donkey's breakfast"). The living conditions meant tuberculosis was rife in both the Merchant Navy and the Royal Navy, where the infected were removed immediately, as Admiral Somerville would discover.[135]

Officers, usually accommodated amidships, had small cabins, although sometimes even these had to be shared. When the ship was at sea, the captain was literally master of all he surveyed, running the ship but also ensuring it traded at a profit, which brought the prospect of a wealthy retirement. He and the other officers would meet and eat in the saloon. While iceboxes provided some fresh food, the ice quickly melted and catering depended upon tinned goods, including milk and butter, as well as dried food, although calls at ports permitted the purchase of some vegetables, fruit, and eggs. The master sought to avoid scurvy, but his acquisition of fresh food was limited by the need to maintain profitability.

Greeks Bearing Gifts

The Greeks proved the other major pillar of trade with Republican Spain, reflecting their postwar success, expanding at an annual rate of 5–10 percent through acquiring cheap ships and operating them profitably, despite rock-bottom freight rates. Between 1914 and 1936, Athens's steamer fleet expanded by 119 percent, from 821,000 grt to 1,800,850 grt, or 606 ships, of which only 13 were modern motor vessels. Indeed, 431 ships (1,102,736 grt) were more than 25 years old, while only 24 (101,054 grt), or 4 percent, were under 15 years old.[136]

Greek ship-owners undercut rivals through using older vessels and lower operating costs. Most crews were drawn from the Aegean islands, often relatves of the owner or master, as were all the presidents of the Greek Ship-owners Association (Enosi Ellinon Efopliston, EEE), such as Michael Pneumaticos (1936–38), and were more cohesive than foreign crews, often speaking the same dialect. Lower manning-levels than their competitors, averaging 19 men per ship, further reduced costs, with all hands expected to cover a wide range of duties and work longer watches and in harsher working conditions than foreign vessels for half of their pay: a master received only £22.10.00 ($112.50) a month, with £7.00.00 ($35.00) for a seaman.[137]

This helped the Greeks erode the British dominance in tramping, and while the world's largest tramping fleet continued to fly the Red Ensign—amounting to 39 percent of tonnage—Greece followed with 16 percent, and from the 1920s switched from its traditional Mediterranean/Black Sea trading routes to the Atlantic and even the Pacific Rim. Such was the Greeks' influence that in January 1935 they created an alliance with British lines to establish the Minimum Rate Scheme, adopted by other European merchant marines in March, which stabilized freight rates and helped push them up in later years.[138] Yet envy of Greek ship-owners provoked a deep vein of Hellenophobia within maritime and naval circles, almost as virulent as anti-semitism, with claims that they were grasping, parsimonious, untrustworthy, exploitative, and with low ethical standards.

The strength of the Greek merchant marine was underpinned by a strong, almost clannish, presence in London where, by 1938, there were 17 offices handling almost half their tramping fleet. This presence was dominated by Aegean owners, who operated flexible cooperative arrangements; half a ship's purchase price being secured in London, often in collaboration with British financial companies with high interest rates. The British also provided financial and brokerage services and charters, with Greek offices assuming responsiblity for organizing insurance and providing fuel to reduce owners' overheads.[139]

The Spanish Civil War offered Greek ship-owners a much-needed opportunity to earn foreign currency and fat profits after many lean years, and while most pursued legitimate trade, some certainly sailed close to the wind. Some Greek-registered shipping lines traded with Spain, a few to Nationalist ports but most to Republican ones, where Greek-registered ships called on 185 occasions during the war.[140] While a few ships were involved in trans-shipment from North African ports, most sailed to Marseilles, and those destined for Spain went down the coast from the French port of Sète.

The authoritarian government of Ioannis Metaxas repressed labor unions, but the Greek Seamen's Union (Naftergatiki Enosi Elladas, NEE) remained extremely influential and their vice-president made many voyages to Spain. Pro-Republican views meant that, on at least three occasions, ships destined for Nationalist ports landed their cargo elsewhere, in one case in Barcelona. Although the ship-owners willingly accepted the risks, the crews were sometimes more reluctant; a Greek ship suddenly stopped unloading munitions at Puerto Rosas, near the Franco-Spanish border, because the crews were spooked and abandoned ship.

Greek maritime activity at this time is underestimated, because of the 34 Greek-owned lines trading with the Republic, two-thirds were registered abroad—half in Great Britain, two in France, and most of the remainder in Panama and Romania, although one was in Italy! The potential protection of the White Ensign meant many vessels transferred to the British registry, with 25 doing so by July 1937. There was great indignation in Royal Navy wardrooms at "pseudo" lines, frequently with Greek-manned ships but occasionally with a British master, although when HMS *Vanoc* boarded the London-registered *Verbormilla*, it was discovered that her master was Polish, with a Russian certificate. Of three "British" ships supporting the northern enclave, only the masters of the *Caper* and the *Mirupanu* were British, while the *Bobie*'s was French.[141]

Most "pseudos" had a single British nominal shareholder, usually the company secretary but sometimes just a clerk. A typical example was the Westcliffe Steamship Company, founded on October 23, 1936, in London by Basil (Vassilios) Pandelis and John Catepodis (also Ioannis Katopodis), with Gordon Till having a nominal holding, this acquiring its first ship, the *Thorpehall*, three days later.[142] The two Greeks also established the Thames Shipping Company, while Pandelis was involved in the Thameside Line, with indications that British businessman and ship-owner Jack Billmeir acted as the companies' consultant.[143] Five largely Greek-owned lines were managed by W. G. Walton, established in 1933, these usually having only a single ship, with Walton acting as their company secretary. In 1937, David Barnett created a Cardiff-based management company, with three lines which had eight ships by the end of 1938. Ships broker J. N. Vassilov of the Union Maritime and Shipping Company was a director in all three lines and helped create the Greek-owned Finchley and Highbury Lines, while joining the board of the Greek-financed Prospero Line formed in August 1938. Many Greek vessels obtained temporary British registration through consuls in foreign ports until that loophole was close in the fall of 1937.

Many of these lines worked closely with Billmeir. Although it is now difficult to determine the exact relationship, he certainly provided brokerage services, arranging charters and finance, which was the source of his fortune.[144] He and Greek owners also indulged in a form of maritime Monopoly, selling to Georgios Mavroleon in 1937 the *Stanbrook*, *Stancourt*, and *Stancroft*, all of which he later repurchased, and the *Stanmore* (iii), while purchasing from T. N. Epiphaniades the *Prekla* (which became the *Stanleigh*), then in 1938 he sold the *Stancliffe* to P. G. Cottaropoulos. He also swapped ships with other lines supplying the Republic, selling the *Sheaf Spear* and *Stanmore* (ii) to France-Navigation.[145]

Non-Intervention

The Iberian Peninsula was a key site on Europe's strategic chessboard and the continent's chancelleries were concerned about its future ruler, leading France, Germany, and Italy to send arms to Spain after the uprising. Fears that foreign intervention might create a proxy war, igniting a European conflagration, led to British pressure turning off the French faucet. However, ideology drove the Fascist powers and the Soviet Union to send men and materiel, ignoring attempts by London and Paris to ensure non-intervention through diplomacy.

French admirals were especially concerned about German and Italian support for the rebels, fearing their Spanish bases might isolate Metropolitan France from its African empire. On July 31, Navy Minister Gasnier-Duparc informed Vice-Admiral Georges Mouget, commander of the 1st Fleet (1er Escadre), of President Leon Blum's concern and his desire to strengthen collaboration with the Royal Navy, despite the strains created by the Abyssinia Crisis and the Anglo-German Treaty.[146] After Blum met Defence Minister Édouard Daladier and Gasnier-Duparc, it was agreed that Atlantic Fleet commander Vice-Admiral François Darlan, accompanied by Rear Admiral Jean Decoux, would visit London, and the following day they met First Sea Lord Chatfield and Deputy Chief of the Naval Staff James.

Darlan said Paris hoped a democratic government would be restored in Spain, aided by an international non-intervention policy, but sought joint military action to pressure Germany and Italy from using the Balearics and Canaries as bases. While the Admiralty, and later the Cabinet, agreed with non-intervention in principle, they felt the French were overreacting and the pair returned empty-handed. Nevertheless, on August 10, chief of staff Durand-Viel wrote to the fleet commanders warning that despite the absence of a short-term threat, the Fascist powers would deliberately exploit the Spanish conflict, and he ordered Mouget to be ready to act in the western Mediterranean.[147] As early as August 4, the Navy Ministry ordered ships to report the movements of foreign merchantmen and warships.[148] The Alsud Command was established on August 18 under Admiral Gensoul, with either a cruiser or the seaplane-carrier *Commandant Teste* in Barcelona, and a cruiser and six destroyers off Morocco or in the western Mediterranean. Gensoul was succeeded by Rear Admirals Emmanuel Ollive, Jean Decoux, Émile Muselier, and Alfred Richard. The Atlantic Fleet separately deployed a destroyer and a sloop off northern Spain.

Eden pushed for an international non-intervention agreement following another precedent of the Third Carlist War.[149] On August 24, the British chiefs of staff warned the Committee for Imperial Defence about the possible Italian occupation of Spanish territory, especially the Balearics. They believed British policy should aim to maintain the integrity of Spanish territory, leading to benevolent neutrality in time of European war. They were also anxious that nothing be done further to alienate Italy.[150]

Meanwhile, Germany's Admiral Carls, fearing that escorting ships carrying military aid to the rebels could lead to an international incident, wanted them to make their own way and enter Nationalist ports at night. Raeder agreed, and on August 22 presented Hitler with the options of ending or escalating intervention. On August 25, the Führer chose the middle ground of limited intervention.[151] Germany, Italy, and most European states signed the Non-Intervention Agreement on August 26, banning exports of war materiel to the Iberian Peninsula, but there was no common definition of the term. Schedules of banned goods usually excluded "soft-skinned" vehicles and oil, which allowed U.S. automotive manufacturers such as Ford, Studebaker, and General Motors, and their European subsidiaries, legitimately to sell some 12,000 vehicles to both sides. In 1937 and 1938, the Nationalists spent the equivalent of $1 million on U.S. trucks, Firestone tires, and machine tools.[152]

The agreement's executive element was the Non-Intervention Committee (NIC), whose first meeting was on September 9.[153] There followed months of wrangling designing an acceptable monitoring system, but the NIC would remain a toothless tiger throughout its existence. Germany, Greece, Poland, Italy, and the Soviet Union ignored their international commitments, yet Eden later argued: "Tattered and full of holes no doubt, but better than total war in Spain and a European war out of that."[154]

Frustration led Eden to suggest in November that the Royal Navy unilaterally enforce non-intervention on foreign merchantmen, an idea strongly opposed by Hoare, now the First Lord of the Admiralty, who had not been consulted. The Cabinet and Baldwin rejected the idea on January 8, saying it lacked international sanction, needed expensive naval mobilization, and implied Britain was taking sides. Other ministers feared incidents with Italy or the Soviet Union, although Eden believed the supremacy of British naval power made this unlikely, and the Cabinet opted for strengthening the non-intervention system.[155] In France, the growing Italian commitment in Spain saw a split between the services, with the army trying to avoid provoking Italy, while the navy took a "gung-ho" attitude and in November Durand-Viel sought joint planning for offensive operations with the Royal Navy. A horrified Admiralty rejected this, arguing the threat was not as great as the French claimed. However, the Marine Nationale strengthened the Mediterranean Fleet, with morale boosted in December by government agreement to a three-year construction program.[156]

On March 9, 1937, the NIC finally agreed in principle to a monitoring system, which was activated at midnight on April 19/20.[157] It was directed by an International Board for Non-Intervention under 57-year-old Vice-Admiral Maarten van Dulm, an experienced officer and efficient administrator who had recently retired after 36 years with the Royal Netherlands Navy, the last two commanding the East India Fleet. He was also an athlete, competing in both the 1924 and 1928 Olympics in the single and team saber competitions, in the latter winning the bronze medal in 1924.

Dulm's Sea Observation network was based in Gibraltar, with deputy administrators at seven designated "observation ports": Dover, Cherbourg, Lisbon, Gibraltar, Madeira, Marseilles, and Palermo (another five were added later). He was supposed to have 550 NIC observers (or control officers), usually retired naval or merchant marine officers, from 17 European nations, with 74 equally divided between Germany and Italy, but there were only 300 when the scheme was implemented. Ships legitimately sailing to Spanish ports would embark observers authorized to inspect both their papers and cargo, supervise loading and unloading, and upon return submitting a report on the voyage. Ships would show they were "under control" by flying a pennant of two black balls on a white background. If the observers reported violations of the Non-Intervention Agreement, the ship's country of registry was obliged to take legal action against either the owners or the master, then report to the NIC. To ensure impartiality, ships sailing to either of the belligerents' ports were assigned observers from countries which generally supported their opponents, or who demonstrated neutrality in the conflict; Germans and Italians sailed to Republican ports, and British, French, and neutral country observers to Nationalist ports. From the summer of 1937, these distinctions were blurred and greater use was made of officers from neutral countries. With no observers permitted in the belligerents' ports, or those of their prime arms suppliers—the Fascist powers and the Soviet Union—the monitoring system was compromised from the start, although some ships carrying war materiel were stopped from leaving ports in the Low Countries.[158]

Dulm and Francis Hemming, the NIC Committee secretary, tried to spin a story of success on August 25, noting that within the first six weeks, 323 ships of the participating nations—together with 415 from non-participating—had been identified, while 79 were investigated as to their registry. But 24 ships sailed to Spain without observers and there were 96 voyages from Germany to Nationalist ports, many by ships carrying war materiel and raising the Panamanian flag when they entered the English Channel, and with considerable understatement they admitted the scheme was of limited value.[159] Nor did the new patrols reduce significantly the harassment of shipping in the Strait, especially of the Russians and minor naval powers, as Salamanca (the Nationalist military headquarters until 1938) ignored protests. The NIC attempted on April 30 to find a formula to prevent commercial cargoes being seized, but this was undermined by British fears it would compromise attempts to appease the Fascist powers.

The Sea Observation scheme was augmented by the Naval Patrol scheme, with the major naval powers operating in specific zones outside Spanish territorial waters. They monitored only those vessels registered to the Non-Intervention Agreement powers, which naturally excluded Spanish vessels or those from non-signatories such as Panama. On paper they could force vessels without the NIC pennant to stop, but they lacked the legal authority to order them into designated ports for inspection. Instead, they could only report suspicious activity, which made the Naval Patrol a cosmetic gesture but one which cost £820,434 ($3.8 million).

The Royal Navy's Home Fleet covered northern Spain from the French border to Cape Busto, west of Gijon, while the French Atlantic Fleet monitored the coast from there to the Portuguese border. Spain's southern coast, from the Portuguese border to Cape de Gata, together with the Canary Islands, was the responsibility of the Royal Navy's Mediterranean Fleet, and from there to Cape Oropesa, just north of Castellon, was watched by the German Navy. The Italian Navy was responsible for the remaining coast to the French border and the waters around Minorca. The French Mediterranean Fleet also patrolled the waters around the remainder of the Balearics, as well as Spanish Morocco.

The Royal Navy assigned a destroyer flotilla (squadron) of some dozen ships, each on rota from the Home and Mediterranean Fleets, while the French deployed vessels from a force of two dozen destroyers and 18 sloops, a third of them from the Atlantic Fleet. Of the Fascist powers, Italy provided half-a-dozen destroyers and two auxiliary cruisers, while Admiral Hermann Boehm's Reconnaissance Force (Aufklärungsstreitkrafte) deployed half-a-dozen ships, from battleships to torpedo boats, occasionally augmented by U-boats operating on the surface, although low visibility from the conning tower made control work hazardous, particularly in heavy seas. The Germans used Melilla for refueling, with oil provided by the Italians, and in April 1937 were permitted to take on stores in Algiers.

Enthusiasm for their new role quickly evaporated, most navies finding it as welcome as a hole in the hull, with frustration at seeing suspect ships under Panamanian colors sailing with impunity. British and French officers felt they were wasting their time to line the pockets of unscrupulous ship-owners, some foreigners using the Red Ensign and the *Tricoleur* as flags of convenience. Admiral Cunningham, who became Deputy Commander of the Mediterranean Fleet in July 1937, observed: "Attracted by the enormous profits to be made by running cargoes into ports of one side or the other, certain British ship-owners were operating whole lines of steamers to break the blockade. They were constantly getting into trouble."[160] One Admiralty official described the task as a "monotonous and disheartening duty," while a U-boat commander commented that avoiding the regulations was "child's play."[161]

Some intercepted ships simply ignored signals and entered port, such as the German freighter *Elise*, carrying war materiel from Bremen, when encountered off Corunna by the French destroyer *Alcyon* on April 28. If the French had come close to boarding her, the Nationalist Navy had orders to "seize" the vessel first, then convey it into port.[162] Nearly a month later, on May 24, the destroyer *Intrépide* halted the

Panamanian *Chepo* in French territorial waters near Port Vendres and discovered she was carrying 4,000 tonnes of munitions, ostensibly to Vera Cruz in Mexico, via Marseilles. As her papers seemed in order and she was Panamanian registered, the destroyer reluctantly allowed her to proceed, only for the Navy Ministry to rebuke her commander for failing to stop the shipment![163]

Yet the Fascist powers were also frustrated, the Italians complaining that the French were allowing Russian ships to sail down the coast within the 3-mile limit, which was untrue, unlike claims Russian ships frequently used false names or flags. Like the Italians, the Germans harbored dark thoughts about the connivance of the Royal Navy and the French Navy in covertly supporting arms supplies to the Republic, such thoughts fed by a constant stream of Nationalist complaints. It led to the bizarre situation where the German Navy, whose prime role from October 6 was shielding arms shipments, believing the British were applying a double standard to support the Republic, and this cooled the warm feelings generated by the 1935 treaty.[164] The Fascist navies became increasingly disgruntled about their monitoring role, and after Republican aircraft attacked their warships in the Balearics, Italy withdrew from the Naval Patrol after only 65 days, immediately followed by Germany. Offers by London and Paris to take over the German and Italian zones were summarily rejected, to the relief of the Nationalists, who feared the effects upon Italian supplies. The Fascist powers remained on the NIC to hamstring its activities, with the unspoken threat of withdrawing if any serious attempt was made to stop the flow of military aid into Nationalist ports. The universal fear of war meant that neither London nor Paris was willing to call the dictators' bluff. But the Royal Navy and the Marine Nationale did not abandon the Naval Patrol until September 1937, leaving only the maritime observer system as the rump of non-intervention.

Non-intervention was tottering not only at sea but also on land. On July 12, France refused to have observers on her Spanish frontier, which remained nominally closed to arms shipment, while Portugal had British observers withdrawn from her Spanish border. Portugal's dictator, António de Oliveira Salazar, naturally opposed the left-wing government in Madrid, making Lisbon a natural destination for German cargoes scheduled for the Nationalists. The *Kamerun*, escorted by the *Köln*, was the first to arrive, followed by DOAL's *Wigbert*. But while there was a peak surge in German ships entering Lisbon from July until September 1936, most were carrying commercial cargoes to what was the safest large port in the Iberian Peninsula.[165] Britain was Portugal's leading commercial partner, a major investor, and controlled the sea-lanes to the colonies, which allowed London to exert pressure restricting the landing of German war materiel in Portugal, forcing the *Usaramo* to sail to Vigo in September. But Lisbon was also influenced by a mutiny of Communist sailors in the destroyer NRP *Dão* and the sloop NRP *Alfonso de Albuquerque* on September 8. The sailors reportedly wished to sail to Spanish ports to support the government, but the mutiny was swiftly and bloodily suppressed. However, it illustrated the problems of becoming too openly involved. Portugal transferred a few shiploads of supplies to the Nationalists and its navy provided gyrostabilizers for the Canarias-class cruisers. Lisbon also allowed German warships to use its ports and anchor in its territorial waters, while German seaplanes joining the Nationalists refueled at the Lisbon naval aviation base of Bom Sucesso, where they received Portuguese bombs. But this was a drop in the ocean compared with the activity of other European powers.

CHAPTER TWO

The Widening War:
October 1936–July 1937

Germany, Italy, and the Soviet Union sank non-intervention by pumping military aid into Spain. Italy was first with extemporized shipments of troops and supplies, while the Germans were soon conducting a systematic program. This was code-named Operation *Magic Fire* (Unternehmen *Feuerzauber*), under Luftwaffe deputy commander General Erhard Milch, who delegated the task to Lieutenant General Helmuth Wilberg. Both had Jewish fathers and were potential scapegoats for failure, although Hitler's deputy and air force commander, Hermann Goering, later decided Milch was a kosher Aryan. Special Staff W (Sonderstab W) was established to coordinate deliveries, and on July 26, 1936, Rear Admiral Eugen Lindau, of the Hamburg Navy Service Office, organized the covert transfer of men and materiel through a Ship Transport Department (Schiffahrtsabteilung) in an operation codenamed the *Rügen Winter Exercise* (*Winterübung Rügen*).

Hamburg ship brokers Matthias Rohde, headed by Henry Aschpurwis, chartered the first ships, which communicated using an ad hoc code supplied by the German Navy, which accidentally supplied the *Lahneck* with this code for a commercial voyage. Lindau envisaged military aid being conveyed by chartering ships, designated Special Ships (*Sonderschiffe*), from lines such as DOAL which regularly traded with Spain, beginning with the *Usaramo*, which departed Flensburg for Cadiz on July 31.[1]

Four lines dominated German trade with Spain: Neptun covering the whole country; OPDR sailing to northern Spain, Spanish Morocco, and the Canaries; Hansa also sailing to northern Spain; and Sloman operating to Mediterranean ports and Majorca. Between July and September, only five vessels were available: the *Kamerun* and *Procida* from OPDR, Sloman's *Girgenti*, and the remainder from DOAL and the Hamburg-Bremer Afrika Line. These made eight voyages to carry 10,867 tonnes of supplies, but owners dragged their feet.[2] Ship-owners were reluctant to expose them when there was an opportunity to benefit from the recovering world economy. Raeder met ship-owners on October 6 and assured them of protection, pointing out the economic advantages of patriotism, with iron ore for rearmament guaranteeing a profitable return cargo.

However, only British underwriters were willing to insure ships travelling to Spain and their high rates made trade with Spain uneconomic, but when Berlin agreed to underwrite insurance costs, Lindau was able to inform the OKM on October 12 that all four lines were now willing to provide Special Ships. During October, eight set sail, five ostensibly chartered by the Junkers aircraft firm, these including two Spanish ships operated by Rhode, and together they brought in 5,686 tonnes of supplies and 474 men.[3] The crews' pay was 20 percent above the normal rate, and they would also receive bonuses to ensure they remained loyal … and silent.[4]

Lethal Cargoes

To match Soviet military aid from October, the Italians decided to increase their flow of supplies. They informed the Germans on October 24, when Foreign Minister Count Galeazzo Ciano, who was Mussolini's son-in-law, met Hitler at Berchtesgaden and asked the Germans to match this effort.[5] Six days later, Rear Admiral Wilhelm Canaris, head of German Military Intelligence (the Abwehr), who was visiting Spain, formally offered Franco a German expeditionary air force. Canaris, who spoke Spanish fluently, in 1915 having briefly monitored shipping from Spain before becoming a U-boat commander, had pursued a conventional career after the war until heading the Abwehr from 1934. When he met his Italian opposite number, General Mario Roatta of the Servizio Informazioni Militari (SIM), he found a like-minded supporter of Franco.[6] Franco accepted the German offer, and between November 7 and 9 some 6,500 men, led by Major General Hugo Sperrle, arrived in Cadiz as the Condor Legion in 25 ships totalling 105,000 grt. A third of these were from Nord-Deutscher Lloyd (NDL), most in the liners *St Louis* and *Berlin* of Strength Through Joy (Kraft durch Freude, KdF), the world's largest travel organization, the "holiday makers" remaining below deck when the ships departed. Total military aid delivered in 1936 amounted to 217, 997 tonnes, while a further 18,774 tonnes was landed during the first quarter of 1937, including 50 tonnes of mustard gas bombs, while three tankers delivered 5,100 tonnes of aviation fuel between November and February.[7] Hitler later announced, on December 22, that military aid to Spain would be sufficient to prosecute the war successfully without compromising German rearmament.

From September, Special Ships loaded at Stettin (Szczecin) and then sailed alone, at a rate of one or two per week, through the English Channel, operating under radio silence until they were off the French island of Ushant (Ouessant) at the entrance to the Bay of Biscay. There, they would use a code, changed monthly, to signal the OKM their location and estimated time of arrival, which was relayed to the Nationalist authorities. Their usual destination was Seville, which became the Germans' prime supply depot, or less frequently Cadiz, but there were occasional voyages to Corunna, Ferrol, and Vigo, the German Navy providing distant escorts. Most voyages were to support either the Condor Legion or the Nationalist Army

Table 2.1. The German Special Ship Program

Year	Voyages out	Delivered		Voyages back	Returned	
		Men	Freight (t)		Men	Freight (t)
Jul. 31, '36–Dec. 31, '37	105 (30)	9,278 (4,246)	73,284 (30,773)	104 (30)	3,615 (3,287)	196,726 (9,041)
1938	49 (49)	6,070 (6,070)	32,068 (32,068)	49 (49)	5,651 (5,651)	5,087 (5,087)
1939	26 (21)	1,498 (1,498)	12,530 (12,530)	26 (21)	7,258 (2,058)	6,607 (6,607)

Based on Source: Jung, 326, 329; Salas Annex 27. Figures in parentheses Aschpurwis & Veltjens

and Air Force, but there were a few voyages specifically to aid the Spanish Navy. The *Nyassa* dropped off supplies for the Nationalist Navy in Corunna in October, while three ships delivered five MTBs (Motor Torpedo Boats, S-boote) from November 10, 1936, until March 5, 1937. There was some confusion over cargo destinations, with tools for aeroengines unloaded at Ferrol when the engines were landed in Seville, while the Nationalist Navy received small arms and ammunition meant for the Army.[8]

Return passages were made with copper and iron pyrites, loaded at Huelva, or Melilla in Spanish Morocco, and fruit from Andalusia. From mid-1937, ships also repatriated men who had completed their tours. There were 180 Special Ship voyages to Spain (Table 2.1), delivering 117,882 tonnes of war material, 62 percent in the first 17 months and 27 percent in 1938, while they returned with 208,420 tonnes of fruit and ore.[9] Spanish exports to Germany rose from the equivalent of $242 million (RM 97.7 million) in 1936 to $585 million (RM 135.9 million) in 1937, while Germany was Spain's largest customer for pyrites.[10] The deployment of the Condor Legion meant the return of German warships to the Strait of Gibraltar, following an agreement with the Italian Navy to divide tactical areas of responsibility, but by the end of the year it was clear the Republican Navy no longer posed a threat.[11]

The activation of the Naval Patrol in March 1937 saw significant changes directed by Goering's crony, the Great War air ace Colonel Josef "Seppl" Veltjens. After the war, he became an arms-dealer, was briefly a Nazi Party member, but quit after arguing with Hitler and ended up on the blacklist of the SS (Schutzstaffel), Hitler's bodyguard, who repeatedly arrested him. Shielded by Goering, Veltjens acted as his front man for shady business dealings, their first in Spain being in August when Veltjens chartered Sloman's *Girgenti* to carry rifles to Corunna for General Mola's forces in northern Spain.[12]

A month later, he was involved in the *Allegro* Incident. He received a $35,000 advance from the Republic to acquire $926,850 worth of arms and ammunition, ostensibly for Yemen, with the first delivery to Barcelona in the *Yorkbrook*. For the second delivery, he acquired the Swedish *Allegro*, renamed *Balboa* but retaining her Swedish crew, which loaded 13,000 boxes with 600 tonnes of small-arms ammunition in Lubeck, but when opened in Barcelona most contained only bricks! It is unclear what happened to the remainder of the cargo or why Veltjens double-crossed his client.[13]

At the end of 1936, Veltjens and Aschpurwis created the Hansagesellschaft Aschpurwis & Veltjens line, which chartered DOAL's *Urundi* to transfer 600 Irish volunteers led by Fascist leader General Eion O'Duffy to Spain, embarking 417 in Galway Bay on December 13 and disembarking them at Ferrol on December 17. They proved a disappointment, and although the *Balboa* was chartered to bring a second contingent, this plan was abandoned.[14] The new line expanded to five ships (13,104 grt), all registered in Panama to avoid foreign interference. Former Sloman Line vessels were used largely for moving personnel, while the *Colon*, designed to carry railway locomotives and rolling stock, was used for the bulky cargoes. Aschpurwis & Veltjens organized 100 Special Ship operations from the spring of 1937, with return cargoes earning fat profits for the owners and Goering, but they also covertly sold arms to the Republic, being paid in Sterling, with shipments arranged through Poland.[15]

Italy's first delivery of military aid was in the *Emilio Morandi* to Melilla on August 3, 1936, and she arrived in Palma de Majorca on August 27 escorted by the destroyer *Malocello*, with supplies for the Majorcan garrison. Italian voyages into late 1936 (see Table 2.2) appear to have been ad hoc missions to meet specific requirements, while the Italian-operated *Aniene* supported air operations, delivering fuel, munitions, spares, and aircraft.[16] Chartering was usually through SIFR, augmented by Società Anonima di Navigazione Italia (SAN Italia)—which incorporated SAN Lloyd Triestino, SAN Adriatica, and Tirrenia—and the Trieste-based Tripcovich, which concentrated on commercial cargoes.[17] There was a surge of activity following Mussolini's December 10 decision to dispatch ground forces of the CTV under Roatta and a Legionary Air Force (Aviazione Legionaria) under Brigadier General Vicenzo Velardi.

Troop transport was aided by Lloyd Triestino's August 1935 acquisition of nine mostly German liners or cargo-liners (110,500 grt), collectively called the Regions (Regioni), to move troops to East Africa. Eight of them plus a hospital ship were among 44 ships (288,234 grt) chartered by Italian State Railroads (Ferrovie dello Stato) to carry the men and equipment to Spain. They made 61 voyages between December 22, 1936, and February 22, 1937, delivering 47,346 men with tanks,

Table 2.2. The German and Italian supply effort, July 1936–March 1937

Quarter	German	Italian
Q3/36	4	6
Q4/36	39	34
Q1/37	12	67

artillery, vehicles, and munitions to Cadiz, Seville, and Huelva. Still under Railroad charter, many ships then sailed to Antwerp and Rotterdam on commercial business. Usually, they sailed alone, but there were 10 convoys, usually of two ships, escorted by the Italian Navy, which deployed 13 cruisers and 22 destroyers. There was also a screen against Republican naval intervention consisting of a further nine cruisers, together with submarines, deployed between Sardinia and Palma. During March and April, there were seven more voyages, which landed another 43,000 tonnes for the CTV in Cadiz. This brought the total to 425,600 tonnes of war materiel, including artillery, ammunition, and vehicles, as well as 2,000 tonnes of phosgene and mustard gas chemical munitions.[18] The British later noted that while 63 Italian ships arrived in Spain's southern ports in 1936, this rose to 183 the following year, although the scale indicates most of these remained genuine commercial activities.[19]

To coordinate activities, Goering visited Mussolini on January 14 and they agreed to accelerate supplies before the Non-Intervention Agreement was implemented.[20] From the second quarter of 1937 to the third quarter of 1938, the Italians dispatched an average of 10 ships a quarter (see Table 2.3), 82 percent by requisitioned Spanish vessels, with a core of armed Italians ensuring the crews' loyalty, but as ships were returned to the Spanish ensign, this dropped to 38 percent from the third quarter of 1938. By the end of the war, 224 voyages brought 74,345 men (94 percent of the Italians sent to Spain), including civilian experts and truck drivers, 1,608 guns, 8,682 vehicles, and 157,908 tonnes of supplies, including 16,720 tonnes of bombs and 76,500 tonnes of supplies for the airmen.[21] They returned with commercial cargoes of minerals and agricultural products.

Four Lloyd Triestino liners, originally converted in 1935 to hospital ships for operations in Abyssinia, made 29 voyages home from Cadiz during the war, although the *Helouan* was lost to a fire off Naples on August 13, 1937.[22] They carried 14,072 sick and wounded men, together with those returning for compassionate reasons,

Table 2.3. Italian shipments of military aid, April 1, 1937–April 1, 1939

Quarter	Ship Movements	Tonnage	Men
Q2/1937	12	16,673	60
Q3/1937	10	19,371	664
Q4/1937	10	10,706	1,107
Q1/1938	10	18,609	48
Q2/1938	8	11,134	1,119
Q3/1938	21	16,004	3,520
Q4/1938	12	8,425	887
Q1/1939	34	11,587	7,114
Totals	117	112,509	14,519

Source: Bargoni. Tonnage is for weapons and military supplies but excludes vehicles. Some tonnage estimated

but in their brigs were 1,685 men who had been court-martialled and sentenced to prolonged terms. From June 1938, the brigs also held Italian members of the International Brigades, and when the *Gradisca* departed Cadiz on June 21, 1938, she included 55 political prisoners with an escort of 10 Carabinieros. The *Aquileia* was used most frequently for this role in 1938, bringing six deported "undesirables" in June and August and 24 political detainees in September, while when she departed Palma on November 2, she had 97 liberated Italian PoWs and 25 political detainees.[23]

Although the Republican Navy was aware of the activity, and an officer suggested "It might be wise to check to see if any of these ships are carrying Italian war material or troops," discretion was the better part of valor.[24] Intercepting them was fraught with difficulties of identification, and even if overcome, forcing a ship with Italian war materiel into Cartagena might have provoked war with Italy.[25] Air power was used against Nationalist ports from July 20 when the British *Ottinge* and the *Hillfern*, delayed in Corunna by a stevedores' strike, were strafed but suffered only minor damage. However, the Republic conducted only intermittent attacks and one led to tragedy.

The Norwegian *Gulnes*, owned by Hans Storaas of Bergen, had arrived in Seville in December 1936 to pick up a cargo of minerals, having unloaded coal at Oporto. On December 7, Republican bombers hit her amidships, causing serious damage, killing her master, Captain Gabriel Kielland, the First Mate, two stokers, and the cook. She was towed to Italy and broken up.[26] Oslo demanded 400,000 kronor (£20,000) in compensation from the Republican government, which paid them only £8,500 in March 1938.

Turning Gold into Lead

State military aid was slower to reach the Republic, apart from a few French shipments across the border, and would come across the Atlantic from Mexico and the Baltic from Poland. The first "commercial" delivery was in the *Jalisco*, acquired on August 5 by the Mexican Navy's Captain Araico, which brought two consignments from France to Alicante in August and September.[27] Mexico's left-wing President, Lázaro Cárdenas del Río, sent weapons from his own arsenals, the first in CTE's *Magallanes*, which arrived in Cartagena on September 2.[28] Cárdenas would dispatch half-a-dozen arms shipments to Spain, mostly to the northern enclave, and arrange for "replacement" Mexican Army weapons to be diverted to Republican ports, but adopted a low profile due to domestic politics.[29]

Mexico also arranged for consignments from Latin America to be sent in French ships via Poland's arms export organization, Syndykat Eksportu Przemysłu Wojennego (SEPEWE). Warsaw had no sympathy for the left-wing Spanish Republic, but because France was Poland's key ally to ensure her southern security, the Poles held their noses and acted as a conduit for arms supplies. Indeed, the Republic became

SEPEWE's leading client, purchasing material worth $34.2 million delivered via the Polish Shipping Agency (Polska Agencja Morska). The first consignment, to Bilbao, departed the international port of Gdynia/Danzig on September 6 in the Inchaustegui line's *Sebastián*, posing as the Mexican *Azteca*.[30] Gdynia provided tighter Polish control and higher storage fees, with faked sales using documents obtained by the brokers from minor diplomats, especially consuls, who grasped a golden opportunity, although Soviet Intelligence sometimes provided the papers.[31] There appears to have been some Polish–Estonian cooperation, with some arms loaded in Tallinin, and much profitable trans-shipment, for example in mid-November 1937, when three Finnish ships transported arms from Estonia to Gdynia to fill the *Jaron/Beny*, destined for Spain.[32]

The Poles dispatched 59 shipments, although not all arrived. Several were snared by the Nationalist blockade, including the Greek *Sylvia* (or *Silvia*) on October 18, 1936, reportedly facilitated by payment to the master, Spyros Katopodi, brother of one of the owners, who had a grudge against the NKVD (Narodny Komissariat Vnutrennikh Del, the People's Commissariat for Internal Affairs, Stalin's Security Service) and the Soviet Union.[33] Nevertheless, the dangers were such that after the loss of the enclave in the fall of 1937, shipments went to ports in western France such as Honfleur and Bordeaux, often in the hulls of Compagnie France-Navigation. This line was created on April 15, 1937, and owned by France's Communist Party, ostensibly for commercial marine transport.[34] Its foundation was influenced by Spanish ambassador Luis Araquistáin Quevedo and a visit to Moscow by French Communist leader Maurice Thorez, yet might have been created on Moscow's direct orders, for many Communist parties had secret radio links with The Centre, as the heart of the Soviet Intelligence organization was called, a fact certainly known to British intelligence, whose man was operating the set![35]

Communist Party members ran the line, including Central Committee member Paul Allard, who was born in Italy as Giulio Ceretti, and company secretary Francine Fromont, with an initial capital of a million francs ($47,000), increased to 5 million francs in August and 25 million in October 1938.[36] From the end of April, five ships left Poland and Romania for Spain with war materiel, often with false names and disguises, with many of the crew being Party members. The fleet rapidly expanded to 14 ships (15,887 grt) by August, many from the Schiaffino Line, purchased for £422,000 ($2.1 million), but during the first half of 1938 it shrank to 10 ships (16,696 grt). Their lethal cargoes had codenames such as the familiar "agricultural machinery," but the French authorities were not deceived.[37] The line made 227 voyages before the end of the Spanish Civil War, using Antwerp and Rotterdam brokers, many on commercial voyages but some on behalf of SEPEWE and the Soviet Union.

Soviet arms shipments were slower to arrive, although after the uprising Hispano–Soviet trade had exploded, beginning on September 26 when the *Neva* brought 3,000 tonnes of food from Odessa to Alicante. By the end of the year, Russia had delivered 277,000 tonnes of cotton, timber, food, and coal worth $7.4 million, rising to 520,000 tonnes worth $25 million in 1937, as well as supplying oil.[38] With the Republic's war industries able to produce only 1 percent of its monthly requirement of 600 tonnes of small-arms ammunition, Madrid requested Soviet military aid as early as July 25.[39]

But it was not until September 14 that Soviet leader Josef Stalin approved a plan by the NKVD, who would supervise the program executed by Marshal Kliment Voroshilov's Defense Ministry, with detailed planning by his Main Intelligence Directorate (Glavnoye Razvedyvatel'noye Upravleniye, GRU) head Semen Uritskii, and the head of the Interior Ministry's Foreign Section, Abram Slutskii, as Operation *Kh* (Operatsiia *X*), this being sent to Stalin at Sochi on September 26. Three days later, it was rubber-stamped by the Central Committee's executive arm, the Politburo, which was responsible for funding each shipment or *Igrek*.[40]

Funding was underpinned by Spain's gold reserves, of which $240 million had already been sent to Paris for military aid. On September 13, the Spanish Cabinet authorized Premier Francisco Largo Caballero and Finance Minister Juan Negrín López to move the remaining 510 tonnes, worth $548 million, to an unspecified "safe place."[41] It was loaded into the *Kim*, *Kuban*, *Neva*, and *Volgoles*, which had all arrived at Cartagena with commercial cargoes, and departed for Odessa on October 25, escorted by the Republican fleet as far as Algiers. They arrived between November 2 and 4 and were unloaded at night by NKVD officers personally selected by the ministry's feared leader, Nikolai Eshov. The bullion was stored in Moscow's Gosbank from November 9, to pay not only for war materiel but also the salaries of Russian specialists. Some was used by the Soviets for their own purposes, but most underpinned finance for the Republic's war effort, channelled through the Moscow-run Banque Commerciale pour l'Europe du Nord (Eurobank), based in Paris.[42]

The gold which paid for arms shipments (known as *Igreks*), I-1/17, actually passed the bullion transports, with the first arriving in Cartagena on October 4 as deck cargo on the tanker *Campeche*. The first Soviet freighter to arrive was the *Komsomol* on October 12, followed three days later by the *Staryi Bolshevik* with Tupolev SB bombers, which would be called Katie (Katiuska), as deck cargo.[43] By November 12, some 6,000 tonnes of war materiel had reportedly been imported, but not all involved weapons and munitions; I-12 in the tanker *Sergo Ordzonikidze* brought 3,900 tonnes of vehicle and aviation gasoline on November 11, followed by I-16 on November 26 with 200 tank crew in the *Chicherin*. There would be 14 *Igreks* in 1936 (see Table 2.4), 38 in 1937, 13 in 1938, and one in 1939, a number of these shipments including materiel loaded in Poland.[44] Soviet military aid began to decline from the spring of 1937, with British Intelligence calculating 13,000 tonnes was dispatched in May 1937, 10,000 tonnes in June that year, 3,750 tonnes in July, and just 2,000 tonnes in August.[45]

Table 2.4. Arms shipments to the Republic

Quarter	Mexico	Poland	Soviet Union	Commercial	Total
Q3/Q4/1936	2	11	15	4	32
Q1/1937	1	12	9	8	30
Q2/1937	–	6	11	5	22
Q3/1937	–	5	5	5	15
Q4/1937	–	4	2	-	6
Q1/1938	–	6	4	3	13
Q2/1938	–	5	6	1	12
Q3/1938	–	1	–	–	1
Q4/1938	–	2	–	–	2
Q1/1939	–	1	2	–	3
Total	3	53	54	26	136

Sources: Howson; Ciechanowski; Manrique/Lucas; Morenos I, 982, 1003, 1020–24, 1034–37, 1039–69, 1090–92, 1149

Notes: Data includes shipments to France. Some commercial estimated from data in Manrique/Lucas

Each *Igrek* was organized by the NKVD, which carefully vetted the crew—both men and the women who embarked as waitresses, nurses, laundry maids, and cleaners—who were mustered at the last minute and confined to the ship. Each ship had a political officer, or Commissar, who with the captain monitored the crew's political "health" and reported upon the ship's return, while the ever-suspicious NKVD usually added an agent secretly.[46] Ships were loaded at night with NKVD guards, those carrying bulk cargoes, such as coal or grain, concealing war materiel behind the legitimate load or covering it with canvas. While some sailed from Murmansk, geography dictated that most Soviet trade with Spain was handled by the Black Sea Merchant Fleet, which deployed 16 ships (56,637 grt) for commercial as well as "Party and Government" (Zadaniye Partii i Pravitel'stva, ZPP) traffic.[47] Despite their false documents, it was impossible to conceal their passage transiting the narrow waters of the Bosphorus, the Sea of Marmara, and the Dardanelles for under the Montreux Convention—signed on July 20, 1936—all merchant ships had to radio their name, nationality, tonnage, destination, and last port of call to receive Turkish authorization. Such calls were easily monitored by consulates which could observe the passage of the ships.[48]

In the Aegean, some ships might anchor in remote Greek islands to change their appearance, using paint and wooden panels, although there was always a risk of being spotted by Italian warships or aircraft from the Dodecanese Islands. One vessel, carrying tank or air crew, pretended to be on passage from British India, with the troops wearing pith helmets, while others pretended to be tourists, slowly strolling the decks in tuxedos![49] These ruses helped ships sail unchallenged past Sicily and

Majorca, while the radio operator, assisted by a cryptographer, transmitted coded signals twice daily to a joint army–NKVD station near Moscow State University in specific Greenwich Meant Time "slots," indicating their exact location and progress. They were paced by legitimate merchantmen, who detected potential threats, sent details to all Russian ships in the vicinity, then acted suspiciously to entice away the Nationalist patrols.[50] The approach to their destination, usually Cartagena or Alicante, was at night, with the ship's lights extinguished, and might be met by Republican warships. Unloading was often compromised by poor Spanish security, with reports of the arrival of Soviet military aid sweeping around the port like wildfire, increasing the threat from air attack. Spanish stevedores proved negligent and clumsy, damaging supplies, while shipments were often left exposed on the dock, partly because the Republic lacked transport to move it inland.

Operation *Kh* overstretched the Soviet Union's commercial fleet of 534 ships (1,156,846 grt), which was straining to support the national economy.[51] Diverting ships deprived the country of valuable foreign currency, including the few freighters capable of carrying large or bulky items, such as the eight Max Hőlz-class vessels, including the *Komsomol*, *Blagoev*, and *Timiryazev*, and even these had to carry crated Katies as deck cargo which might be swept overboard in storms.[52] Stalin quickly decided he did not wish to be seen flagrantly flouting the Non-Intervention Agreement, so I-8, in the *Blagoev* on November 4, was the last in a Soviet hull. They were replaced by foreign ones, starting with the Norwegian *Linhaug*, which brought I-11 to Cartagena on November 10, with many chartered in Rotterdam through Neederlandsche Bevrachtingskantoor Van Driel.[53] The Russians may also have chartered vessels for dual-use cargoes. Indeed, on December 2, the British authorities delayed the Murrell Steamship Company's West Hartlepool-registered *Thurston* at Malta before deciding her 100 Russian-built trucks were not war materiel.[54]

Spanish ships were the obvious choice for arms deliveries, with the Basque P. Aldecoa line's *Aldecoa* landing I-9, I-21, and I-34 between November 1936 and June 1937, with a special shipment on April 7 of 4 tonnes of mustard gas.[55] Yet there were problems, for the Russians lacked detailed information on foreign vessels' capacities and capabilities, while there was no guarantee that Spanish ships would succeed. Indeed, on July 8, the crew of the *Iciar* refused to sail to Spain with I-35, which was transferred to another Spanish ship, the *Darro*.[56] The crew's pessimism was well founded, for the *Iciar* was captured on her next voyage to Spain in August 1937. Despite all these problems, Soviet historians assert that 64 of 66 shipments made during the Civil War reached their destination.[57] Operation *Kh* shipments also involved consignments from other nations; I-10, I-11, and I-26 were actually SWEPE cargoes, while I-43 to I-46 were Czech weapons brought in France-Navigation ships. By the end of 1938, the total value of the operation's deliveries came to $171,438,789.[58] Soviet arms prevented the fall of Madrid, but Nationalist pressure upon the city meant the government moved to Valencia.

Both sides received war materiel from the Greeks, whose ships frequently flew the Panamanian flag. The Republic ordered ammunition in September 1936 from the Greek Powder and Cartridge Company (Etaria Ellinikou Pyritidopoieiou kai Kalykopoieiou, Pyrkal), owned by the prominent industrialist Prodromos Bodosakis-Athanasiadis, with Prime Minister Metaxas willing to turn a blind eye to the activities of Bodosakis and ship-owners, munitions providing some 12 percent of Greek exports in 1937.[59] Most munitions for the Republic appear to have been carried by G. M. Mavroleon's *Cap Ferrat*, *Katina*, *Kimon*, and *Nephaligeretis*, augmented in 1937 by four ships purchased from Billmeir which became the *Naukratoussa* (*Stanmore*), *Neoptolemos* (*Stancroft*), *Nepheligeretis* (*Stancourt*), and *Polyfloisvios* (*Stanbroke*), the *Neoptolemos* and *Polyfloisvios* returning to Billmeir in 1937 and 1938 respectively.[60] On July 15, 1937, an NIC observer in Marseilles discovered shells in the hold of the *Naukratoussa*, but after receiving the master's assurances they were destined for Piraeus, she was allowed to depart on July 19, only to be unloaded in Barcelona. At exactly the same time, the *Nepheligeretis*, also known as the *Melitios Venezianos*, was unloading in Valencia munitions which she too had loaded in Marseilles while flying a non-intervention pennant. Ships frequently changed their names, appearances, and registrations, sometimes in mid-voyage: the larger *Kimon* also assumed the names *Leonia* and *Ariston* to deliver 1,500 tonnes of munitions between March 3 and June 30, 1937.[61]

The first deliveries appear to have been made at the end of 1936, with the Nationalists claiming 18 Greek munitions shipments to the Republic from January 3, 1937 to May 11, 1938. Six shipments followed during the second half of 1937. Ships were chartered by Greek agents in Marseilles and loaded in Piraeus, accompanied by documents usually naming Vera Cruz as the destination, courtesy of the Mexican Chargé d'Affaires in Athens, Máximo José Kahn Mussabaun. Extrapolating data from 1937 figures suggests there were 50 arms shipments to the Republic involving 25,000 tonnes of war material worth some £3 million ($15 million), with Greek-registered vessels usually carrying munitions and Panamanian ones carrying weapons.[62] However, three Greek-registered vessels carried some of SEPEWE's earliest consignments, while on February 27, 1937, an agreement was signed allowing Soviet military cargoes to be carried in Greek ships. The *Kimon* carried one of the first such consignments, the agreement being renewed a year later.[63]

A dozen munitions shipments totalling 5,000 tonnes, worth some £1.5 million ($8 million), were made to the Nationalists by Bodosakis's Davaris Line sailing to Huelva or Malaga.[64] Nationalist naval intelligence monitored Greek duplicity, which was deeply resented by the Nationalists. In May 1938, they presented the Greek diplomatic agent, retired Rear Admiral Perikles Argyropoulos, with documentary evidence of the Greek Navy selling 30 6.1-inch (155mm) guns to the Republic. Metaxas may have been personally involved in the arms shipments, and was certainly aware of them, but allowed them to be handled by his éminence grise, Ioannis Diakos, and his friend Bosakis to provide plausible deniability.[65]

Billmeir's maritime shell-game meant he was frequently accused of being an arms-smuggler, although this does not appear to have been the case. However, on October 30, the Royal Navy reported the Bramhall Shipping Company's ship the *Bramhall* unloading at Alicante 900 tons of weapons obtained by the anarchist Confederación Nacional de Trabajo (CNT) in Hamburg.[66] Reports that another Bramhall line ship, the *Hillfern*, was loading arms for Spain in Danzig/Gdansk led to the line's manager, Claude Angel, being summoned to a meeting with Sir Julian Foley, head of the British Board of Trade's Mercantile Marine Department. Angel admitted the cargo was destined for Bilbao and claimed he would lose money if the charter was not completed, but reluctantly agreed to cancel the charter and pledge not to send any more arms to Spain. But on November 10, he informed Foley he had been unable to prevent the *Hillfern*'s departure and that the cargo had been discharged in Bilbao. Other lines were more cautious, the Glasgow-based Maclay and MacIntyre consulting the Board of Trade when offered a Russian charter to carry cargo to Spain. Officials warned that the voyage might be dangerous and Royal Navy protection was not automatically available. The Admiralty's jaundiced comment was: "The Russians are not doing this to send Christmas crackers to Spain."[67]

Delivering Black Gold

Ships, vehicles, and aircraft all needed fuel, but in July 1936 the Spanish Petroleum, Oil, and Lubricants (POL) monopoly CAMPSA had only 16 tankers (78,025 grt).[68] CAMPSA depended upon the American Texas Company, popularly called Texaco—although this did not become its formal name until 1959—to supply most of Spain's oil.[69]

Texaco's chairman, Norwegian immigrant and former ship's master Captain Thorkill Rieber, had worked his way up from deckhand and was a fascist-admiring Anglophobe. He diverted five tankers bound for mainland Spain to the Nationalist refinery at Tenerife in the Canaries, with the first to arrive being the Norwegian *Solitaire*, with 5,000 tons of crude from Bordeaux, but from 1937 they also went to Vigo. In October, Rieber arranged for refined products to be delivered from the Port Arthur, Texas, oil refinery and distributed from Tenerife to all the Nationalist-controlled ports in Texaco vessels and some Spanish tankers. The *Campas* operated to and from Seville, the *Tiflis* from Vigo, while the *Badalona* supported naval bases, augmenting the small amounts which Germany and Italy could spare from their limited stocks.[70]

Rieber delivered a total of 1,866,000 tonnes worth $6 million and also provided the Nationalists with intelligence on Republican oil transport.[71] He refused U.S. President Franklin D. Roosevelt's request to cease trading and arranging credit with the Nationalists, and was fined $22,000 in 1937 for violating the Neutrality Act. Growing domestic political pressure forced Rieber to replace Texaco vessels from

Table 2.5. POL supplies to the Spanish Republic (tonnes)

Country	1936	1937	1938	Total
USSR	111,716	163,841	159,000	434,557
Romania	66,279	203,804	238,277	508,360
Mexico	1,398	1,604	3,380	6,382
Total	179,393	369,249	400,657	949,299

Source: Roizin, *Fuel, the blood of war*

1938 with tankers from Norway, which had the world's third-biggest tanker fleet, with 229 hulls (1,657,782 grt) or 15.5 percent of the world total, most of them modern motor vessels.[72] Shipping lines such as Fearnley & Eger, Leif Hoegh, and J. Hansen loaded oil ostensibly bound for Antwerp or Rotterdam, but at sea diverted to Nationalist ports. Fearnley & Eger's *Garonne* made five voyages from September 1938 to March 1939, mostly to Bilbao and Santander. Curiously, none of Ludwig Mowinckel's tankers were involved in this trade, although his freighters regularly called in Nationalists ports en route to Latin America. Directly and indirectly, 53 Norwegian tankers made 74 voyages to Nationalist Spain, half from Port Arthur, usually on behalf of Texaco but some chartered by Standard Oil of New Jersey (which became Esso), Standard Oil of New York (or Socony, later Mobil), and Royal Dutch Shell. Total oil sales to the Nationalists were 3.5 million tonnes, worth $20 million.[73]

Mexico supplied some oil to the Republic, but Eastern Europe was the prime source, especially Romania. This came through French ports, usually Marseilles, and continued even after Romania banned CAMPSA in mid-1937 due to German pressure.[74] On August 17, 1936, the Soviet Union's Politburo agreed to sell the Republic "fuel oil at a reduced price in the required quantity on the most favorable terms," and between August 15 and October 3, eight Soviet vessels brought in 60,000 tonnes. Madrid's Finance Ministry delegated all transport arrangements to CAMPSA, which worked with the Soviet Embassy's commercial attaché. However, most of the Republic's oil came in foreign hulls, including the Hellenic Tramp Steamship's *Ionia, Iolkos,* and *Iossifoglu,* which were given British registrations in 1937, becoming the *Romford, Woodford,* and *Ilford* respectively, but still with Greek crews.[75] During the war, CAMPSA acquired three ships—*English Tanker, Micoene,* and *Saustan*—which they ran under flags of convenience. The Italians estimated that between September 1936 and December 1937, the Republic received nearly 795,000 tonnes of POL (See Tables 2.5 and 2.6) from Eastern Europe.[76]

Danger at Sea

Moscow's fears for the safety of its ships were demonstrated on December 14 by the fate of the motor ship *Komsomol.* She had delivered war materiel on October 12

Table 2.6. POL deliveries to the Republic from Eastern Europe (tonnes)

Quarter	Gasoline	Oil	Total
Q3/36	2,500	37,877	40,377
Q4/36	55,152	125,744	180,896
Q1/37	92,200	77,050	169,250
Q2/37	45,050	101,150	146,200
Q3/37	52,900	49,170	102,070
Q4/37	108,510	47,340	155,850
Q1/38	67,550	39,948	107,498
Q2/38*	59,624	74,430	134,054
Total	483,486	552,709	1,036,195

Source: Rapalino, Appendix VII
Note: *includes July 1938

and then resumed commercial operations, loading 6,900 tonnes of manganese ore at Poti before departing for Ghent on December 5. Italian destroyers spotted her passing through the Sicilian Channel and reported to the cruiser *Canarias*, flying the flag of Francisco Moreno, who was patrolling the approaches to the Alboran Sea with two auxiliary cruisers.

They intercepted the *Komsomol* 30 miles south of the Spanish coast, identifying her through the photograph in her file, fired a warning shot, and sent a boarding party. When they arrived, they ordered her master, Captain Grigory Mezentsev, and his crew of 38, including two women, to abandon ship.[77] Once they boarded the cruiser, Captain Moreno, on his own initiative, sank the freighter with gunfire. He claimed she was, or might have been, carrying war materiel, and threats of air or submarine attack made an inspection impossible, yet in heaving-to to dispatch a boarding party he was exposing his ship to these threats. He could have forced the freighter to sail to Ceuta for inspection, just as the Strait Flotilla did with the two Soviet ships only days earlier.[78] On April 2, he would also sink the Greek-owned *Poli* in identical circumstances when she was in ballast from Bagnoni to Nationalist-held Melilla to pick up minerals, and had earlier been accused of "smuggling." Her owner, Emmanuele Vintiades, who lived in Genoa, replaced her with a Nationalist merchantman, the *Compostela*.

Moreno's actions seem to have been personal protests against arms shipments to the Republic. The sinking of the *Poli* alarmed Franco, who feared it would provoke an intervention by the French or the Russian Black Sea Fleet, according to Lieutenant Colonel Emilio Faldella, Italian liaison officer at Franco's headquarters in a telegram to Rome that night. He passed the buck neatly by coyly suggesting he would follow whatever actions his friends recommended.[79] Ivan Maisky, the Russian ambassador in London and national NIC representative, certainly wanted Soviet warships to escort

Soviet supply ships in the western Mediterranean. But Navy Minister (Commissar of the Soviet Navy) Admiral Vladimir Orlov did not wish to expose his ships and found various excuses for inaction.[80]

Mezentsev and his crew were imprisoned for 10 months, with Moscow uncertain about their fate until the Italian ambassador in Moscow informed Foreign Minister Maksim Litvinov that the crew, and that of another Russian ship, were interned in "insurgent" territory. Yet the Soviet authorities denied all knowledge of their fate to the crews' dependents and stopped the crews' pay. When the crews returned in October and November 1937, they were feted, presented with new clothing and a gratuity equivalent to a month's pay, but no back pay.[81] The *Poli's* crew of 19 Greeks and an Albanian were also imprisoned before being transferred first to Genoa and then the Piraeus.

Seeking the Golden Fleece

Many ship-owners, led by the British, were prepared to accept increased risks because the Spanish Civil War created commercial opportunities. The Nationalists would claim that of the 2,825 (7,035,500 grt) ships which entered enemy ports between January 1, 1937, and March 31, 1939, 1,599 (56.5 percent) were British, 270 (9.5 percent) were French, and 185 (6.5 percent) were Greek, while 56 were of unknown registration.[82] Britain was the Republic's prime export customer, although her own exports to Spain almost halved from £10.5 million in 1936 to £5.6 million in 1938. But Britain remained a major customer of Spanish iron ore, totaling 719,897 tonnes in 1936, 745,376 tonnes in 1937, and 987,835 tonnes in 1938, freight rates to Republican ports being twice those to Nationalist ones.[83] The British were also involved in traffic from Black Sea (see Tables 2.7 and 2.8) ports which were the source of war materiel, food, POL, manufactured products, and raw materials.

Before the Civil War, freight rates had steadily declined from 21.30 shillings ($5.32) per ton in 1930 to 19.53 shillings ($4.90) in 1935, although they rose to

Table 2.7. Italian assessment of ships sailing to Republican ports from Black Sea ports, 1936

Period	Ships							
	Russian	Republican	British	Greek	Panamanian	French	Other	Total
September–October	13	4	–	–	–	–	–	17
October–November	17	2	2	3	–	–	–	24
December	17	4	–	–	–	–	–	21
Total	47	10	2	3	–	–	–	62

Source: Rapalino, Appendix VI

Table 2.8. Italian assessment of ships sailing to Republican ports from Black Sea ports, January–July 1937

Period	Russian	Republican	British	Greek	Panamanian	French	Other	Total
January	11	10	–	–	–	–	1	22
February	3	14	1	5	–	–	1	24
March	–	15	5	3	1	–	–	24
April	2	19	5	2	–	–	–	28
May	–	14	5	2	1	–	4	26
June	–	10	11	3	2	–	–	26
July	–	10	10	1	1	1	1	24
Total	16	92	37	16	5	1	7	174

Source: Rapalino, Appendix VI

33.95 shillings ($8.48) in 1937.[84] As one writer noted: "After fifteen years of almost continuously depressed freight rates, it was difficult to keep out of a trade which was likely to yield some handsome returns ... Any ship involved in the trade had to pay an increased war risk insurance for the hull, insurance for the crews, and a war bonus to the crews of the ships."[85] The Abbey Line's first voyage, when the *Neath Abbey* unloaded from Rotterdam at Alicante by May Day 1937, made a £2,369 ($11,800) profit, the equivalent of a whole year before then, while her voyage to Liverpool made another profit of nearly £1,665 ($8,300). Most of the £45,000 ($225,000) in profits it generated from July 1934 to February 1939 were through trading with the Republic.[86] A cargo worth £5,000 ($25,000) would generate a £2,700 ($13,500) profit, even with increased costs, with ship-owners boosting profits by operating elderly "rust-buckets" which generated lower war risk insurance premiums, typically 20–25 percent of the cargo's value, than more modern vessels. In January 1937, they accepted seamen's demands for a 50 percent daily bonus, or £2 ($10) for ships trading with Spanish ports, covering the 24 hours before the ship entered such a port to 24 hours afterwards, the Depression ensuring there was never a shortage of seamen.[87]

The Soviet Union helped the Republic charter vessels and pay the owners bonuses through the Moscow Narodny Bank, Officina Commercial España, and later the Mid-Atlantic Shipping Company. The latter was a Republican front organization created in London on July 21, 1937, whose directors were the Spaniard José Ignacio Aldama, the Briton Edward Leader Burbidge, and the Philippine-born American citizen Marino de Gamboa, who had spent most of his life in Bilbao. It had half-a-dozen British and Estonian-registered ships, and following a Republican government decree of April 19, 1938, managed all Sota y Aznar vessels in foreign ports.[88] Time-charters could create complex problems for owners, as the Abbey Line discovered. The Republic had a £4,750 ($23,750) per month time-charter on the *Neath Abbey*, which was ordered to Odessa in January 1938. The line was reluctant due to the risks, but the crew said they were willing to make the voyage and the Spanish agreed a one-off bonus of £2,500 ($12,500) for fuel and extra expenditure.

British activity was dominated by Charles Strubin and Jack Billmeir. Strubin was born in Switzerland's Basel-Land canton as Karl-Ernst Strübin, emigrating to England before the Great War.[89] In March 1928, he founded Charles Strubin & Company, with offices in the docks near Tower Bridge, Grimsey, Latham & Co. acting as his agents. He operated half-a-dozen vessels at a time and had a wide range of contacts, especially in the Baltic States, where he acquired a number of Estonian vessels from late 1936. He shared his home near Slough with Estonian shipowner Evald John Jakobson. He also acted as an agent with Mid-Atlantic, as well as working closely with Claude Angel and Alfred Pope.

Angel began trading in 1916, with offices in Cardiff, operating from 1934 as Angel, Son & Company. During the Civil War, he would expand his fleet to a dozen vessels, including the *Hillfern*.[90] Under his company's old title, Angel, Dalling and Company, he owned the *Bramden* and the *Bramhall*.[91] Pope's former coal-exporting business helped him acquire the majestic Seabank Hotel in Porthcawl, living and working on the top floor. He had an interest in the Kenfig Pool Export and Import Company, and on December 19, 1936, established the Veronica Steamship Company, named after his wife, and soon acquired the *Joyce Llewellyn* (later *Seabank Spray*), the *Seven Seas Spray*, and the *Kenfig Pool* (later *Seabank*). His business partner was Gibraltar resident Thomas McEwen, who had worked in Spain for 30 years and organized time-charter work with the Basque and Republican governments; one of his relatives, W. H. McEwen, owned the Gibraltar-registered *Bobie*, which became involved in the infamous Santona Agreement of September 1937.[92]

Billmeir, born Billmeier, left school in August 1914 to work in a shipbroker office in the City of London, changing his surname when he joined the Baltic Exchange in 1926.[93] Commercial success did not begin until 1931, when he formed J. A. Billmeir and Company for ship management, followed in 1934 by the Stanhope Steamship Company, with two small coasters. Seeing the potential market in Republican Spain, he expanded Stanhope to seven ships by the end of 1936, bought 21 in 1937, including three tankers—but not all for Spanish operations—and nine in 1938, the loans guaranteed by another ship-owner, Halford Constant. His fleet averaged about 25 hulls, declining to about 20 when the Civil War ended, and in addition to buying or selling ships to Greek lines he sold two to France-Navigation.[94]

He reportedly made £3 million ($15 million) from trading with the Republic, allowing him to move from a small office in Bury Street to a new building in Bishopsgate. But his fortune did not come purely from the Stanhope Line, which made profits of £62,373 ($311,865) in 1937, £137,632 ($688,160) in 1938, and £99,999 ($499,995) in 1939, with dividends of £7,620 ($38,100), £8,276 ($41,380), and £18,461 ($92,305) respectively.[95] He was also the director of other lines, such as Newbegin (and Edward Newbegin was a director of his line), and was closely linked with the Greek shipping community in London while also providing brokerage and financial services. However, claims he directly and indirectly controlled 140 ships through three companies are exaggerated.[96] It was probably this aspect which allowed him to become a millionaire and in 1937 to acquire the 216-acre Westbrook estate, near Farnham, West Surrey—which was sold in December 2021 for £24.5 million ($30.5 million)—while the following year he bought Chestfield Golf Club.[97] Billmeir also acquired a yacht, with guests including his friend Winston Churchill; he was an accomplished yachtsman and a friend described him as "the jolliest millionaire I ever knew."[98] He joined one of the great City guilds, The Worshipful Company of Shipwrights, and rose to the position of Prime Warden in 1962–63. The Guild's Billmeir Award Scheme continues to encourage young boat builders.[99]

The only war materiel Billmeir is known to have supplied, as he admitted to Sir Julian Foley in October 1936, were three aircraft in the *Stanmore* which were offered to the Nationalists and sold to the Republicans. He claimed he was unaware of the cargo until it was loaded, but had already decided to confine his activities in Spain to legitimate commercial activities such as carrying coal and food. He appears to have done so, but not everyone was so scrupulous; Claude Angel was certainly involved with Strubin in a number of arms shipments, including the Estonian-registered *Yorkbrook*, which they jointly owned.

Other entrepreneurs included Cardiff-based David Barnett, who would manage up to 15 London-registered ships trading with the Republic for the Atlantic and Mediterranean Trading Company, the Continental Transit Company, and the African and Continental Steamship Company (later African and Continental Steamship and Trading Company). The latter line had five ships operating out of Oran and Marseilles, while six ships operated by Counties Steamship Management served Republican contracts.[100] The Cardiff-based Arlon Steamship Company had four modern tankers; three carrying aviation gasoline from French refineries to Valencia and Barcelona, with one operating from Oran to Alicante and Barcelona. On November 25, the Thameside Shipping company was established with Gordon Till, acquiring its first ship, the *Marvia*, five days later. In Wales, the Dillwyn Steamship company was created in Swansea on January 23, 1937, and operated with Claude Angel, who apparently purchased its first ship, the *Marie Llewellyn*. The established Tyneside line of Sheffield-born W. A. Souter also became involved in trading with the Republic, together with the Souter-owned Sheaf Steam Shipping Company.

Belgian, Dutch, French, Greek, Scandinavian, and Baltic State ship-owners also sought to capitalize upon the war's commercial opportunities. In addition to France-Navigation, a number of French lines traded with Spain, including the Paris-based Scotia Corporation, under John Jensen and Francois León. This was probably another Republican front organization, with a fleet of four vessels, some shipping arms flying the Panamanian flag, as did the five ships of the Antwerp-based Societé Belge des Enterprises Commerciales, created in 1937 but wound up the following year, and associated with Van Driel in Rotterdam. Two Marseille-based Greek businessmen, P. G. Cottaropoulos and G. Theophylatos, had a fleet of four ships, but later sold one to France-Navigation, which also supplied POL. Management arrangements were sometimes complex. The *Navarinon*, for example, sailed under a Greek flag but was owned by Societé Jean Miloas of Paris and managed by Strubin in London.[101]

Intelligence

London had detailed knowledge of Italian naval support for the Nationalists through communications intelligence (Comint) monitoring radio traffic, based upon commercial Enigma K-system machines. From 1935, the Naval Section of the British Government Code & Cypher School (GC&CS) tracked Italian warships and also read Italian Air Force (Regia Aeronautica) communications throughout most of the Spanish Civil War.[102] German Navy codes, however, based upon more advanced Enigmas, remained opaque until 1940, despite all the efforts of the British Naval Intelligence Division (NID). It is likely that French Comint also provided Paris with a detailed picture of Italian activity.[103]

The Italian Navy Secret Intelligence Service (Servizio Informazioni Segrete della Regia Marina, SISRM) could read some British and French naval codes intercepted by Branch B (*Beta*) under Commander Mario De Monte, who also provided Comint facilities for Italian Air Force Intelligence.[104] Since 1934, they had read the Royal Navy's non-confidential Administrative Code and monitored Anglo-French naval and maritime activity through seven stations—including sites in Sicily, Sardinia, Tripoli, Benghazi, and Rhodes—which also tracked merchantmen supplying the Republic.[105] They were assisted by the German Observation Service (Beobachtungsdienst, B-Dienst), but cooperation was half-hearted. The Germans did not inform their friends they had cracked the Royal Navy's operational Naval Cipher Code #1 in 1937 and had been monitoring Royal Navy and merchant ship movements since the Abyssinia Crisis, boosted in 1936 by a secret station on the top floor of Seville's Hotel Cristina.[106] The Nationalist Navy established its own organization under Lieutenant Antonio Blanco Gárcia, although the Naval Staff's Communications, Cipher and Photography section was established only in the fall of 1937.[107] The Republicans certainly had similar facilities, for seven of their cryptographers joined the French Army's Comint service in 1939.[108]

Republican maritime traffic was also monitored by human intelligence (Humint, or spies), including an Italian network based in Malta.[109] As head of SIM since 1934, Roatta had organized spy rings in France, the Mediterranean states, and the Balkans. SIM's executive directors, Colonels Paolo Angioi and Donato Tripiccione, continued the work while he was in Spain, as well as organizing sabotage operations in France against Republican ships. In Istanbul, from the summer of 1937, the SIM network included Soviet Trotskyists and defectors.[110] SIM assisted the Nationalist Military

Information and Police Service (Servicio de Información y Policía Militaria, SIPM), under Colonel José Ungría Jiménez, to establish agents in Algiers, Bordeaux, Le Havre, Marseilles, Oran, St Nazaire, Romania, and Istanbul. Networks in western France were run by Major Julián Troncoso Sagredo, based in Irun, those in southern France being under José Bertrán y Missitu.[111]

Vice-Admiral Cervera, the Nationalist Naval chief of staff, wanted a dedicated network and selected as its leader, on August 4, 1936, Lieutenant Commander Manuel Espinosa Rodríguez, an electrical engineer on the cruiser *Canarias* who was recovering from liver disease. He had met future Abwehr chief Canaris during a training mission to Germany in 1930 but was rebuffed when flown to Rome to seek Italian assistance. After Commander Werner Lange, German Naval Attaché in Rome, arranged an introduction to Canarias, Espinosa went to Berlin, where the Abwehr chief agreed to support him with a fortnight's training course, a camera, and a false passport.[112] Aided by Spanish diplomats, Espinosa established networks in Bulgaria, Romania, and then Greece, whose reports were couriered to Spain, although details on Marseilles traffic were radioed to Majorca from a Monte Carlo-berthed yacht. Running the networks was a challenge for Espinosa, eased when he became Deputy Naval Attaché in Rome from December 1937 until October 1938 and then Naval Attaché in Bucharest. While Nationalist sources are extremely complementary about Espinosa's work, there remain doubts about the quality of Nationalist naval intelligence, especially regarding maritime traffic. The most difficult task in intelligence is assessing information, and it appears the stream of reports reaching Cervera was often based upon conjecture.

In January 1937, Ciano proposed a sabotage campaign to Army chief of staff General Alberto Pariani, who delegated the task to SIM's Angioi, who in turn assigned it to Carabiniero Colonel Santo Emanuele. He created an organization called Red Cross (Crociera Ruiz), with three groups each of 10 agents: one in Marseilles and the others in southern French towns. He used members of the French Fascist terrorist organization generally known as The Cowl (La Cagoule), financed by wealthy sympathizers, including cosmetics company L'Oréal, which aimed to overthrow the country's left-wing government.[113] The Marseilles group placed bombs or incendiaries which damaged four ships in February and March 1937.[114]

Left wingers, primarily Communists, also sabotaged "Fascist" ships in a campaign loosely organized by a German Communist seaman, Ernst Wollweber, leader of the International Union of Seamen and Harbor Workers, with cells in Scandinavian and European ports. From 1937, his Organization Against Fascism and in Support of the USSR, usually called the Wollweber League, conducted 21 random attacks against German, Italian, and Japanese ships, including two on the Polish liner *Bartoroy*, apparently because she sailed to Nationalist ports. There were only two confirmed successes with bombs: on November 18, 1937, the Italian *Boccaccio* (3,027 grt), carrying 2,300 tonnes of metal to Genoa, was sunk off Brest from a bomb planted in Antwerp, an officer being killed, while on March 19, 1938, the German freighter *Claus Böge* (2,340 grt), sailing in ballast from Oslo to Huelva, was sunk off Esbjerg.[115]

The First Submarine Campaign

Franco, alarmed by the appearance of Soviet military aid, saw the heads of the German and Italian military missions, Lieutenant Colonels Walter Warlimont and Emilio Faldella, on October 16, requesting they blockade Republican ports. He asked for two submarines and two destroyers, and later for Italian aircraft, to interdict the enemy sea-lanes from Majorca and Sardinia.[116] Roatta was sceptical about Franco's claims, but on October 27 the Italian Naval Staff ordered the Sicilian Naval Command (Comandante Militare Marittimo della Sicilia) to monitor the Strait of Sicily using four cruisers and eight destroyers, with air support. They detected at least one heavily disguised Russian steamer, while Comint had monitored another 51 by mid-November, when fears of Soviet intervention led Rome to raise the defensive states of the Dodecanese Islands in the Aegean and the Libyan coast.

Neither Berlin nor Rome wished to supply submarines, but Warlimont informed Roatta on October 12 that Berlin might change its mind. Fearing growing German influence and their potential presence in "Our Sea," Mussolini, who was also Navy Minister, grew worried. The Italian naval staff were understandably reluctant to transfer submarines which Mussolini knew could not be manned by the Nationalists, then the naval mission head, Captain (later Rear Admiral) Giovanni Ferretti, suggested deploying two Italian boats in the western Mediterranean, to which Cervera agreed. Spanish officers would be embarked as nominal commanders, which allowed Mussolini to overrule objections from chief of staff Admiral Domenico Cavagnari. On October 27, the Topazio-class coastal boats *Naiade* and *Topazio* departed for La Maddalena in Sardinia.[117]

Despite its lack of Great War success—sinking just three steamers (7,243 grt) in the Adriatic during three years, while their Allies sank four (2,000 grt)—the postwar Italian submarine force had been expanded. By 1936, it had 88 boats: 11 ocean-going cruisers (*sommergibile grande crociera*) similar to the U.S. Navy's Fleet boats, 17 sea-going boats (*sommergibile media crociera*), three minelayers (*sommergibile posamine*), and 57 coastal boats (*sommergibile piccola crociera*). They were poorly designed, with large conning towers (now called "sails") increasing visibility on the surface, slowing diving times to two minutes (double that of their contemporaries), and causing sluggish underwater performance. Furthermore, boats had only four forward torpedo tubes instead of the normal six. Their doctrine was based upon short patrols in narrow zones at 30 meters with a passive sonar watch, augmented by occasional searches with a periscope.[118] The emphasis was upon submerged attacks launching one or two torpedoes, rather than a larger spread, because there were few reloads in the larger boats and none in the smaller ones, with a mixture of heavyweight (21-inch, 533mm) and lightweight (17.1-inch, 450mm) weapons, the latter against merchantmen. The Navy Ministry restricted attacks to clearly identified Spanish or Russian merchantmen and warships, former submariner Canaris later noting the instructions made recognition almost impossible.[119]

Germany's Great War unrestricted, sink-on-sight submarine offensives horrified the world, and postwar politicians made submarines follow surface ship ("prize") rules which demanded merchant vessels' papers be checked before they were attacked. Sinking was permitted only after everyone on board was in lifeboats. These rules featured in Articles 1 and 22 respectively of the 1922 Washington and 1930 London Treaties, the latter a supplementary agreement to the Washington Treaty, as well as the 1936 Protocol on Submarine Warfare which Italy signed on November 6, two days before the legionary submarines (*sommergibile legionari*) departed on the first patrols. International law on submarine warfare, as with the use of chemical weapons and even non-intervention, were sacrificial victims on the altar of the Cardboard Ceasar's sacred ego.[120]

Their mission was both to prevent the supply of arms and to erode Republican naval strength. The Italian naval staff informed their Nationalist counterparts of the deployment only on November 13, but the campaign did not begin well; *Naiade* returned early due to mechanical failure, while *Topazio*'s 12-day patrol was fruitless, the pair being relieved by submarine cruiser *Antonio Sciesa* and the sea-going *Evangelista Torricelli*.[121] On November 22, the *Torricelli*, under Lieutenant Commander Giuseppe Zarpellon, attacked the cruisers *Cervantes* and *Méndez Núñez*—identified by Lieutenant Commander Arturo Génova Torruella, former Naval Attaché in Paris and now Naval Attaché in Rome—on his second patrol, having previously been in *Naiade*. Zarpellon hit the *Cervantes*, flooding the engine room, but her commander, Lieutenant Commander Luis Gonzáles de Ubieta y González del Campillo, succeeded in reaching the dockyard. Nevertheless, she was out of action until April 11, 1938. Zarpellon avoided a search by three destroyers and was the last boat to return to base on December 2, his after-action report bitterly complaining about the Navy Ministry's restrictions. To save Italian blushes, Franco claimed on November 24 that submarine *B-5* had defected, while the waters were further muddied when experts examining fragments of the torpedoes concluded they were launched by a German boat!

On the night of November 26/27, Roatta urged interdiction of Republican sea-lanes, in cooperation with the Germans if necessary, while the following day, the Nationalists asked their friends to "torpedo every blacked-out ship north of Majorca."[122] The issue was discussed on December 6 when Goering, Raeder, Canaris, and Defense Minister Field Marshal Werner von Blomberg met Mussolini, Ciano, and the Italian service chiefs at the Duce's official residence, the Palazzo Venezia. Mussolini again dismissed Admiral Cavagnari's concerns and agreed to intensify the submarine campaign by deploying up to eight boats at a time, but observed he would rather the Germans used air power than submarines (U-boats) against Republican ships.[123]

Raeder and Blomberg, delighted there was no major commitment of German naval forces in the Mediterranean, quickly withdrew all vessels west of Gibraltar, washing their hands of any responsibility for the consequences of an Italian submarine campaign. While Raeder was willing to make a token contribution, he recognized Germany could not be seen repeating "barbaric" unrestricted submarine attacks. Yet he made no attempt to dissuade the Italians, and may have encouraged them by backing out gracefully.[124]

In early December, British Comint heard Salamanca order the dispatch of three submarine specialists to Rome.[125] The Italian submarine campaign resumed from December 9, when seven boats slipped their moorings to ensure that four or five were on station at a time during January and February. Their commanders' orders bluntly stated: "Sink Republican warships, sink cargo ships clearly recognized as Red Spanish or Russian and sink ships without lights transiting the submarine's sector."[126] Most of the patrols were off Cartagena, Barcelona, and Valencia and tended to last just over a fortnight, of which 10 days were on station, the boats surfacing at night to recharge batteries and hunt their prey.

But there were meagre results: only 15 attacks, together with six shore bombardments, 28 torpedoes being launched and two ships (2,946 grt) hit and beached, but their cargoes being salvaged. On the evening of January 31/February 1, Lieutenant Commander Vittorio Moccagatta's *Ciro Menotti* attacked the freighter *Delfín*, carrying flour to Malaga. It is unclear whether Moccagatta's torpedoes hit the ship, or the sight of them caused her master to run her aground east of Malaga, where a German seaplane finished her off a few days later. On the evening of February 9, Lieutenant Commander Primo Longobardo in the *Galileo Ferraris* encountered the freighter *Navarra* 7 miles north of Tarragona, as she sailed to Barcelona from Marseilles. His torpedoes so damaged her that she became a constructive total loss. Most of the crew survived, but a passenger, the French Communist Deputy Marcel Basset, perished. The Republican Navy's limited antisubmarine warfare (ASW) capability hamstrung Valencia's defensive options, but the *Enrico Tazzoli* was damaged by depth charges following an attack upon two Republican destroyers on the night of December 26/27. During the summer, ASW flotillas were activated at Barcelona, Almeria, and Valencia using auxiliary patrol boats and various minor warships.

The Republicans naturally suspected Italian involvement, and conclusive evidence was provided by the *Jalea* on the night of December 25/26, when a torpedo launched at a freighter near Prat Llobregat was recovered intact upon a beach. The Italians were generally satisfied with the campaign, Rear Admiral Antonio Legnani—Fleet Submarine Commander (Comando Squadra Sommergerbili, Mariscoscom) from February 15, 1937—later claiming there was a significant decline in the volume

Table 2.9. The first Italian submarine campaign

Month	Boats dispatched	Succesful patrols
November	4	3
December	11	10
January	15	11
February	11	5
Total	41	29

Source: Bargoni I

of traffic between December 1, 1936, and January 15, 1937.[127] However, it also raised serious questions about the submarine arm and its capabilities. For example, three boats were driven from their patrol zones in January by heavy seas, something which would rarely happen a few years later with U-boats in the Atlantic and the U.S. Navy in the Pacific, while there was a tendency to lose trim when torpedoes were launched. The campaign abruptly ended in mid-February as preparations for the Naval Patrol gathered pace. The last six boats dispatched were all recalled by February 15 (see Table 2.9), the final one dropping anchor on February 18.[128] The campaign disappointed the Nationalists, who believed the Italians should have flown caution to the winds, but even Rome had to observe some diplomatic niceties.

Germany reluctantly authorized a limited U-boat deployment on November 2. Submarine Commander (Führer der U-booten) Captain Karl Dönitz—no stranger to the Mediterranean, having been captured near Malta in October 1918—selected the first of the Type VIIA long-range submarines which would spearhead future operations in a war against Britain and France, U-33 and U-34, the former being commissioned only on July 25. The mission, Operation Ursula (Unternehmen Ursula) was organized by Dönitz and Rear Admiral Boehm, Commander of Reconnaissance Forces (Befehlshaber der Aufklärungsstreitkräfte), who became Commander of Naval Force in Spain (Befehlshaber deutschen Seestreitkräfte vor der Spanischen Küste) on November 14.[129] Experienced officers were placed in command; U-34's Lieutenant Harald Grosse had delivered E-1 to Turkey, while he and Senior Lieutenant Kurt Freiwald were to conduct only daylight underwater attacks and would communicate with Boehm using one-off codes.

On November 17, Commander Lange and the head of the OKM's Operations Department, Lieutenant Commander Hellmuth Heye, met Italian deputy chief of staff Admiral Vladimiro Pini and 1st Fleet chief of staff Rear Admiral Oscar di Giamberardino to coordinate operations. It was decided the U-boats would not embark Spanish officers, but might use Maddalena for repairs, sailing on the surface flying an Italian flag.[130] Grosse and Freiwald secretly departed Wilhelmshaven on the night of November 20/21, with no attempt to inform the Nationalists of Ursula, while OKM waited until the boats were about to enter the Strait of Gibraltar on

November 26 before informing Rome. They crossed the Strait on the surface at night and reached their patrol zones from November 29. There were nine abortive attacks, which, like those of the Italians, encountered torpedo problems. The campaign abruptly ended on December 11 when they were recalled following the Palazzo Venezia meeting, the boats returning to Wilhelmshaven on December 20.

As the returning Grosse approached the Strait submerged on the afternoon of December 12, he spotted the Republican submarine *C-3* on the surface amid trawlers and patrol craft, most of her crew having just finished lunch. He launched a single torpedo which cut her in two, sinking the vessel in seconds, confirmed by sonar as Grosse did not dare risk using his periscope. Only three of the 50 crew survived; one of them a former Merchant Navy officer acting as watch-keeper who had been speaking to the commanding officer when the torpedo hit, and the others on a garbage disposal detail. Later, the Nationalists claimed commander Sub-Lieutenant Antonio Arbona Pastor had sabotaged the boat, while the head of the Republican submarine force, Lieutenant Commander Remigio Verdiá Jolí, concluded the boat was lost to a battery explosion.[131]

All the Type VIIA U-boats would deploy to the Mediterranean from June 1, 1937, until December 4, 1938, together with four Type II coastal boats, both to gain experience in these waters and to support the Naval Patrol, making 26 and five patrols respectively. On June 30 the surfaced *U-35* off Santander encountered a Republican convoy escorted by two destroyers which failed to see the NIC "stripes." One rapidly approached and the boat dived to begin an attack on the destroyer but could not get into a firing position and both ships then withdrew.

The Admirals' Conference and New Submarine Offensive

Senior officials of the Fascist navies and their Nationalist friends met at Ceuta on December 10 and in "The Admirals' Conference" in the *Canarias* at Cadiz on December 29. They discussed the blockade and interdicting the Republican sea-lanes, although Cervera felt his allies did not understand his problems. The Ceuta meeting was Boehm's swansong, as he was relieved on December 16 by Admiral Hermann von Fishel, who attended "The Admirals' Conference" with Rear Admiral Angelo Iachino, Cervera, Moreno, and Ferretti.[132] Cervera made it clear he would control the blockade, and in a heated discussion in Cadiz he rejected a tri-national task force, although he reluctantly allowed liaison officers access to the Nationalist navy's southern and eastern blockade headquarters in Cadiz.[133]

Cervera's "shopping list" rose to six destroyers and six submarines, but at Cadiz he called for submarine operations augmented by minelaying and Italian assistance to create a base in Majorca. Diplomatic hurdles prevented the transfer of ships, but his allies diplomatically said the situation would be reviewed if Soviet submarines appeared, and as a sop agreed to provide MTBs and to support minelaying.

The meeting established rules for collaboration "directed by the Spanish Admiral with the collaboration of the German and Italian Navies," which became the blueprint for interdicting Republican sea-lanes. They would concentrate upon the Strait and Majorca, supported by Italian air power, while Rome's submarines would deploy in the western Mediterranean, with a couple disguised as Nationalist boats.

Discussions between Génova and Admiral Edoardo Simili, Mussolini's Naval Chief of Cabinet, continued into the spring. Rome agreed to provide the *Archimedes* and her sister ship *Torricelli*, which became the Nationalist *General Sanjurjo* and *General Mola*, respectively, although referred to as *C-3* and *C-5* to maintain the fiction they were defecting boats.[134] They departed La Spezia on April 17, with 20 percent of each boat's 55-man crew being Italians; an engineer, two electricians, a helmsman, two sonar operators, two gunners, and three torpedo men, the commander and the remainder being Spanish.[135]

After working up in Pollensa Bay, their first patrols began on May 13 under Lieutenant Commanders Pablo Suances Jáudenes (*Sanjurjo*) and Rafael Fernández de Bobadilla y Ragel (*Mola*), Suances having the first success off Cape Tordera on May 30 against the ferry *Ciudad de Barcelona*. She was sailing from Marseilles to Valencia with war materiel, cotton, and food, a crew of 60, and 312 passengers, most of whom were International Brigade volunteers from Great Britain, Scandanavia, North America, and Australia together with some French airmen. Suances's first torpedo missed and the ferry turned towards the coast, but a second torpedo hit her astern and she sank in three minutes, taking down four crew and 187 passengers. He would later sink two schooners, after giving their crews time to take to the lifeboats, and on June 4 damaged the tanker *Campero* near Palamos.[136] On June 26, Bobadilla surfaced 28 miles north of Alicante and sank the freighter *Cabo de Palos*, carrying food, salt, and ammonia from Odessa to Valencia, with the loss of five crew, but the remaining 45—including a female nurse—were picked up by a fishing boat.

The second patrols began in mid-July, with the *Sanjurjo* intercepting a convoy consisting of the freighter *Andutz Mendi* and the tankers *Zorroza* and *Saustan* near Sète on July 29. The freighter had left Port Vendres and had barely rendezvoused with the tankers when the submarine made a surface attack, concentrating upon the *Andutz Mendi*. Machine-gun fire killed many of her crew and some leapt overboard in panic; the ship was set ablaze and abandoned, the master and seven survivors rowing to shore. French authorities and fishermen salvaged the vessel and three days later she was brought into Sète, but 20 men had lost their lives. At the end of July, the *Mola* made an unsuccessful surface attack upon another two-ship mini-convoy some 50 kilometres north of Barcelona, being driven off by accurate coastal artillery fire. Thus ended a campaign which sank four Spanish ships (10,627 grt) and damaged two (7,983 grt), but both boats required refits, the *Mola* having suffered electrical problems and a leak, and they returned to Spezia.

The Mine Threat

Nationalist minelaying plans were hampered by the limited prewar mine stock divided between Ferrol and Cartagena. The majority were conventional "horned" contact Vickers H Mk V weapons with a 100-kg load, augmented by Vickers-Elia H-16A, designed by Italy's Captain G. Elia, with a 54-kg charge in a form of lethal fruit machine which achieved the jackpot when the target struck its lever. Both were produced under licence by the SECN, but the Nationalists appear to have expended most of their stock off the Cantabrian coast during 1936.[137] There were the two new minelayers, *Júpiter* and *Vulcano*, and some auxiliary vessels, but the prewar navy's submarines had no minelaying capabilities, so Italian boats lacked plausible deniability. The Nationalists relied upon bluff by announcing their intention to mine enemy coasts on October 3, 1936, and the eastern seaboard on December 8, ignoring British and French protests. A few weeks later, Cervera radioed an order en clair for minelaying off Barcelona and Cape de Begur, although six weeks elapsed before these orders were executed.[138]

This followed the arrival, at Warlimont's request, of the OPDR freighter *August Schultze* in Ferrol on December 16 with 500 naval mines. Simultaneously, the German naval mission, the North Sea Office (Nordsee Büro), provided mine warfare experts to facilitate the deployment of the EMC II, which had a 300-kg charge and could be moored at depths of 100–500 meters.[139] There were disputes between the Germans and their allies about the optimum use of the weapons, leading one exasperated German officer to tell Raeder: "Concerning the theme, Cooperation, it does not exist! Our inquiries are looked upon as supervision and are disliked."[140]

Eventually, nearly half were laid, most north of Barcelona; 60 off Cape Creus on the night of February 22/23 and three days later 63 off Cape de Begur, while on the night of April 6/7 two former German MTBs laid a small field just east of Almeria. The impact was almost immediate—but not as Salamanca had expected. On February 25, the Union Castle liner *Llandovery Castle*, with 300 passengers, was making for Port Natal in South Africa via Marseilles and the Suez Canal when there was what her master, Captain Clarence Aylen, later described as "a heavy explosion forward" 2 miles southeast of Cape Creus. This left a 9-meter hole in the hull that flooded the two forward holds, leaving her down by the head and with a severe list which would have prevented the launching of half the lifeboats. The British press later claimed some of the passengers spent the evening dancing, although Captain Aylen would surely have insisted on his passengers being at their lifeboat muster stations.[141]

The liner limped to Port Vendres, where the authorities denied her access for fear she would sink. The passengers were disembarked and a cofferdam was erected, allowing her to proceed to Genoa for repairs, but 29 crew members, mostly from the Black Gang, said she was not safe and demanded a bonus together with a discharge.

Even when shown a certificate of seaworthiness, 13 of them refused to sail and were taken to London. There, on May 14, a British court found them guilty of wilful disobedience and impeding navigation, and they were jailed for between six and 12 weeks with hard labor.[142]

Two mine victims passed the liner as they departed Port Vendres. The French freighter *Maria Thérésa Le Borgne* was sailing from Marseilles to Oran, aware of the French Navy Ministry's advice that ships sail in depths of more than 200 meters.[143] Just just before dawn on March 1, while 10 miles south by southeast of Cape Creus, an explosion flooded the two forward holds, but she managed to reach Palamos where she was beached. As attempts were made to salvage her, an air attack on March 5 slightly injured the First Mate, but she was floated off on July 15 and sailed to Marseilles. On March 4, the Greek tanker *Loukia*, proceeding to Barcelona with 3,500 tonnes of gasoline from Baku, was mined in rough weather 2 miles off Cape Sebastion, exploding and killing all but one of her 23-man crew.

Yet the most serious international incident was due to one of the MTB's mines. On the afternoon of May 13, the destroyer HMS *Hunter* entered Almeria and prepared to drop anchor 5 miles offshore. She had barely come to a stop in 100 fathoms (183 meters) when there was an explosion on the port side near the bridge. A column of oil and water rose to the height of the mast and 900 tons of water flooded the boiler rooms, leaving the ship listing and down by the bow with a wrecked radio room.[144] There were 32 casualties, including eight dead and six seriously burned, her commander Lieutenant Commander Bryan Scurfield rescuing five men at great risk to himself.[145] As damage-control operations began, the Republican destroyer *Lazaga* sailed into the mined area to tow out the *Hunter*, pick up survivors, and take the wounded to the *Jaime I*.

The following day, the cruiser HMS *Arethusa* and two destroyers arrived, divers determining that the explosion, which was originally thought to have been caused by a torpedo, was due to a mine. After emergency repairs, the cruiser towed the destroyer stern-first to Gibraltar for temporary repairs, then to Malta, where she was made operational by November. Fragments showed the ship had hit a German-made mine. The British government claimed £135,000 compensation from the Nationalists, who denied all responsibility. The threat remained, and on May 19 HMS *Fortune* reported sinking a floating mine with rifle fire, while the Admiralty and the Mediterranean Fleet discussed replacing the valuable Naval Patrol destroyers with nine auxiliary patrol boats. This idea was abandoned on May 27 because they could be manned only by stripping other warships, but during the summer the 1st Minesweeping Squadron was sent to the Mediterranean.

Opposition to minelaying came, surprisingly, from Rome, for drifting mines posed a serious threat to Italian shipping, especially vessels supplying the Nationalists. Francisco Moreno, a vice-admiral from July 29, and his superiors initially ignored Italian protests, which were later supported by Berlin following the *Llandovery*

Castle incident. Both pointed out that the mines could be a source of acute political embarrassment to the Franco government, when it was attempting to gain additional diplomatic recognition abroad. Germany ceased supplying mines after their weapons sank a total of five merchant ships (7,668 grt), damaging two more (12,208 grt) and a destroyer. The Nationalists, by now appreciating the problems caused, reluctantly agreed to lay no more.

In November 1937, however, the USS *Manley* reported increased mining activity between Cape Sant'Antonio and Tortosa, although the Nationalists staged only one more offensive operation. This was on February 28, 1938, when the *Júpiter* and *Vulcano* laid 109 mines off Valencia, but the Republican Navy's mine countermeasures (MCM) force operated twice daily to clear a mile-wide channel 1 mile from the coast.[146] Apart from a report that the French schooner *Belle Hirondelle* was sunk, possibly by a mine, 10 miles off Las Palmas on May 2, there were no more immediate victims of the two minefields.[147] Drifting weapons did account for three more vessels during the Spanish Civil War; there were two in 1939, and the Spanish schooner *Cala Esperanza* (also *Cala Engosaura*) was lost with all hands off Castellon on November 25, 1937.

Death from the Sky

Ships faced threats not only from under the water but also from the skies, despite both sides having a limited maritime reconnaissance capability. The Republican Air Force's 71st Group had a heterogeneous collection of aircraft, including Savoia S.62 and Dornier Whale (*Wal*) flying boats plus lumbering French bombers. Early in 1937, four Katies formed the Naval Support Detachment (Destacamento de Apoyo Naval), which was absorbed by the 12th Bomber Group in April.[148]

Ship recognition and bomb aiming were poor, and following a Republican attack upon the French destroyer *Maillé-Brezé* on January 18, the French Navy Ministry authorized ships "to retaliate immediately against any attack directed against them."[149] Following a meeting between Foreign Minister Yvon Delbos and Chief of the Naval Staff Vice-Admiral Darlan, the Navy Ministry amended its instructions on January 27, saying: "It is always necessary to defend oneself and react when the honor of the flag is engaged, or in case of attack against any French building whatever it is and this independently of any control of the nationality."[150] The self-confident and assertive Darlan had leapfrogged colleagues to succeed Durand-Viel, and although a political conservative, he supported Blum's social reforms. He believed Italy was the greatest threat to French security, hence his concern over the Italian presence in the Balearics, but regarded the British with suspicion for accepting Franco-Italian naval parity in postwar treaties.[151]

The Royal Navy also faced attacks; the battleship HMS *Royal Oak* off Gibraltar on February 2 and two destroyers off Algeria's Cape Tenez on February 13. There were no casualties, but on February 22, while off Valencia, an air-defense shell hit the battleship, injuring five, including her commander, Captain Thomas Drew. Nevertheless, the British deemed this "An act of God" and took no action. On April 6, the destroyer HMS *Gallant* was attacked off Cape Huertas, forcing her to take evasive maneuvers and fire 21 rounds from the 4.7-inch guns. The incident led the Admiralty to instruct warships operating within 150 miles of Spanish territory to keep some air-defense guns manned.

Merchantmen were also attacked, especially French vessels, with three bombed without casualties between February 3 and March 10, together with the Greek *Memas*. The only damage was in the last attack, upon the Marseilles-based Compagnie de Navigation Mixte (CNM) freighter *Djebel Antar* 115 miles east of Majorca, sailing to Marseilles. This last attack renewed calls to arm merchantmen, but they were rejected by the Navy Ministry on March 8. Consequently, from March 12, crews refused to sail from Marseilles unless either given an escort, wartime convoys were reinstated, or their ships received antiaircraft guns, but the ministry stood firm. On March 15, Navy Minister Gasnier-Duparc sent a soothing letter noting that warships offered protection outside the 3-mile-limit, while within Republican ports there were "safe zones." The sailors returned to sea, reassured less by his words than by the four cruisers patrolling the western Mediterranean. The attacks worried Norwegian ship-owners, whose tankers were vital for national security, and to meet their concerns the Navy Ministry in April permitted warships to support foreign vessels trading with French ports.[152]

April also saw a series of incidents involving Nationalist aircraft off French North Africa. On April 11, the Spanish *Mar Caribe* was attacked in French territorial waters off Cape Attia (near Philippeville) and sought sanctuary at Bougie (now Béjaïa). French naval authorities in North Africa were authorized to deny French air space to foreign aircraft and force them to land, an empty threat as there were few fighters or air-defense guns, and on April 17 a defiant Nationalist reconnaissance aircraft flew over Bougie.

The most serious international incident was created by the Russian-led 12th Group in May. Soviet naval adviser Captain Nikolai Kuznetsov (Commodore from August 1937) asked the group's commander, Captain Ivan Proskurov, to attack Nationalist cruisers in the Balearics, but only during a battlefield lull following an attack upon the *Jaime I* did Proskurov act.[153] He attacked Palma on May 23 with the 71st Group, inflicting minor damage upon the cruiser *Baleares*, and the following evening Proskurov led five Katies against Italian warships.

The NIC wanted to establish a secure zone in Palma for Naval Patrol ships, but the Republican authorities in Valencia refused to sanction "foreign interference in Spain's territorial waters." In the harbor were the *Baleares* and eight foreign warships, half of them Italian—four destroyers and the auxiliary cruiser *Barletta*—as well as the Società Italiana Petroliere d'Oriente tanker *Nevona*. The Katies peppered the Italian ships with fragmentation bombs, wounding one man but causing no significant damage, while nearby British and German ships escaped damage. However, an attack early the following morning struck the *Barletta*'s officers' quarters, killing six and wounding three, including the commanding officer, Lieutenant Commander Rafaelo Lauro. Another bomb sun the 93 grt schooner *Cala Mayor*.[154] The *Barletta*, which rotated patrol duties with her sister ship, the *Adriatico*, departed for repairs in La Spezia on May 28, and on that day Italy protested vigorously to the NIC. The heavy cruiser *Bolzano* and four destroyers arrived in Palma to ensure there was no repeat.[155]

These attacks led to the OKM ordering Admiral Hermann von Fischel to transfer to a safer harbor, and on May 24 the pocket battleship *Deutschland* and torpedo boat *Leopard* sailed to Ibiza, without informing the Republican government. Valencia quickly learned, probably from Comint, that a major warship would arrive in Ibiza, and believing it to be a Canarias-class cruiser, dispatched a task force of the cruisers *Libertad* and *Méndez Núñez* and eight destroyers to shell the harbor. The German ships arrived on the afternoon of May 29, together with a tanker which would refuel them the following day. Preparations began for an evening reception of local dignitaries, and to greet them a band began to play upon the quarter deck. Fisher went for a bath and the crews assembled in their messes for supper.

Proskurov and two bombers had taken off from Los Alcazares, witnessed by Republican Air Force commander General Ignacio Hidalgo de Cisneros y López de Montenegro, and arrived over Ibiza some 20 minutes after the Germans arrived. The Germans literally never saw what hit them, the bombers swooping out of the setting sun and each dropping two 250-kg bombs from 3,300 feet (1,000 meters). The first bomber missed, but the second hit the *Deutschland*'s paint store and destroyed the catapult and the ship's observation floatplane, causing fires which spread into the mess deck, engulfing the hungry sailors and threatening the forward magazine, which was flooded as a precaution. The crew went to general quarters, and as fire-fighting parties played their hoses, the boatload of dignitaries was waved away just as shells from the Republican task force began to fall. They swiftly ceased when the Republicans realized the target was German, and the raiders withdrew. The attack left 23 dead, 19 seriously injured, and 64 slightly wounded, but the survivors' priority was to fight the fires, which were quenched after two hours. Proskurov returned and informed Hildalgo de Cisneros they had sunk a Canarias-class cruiser.[156] The following day, after an exchange of boarding calls with the USS *Kane*, the *Deutschland* sailed to Gibraltar to obtain medical treatment, rendezvousing with the *Scheer*. They reached the British base, where the dead were buried, followed by five more who succumbed to their injuries by June, bringing the death toll to 31. All were later exhumed for a funeral service in Germany.[157]

The attack caused consternation in Berlin, with the Germans initially believing shells had damaged the *Deutschland*, but Raeder rejected staff proposals for bombarding an unspecified target in retaliation, a policy backed by Hitler who was incandescent with rage. When it became clear that bombs had damaged the ship, there was some nervous checking of records at Nationalist air headquarters before Valencia admitted responsibility. This added fuel to the flames and Hitler demanded either Valencia or Cartagena be shelled. When Raeder pointed out that both possessed formidable coast defenses, he opted instead for Almeria, apparently because Raeder falsely assured him the *Jaime I* was there.

The *Scheer* and four torpedo boats shelled the port on the morning of May 31, the 21st anniversary of the battle of Jutland, leading the ships to fly the old Imperial Navy's battle flag, although neither Fischel nor Captain Otto Ciliax, commanding the *Scheer*, had participated in the 1916 battle. The town was covered with mist, so the warships used the tops of the taller buildings visible above the murk as ranging posts. They fired 275 shells, including 94 11-inch, inflicting 74 civilian casualties, 19 fatal, and destroying 30 buildings. Coast defense batteries ineffectively fired back 60 rounds. Meanwhile, the German ambassador to London, Joachim von Ribbentrop, informed the NIC that unless Germany received guarantees there would be no more attacks, his country would withdraw from the Naval Patrol, which it promptly did, followed by Italy, although Berlin had wanted Rome to remain.[158]

Defense Minister Indalecío Prieto Tuero proposed new attacks upon German warships to provoke a European war, but as this idea appalled Moscow, Communist ministers reined in the government and an appeal to the League of Nations saw it wring its hands ineffectively as usual. The diplomatic temperature briefly died down, and after a fortnight the Germans and Italians resumed patrols, Berlin reinforcing its Mediterranean presence with the cruisers *Köln* and *Leipzig*, two torpedo boats, and four Type VIIA submarines, including the "Ursula" boats. Then on June 15, the *Leipzig's* sonar detected the sound of three incoming torpedoes, although the sceptical commanding officer, Captain Otto Schenk, did not report the incident to the OKM. Three days later, when the cruiser and the torpedo boats were 20 miles off Oran, sonar again reported an incoming torpedo and a lookout reported a disturbance on the surface, suggesting the presence of a submarine.[159]

The OKM authorized its three submarines operating in the western Mediterranean to attack Republican warships and merchantmen, while on June 19, Raeder alerted the 2nd U-boat Flotilla to send half-a-dozen boats to the Mediterranean. Ribbentrop called for a four-power naval demonstration off Valencia and a strong protest letter to the Republican government as the OKM rescinded the orders. This had been done because Fischel doubted the reports, with tests showing the "torpedo" noises were generated by the ship's machinery. Fischel told the OKM: "Reports received from *Leipzig* indicate false observations. The probability that within three days, three or four submarines tried to fire at *Leipzig* is most unlikely. The same applies to a joint attack by two submarines."[160] The cruiser *Nürnberg* later reported submarine attacks based upon sonar data on June 25 and July 16, but by now the OKM was extremely skeptical. The Royal Navy was concerned by the implications of the "attack," and on June 24 Admiral Dudley Pound, commander of the Mediterranean Fleet, prepared contingency plans to hunt-down submarines which attacked, or appeared about to attack, his ships.[161]

None of the three Republican boats at sea were operating off Oran, and Valencia justifiably denied responsibility.[162] Nevertheless, the German Foreign Ministry considered demanding the surrender of all Republican submarines and their internment in Gibraltar, a plan rejected because Italy feared it would set a precedent for its forces in Spain. With no response to the alleged attacks, Ribbentrop withdrew Germany from the Naval Patrol on June 23 and Italy followed suit, having completed only two patrols with destroyers, but all the German surface units made a short show of strength from that date.

The German Navy had returned to the Naval Patrol to hinder the supply of military aid to the Republic, but quickly concluded this was unnecessary and sought another excuse to withdraw.[163] When they realized neither Germany nor Italy would return, the British and French proposed on June 29 they relieve the Germans, but even in cost-conscious London and Paris this received lukewarm support, as did Germany's proposals to grant both sides belligerent rights. A fig leaf of non-intervention was retained when the British proposal for retaining the shipborne observer scheme was accepted on July 27, again because of financial rather than ethical concerns. Meanwhile, ships continued to bring in war materiel. Indeed, it was estimated that between April and July, at least 42 ships evaded inspection; to all intents and purposes, the Non-Intervention Agreement was now a dead letter.[164]

Friends with Strategic Benefits

While the Nationalists' dependence upon their Fascist allies affronted Spanish pride, it was vital to enforce the blockade. Material and advisory support came through 100 naval experts and advisors, the Italian mission under Ferretti, and the German "North Sea Office" under their Attaché, Commander Kurt Meyer-Döhner.[165]

The Italian mission in Cadiz was the most important, and relations between the two were generally very good, with Italian-built radio stations strengthening Nationalist communications. Ferretti was an old friend of Cervera, and on his own initiative established a common code for the two navies, which was extended to the Germans. The Germans reorganized the San Fernando Naval College near Cadiz upon their own training curriculum and manuals, with a separate detachment of petty-officer instructors.

Both Germany and Italy were reluctant to break the non-intervention agreement too blatantly, but did provide weapons and equipment for ships. As well as mines, the Germans supplied eight 3.45-inch (88mm) and 4.1-inch (105mm) guns, together with 68 air-defense guns and 28 5.9-inch (150mm) coast-defense guns, fire directors, radios, sonars, and engineering and electrical items. The Italians provided 44 3-inch (76mm) and 4.7-inch (120mm) guns and 23 air-defense guns for ships. Rome would supply $5.18 million (84.8 million lira) of naval aid, including torpedoes, munitions, 1,464 tonnes of MTB gasoline, and 255 tonnes of coal, together with communications, electrical, and engineering materiel. They also established a base for auxiliary cruisers on the island of Favignana, west of Sicily, with a coal barge, a water tanker, and, from June, the captured Republican freighter *Mina Piquera* as a support ship, while their Cagliari naval base was used for refits and held stores.[166]

Spanish reluctance to accept advice caused frustration, with the Germans and Italians frequently criticizing Cervera, whom they felt was too cautious, even urging his removal, but Franco stubbornly refused.[167] The proud leaders of a navy which could trace its history to the 14th century also rejected proposals for "joint" naval commands from allies barely half-a-century old. Nevertheless, Cervera appreciated the material support he received, especially from the Italians, who spent the first half of 1937 creating the infrastructure to strengthen the Nationalist blockade in the western Mediterranean. The prewar Spanish Navy followed the example of the British, French, and American fleets of the 18th century and early 19th century and used the huge natural harbor of Port Mahon in Minorca as its base in the Balearics, but from July 1936 this was firmly in Republican hands.[168]

The Nationalists had auxiliary patrol boats in Palma, while the Italians maintained air squadrons at Son Sant Joan airfield and the Spanish Navy's seaplane base in Pollensa Bay, so Cervera decided on November 28 to create a naval base at Palma de Majorca, with Italian support which he secured at "The Admirals' Conference."[169] On January 22, Captain Francisco Bastarreche Díez de Bulnes, first commander of the *Canarias*, assumed command of the base (Jefe de la Base Naval de Palma). He was promoted to rear admiral on March 7 to blockade the eastern coast of Spain, reinforced by a pair of auxiliary cruisers and, from time to time, the Canarias-class cruisers supported by the Italian Navy oilers.[170] The auxiliary cruisers patrolled between Marseilles and Barcelona, and from the end of February 1937 operated in the Sicilian Channel and as far east as Cape Matapan in Greece, from their Favignana base. This base was temporarily closed in October, the *Mina Piquera* being transferred to Palma, but reopened the following year.

The Italian presence in Majorca was of universal concern. The antics of "Count Rossi" fed Nationalist fears of a land-grab, and they successfully demanded the major's removal. An Italian base also threatened the sea-lanes between Metropolitan France and her African colonies, as well as Britain's imperial communications through the Mediterranean to India and East Africa. From March 11, the French Navy stationed a ship in Palma to monitor the situation.[171] The Italian presence was the greatest impediment to London's desire to improve relations with Rome, although the Foreign Office believed a gentlemen's agreement signed on January 2 was the first step in this direction. This regulated British and Italian interests within the

Mediterranean, with non-interference commitments towards the region's states and shipping in the Mediterranean. The Balearics were included, but British Comint monitored communications between Majorca and Rome, and tracked the *Aniene*'s frequent supply runs, gathering evidence that the agreement was not worth the paper it was written on. By July, the Cabinet had concluded that Italy was no longer a reliable friend and defenses within the Mediterranean needed to be strengthened.[172]

Malaga

With Mussolini determined the CTV should quickly be "blooded," they spearheaded an offensive from January 17 to capture the remaining Andalusian provinces of Malaga and Granada by February 8.[173] From January 11, Malaga faced aerial and naval bombardment by the *Baleares* and *Canarias* which caught the Danish *Signe* and Norwegian *Saga* docked awaiting cargoes of fruit, with splinters injuring some of the crew. However, both had steam up and promptly departed for Gibraltar.

As the Nationalists closed on Malaga, the Republican Fleet ignored the government's ever-more strident demands to support the port's defenders, who were unable to destroy the facilities. By contrast, the Italian Navy was extremely active, with two submarines used for shore bombardment. An ambitious plan for an Italian MTB attack upon Malaga harbor on February 5 was thwarted by thick fog, but these vessels would sail defensive patrols until late April, when they were transferred to the Nationalist Navy. On February 8, the Italian destroyers *Maestrale* and *Sciroco* escorted the freighters *Tevere* and *Sicilia* from Tangiers into Malaga. The previous day, Claude Angel's *Hilfern*, which was berthed in Malaga, departed, only to be stopped outside the port by the *Canarias* and *Cervera*. She was freed with the arrival of a British destroyer, HMS *Brazen*, but briefly stopped to land two Spanish stowaways. The Nationalists captured two intact freighters (4,761 grt) and two scuttled ships (1,985 grt) which were both salvaged, but on February 13 the Greek steamer *Mariopi* collided with the *Canarias*, which required major repairs in Ferrol.

Following the Malaga campaign, the Italian Navy twice shelled Valencia, starting on the evening of February 14 when the light cruiser *Eugenio di Savoia* dashed from Maddalena to fire nine salvos into the city center in five minutes. The following day, her sister ship, *Emanuele Filiberto Duca d'Aosta*, accompanied by the cruiser *Raimondo Montecuccoli*, departed Maddalena with the 2nd Fleet (2a Squadra). Commander Admiral Romeo Bernotti embarked, and to ensure no interference he deployed eight cruisers, a dozen destroyers, and six submarines as a screen. The *d'Aosta* fired 30 salvos in nine minutes, but the coast defense batteries engaged her and inflicted minor damage to the hull and stern turret. The shelling left many British masters uneasy, and for some weeks they would sail out of the harbor and anchor near heavy cruiser HMS *Shropshire*, where they felt safer, but Italian offensive naval operations ceased with the establishment of the Naval Patrol scheme.[174]

Two Navies

The Nationalist Navy benefitted from allied technical support and the Hispano-Marroquí de Transportes (Hisma) created at Tetuan in July 1936 to handle German trade and support responded to 121 requests for hull plating, cabling, machinery, communications, and fire control equipment, as well as weapons and ammunition. However, the new cruisers were handicapped by the lack of dedicated fire directors, and in clashes with enemy cruisers often came off worse. While the Fascist powers provided only half-a-dozen MTBs—two obsolete MAS from Italy and four German S-booten in the first half of 1937—they proved disappointments and ended the war acting as patrol boats.[175]

The end of 1936 saw Cervera become chief of staff with his headquarters in Salamanca. In addition to Bastarreche's command, Admiral Castro became commander of northern naval operations, and there was also a small Africa Naval Command under Admiral Ruiz, based in Ceuta. Cervera faced problems with Nationalist General Headquarters and Franco, for while the admiral was willing to risk ships to dominate the waters off Republican Spain, Franco feared losing them and the effect upon national morale. Nationalist fleet operations consisted of blockade and MCM patrols, escorting individual supply ships or "convoys" of a couple of ships, commerce raiding, and the occasional shore bombardment.

By contrast, the Republican Fleet remained passive, despite Prieto's appointment first as Navy and Air Force Minister on September 5, 1936, then as Defense Minister in March 1937, with most operations consisting of coastal and MCM sweeps. From the spring of 1937, each week they also escorted a convoy of ships, aided by the transfer of the *Méndez Núñez* and two destroyers to Barcelona at the end of 1936.[176] Kuznetsov would later report to Moscow that this was "a thankless, dangerous and full-time task whose importance was not understood outside the navy."[177] While returning from a shore-bombardment mission against Malaga on April 23, the ill-fated *Jaime I* ran aground at Almeria, then an Italian air attack on May 21 caused damage around No 3 Turret (X Turret in Royal Navy nomenclature), leading the battleship to sail to Cartagena for repairs. On the afternoon of June 17, the aft magazine detonated, possibly due to sparks from a welding machine, wrecking the ship and killing 179 crew, with some 200 injured. One of the survivors was Lieutenant Commander Valentin Bogdenko, the Soviet gunner advisor, who would become Pacific Fleet chief of staff in 1941. Although raised, the *Jaime I* was a constructive total loss.[178]

Under Prieto, the navy returned to traditional values, authorizing ship commanders on November 19 to ignore the ship's committees, which were replaced by political commissars in May 1937. The Naval Staff was reformed on December 26 by mobilizing former Naval College instructors, but finding officers to replace those jailed or killed after the uprising proved difficult. To plug the gap, some 111

Merchant Navy officers were press-ganged in March 1937, but most ship commanders had been only junior officers in July 1936.[179]

The Soviet Union would send 77 officers to Spain, led by former Black Sea Fleet cruiser commander Kuznetsov, who arrived on August 27, 1936, and was replaced in January 1938 by Commodore Vladimir Alafuzov. Few Russians spoke Spanish, so only a handful served in Republican warships, including Maria Skavronskaya in the cruiser *Libertad*, who appears to have been the only woman to go to sea in a Spanish warship during the Civil War. The Russians provided technical expertise, two acting as gunnery officers in the *Jaime I* and *Méndez Núñez*, but the irresistible force met the immovable object, with the Russians complaining about poor maintenance, for which they blamed the naval bureaucracy. The Spanish Republicans, like their foes, were also reluctant to accept advice but, at Russian prompting, exercises increased, while technical courses helped to improve crew quality.[180]

Five Soviet officers commanded submarines, but even they were unable to improve their efficiency and they sank only a fishing vessel on September 14, 1936.[181] The boats were poorly supported, with some barely capable of diving, while the high standards of discipline and technical expertise vital for a submarine crew were undermined by boat committees. The disappearance in the Bay of Biscay of the *C-5* in December 1936, while ascribed by Spanish historians as the gallant act of self-sacrifice by her Nationalist sympathizer commanding officer, was almost certainly lost to human or mechanical failure.[182] Submarine operations were also restricted by a government which feared that sinking a German or Italian merchantman would give Berlin and Rome an excuse to openly join the conflict.

The Russians could provide little material help, apart from 18 radio and direction-finding stations, as well as four G-5 class MTBs (Torpedo Cutters) which arrived with commanders in Cartagena, with eight torpedoes, on the *Cabo San Tomé* on May 1, 1937.[183] A covert contract for Type 40K MTBs was placed with Charles Picker, of the Lorraine Dietrich company, with work by the British company Aero-Marine Engines, but the Spanish Civil War ended before any were delivered.[184] Russian, Baltic State, and Mexican sources provided the Republic with naval guns ranging from 14 3-inch (75mm) to 4.7-inch (120mm) and some 50 antiaircraft guns, but limited ammunition.[185]

On May 2, tensions within the left-wing authorities in Barcelona led to a three-day mini-civil war, partly ended by using the *Jaime I* and a couple of destroyers to bring in paramilitary forces which imposed peace at bayonet point. As a result, Catalonia lost its autonomous state within the Republic, while Premier Francisco Largo Caballero, who had been in power since September 4, was forced to resign, being replaced by Juan Negrín. The new premier continued to extend central government control and sought foreign intervention to achieve a political solution to the country's divisions, both making him more reliant upon the Communists and the Soviet Union, although he was never a sympathizer.

The Growing Threats

Cervera recognized the value of air power but frustratingly lacked the means to exploit it because he controlled a limited seaplane force for maritime reconnaissance, with 25 Savoia S.62s, the Dornier Whale and Cant Z.501 Gull (Gabbiano) flying boats covering the Strait, and a trio of Gulls at Pollensa Bay. However, the creation of the Spanish Air Force (Aviación Nacional) in the spring meant he lost operational control of them.[186] They were augmented by the Condor Legion's floatplane squadron AS/88, based on its He 59, known as Big or Clown Boots (Zapatones), and He 60 in the Strait, later moving from Cadiz to Malaga. The Big Boots, or Boots, could carry 250-kg bombs, and on January 30 one piloted by future torpedo-bomber ace Lieutenant Werner Klumper finished off the beached *Delfin* and bombed the *Jaime I* in Almeria. On June 8, the He 60s were handed over to the Nationalist Air Force, while the Boots transferred to Pollensa Bay, flying missions in pairs to Cadiz one day and returning to Majorca the next.[187]

To interdict the sea-lanes and strike the ports, Cervera depended upon his allies, especially the Italian bombers on Majorca; on November 19, 1936, Blomberg approved Rome's plans to strengthen its air base on the island.[188] The Germans and Italians held frequent discussions about a bombing campaign against the ports, but the few raids had little effect against fierce air-defense fire, augmented in Alicante on November 5 and November 22 by the guns of the Italian-built Argentinian heavy cruiser ARA *Veinticinco de Mayo*. Attacks upon Cartagena forced the fleet to anchor outside the harbour at night, exposing the ships to submarine attack.[189] The Fascist powers lacked bombers, both to cut the flow of supplies and support battlefield operations, and Goering wrongly concluded in 1936 the Italians were, at best, half-hearted about the maritime interdiction mission.

In fact, Palma informed Salamanca on November 11, 1936, of plans to expand the airfields to strike Republican ports.[190] The Italian bombers were nominally under the Commander of Majorca Air Forces (Jefe de las Fuerzas Aéreas de Mallorca), Franco's brother Ramón, a lieutenant colonel who was Air Attaché in Washington at the outbreak of the war and then commander at Pollensa Bay. His brother appointed him without reference to Nationalist air chief General Alfredo Kindelán y Duany, who loathed him, as did the base's officers, due to Ramón's Republican beliefs.[191] He won over his critics through his leadership, flying 51 sorties, and on March 29, 1937, helped to capture a merchantman.[192]

The bombers were always firmly under Italian command, and from May this was General Velardi, the first Legionary Air leader, who would remain until the spring of 1938. Roatta had dismissed him following a dispute over his reports to Rome, and his new appointment was the Air Ministry's gesture of disdain towards Italy's supremo in Spain. But he had less than a dozen Bat bombers, briefly augmented in March by a pair of Savoia-Marchetti S.79 Sparrowhawk (Sparviero) or Hawk high-speed bombers staging through Palma en route to the Spanish mainland. During the first half of 1937, the Bats made only seven attacks upon ports, with three in July, involving some 45 sorties and 60 tonnes of bombs, but most raids were upon naval bases, factories, and airfields. A trickle of reinforcements from May saw Velardi expand to a dozen Bats.[193]

The Hawks had an early success on March 5 when they attacked the Republican merchantman *Legazpi* sailing from Puerto Rosas to Barcelona, causing the crew to abandon ship and run aground north of Barcelona. The crew refloated her and sailed to Benicarlo, but two months later, on May 19, Hawk bombs set her ablaze as she unloaded medical supplies and equipment at Benicasim, just north of Castellon. One crewman was killed and eight badly injured, these being treated by three British medical staff, but the ship sank with the loss of her cargo. Although salvaged, she was a constructive total loss, the success leading Velardi to demand two squadrons of Hawks,

Majorca-based Bats and Boots harassed the western Mediterranean from March to July. The Spanish motor vessel *Araya Mendi*, sailing to Algiers, was set on fire on March 25 but reached her destination, while two more Spanish vessels escaped unharmed from seaplane attacks. On June 18, a Spanish Gull spotted a freighter identified as the Spanish *Mar Bianca* heading west off the Algerian coast. Two Bats bombed her off Oran, causing flooding forward, but there were no injuries. Unfortunately, she was the Genoa-registered *Madda*, carrying cotton seed cake from Port Sudan to Glasgow. Her radio pleas for aid were answered by the Italian destroyer *Nicolo Zeno*, which, ironically, sailed from Palma, escorting her to Gibraltar, from where she resumed her voyage four days later after emergency repairs. Rome, naturally, blamed "Government aircraft" for the incident, but Velardi, who admitted the attack, blamed his allies for misidentifying the ship.[194] In late July there was a flurry of attacks by seaplanes upon foreign merchantmen. On July 30, three Boots bombed and hit the Greek *Laris* (formerly *Katina II*), flying a Panamanian flag under a false name, *Shepo* or *Chepu*, carrying aero-engines and munitions, causing her to run her aground near the small Catalonian port of Blanes, but the cargo was salvaged. The escort of three destroyers and torpedo boats were all damaged, but their air-defense barrage caused one of the attackers to make a forced landing, being towed back to Pollensa Bay by the *Canarias*.[195]

Velardi's Bats also raided ports, nearly sinking the Newcastle Newbegin Line's steamer *Greatend* on May 24 while unloading grain at Almeria.[196] Nine days later, the *Cabo Creux*, also known as the *Kardin*, was sunk in the inner harbor of Valencia with the loss of seven dead, but was later refloated, while two British ships suffered slight splinter damage. In June, the Spanish tanker *Campero*, which had survived a submarine attack, was damaged when a bomb detonated a nearby ammunition barge.[197] On July 24, a near miss during a raid on Valencia caused a leak in the forward hold of the British *St Quentin*, ruining 200 tons of sugar.

While most of these attacks were by Nationalist aircraft, Republican airmen were occasionally involved. On July 26, a French-built Potez 25 bombed the French submarine *Thétis* off Port Vendres as she was escorting the packet *El Mansour*, the submarine replying with machine-gun fire. The French protested, but Valencia retorted the French should stop using submarines as escorts.[198]

During the early summer, Cervera again emphasized the importance of an air-sea blockade and on May 17 called for a combined naval-air command. Kindélan agreed, but the two services could not agree who should have overall authority, with the air staff arguing on July 22 that the navy lacked infrastructure and resources to support an air-sea campaign. Cervera did not confine his efforts to his countrymen, writing on July 5 to Velardi's Legionary Air successor, General Mario Bernasconi, stressing the importance of intensifying air attacks and asking that Velardi join Nationalist air and naval leaders and the Germans to form an aerial blockade central staff.[199] Following his efforts, on July 15, Franco's headquarters issued Directive 318, calling on air forces to: "Intensify offensive aerial operations against the enemy Fleet, communications and ports in collaboration with the fleet's naval blockade of the Mediterranean." A week later, a two-day meeting considered how to achieve these goals and suggested they could be achieved by acquiring seven surface warships and two more submarines.[200] But it was Italian submarines which would trigger the next Spanish Civil War diplomatic crisis.

CHAPTER THREE

The Northern Blockade, August 1936–October 1937

After the uprising, the Republic held a mineral-rich enclave along 190 miles of the Biscay coast from Gijon to the French border, but while coal and iron ore were abundant, the region lacked the agricultural resources to support the population. Autonomous governments recognizing the Republic were established by the Basques, with their capital at Bilbao, the Santanderinos at Santander, and the Asturians in Gijon, their political hue becoming redder from east to west. The enclave's existence had left uprising mastermind General Mola in despair, but Veltjens's arms consignment in the *Girgenti* on August 26 restored his spirits, the ship returning with iron ore and the bodies of two German airmen.[1] Boosted by the arms delivery, Mola isolated the enclave on September 4 by taking Irun on the French border. This left the enclave dependent upon traffic across the Bay of Biscay and the Cantabrian Sea (Mar Cantábrico) in an area traditionally dominated by the British merchant marine, which increased potential clashes between the Nationalists and the Royal Navy.[2]

The Nationalist Blockade

The first incident involved the *Cervera* under Commander Salvador Moreno Fernández, which was providing fire support for rebels besieged in Gijon's Simancas Barracks. The shells seriously injured six German citizens, but "neutral" Admiral Carls rejected Madrid's request he sink the "pirate."[3] Despite the fighting, the British sailing yacht *Blue Shadow*, owned by the American-born Mrs Eloise Drake, put into Gijon for repairs while sailing to Oporto.

The yacht and Mrs Drake, who was divorcing her husband, were both skippered by Bermuda-born fantasist "Captain" Rupert Saville, who once claimed to be the son of a former Spanish ambassador to London.[4] The yacht departed Fowey in Cornwall in September 1935 on a cruise with eight passengers, but the following month her engine flooded in the English Channel and she had to be towed to safety by a French collier, the passengers disembarking. The couple and a two-man crew then sailed the eastern Mediterranean and the Bay of Biscay.[5]

On August 9, Saville was informed by the Royal Navy destroyer HMS *Comet*, which was laying offshore, that the *Cervera* was approaching to renew shelling the city, and he prudently decided to put out to sea. But as he made for the destroyer, for unknown reasons, Moreno fired upon her with the cruiser's 3-pounder (47mm) tertiary armament, killing Saville and injuring the lady.[6] The destroyer took off Saville's body and the survivors to the French fishing port and seaside resort of St-Jean-de-Luz. The damaged yacht was towed to Musel and Mrs Drake later sold her, while Moreno recognized his error and apologized. The cruiser would run a deadly shuttle trip between Gijon and Ferrol until August 16, when the besiegers entered the barracks, whose garrison called down fire from the cruiser to kill both defenders and attackers.[7]

On that day, Madrid dispatched northwards five submarines, a herd of sheep rather than a wolf-pack due to the boats' poor condition, *C-2* being able to dive for only two hours, with ill-trained crews and unenthusiastic commanding officers.[8] They achieved little, a torpedo hitting the *España* on August 31 but the warhead failing to detonate, sinking a small fishing boat and capturing a second, then losing *B-6*, which was surprised on the surface by two patrol boats. A more serious challenge to the Nationalists was the arrival of the task force led by the *Jaime I*, and in response Castro laid mines off Bilbao, sinking a fishing boat and a couple of minesweepers, and briefly closing Bilbao and Santander to international traffic on September 14.[9]

The task force returned south on October 13, leaving the destroyer *José Luis Díez*, a torpedo boat, three submarines, and four auxiliary patrol boats which, from November, came under Commander (later Rear Admiral) Valentín Fuentes López, as Commander, Cantabrian Naval Forces (Jefé de las Fuerzas Navales del Cantábrico). The destroyer so rarely left Bilbao, allegedly due to engine problems, that she was nicknamed "Homebird Joe" (*Pepe, el del Puerto*), and when she went to Bordeaux for repairs her officers promptly defected. Fuentes had no authority over the Basque Auxiliary Navy (Eusko Itsas Gudarostea) based at the little harbor of Portugalete (also Portugaldeta), near the mouth of the River Nervion. This had two-dozen fishing and harbor vessels, converted into inshore minesweepers and patrol boats, while Basque naval power would be projected by four Pesquerías y Secaderos de Bacalao de España (Psybe) deep-sea trawlers (*bous*), armed with 3.9-inch guns from the *Jaime I* and armored with steel plates.[10]

As early as December 20, the Nationalists stated that northern ports were closed, but it was not until February 25, 1937, that they formally blockaded the Cantabrian coast at Bilbao/Santander and the Asturian ports of Ribadesella, Gijon, and Aviles.[11] To enforce the blockade, Castro had only a pair of torpedo boats and a Coast Guard cutter, although he energetically added auxiliary patrol boats and restored the battleship *España*, the *Cervera*, and the destroyer *Velasco* to operational status. The cruiser departed on its first mission on July 26 and the others became operational on August 12.[12] During late 1936, the *Velasco* would approach ships sailing towards Bilbao and try to persuade them to sell their cargoes in Ferrol, while the destroyer HMS *Foxhound* reported that German war materiel was being unloaded both there and at Corunna. In the latter part of the year, the destroyer helped the colliers *Greatend* and *Greathead* avoid interference from Nationalist forces.[13]

Forward bases were established at Ribadeo (also Rivadeo), between Ferrol and Gijon, and Pasajes de San Pedro (Pasajes, also Pasaia) near the French border, although the Nationalists had first to raise the block ship *Jata Mendi* (4,250 grt) from the approaches. From these bases they would deploy up to seven *bous* converted to auxiliary patrol boats, although strictly they returned to this role for most were former Royal Navy Castle or Mersey-class vessels. They received 3-inch (75/76mm) guns taken out of stores, and would be augmented by three auxiliary cruisers, armed merchant cruisers (AMC) in British terminology.

With naval radar being developed only by the major powers, Nationalist vessels relied upon visual observation which, at best, extended only to the horizon and was impeded by rain, fog, mist, and haze. Some patrol boats even lacked radios or had unreliable sets. Blockade-runners might be detected through dense plumes of smoke as coal-fired furnaces were stoked to provide maximum speed, which the patrol boats could not match. Indeed, the former British Castle-class vessels had a maximum speed of only 10.5 knots, which was why they often had to fire shots across the bows to make their prey heave-to. There were only a dozen vessels capable of operating in most weathers and not more than half were on station at any one time, with the remainder in passage or in harbor.

Merchantmen Under Threat

Some two-thirds of the Spanish merchant fleet, 205 mostly Basque-owned and manned vessels (580,521 grt), was in Atlantic waters, with at least two vessels (3,379 grt) laid up for the duration of the conflict, while five (21,274 grt) were acting as prison ships.[14] Between November 1936 and February 1937, some 70 ships landed cargoes in northern ports, half of them Spanish, with a core of some 40 freighters (126,000 grt), while half-a-dozen Spanish coasters augmented by converted trawlers plied their trade along the Cantabrian coast. Almost all the POL for the enclave was provided by the tanker *Campaomor* from Philadelphia, Galveston, and Mexico, while the tanker *Gobeo* broke through the Strait to reach Bilbao with 2,000 tonnes of gasoline and 1,300 tonnes of naval fuel oil. A dozen Basque ships also broke through the Strait blockade, the *Cabo Prior* twice, while five ships sailed in the opposite direction.

Bilbao was extremely busy, with 153 departures, 97 (63 percent) Spanish, between August 1, 1936, and March 31, 1937 (see Table 3.1), many carrying iron ore to meet the demand of recovering industries.[15] The trade was hazardous, and when the collier *Arriluce* (also *Arriluze*) was intercepted by the *Cervera* on August 19 while carrying munitions and gun carriages from Valencia to Gijon, she ran aground and became a constructive total loss. A week later, on August 26, the *Velasco* sank the *Konstan* on a similar mission. In a magnanimous gesture, unprecedented in the conflict, the destroyer's commander, Lieutenant Commander Manuel Calderón y López-Bago, arranged transport for the crew back to Bilbao. In early November, the Nationalists seized the *Manu* and *Araitz-Mendi*, which had been attempting to bring food, coal, and military supplies into Bilbao.[16]

The *Araitz-Mendi* belonged to Spain's largest fleet, the Compañia Naviera Sota y Aznar, whose fate reflected changing fortunes following the uprising. The company board consisted of the liberal, Basque nationalist Sota family, who dominated it, and their conservative monarchist cousins, the Aznars. The Anglophile Ramón de la Sota y Llano had received an honorary knighthood for allowing the British to use his ships in the Great War, but died a month after the uprising and his son, Luis Ramón de la Sota y Aburto, assumed control. Both ensured the majority of the fleet—39 out of 44 vessels—supported the Basque/Republican cause by trading around the Atlantic basin, but ships and associated companies within the Nationalist zone came under the Aznars' control. Under José Luis Aznar Zavala, all the Sota assets, including ships in Nationalist Spain, were placed in 1938 under Naviera Aznar S.A. Sota went into exile in 1937 and, like many Republicans, emigrated to Latin America, where he died in 1978, while Aznar prospered until the 1970s, when the line went into decline, and was declared bankrupt in 1983.[17]

For much of the conflict, Fuentes's ships cowered in harbor, the *C-5*'s crew fleeing into a nearby railroad tunnel at even the hint of an air raid. The only challenge to the blockade was Republican air power, which damaged two patrol boats, although one inquisitive seaplane was driven off with fireworks! A Nationalist bomber attacked the destroyer USS *Kane* on August 17, despite the fact she was displaying a large Star-Spangled Banner horizontally like an awning at the stern, and when that failed to dissuade the attacker, she too resorted to gunfire.[18] There were some minor clashes, which saw each side acquire a patrol boat through the age-old tactic of boarding, while the Republic acquired another, renamed *Donostia*, through defection. The Nationalists' shortage of hulls made them extremely sensitive to losses and reluctant to expose their miniscule fleet to attrition.[19]

Castro's attempts to enforce the blockade and prevent arms imports were further impeded by the enclave's growing reliance upon foreign shipping. Cervera's kid-glove policy towards the British was especially important because they dominated this trade. Of nearly 278,000 tonnes of iron ore exported through Bilbao in 1936, all but 32,000 tonnes (11.5 percent) went to British ports, this pattern continuing until mid-April (see Table 3.1). Germany received only 8,500 tonnes during August in the German *Kurland* and Spanish *Elanchove*. In March, one of the departing ships was the *Hillfern*, which had brought in a weapons consignment and departed with 1,400 tonnes of ore for Tyneside.[20] Even with non-British vessels there were problems;

Table 3.1. Ships departing Bilbao with iron ore, August 1, 1936–April 14 ,1937

Month	Ships (cargo tonnage)			Total
	Spanish	British	Other	
August 1936	3 (9,900)	19 (52,180)	3 (7,660)	25 (69,740)
September	18 (64,850)	4 (6,980)	–	22 (71,830)
October	14 (69,800)	–	–	14 (69,800)
November	10 (48,400)	–	–	10 (48,400)
December	5 (18,100)	–	–	5 (18,100)
Total	50 (211,050)	23 (59,160)	3 (7,660)	76 (277,870)
January 1937	15 (58,675)	7 (19,650)	–	22 (78,325)
February	22 (91,950)	10 (32,900)		32 (124,850)
March	10 (43,750)	11 (34,210)	2 (3,700)	23 (81,660)
April 1–14	1 (3,600)	4 (10,660)	3 (8,050)	8 (22,310)
Total	48 (197,975)	32 (97,420)	5 (11,750)	85 (307,145)

Source: Salas, Intervención Annex 20

when a patrol boat tried to examine the papers of the Estonian *Lena* on August 23, she ignored a shot across her bows and steamed up the River Nervion to Bilbao.

The first Basque arms deliveries were in August and early September, with five trips down the coast from France in trawlers, while major shipments began on September 24, when the Basque *Itxas-Alde* unloaded Polish-supplied weapons at Santander and the *Jalisco* brought Mexican arms to Bilbao. By the end of March, eight more shipments had been made to Santander and six to Bilbao, some originating in the Soviet Union (see Table 3.2), but no consignments appear to have been made to Gijon due to poor dockside facilities.

The first Soviet consignment, I-7, arrived on November 1 when the modern Russian ship *A. Andriev* sailed up the Nervion to be met by Basque Navy Minister Joaquín de Egia y Untzueta. When she entered the Nervion, the crew was alarmed to see the German light cruiser *Köln* in Portugalete, sheltering from a storm. During her

Table 3.2. Arms shipments to the northern enclave

Quarter	Mexico	Poland	Soviet Union	Commercial	Total
Q3/Q4/1936	–	3	3	2	8
Q1/1937	1	8	–	3	12
Q2/1937	–	1	2	4	7
Q3/1937	–	–	–	3	3
Q4/1937	–	1	–	–	1

Sources: Howson; Manrique/Lucas Molina; Morenos I, 982, 1003, 1020–24, 1034–37, 1039–69, 1090–92, 1149

return voyage, the freighter received a radio signal to stop at Hamburg, but the on-board NKVD officer insisted she sail directly to Leningrad.[21] The blockading forces had little success stopping these shipments, apart from two Polish shipments in the *Sylvia* and the Norwegian *Rona* in October and November, the latter's master bribed to deliver his cargo to Ferrol.[22]

The British Security Service (MI5) reported on March 24 that the Basques were trying to acquire the London, Midland and Scottish Railway Company (LMS) freighter *Douglas* to bring in arms. Billmeir acquired the ship on April 1 as the *Stancourt*, and the Republican Consul in Bayonne chartered her for £1,100 ($5,500) a month by to bring in food from Antwerp to Santander.[23] For these reasons, the Nationalists appear to have focussed their inspection efforts from late 1936 upon "the usual suspects," stopping two Russian ships on November 17 and two French ones between November 13 and December 20, to restrict the supply of food into Bilbao by deterring the fainthearted.[24]

The *Palos* Incident

Basque retaliation sparked an international incident on December 20 when four navy *bous* on an exercise/patrol stopped the German merchantman *Pluto* 6 miles north of Cape Machichaco and forced her to enter Bilbao to examine her papers. The *Pluto* was released at the insistence of Republican Navy headquarters, but on Christmas Day the *Bizkaya* ended the season of goodwill in the Bay of Biscay by stopping and boarding the German OPDR freighter *Palos* north of Cape Ogoño.

She was not a Special Ship and was carrying a mixed cargo to a Nationalist port from Hamburg via Rotterdam. Her master protested the search because the *Bizkaya* was not from an internationally recognized maritime organization, but was still forced into Bilbao. There, the Basques unloaded celluloid and telephones, which they judged to be war materiel, and jailed a Nationalist official who was a passenger.[25] The incident raised important questions about belligerent rights; while Berlin was happy to feed the NIC a steady stream of reports of arms shipments to the Republic, it believed the "Reds" had no right to stop and inspect German ships.[26]

Strident protests from Berlin demanded the release of the *Palos*, underlined by the arrival off Bilbao of the light cruiser *Königsberg*. At dusk on December 28, the OKM authorized Carls to seize Republican merchantmen to use as pawns in securing the *Palos*'s release, which actually occurred the following day, but without either her "military" cargo or the passenger. In retaliation, on New Year's Day, the battleship *Admiral Graf Spee*, flying Carls's flag, seized the Spanish freighter *Aragon* as she sailed from Bilbao to Santander within the 3-mile limit, while the *Königsberg* pursued the Spanish *Soton* to Santander, where she ran her aground at the port entrance.

On January 3, the OKM handed Neurath a plan for sterner measures, including seizing more steamers, attacking "Red" naval forces, or even shelling a port, but only the first was approved. Later in the day, the OKM authorized Carls to demand the release of the remainder of the *Palos*'s cargo and her passenger, but to take no other action until he received a response. He sent his ultimatum to "the Red Ruler" (*den roten Machthaber*) of Bilbao, but was ignored. Later in the day, the *Königsberg* seized the Spanish *Marta Junquera*, carrying 600 tonnes of food from Bilbao to Santander, and she later became a support vessel for the Ribadeo Flotilla. The OKM publicly stated it would take more severe measures unless all the cargo of the *Palos* and the missing passenger were returned, while the Foreign Ministry threatened to attack Republican warships and shell ports as well as seizing more ships. The Basque government remained obdurate, but Valencia was more accommodating, offering to release the cargo once an inspection by NIC representatives confirmed it was not war materiel. When it was not returned, Carls turned over the captured ships to the Nationalists on January 7 after releasing their crews.

Meanwhile, there was a noticeable tightening of the Nationalist blockade, especially of Bilbao, leading to the harassment of several foreign vessels during the first quarter of 1937. On New Year's Day, the British *Blackhill*, sailing to Santander to collect iron ore, was intercepted by 20 miles northwest of Pasajes by a patrol boat which fired 30 rounds, all fortunately falling short, and the master rang up full speed to escape.[27] The enclave was as desperate for food as it was for arms, and on January 9, the destroyer *Velasco* stopped the Russian *Smidovich*, carrying 3,337 tonnes of grain and lentils from Leningrad to Bilbao, and took her to Pasajes. The crew was jailed for nine months before being repatriated, with both cargo and ship seized, becoming the Nationalist *Castillo Peñafiel*. When the Soviet seamen returned home, they received a month's salary and clothing as compensation for their hardship, while the crews of two other Soviet freighters briefly detained in January were also released. Later in the month, the Norwegian *Carrier* was intercepted off Aviles with a cargo for a mining company and forced into Corunna, where her cargo was seized.[28]

Nationalist warships extended operations along the French coast during February, shelling the Spanish *Maria Amalia* off Bayonne on February 3, although she escaped. During March, Spanish ships were attacked within France's territorial waters. On March 10, a patrol boat shelled and hit the *Conde de Figuera* and *Conde de Zubiria* off Ushant, the French Navy sending a seaplane and the Coast Guard a cutter to intervene. The seaplane drove off the warship and the cutter escorted the steamer to Brest, where wounded seamen were disembarked. On March 29, off Capbreton, 10 miles north of Bayonne, two Nationalist ships fired upon the *Mar Caspio*, carrying 2,000 tons of coal from Newcastle to Bayonne, forcing her master to run her aground on the bar of the River Adour, where she became a total loss. Earlier, on March 6, Nationalist patrol boats had stopped a French ship 12 miles off Britanny's Ile de Yeu to inspect her papers, while on March 28, 20 miles off Santander, a warship fired six shells across the bow of the London-registered *Magdalena*, sailing from Tunis's port of La Goulette to Bayonne, before allowing her to proceed. On March 29, the Nationalists announced they expected British vessels to heave-to when ordered by their warships, claiming with some accuracy that some of the dozen "British" ships trading with Bilbao were "pseudos," but the significance of the demand was not recognized. The following day, a patrol boat fired across the bows of the French *Cap Falcon* 15 miles off Santander, forcing her stop for inspection before she was allowed to proceed.

The *Mar Cantábrico* Incident

The blockading force was strengthened during March by the minelayer *Júpiter* and two auxiliary cruisers, while the *Canarias* under Francisco Moreno was temporarily assigned and scored one of the most spectacular successes against the Basque-owned, diesel-powered *Mar Cantábrico* of Cia Maritima del Nervion. The freighter had beaten the Strait blockade and was chartered by a Latvian-born U.S. citizen, Robert Cuse, to carry $2,775,000 worth of aero-engines from New York to Bilbao after receiving a reluctantly granted State Department license.[29] When the House reconvened on January 6, an Isolationist Congress overwhelming supported resolutions introduced by two Democrat politicians, Senator Key D. Pittman (Nevada) and Representative Samuel D. McReynolds (Tennessee), banning U.S. arms exports to Spain. However, a technical error meant the legislation came into effect only on January 8. The previous day, Cuse hastily departed New York with some of his engines, eight American aircraft and food, sailing to Vera Cruz, where the ship picked up a weapons consignment, including some 2,000 tonnes of munitions, before departing eastwards on February 19, with the crew trying to disguise her appearance as the British Elder Dempster Line cargo-liner *Adda*, complete with Red Ensign.[30]

The *Canarias* had departed Ferrol on March 3 for the Mediterranean, but the following day was ordered to intercept the *Mar Cantábrico* and the Spanish freighter *Galdames*, heading to Bilbao from Bayonne. The latter carried ammunition, 4 tonnes of nickel for coinage, and passengers, including 140 male civilians and soldiers, but heavy seas and fog scattered her escort of four patrol boats. Seeking her, Moreno, by good fortune, encountered the Bilbao-bound British *Yorkbrook* with 460 tons of war materiel, whose escort, the destroyer *Díez*, promptly abandoned her charge.[31]

As Moreno shepherded the *Yorkbrook* towards Pasajes on the morning of March 5, he encountered the patrol boat *Gipuzkoa* off Cape Machichaco (also Cape Matxitxako), and despite poor visibility quickly set her ablaze, causing 17 casualties, including five dead. Nevertheless, coastal defense batteries covered her entry into the Nervion, where she ran aground at Portugalete. The diversion allowed another patrol boat to cut out the *Yorkbrook*, which hastily made for Bermeo, then sailed on to Bilbao, where it unloaded its cargo before returning to Tyneside on March 19. The cruiser now encountered the *Galdames*, firing a shot which jammed the merchantman's rudder and reportedly killed a woman and three children, while desperate passengers leapt overboard. The two remaining patrol boats, the former Nationalist *Donostia* and the *Nabarra*, tried to shield the merchantman while vainly seeking assistance from the *Díez*. The *Donostia* was driven into French waters, while the *Nabarra* was sunk with the loss of 29 lives, including her commander. The cruiser recovered 20 survivors, who were treated well. During their court martial, Moreno successfully requested that none be executed, another rare example of Nationalist mercy. The *Galdames* was forced into a Nationalist port, where many of her passengers were quickly imprisoned and several were executed, including Manuel Carrsco Formiguera, a member of the Basque government.

The *Donostia* reached Arachón on March 6, then sailed to La Pallice, where she remained until the end of the war. As early as August 2, 1936, the French Navy Ministry had instructed all regional maritime authorities to ban deliveries of fuel oil and munitions to Republican warships and insist upon their departure as soon as possible, and while these rules were later eased, the French interned warships who overstayed their welcome.[32] The *Díez* went to Bordeaux, where the officers promptly defected. However, most of the crew remained loyal and, under a new commander, returned to Santander, encountering en route the *España* and the auxiliary cruiser *Ciudad de Palma* but evading them at high speed.

Meanwhile, the *Mar Cantábrico* sailed towards Santander but, in an astonishing lapse of security, Defense Minister Prieto kept seeking updates on its progress, which he relayed by radio to Basque President José Antonio Aguirre y Lecube. The messages were intercepted by the Nationalists, and on the afternoon of March 8 the freighter saw the *Canarias* come over the horizon.[33] The *Mar Cantábrico* maintained she was the British *Adda* and radioed for Royal Navy assistance, which briefly confused Moreno, the signal being intercepted by *Adda*'s sister, the *Aba*. Seven hours later, four destroyers of the Royal Navy's 5th Flotilla arrived, but by now the Admiralty was smelling a rat. The destroyers realized this was not the *Adda*, indeed her original name was still visible, so refused to help, leaving the *Mar Cantábrico* to surrender. She sailed to Ferrol, where her cargo was unloaded and many of her 26-man crew were executed; some may have been summarily executed by the boarding party, as French fishing vessels reported picking up two bodies which had been shot in the head. The freighter was requisitioned to become an auxiliary cruiser, turning from prey to being the hunter.[34]

Tightening the Bilbao Blockade

During April, Valencia reinforced Fuentes with the destroyer *Císcar* and the submarines *C-4* and *C-6*, but they too stubbornly remained in Bilbao. In a rare sortie on May 21, the *Císcar* collided with and sank a minesweeper, while *C-6* unsuccessfully attacked the *Cervera* on May 13, her ill-disciplined crew seeming happiest when "mechanical problems" forced the boat to remain in harbor. On May 31, exasperated by the Republican warships' under-performance, the Basque government seized and manned the *Díez*, *Císcar*, and *C-6*, the latter under the Russian Lieutenant Commander Ivan Burmitsov, but even this brought no improvement.[35]

Having failed to take Madrid, General Franco decided to roll-up the northern enclave. At the end of March, Mola began an offensive which slowly pushed the Basque forces back towards Bilbao.[36] The Nationalist Navy supported the offensive by tightening its blockade, capturing two arms shipments from Gdynia to Santander: the Greek *Nagos* on April 5 and the Panamanian *Hordena* on April 16, the latter proving a major prize for her cargo was worth the equivalent of $1.7 million, including 23 light bombers and 1,400 tonnes of ammunition.[37] A few weeks before the Nationalists began their advance upon Bilbao, the Basque Francisco Basterrechea Zaldívar, the Republic's arms-purchasing agent in France, warned Prieto that without the support of the Republican Navy it would be impossible to use Spanish ships to transport cargoes to Bilbao; instead, Valencia should transfer 15 Basque vessels to the Red Ensign.[38] As heralded by the taking of the *Smidovich*, the Nationalists intended starving the Basques into surrender. On April 6, the Nationalists ramped up the situation by announcing that they regarded food as contraband, just as the Basque government chartered a dozen British vessels to bring in food and take out iron ore.[39] By now, food shortages in Bilbao meant that any cat from a British ship which sought to explore the docks risked losing its ninth life in a Basque pot.

On March 19, NIC co-chairman Ivor Windsor-Clive, the Earl of Plymouth, told Parliament, apparently without consulting the Admiralty: "The Non-Intervention Agreement does not prohibit the carrying of food to Spain by ships of the participating nations. His Majesty's Government, would, in fact, protest against any interference on the high seas with British ships carrying food or other commodities and the Navy would prevent such interference whenever it could."[40] On the same day, Franco protested against British ships commercially trading with "the Reds."[41] By early April, a number of vessels had slipped through the blockade, including the *Coquetdale* and her sister ship, the *Brinkburn*; the former's deck cargo extended to the height of the superstructure fore and aft, while the latter brought potatoes from Antwerp and was the last ship to enter the Nervion before the blockade intensified.

The British were blindly sailing into a crisis, for they failed to realize the tightening of the blockade heralded a major offensive to take Bilbao. The crisis had been caused by the Foreign Office and the Admiralty pursuing separate policies. Only on March 24 did Foreign Secretary Anthony Eden belatedly inform the Cabinet that he would consult with the Admiralty if Nationalist ships stopped British ships. At the beginning of April, the Royal Navy was conducting its usual routines; the RFA oiler *Prestol* was refuelling the destroyer HMS *Brilliant* in Corunna, while Commander Clifford Caslon of HMS *Blanche*, the senior naval officer in the area, was completing a formal visit to Corunna. There, the local commander informed him the Spanish did not recognize the concept of neutrality in this struggle, although the destroyer had rescued his niece and her children from Cartagena earlier in the conflict. At the end of March, the Royal Navy had reduced deployment off northern Spain to four destroyers: two off Bilbao, one off Santander and the other watching the Nationalist ports of Vigo or Corunna. As Caslon departed from Corunna on the evening of April 5, HMS *Brazen*, which was temporarily the Royal Navy's sole representative off Bilbao, reported the Nationalists were tightening their blockade.[42]

This was demonstrated twice the following day, with implications to British interests. The Panamanian-registered freighter *Andra*, owned by the Antwerp company Socdeco, had landed Polish arms in Santander on March 31, and under a Welsh charter was sailing in ballast to Castro Urdiales to pick up iron ore when she was intercepted in thick fog and sunk 10 miles off Santona by the patrol boat *Galerna*.[43] Further down the coast, the master of the Westcliffe line's *Thorpehall*, Captain Joseph Andrews—carrying food from Alicante—announced to HMS *Brazen* his intention of entering Bilbao.[44] She had earlier been cleared to sail after inspection by both a Nationalist warship and the British authorities, but the *Galerna* now arrived and reinforced her demand to inspect the ship's papers with a shot across her bows. When *Brazen* arrived, she found the gunboat supported by the *Cervera* under Francisco Moreno's brother, Commander Salvador Moreno. *Brazen's* commander sent his crew to general quarters as the destroyer placed herself between the Spanish warships.[45]

Caslon now came up with HMS *Blanche* and HMS *Beagle* and began a long negotiation over unreliable radio links. He confirmed the ship had been searched by the NIC observer at Gibraltar and was carrying only food, believing that Moreno was under the misapprehension she was carrying war materiel. Moreno refused to back down, and some two hours elapsed before a shocked Caslon realized the Nationalists seriously regarded food as contraband and for this reason were determined to deny the freighter access to the port. As a precaution, the destroyers turned their torpedo tubes towards the cruiser, but by now the *Graf Spee*, with Carls aboard, had arrived to monitor the situation and, apparently, to advise Moreno to withdraw. As the talks continued, the *Thorpehall* crept towards Bilbao and crossed the 3-mile limit. Fear of Bilbao's five coastal defense batteries meant the Nationalist ships did not attempt to intercept and they withdrew, haughtily ignoring Caslon's attempts to explain the British position. Moreno returned that afternoon, but the British destroyers again turned their torpedo tubes towards him and deployed for an attack, compelling a second withdrawal. Reporting the incident to the Home Fleet commander in chief, Admiral Sir Roger Backhouse, Caslon observed in passing that "the blockade is effective" and recommended either sending naval reinforcements or banning British merchantmen from entering Bilbao. The Cabinet was left to grasp the nettle.

British minds were further concentrated by the issue of mining. Castro had expended much of his mine stock to contain the Republican task force during the fall, but at the end of September the merchantman *Genovera* brought in another 200 mines for the northern theater. On January 8, Franco claimed to have mined

Republican waters, both on the Cantabrian and Mediterranean coasts, although the latter at that time was an idle boast.[46] In the weeks before Mola's campaign began, Castro laid some mines off Bilbao and, in view of events in the Mediterranean, their presence meant British warships temporarily refused to enter northern ports until the approaches had been cleared. The Basques appear to have done this with considerable efficiency, removing 200 mines between February and mid-June.[47] The Nationalist claims were dismissed by Republican supporters and the Basque government, whose MCM success was confirmed by former boy sailor and retired naval officer Commander Harry Pursey, now working as a pro-Republican journalist.[48] But the threat still existed, mines sinking a Basque patrol boat and a minesweeper, with 23 dead, including the senior MCM officer.

The U.S. Navy shared this view of the mine threat, although bad weather prevented the USS *Hatfield* visiting St-Jean-de-Luz to seek detailed information. Nevertheless, the following month, Rear Admiral Fairfield reported: "These mines are drifting off-shore and may be encountered in areas normally used by shipping."[49] The Germans predictably reported: "The coast was blockaded so effectively that not even a fishing vessel could move out."[50] While there was, therefore, genuine cause for concern, this provided welcome ammunition for the Admiralty and British ambassador Chilton to emphasize the effectiveness of the blockade.

The Cabinet discussed the implications of the *Thorpehall* incident on April 8.[51] Appeaser and Nationalist sympathizer Sir Samuel Hoare wanted Whitehall to recognize the Nationalist blockade and opposed providing Royal Navy support for nine British vessels now scheduled to enter Bilbao.[52] Eden was more sympathetic to the Basques, while his Cabinet colleagues, even Trade and Industry Minister Runciman, displayed surprisingly little sympathy for supporting British shipping. This was because they were aware that some ship-owners had only recently wrapped the Red Ensign around the vessels and were profiteering.[53] Prime Minister Baldwin remained silent during the debate and the Cabinet decided to dissuade British ships from entering Bilbao by intimating the Royal Navy would not help them, while simultaneously creating a committee to study the matter in detail.

The committee met that afternoon, with Hoare emphasizing the "grave risks," but Runciman now favored supporting British ships legitimately trading with Bilbao, especially as they were bringing back much-needed iron ore. There followed a typical British "fudge" which guaranteed ships protection up to the 3-mile limit while emphasizing the hazards of operating off Bilbao. Simultaneously, London informed the Nationalists that the British still denied either side belligerent rights and demanded British ships be allowed to sail without interference unless they were carrying war materiel. However, this policy was subject to frequent modification as the government tacked its way through the international squalls. Eden informed a Parliament angry at the lack of Royal Navy support that ships which ignored the Board of Trade instruction would be given naval protection to the internationally recognized 3-mile limit. However, Spain claimed a 6-mile limit, and on April 22 the Nationalist Naval Staff informed the fleet the 6-mile limit was official policy.[54] On April 12, Baldwin told Parliament: "His Majesty's Government cannot recognise, nor concede, belligerent rights and they cannot tolerate any interference with British shipping at sea. They are, however, warning British shipping that, in view of conditions at present prevailing in the neighbourhood of Bilbao, they should not, for practical reasons and in view of the risks [from] which it is at present impossible to protect them, go into that area as the conditions prevail."[55] There was a taint of duplicity about British policy, with discreet warnings to ship-owners, by private communication not radio, not to risk breaking the Bilbao blockade while simultaneously trying to show the Nationalists they were not submitting to force, and the Basques that London was publicly not trying to impede freighters entering the Nervion.[56]

The mines put the British on the horns of a dilemma: should merchantmen be prevented from placing themselves in harm's way or should they be allowed to risk being mined? The Cabinet now began to question the Admiralty's claims, and the 4th Destroyer Flotilla's commander, Captain Rhoderick McGrigor, informed Home Fleet commander Backhouse that while mines had been seen on March 24 and March 31, he was confident Basque minesweeping ensured it was safe to sail to Bilbao. Backhouse ordered that this message should not be passed to either the Foreign Office or the Board of Trade. When Vice-Admiral Geoffrey Blake, commander of the Battlecruiser Squadron, assumed command of the Royal Navy in the Cantabrian Sea, he was informed on April 12: "If a British ship proceeding to Bilbao despite Government advice calls on you for protection in a particular case you should render protection on the High Seas."[57] Two days later, however, Blake reported that the Bilbao blockade consisted of only one warship, which meant it was ineffective, a point underlined by the Spanish Embassy, which published a list of ships which had entered and left Bilbao between April 7 and 13. In his memoirs, Cervera admitted he lacked hulls for an effective blockade, while a postwar Spanish account claimed military aid worth the equivalent of 275 million French francs ($11.1 million) reached the northern enclave in March.[58] The *Thorpehall* departed on April 15, intervention by HMS *Brazen* allowing her to proceed after being intercepted by the battleship *España*, and she too confirmed the absence of mines off Bilbao. By now, ship-owners were seeking permission at least to proceed to Santander, the South Wales iron and steel industry complained about a shortage of ore, and press reports portrayed the ship masters as "bluff British sea-dogs whom only government orders restrained from gallantly running an imaginary blockade with food for starving women and children."[59] On April 16, the Cabinet committee pondering the issue realized that accepting Nationalist claims might prevent British ships entering any Spanish port, and now confirmed the policy of protecting merchantmen on the high seas.

Meanwhile, on April 8, Caslon, on his own initiative, radioed all British merchantmen within 100 miles of Bilbao to sail to St-Jean-de-Luz and there await further orders, ships without transceivers often hearing the message on the master's commercial radio. The following day, the Admiralty instructed him not to use the airwaves to contact ships. Nevertheless, Their Lordships (the Lords Commissioners of the Admiralty, in charge of the operational and administrative control of the Royal Navy) commended and encouraged Caslon who was backed by the Board of Trade, and his greyhounds of the sea acted as sheepdogs, rounding up and herding merchantmen to St-Jean. The port was popular with the French and Spanish aristocracy, as well as composer Maurice Ravel, and had historic associations: in 1660, Louis XIV and Maria Teresa were married in the cathedral, while from 1813–14 it acted as the Duke of Wellington's headquarters in the war against Napoleon's French. The harbor is suitable for fishing boats and smaller merchantmen, larger vessels having to anchor offshore. In 1940, much of the Polish Army in France would escape through the port, carried to seagoing ships by fishing boats in a second Dunkirk.

On April 9, Caslon wrote to masters of ships: "You are not to leave St-Jean-de-Luz for any port in the hands of the Spanish Government on the North of Spain until further orders." The following day, the Board of Trade underlined these instructions by ordering the British Consul in Bordeaux to inform masters they were not to attempt to enter Basque ports due to the dangerous situation. However, the situation was aggravated by a serious misunderstanding at Nationalist military headquarters in Salamanca.[60] Having read Moreno's report of the *Thorpehall* incident, overheard Caslon's radio instructions, and seen the build-up of British ships, Nationalist Naval Intelligence—as so often—added two and two to get five, concluding that Perfidious Albion planned to run a convoy into Bilbao with Royal Navy support.[61] Major Troncoso's spies had identified four food ships in St-Jean, and Salamanca informed him the navy was determined to enforce the blockade, so he informed his friend Chilton on April 9 that Nationalist warships would resist attempts to break the blockade "by all available means," including laying more mines off Bilbao.

This was leaked and the press broke the news the following day, causing great public indignation. In response, Eden, Hoare, and Runciman agreed to dispatch the battlecruiser HMS *Hood*, the symbol of British naval power, flying Blake's flag to the Cantabrian Sea, together with the battleship HMS *Royal Oak* and heavy cruiser HMS *Shropshire*. The battlecruiser had been recommissioned in September after a refit and was scheduled to join the Mediterranean Fleet, where Blake was to join her, but an accident meant she needed repairs in Portsmouth, where the admiral boarded her on November 28.[62] They also persuaded a reluctant Baldwin to summon a rare Sunday evening meeting of the Cabinet on April 11. As usual, Hoare threw out objections like jettisoning cargo to save a sinking ship, highlighting the potential threat from the obsolete *España*, and even advocated banning food shipments to Bilbao. A compromise was arranged in which Chilton would inform the Nationalists that the Royal Navy would not tolerate any interference with British shipping on the high seas, but that London would continue advising ships not to proceed to Bilbao. The Admiralty was instructed to inform British ships that protection would be withdrawn from any vessel wishing to sail to Bilbao.

What the Admiralty chose to ignore was a Spanish Embassy report, confirmed by the British Consul, that 32 ships docked at Bilbao and seven departed during the first half of April, although most began departing from April 14.[63] They were led by the Sunderland-registered *Brinkburn*, which returned unmolested to her home port on April 20 with a cargo of iron ore. The other ships followed without incident, although when the *Coquetdale* returned to the Northeast to take on a cargo of coal for Bilbao, several of the crew refused to return to the warzone and had to be replaced. Refusing to sail had legal and financial implications. Seamen faced charges with fines or even jail for refusing to obey an order, and they could also lose their unemployment benefit, until this threat was quashed following a test case at the South Shields Court of Referees in March 1937.

The St-Jean-de-Luz Dilemma

In St-Jean-de-Luz, the masters pondered their next moves, especially the four ships identified by Troncoso: the *Hamsterley*, *Marie Llewellyn*, *Macgregor*, and *Sarastone*. Most of them were loaded in Antwerp, and some of them, including the *Marie Llewellyn*, lacked transceivers. The Newcastle-registered *Hamsterley*, under Captain A. H. Still, carried peas and beans, but press attention focused upon the three Welsh-owned ships, whose masters were all surnamed Jones. To distinguish between them, *The Times*'s David Scott nicknamed them according to their cargoes, and this was widely accepted.[64] The *Marie Llewellyn*, under Captain David John "Potato" Jones, had 1,000 tons of potatoes, Captain Owen "Corn Cob" Jones's *Macgregor* had grain, while Captain John "Ham and Egg" Jones's *Sarastone* actually carried potatoes and grain. On April 11, they were joined by the Veronica Steamship Company's *Seven Seas Spray* under another Welsh master, Captain William Roberts, carrying 4,000 tons of tinned food, salt, cognac, hams, peas, nuts, drums of olive oil, and barrels of wine, as well as horse fodder from Alicante. Despite warnings from HMS *Blanche*, the *Seven Seas Spray* attempted to slip into Bilbao by running along the coast outside Spanish territorial waters, but was intercepted by the *Cervera* on April 10 and shepherded past Bilbao, before heeding the Board of Trade instruction. On the evening she arrived, "Corn Cob" Jones departed for Bayonne to await further orders.

None of the ships had refrigerated holds, and as the cargoes rotted the masters fretted on the prospect of a profitless voyage. Many began to express their doubts, both about the effectiveness of the blockade and the mine threat. Captain Still said he was willing to sail with other ships, but the ship's owner, Mr Walter Vaughan, ordered him to remain where he was. "Potato" Jones, whose appearance and speech resembled the English newspaper cartoon figure Colonel Blimp, told the press: "Spanish Navy? Never heard of it since the Armada." He added: "It makes me sick thinking of these Spanish Dons strutting around the quarter-deck of their miserable ships intimidating the British Navy and interfering with shipping." These views made him popular with the British public, who shared these views, but Jones had a double financial interest in delivering his cargo because he was part-owner of the Dillwyn Steamship Company.

The desperate Basque government offered the masters 5,000 French francs ($200) for each ship which departed on April 17, with 1,000 francs for each succeeding day, assuring them of protection within the 3-mile limit and that the port's entrance had been swept of mines. Bilbao cited the example of the *Thorpehall*, which entered the port on April 6 and then departed for Gijon, where it arrived on April 19, but the owners then ordered her to obey Board of Trade instructions and sail to La Pallice. The Nationalist threat was underlined when the French trawler *Roche Rouge*, attempting to evacuate men from a Belgian company, was intercepted off Pasajes on April 19, but managed to escape and return to St-Jean.[65] Nevertheless, during the afternoon of April 15, "Potato" Jones suddenly departed without informing the harbour master and was seen battling his way westward through a heavy swell and torrential rain.[66] She was intercepted by HMS *Brazen* and forced to return to the port, where he denied trying to break the blockade and blustered that he had wanted to sail to Bayonne to get fresh water. Two days later, he again departed with a ruined cargo for Alicante, where he would pick up a cargo of fruit for Antwerp.

The British Chamber of Shipping met on April 14 to consider the blockade issue, and on April 17 advised ship-owners considering trade with Spain to operate at their own discretion. If they judged that entry into a port under blockade, or with the threat of hostilities, was an unacceptable risk, then they should take their cargoes to a safe port, which would be regarded as the original destination, and there unload to ensure payment.[67] The dilemma for the masters was that in delivering their cargoes they risked their ships, but remaining moored saw rising costs due to war risk insurance and crew bonuses. On April 19, the French ordered "Ham and Egg" Jones to Bordeaux on suspicion of carrying war materiel, and while dock workers originally agreed to unload the rotting food, when they realized NIC officers intended inspecting the whole cargo they walked off the ship. A fortnight elapsed before they resumed work, the only item confiscated being a consignment of nickel coins which the NIC deemed might be used to manufacture munitions. The rest of the cargo, minus the rotten food, was reloaded and the ship was allowed to leave, but during her stay in Bordeaux the blockade was broken.

The Blockade is Broken

The *Seven Seas Spray* was a World War I H-Type standard freighter, the equivalent of a World War II Liberty ship, initially owned by the Good Hope Shipping Company but then sold to the Veronica Line, both owned by Welshman Alfred Pope, who publicly stated it was foolish to attempt to break the blockade. After the ship arrived in St-Jean, he sent his partner, Thomas McEwen, to discuss the situation with Roberts and they agreed the ship should try to reach Bilbao. While the men were willing to risk ship, cargo, and crew, in those more chauvinistic times they were concerned about the fate of the two female members of the ship's complement. These were the widower Roberts's daughter, Florence (or Fifi) and Mrs Beatrice Docker, wife of Chief Engineer William Docker, who both decided to stay. On the evening of April 19, the *Seven Seas Spray* raised anchor and departed, without informing the authorities, whose order to stop they ignored. By chance, the 4th Destroyer Flotilla was relieved that day by Captain Victor Danckwerts's 6th Destroyer Flotilla.[68]

Roberts did not use his navigation lights, so a passing warship did not see him, and he sailed down the coast until around dawn. Then, when he was 10 miles off the coast, a British destroyer approached and asked "Where bound?" Roberts boldly replied "Bilbao," and, having warned him he did so at his own risk, the destroyer wished him "Good Luck." At the entrance to the harbour at 0800 hours he was met by Fuentes's destroyers and two Basque patrol boats, the triumphant flotilla sailing up the river with Roberts and his 20-year-old daughter on the bridge and cheering crowds on both banks. A grateful Basque government gave Roberts a silver cigarette case and his photogenic daughter a bracelet. Pope later told the press that the actions of his ship had shown the blockade was "nothing but boast and tommy rot." Fifi would write about her adventures to her old school, Penarth County Grammar (now Stanwell School), which would later adopt the vessel. By contrast, 43-year-old Mrs Docker appears to have been airbrushed out of the press coverage, although Roberts informed the *Western Daily Mail*: "I had the loyal co-operation of officers, engineers and crew, and the ladies entered into the venture with zest."[69]

Runciman was now demanding an end to the ban on merchantmen entering Bilbao, noting that both ship-owners and the South Wales steel industry—which had 18 ships ready to carry ore—would support the move. Hoare refused to listen. However, the situation was drifting out of his control as potential blockade-runners began to sail out of St-Jean. The furious Nationalists again spoke of intensifying the blockade, the opportunity arising on April 23, St George's Day, and featuring "Corn Cob" Jones. The *Macgregor* had returned to St-Jean on April 21 and Jones discussed his plans to break the blockade with Vice-Admiral Blake, who now believed it was ineffective and was determined to escort British merchantmen to the internationally recognized 3-mile limit. He assured Jones, together with Captains Still (*Hamsterley*) and Gwilym Prance (*Stanbrook*), that *Hood*, accompanied by the destroyer HMS *Firedrake*, would be waiting off Bilbao when they arrived. When Blake informed the Admiralty, their Lordships initially protested, fearing the Royal Navy would be responsible for convoys into Bilbao, but eventually conceded to the admiral's point of view.[70]

On the moonlit evening of April 22, the three freighters departed St-Jean carrying 8,500 tons of food. Troncoso's agents promptly telephoned the news and the patrol boat *Galerna* met them 10 miles off Bilbao when they arrived the following morning, greeting them with a shot across the *Macgregor*'s bow. HMS *Firedrake* intervened and Moreno's *Cervera* went to general quarters, signalling: "Please tell steamers not to enter Bilbao." Blake warned Moreno to "stop interfering" and they argued for three hours on the legality of the 6 or 3-mile limit, then the *Galerna* fired another shot across the bows of the three merchantmen. The destroyer went to general quarters and pointed her guns at the patrol boat, which came under fire from shore batteries and sheered-off as *Hood* also came up. Moreno now pointed his guns at the *Macgregor* and as the situation grew more tense, Blake ordered *Hood*'s commander, Captain Arthur "Toby" Pridham, to turn the main armament towards the cruiser, but not directly at her.[71] The Gunnery Officer, Commander John Terry, misunderstood the order and Moreno briefly found himself looking down eight barrels of 15-inch rifled Universal Translator guns before a furious Blake ensured his orders were obeyed.[72]

Two Basque patrol boats came out to escort the merchantmen inside the 3-mile limit and engaged the *Galerna*, although some shells fell near *Firedrake*, which ordered them to cease. Faced with force majeure, Moreno withdrew with teeth-clenched dignity and the food-ship convoy triumphantly sailed up the Nervion, cheered by huge crowds. Captain Prance later radioed Billmeir: "No sign of mines or Franco."[73] Although the *Hamsterley* was later hit during an air raid, Captain Still was able to depart on May 5, carrying precious iron ore."[74] Three days later, Blake was relieved as senior naval officer by Rear Admiral Charles Ramsey, commander of the 2nd Battle Squadron, flying his flag in the battleship HMS *Royal Oak* and accompanied by her sister ship HMS *Resolution*.[75] The *Hood* returned home for the Coronation Naval Review, during which King George VI knighted Blake.

The experience of Captain Charles Dick gives some idea of the situation at this time. He joined a largely Dutch-manned ship, the *Olavus*, at Nantes, intending to pick up a cargo of iron ore for Ijmuiden in the Netherlands, but the crew was extremely reluctant. Despite this, he sailed to Bilbao and the *Cervera* fired a warning shot when the *Olavus* entered the 6-mile-limit. Basque coastal batteries fired their own warning shots, which fell just astern of Dick's ship, panicking the crew, who forced him to turn back and spend the night cruising off the Nervion with navigational lights switched off. At dawn, with no sign of any Nationalist warship, he was able to pick up the pilot. As they sailed up the river, there was an air raid and the pilot leapt over the side and swam to shore. On the homeward voyage, the ship was intercepted by the *España*, which ordered her to change course, but luckily HMS *Hood* appeared and escorted her into international waters. Captain Dick, who later shipped food to Alicante and Barcelona, observed: "It was just another job of work and not as bad as the First World War."[76]

On April 28, the *Backworth*, carrying food and medical supplies raised by charities, was escorted by the destroyer HMS *Fury* to the 3-mile limit. *Fury* advised the master, Captain Thomas "Hard Nut" Russell, to sail to St-Jean, but the freighter sailed into the Nervion, with lifeboats ready for launching.[77] Other ships followed, including another small convoy on April 29, with prior arrangement with Rear Admiral Ramsey, and by the end of the month 71 ships had entered Bilbao, with another 32 in Santander.[78] Some British masters and crews reduced their rations during the passage, leaving the rest to be distributed among the civilian population, while other crews, before departing St-Jean, purchased up to 10 shillings ($2.45) of bread which they handed out to civilians.

With so much attention paid to Bilbao, arms shipments were increasingly made to Gijon and Santander, with at least three in April and two in the first half of May, the last by France-Navigation ships.[79] The blockade at both ports was as uneven as Bilbao, but grew tighter, forcing ships to wait outside territorial waters ready dash in.[80] Yet even international waters were not always safe; on April 25, a shot was fired across the bows of the *Oakgrove* as she sought to enter Santander, but the arrival of HMS *Fury* forced the Spanish warship away, an act later described as a "humiliation."[81] The following day, the *Royal Oak* successfully dissuaded the *Consett* from entering the port, aided by the menacing presence of the *España*, and she sailed to St-Jean. Similar attempts by the Spanish destroyer with the British "pseudo" *Jenny* were hampered because her French master spoke little English. On April 30, the *Consett*, which had no radio, made another vain effort to enter Santander, but veered off following warning shots from the *España*.

Meanwhile, the Nationalist Navy conducted occasional mine-laying operations off Santander. The *Júpiter* lay about 20 German mines on April 20, while on the night of April 29/30, the destroyer *Velasco* attempted to lay 60 Vickers "eggs" off Bilbao but was thwarted by alert Basque coast defenses.[82] The *Velasco* was still carrying 53 mines when she was summoned to support the *España*, which had relieved the *Cervera* off Santander on April 24 and intercepted a message that another Consett ship, the *Knitsley*, planned to enter the small port of Castro Urdiales with a cargo of coal. The destroyer intercepted the collier and fired a warning shot, which was ignored.

The watching *España* now drifted into a minefield laid some weeks earlier, possibly by the *Velasco*, and detonated a mine, which flooded her engine room and caused her slowly to list to port. To add insult to injury, two Gourdou-Leseurre GL-32 fighter/dive-bombers attacked the battleship with half-a-dozen 50-kg bombs, but were driven off by air-defense guns. It became clear the battleship could not be saved and the *Velasco* came alongside to rescue all but three of the crew before the battleship capsized and sank, having ironically justified the Nationalist Navy's much-vaunted mine threat.[83] The air attack worried the Admiralty, fearing bombs had sunk the *España*, so there was a collective sigh of relief when the real cause of her loss was determined. The Royal Navy remained confident bombers proved no threat to capital ships at sea … until December 10, 1941, and the sinking of the battleship HMS *Prince of Wales* and battlecruiser HMS *Repulse* off Malaya by Japanese aircraft. Meanwhile, the *Knitsley* quietly entered port and returned safely to Sunderland, where 11 members of the crew refused to sail on another voyage to Spain without receiving more than the agreed war-zone bonus. At a court in Sunderland on June 18, they were convicted of conspiring to impede the ship's progress and fined 40 shillings ($9.80) each, although the master, Captain Frederick Robinson, agreed the trip had been much more dangerous than a normal commercial voyage.[84]

The Fall of Bilbao

During May, 95 ships entered Bilbao while 59 reached Santander, but increasingly ships were being diverted to Gijon, where congestion kept them for up to three weeks.[85] Ships entering Bilbao included CTE's trans-Atlantic liner *Habana* and the Sota's 1,266 grt steam yacht *Goizeko-Izarra*. The latter was built as the *Warrior* for American multi-millionaire Frederick William Vanderbilt, requisitioned by the Royal Navy in 1917, and acquired after the war by Ramón de la Sota Llano.[86] Even Basque shipowners were despondent, and from January to April, Runciman revealed that 37 ships under 1,000 grt were transferred to the British registry, with another 10 registered in British overseas dominions and protectorates.[87]

From the end of April, the Basque government began evacuating noncombatants from Bilbao, arranging for the ships already in the port to carry 5,000 women and children to France. In anticipation of this, French ministers—chaired by Foreign Minister Delbos—met on April 30 and assigned five ships to take refugees to La Pallice or Pauillac, with the powerful French trades union, the Confédération *Générale de Travail* (CGT), closely involved in preparations to receive them. The Atlantic Fleet commander, Vice-Admiral Count Jean de Laborde, was ordered to have the light cruiser *Émile Bertin* and half-a-dozen destroyers ready to cover the evacuation but, as part of the Naval Patrol, he had already deployed ships from the nine-strong 2nd Destroyer Flotilla (2eme Flotille de Torpilleurs) and seven sloops.[88] The following day, the situation had deteriorated so badly that both Paris and London ordered the evacuation to begin immediately, the sloop *Somme* being sent to Castro Urdiales to evacuate French and Belgian citizens. On the same day, a clash between the *Ciscar* and the *Galerna* saw HMS *Faulkner* straddled but undamaged.[89]

On May 3, Paris ordered the liner *Meknès* and the freighter *Montesquieu* to begin the evacuation, while the freighters *Carimare*, *Château Margaux*, and *Château Palmer* assembled at Bordeaux for added capacity, although the French remained worried about mines. Two days later, the Basque diaspora began in earnest with the departure of the *Hamsterley*, which was pursued by a Nationalist warship that fired across her bow, but reached the safety of international waters observed by HMS *Royal Oak*. The same evening, 3,300 women and children embarked in the

Habana and *Goizeko-Izarra* to sail for Pallice, although many had been promised a haven in Great Britain.

They departed on the morning of May 6, flying the Basque and International Red Cross flags, escorted to the 3-mile limit by the *Císcar* and two patrol boats. They were met just beyond the limit by the *Royal Oak* and various destroyers with orders to shield them in international waters. The *Cervera* was at general quarters and also waiting, and Moreno informed Ramsey: "I have orders from my government to stop any Spanish ship leaving Bilbao. I protest if you stop me from exercising my rights." Ramsey replied: "These ships are carrying non-combatant refugees certified by British Consul. I have orders from my government to protect these ships on the high seas. I have noted your protest and will inform my government." Moreno tried to cross the battleship's bows to come alongside the Spanish ships, whom he instructed to sail to a Nationalist port, where, he ambiguously informed them, his government would "take care of" (*atendidos*) them. Ramsey insisted his orders were to conduct the ships to French ports; faced again with *force majeure*, Moreno stood down his crew and withdrew in impotent fury.[90] Between May 3 and 10, the Basque, British, and French ships landed 4,873 refugees, including 3,050 children.[91]

First Sea Lord Admiral Chatfield continued to fret about the Nationalist blockade, and on April 28 informed the Cabinet Committee on the Protection of British Shipping 1937 that "interference" might be regarded as taking sides, provoking Germany and Italy. Home Fleet commander Admiral Backhouse pressed for granting both sides belligerent rights in a letter to Chatfield on July 4, observing: "We cannot evacuate refugees indefinitely." Backhouse commented that Government policy regarding the northern coast was very pro-Republican and noted that Franco restored order quickly. Chatfield replied that he was against granting both sides belligerent rights, not only because he feared it would lead to further incidents but also because it required a network of observers in all Spanish ports, which was unacceptable to either side.[92]

The *Habana* and *Goizeko-Izarra* would make several rescue voyages, both from Bilbao and Santander, shielded by the Royal Navy, with the liner even carrying 4,000 refugees to Southampton, Sato selling the yacht to British industrialist Sir Hugo Cunliffe-Owen, chairman of the British-American Tobacco Company and a well-known racehorse owner.[93] British ships also carried away refugees; the *Hamsterley* was followed by the *Backworth*, along with the *Macgregor* and the *Thorpehall*. These ships had holds full of iron ore but very limited accommodation, and despite all the crews' efforts, the voyage was very uncomfortable for their unhappy passengers, especially as they had left most of their food in Bilbao.[94] The port itself was increasingly dangerous due to air raids; on May 23, bomb splinters showered the *Oakgrove* and injured two of her crew. Gijon's port, Musel, was also under attack by German bombers, which hit the bridge of the Bilbao-registered *Itxas-Ondo* on March 25, killing the master and injuring several crewmen.[95]

French humanitarian efforts increased, and on May 6 the *Château Margaux* and *Château Palmer* were escorted to Bilbao by the destroyer *le Fantasque*, being joined two days later by the *Carimare*, *Château Margaux*, and *Château Palmer*. All were escorted to the 3-mile limit by the *Somme*, despite Moreno's efforts, which were rebuked by Rear Admiral Jean-Ernest Odend'hal, commander of the 2nd Light Squadron (2eme Escadre Légère), who was ordered to shield the French ships.[96] They all departed the following day with some 1,960 refugees. Again the *Cervera* approached, protesting about French partisanship and violation of "an effective blockade," but was ignored and the refugee ships arrived safely at Paulliac on May 10. Three British ships—the *Marvia*, *Thurston*, and *Stancourt*—followed on May 10, then the *Habana* and *Goizeko-Izarra* took out another 4,000 refugees four days later, followed by a further run to Southampton on May 20. After another two days, there was a new multi-national convoy.

Paris was already reviewing the whole evacuation issue, scaling back the naval support from May 9. Two days later, a naval staff officer, Rear Admiral Réné-Émil Godfroy, sent Navy Minister Gasnier-Duparc a note claiming the refugees were all "comfortable people" travelling with their servants and that they seemed afraid of the Communists, with many willing to return to Nationalist Spain. He claimed there was a considerable risk from mines, artillery fire, and incidents with Nationalist warships, requesting the minister "refrain from pursuing rather dangerous operations" which had no humanitarian basis. Consequently, by May 12, the evacuation policy was in the waste bin.[97]

French Communists were undaunted, and as the Nationalists closed in on Bilbao's defenses at the beginning of June, they sent a delegation—consisting of Party Treasurer Émile Dutilleul, Central Committee member Giulio Ceretti (also known as Pierre Allard), and sympathizing non-Party member physicist Paul Langevin—to meet President Blum. They wanted to use France-Navigation to evacuate refugees but were seeking French naval support. Following the meeting, Vice-Admiral Laborde was ordered on June 2 to assign a destroyer to escort three of the line's freighters from the Verdon to Bilbao, where the *Ploubazlanec* arrived on June 5 with food. She departed for Verdon with 300 children on June 13, and that day the *Trégastel* and the *Perros-Guirec* set sail for Bilbao from Bordeaux, escorted by a sloop. When they arrived off Bilbao the next day, a British destroyer warned them the port was under constant air attack and the freighters returned to Bordeaux.[98]

With the fall of Bilbao inevitable, the pace of evacuation increased in June. Shielded by the Royal Navy, the *Habana* made three runs to La Pallice between June 1 and 13, while the *Goizeko-Izarra*—now the British-owned *Warrior*—made its last on June 14, when foreign evacuation voyages ended with the departure of the last British freighter, the *Thurston*. Most of the ships entering the Nervion in early June brought food, but the Newcastle steamer *Alice Marie* arrived from Blyth also carrying coal, ambulances, motorcycles, and medical equipment, later departing with iron ore and 500 refugees.

One of the last British ships down the Nervion was the *Seabank* (formerly *Joyce Llewellyn*, not to be confused with the *Seabank Spray*) with the contents of the city's British banks and the Bank of Bilbao, as well as 9,000 boxes of gold and securities. She cruised off La Pallice for a week, planning to meet the Spanish *Axpe-Mendi* in French waters and transfer her cargo, but on June 25 a French warship ordered both ships to put into La Pallice. Paris planned to unload the cargo, but for several weeks dock workers declined to do so; when they eventually relented, it was placed in bond by French customs officials while the courts sorted out legal claims. There was a brief moment of alarm when the *Císcar* arrived at La Pallice with 100 refugees, leading to fears she would seize the golden cargo. To prevent this, the destroyer *l'Audacieux* was dispatched to the port ande HMS *Bulldog* was stationed offshore. The *Císcar* was moored alongside the *Seabank*, and there were reported tensions between the two crews. The Spanish destroyer's passengers were disembarked after prolonged discussions, and on June 18 she departed, defiantly pointing her guns at *l'Audacieux*. Two days later, she met the *Díez*, which had brought 100 refugees to Verdon, with both sailing to Santander, which was also the destination for the *Seabank* and *Axpe-Mendi* when they sailed on August 24.[99] On June 15, the *Thorpehall* departed Bilbao with £200,000 ($1 million) worth of valuables and securities from banks, but when she arrived in La Pallice she lacked documentations and was unable to unload her cargo. She had to depart on June 25, but eventually arrived at the Dutch port of Flushing (Vlissingen) on July 2, where she was promptly arrested by the police and her cargo impounded by the authorities. Attempts by Basques and Valencia to recover the property were rejected by the Dutch court.[100]

There was an exodus of Republican naval forces from June 15, accelerated by an air raid on Portugalete which sank or badly damaged four minesweepers. The destroyers departed for France loaded with military and political leaders, together with refugees, while the patrol boats sailed westwards to Santona, followed three days later by most of the surviving minesweepers. The *D-5* and *D-6* sailed for Belgium to act as arms transporters, but when they put into La Pallice on August 5, the French authorities ordered them to Les Sables d'Olonne, an American Expeditionary Force landing point in the Great War, where they were interned. Some Basque merchantmen and fishing vessels attempted to escape with refugees on June 18, but almost all were siezed by a task group of four patrol boats and a torpedo boat under Captain Felix Bastarrache.[101] Nevertheless, it was estimated that 9,000 refugees were brought out of Bilbao between May 10 and June 16, a third of them in French ships.[102]

With the fall of the port on June 19, the Nationalist Navy arrived with a flotilla of four patrol boats and the hospital ship *Nodriza*, which together with three merchantmen were led up the Nervion by the auxiliary cruiser *Ciudad de Palma* and acquired much valuable naval materiel.[103] There was a disappointing haul of merchant ships in Bilbao, with only nine freighters (27,737 grt), of which the *Bodon* (841 grt) was virtually a hulk. Upon the fall of Bilbao, the Admiralty decided the crisis had passed and recalled Ramsey and the *Royal Oak*, leaving Captain Sir Lionel Sturdee in the battleship *Resolution* as the senior naval officer. Nevertheless, tensions remained, and on June 21 the British *Genthills* was fired upon in the Bay of Biscay.

Under Nationalist control, Bilbao had the lion's share of imports at 947,031 tonnes, much of it coal, but more than half of Nationalist exports in 1938—including 2.2 million tonnes of iron pyrites—went from Huelva, often in German ships carrying iron ore from Spanish Morocco.[104] Germany's OPD resumed services to the port in July. During 1937, Germany would import 1.62 million tons of Spanish iron ore, and the Germans hoped to have exclusive access to the precious mineral organized by ROWAK (Rŏhstoffe und Waren Einkaufgesellschaft).[105] Exports of Basque iron ore did not begin until August, when 45,000 tonnes was dispatched, but the pace rapidly picked up to 100,000 tons in September and 345,000 tons in the last quarter of 1937. During 1937, 1.62 million tonnes of Spanish iron ore was shipped to Germany, along with 963,000 tonnes of other ores.[106]

Despite Nationalist assurances that British ships would be permitted to use Bilbao, during July it proved almost impossible to obtain permits. As Britain remained a major trading partner with Spain following secret negotiations with the Foreign Office, Burgos eventually agreed that British ships could resume exporting Basque iron ore. The first delivery to Cardiff was led by the shipping company Constants (South Wales), with the cargo arriving on August 28. Other ship-owners followed, but incoming vessels had to give 72 hours' notice to ensure a berth and a pilot. Furthermore, on August 3, the Board of Trade warned that the Nationalists would deny access to ships which had been trading with Republican ports, except in cases of emergency, and then would be allowed to remain for only 24 hours.[107] Trade with the Republic was especially profitable, particularly to the northern enclave. Runciman informed the Commons on May 4 that rates to Republican ports in the Mediterranean were 25 shillings ($6.25) a ton, compared with 12 shillings ($3.00) to French ports, while to Bilbao it was 22 shillings ($5.50), against 7 shillings ($1.75) to Bayonne. Time charter rates to Republican ports were more than 15 shillings ($3.80) per ton on deadweight.[108]

The Santander Blockade

Santander was now in the sights of General Franco and his navy, and although his offensive was delayed until mid-August, few in the enclave were optimistic and flight was foremost in many minds.[109] As early as June 16, President Blum ordered the *Marine Nationale* to escort ships making for Santander on humanitarian missions. The destroyer *Orage* and the sloop *L'Épinal* escorted the liner *Marrakech* and France-Maritime's *Ploubazlanec*, *Trégastel*, and *Perros-Guirec* to Santander on June 20, where they picked up 1,000 refugees and departed the next day.[110] On June 19, five British ships—the *Hillfern*, *Kenfig Pool*, *African Trader*, *Surreybrook*, and *Latymer*—departed with refugees for France. When the Hong Kong-registered *Marion Moller*, carrying 2,000 women and children, departed four days later, she was stopped by the *Cuidad de Palma* in international waters and sent a distress call, to which the destroyer HMS *Boadicea* responded. The Spanish commander believed there were soldiers, or potential conscripts, among her passengers and passed his concerns to the French authorities, so the freighter was sent to Pauillac, near Bordeaux, where soldiers and potential conscripts were indeed discovered, all of whom were interned.[111]

By covering a shorter length of coast, the blockade was strengthened and remained unchallenged by the Republican Navy. When the *Cervera* bombarded Santona on June 18, a Basque patrol boat fired back, leading the Santanderino authorities to disarm her, although later she was rearmed. Basque minesweepers continued to clear the sea lanes into Santander, but when the destroyers returned to the enclave on June 21, most of the Basque crews were replaced by Santanderinos. On August 1, Fuentes gained control of them on behalf of the Valencia government, and four days later the patrol boats replaced the Basque ensign with that of the Republic.

The blockade's grip was quickly demonstrated on July 4 when the departing *Trégastel* was stopped 2 miles outside Santander by the *Cervera* and forced to go to Plencia, although released a week later. On July 8, the French trawler *Liberté*, carrying supplies for a Belgian factory near Las Arenas, was stopped and eventually seized as a prize.[112] Ships continued to assemble in international waters off Santander, although Sturdee on the *Resolution* repeatedly warned them against trying to enter the port, just as the harbor authorities encouraged them to make the effort. Even the *Seven Seas Spray*, which arrived with a cargo from Valencia on July 5, was forced to make for Bayonne so that Captain Roberts could contact owner Alfred Pope. Tensions between the Royal Navy and the Nationalist naval leadership rose from July 6 when the British *Gordonia* was stopped by a torpedo boat and the *Cervera*, the latter ordering her to sail to a Nationalist port; the destroyers HMS *Bulldog* and *Escapade* did not intervene because the *Gordonia's* master obeyed and they believed she was a prize.

At this point Ramsey, having resumed the role as senior naval officer, arrived in the *Royal Oak* and decided that, as there was no prize crew and the *Gordonia* was in international waters, she should be escorted to Bordeaux, despite Moreno's strong protests. After later talking to the *Gordonia's* master and owners, Ramsey realized he was wrong, but secured a written undertaking from them not to attempt to re-enter Santander. When he conveyed his apologies to Moreno, the Spaniard understandably refused to accept them. Following discussions with the Admiralty, the Royal Navy was now instructed not interfere if a Nationalist warship stopped a merchantman within territorial waters, provided it had made a clear signal and fired warning shots. The policy was radioed to Moreno, and Ramsey decided to observe the rules scrupulously to prevent the Nationalist Navy again finding itself in a humiliating position.[113]

The *Gordonia* incident led the French Navy, never an enthusiastic supporter of operations in the Cantabrian Sea, to reconsider its policy. On July 12, France's Navy Ministry sent the sloop *Arras* to survey the situation and found the Nationalists had the *Cervera*, the minelayer *Júpiter*, and many patrol boats watched by the Royal Navy's battleship HMS *Royal Oak* and two destroyers.[114] Ships waiting off Santander included the *Molton*, the *Sarastone*, as well as Pope's *Kenfig Pool*. The last vessel's master claimed she would enter Santander at all costs, but when he attempted to do so, the appearance of the *Cervera* forced him back into international waters. The *Molton*, under Captain R. H. Stears, was owned by one of the most famous men in Britain, William "Sporting Bill" Tatem, First Baron Glanely of St Fagans, a philanthropist who made his money in shipping and whose horses won all five British Classic races. From a clerk in a shipping company, he established his own shipping line with 16 vessels in 1914, and during the war he was elevated to the peerage. He survived the Depression with a smaller, but more modern, fleet, and on July 1 he chartered his two oldest ships, the *Molton* and the *Pilton*, to bring out Basque refugees.[115] On the morning of July 14, however, the *Molton* was captured by the *Cervera* within the 3-mile limit, watched by HMS *Royal Oak*, which was powerless to intervene. When the ship was escorted to Bilbao, the *Stanhill*, carrying refugees, exploited the distraction to dash from Santander into international waters, while a fortnight later the *Pilton* brought refugees from Aviles to France.[116]

The fate of the *Molton* was cited by British warships the following day as they warned off several ships, including "Potato" Jones's *Marie Llewellyn*, now renamed the *Kellwyn*, which all decided to sail to Gijon, which was less closely patrolled. Jones broke through and later brought out 800 refugees. The *Sarastone* and Captain Reginald Jones's *Candleston Castle* followed suit, but as they crossed the 3-mile limit on July 17, they were intercepted near the port of Musel by the *Cervera*. The *Sarastone* sailed close to the shore, covered by coast-defense batteries, and entered Gijon, but the *Candleston Castle* was captured and forced to sail to Ferrol. She and the *Molton* would be held by the Nationalists until September 10, while the Nationalists deployed the *Júpiter* and a patrol boat as permanent close blockade off the Asturias, where only four ships entered during July.[117] On July 19, nine ships carrying 16,000 refugees departed Santander, and once across the 3-mile limit were escorted by the Royal Navy to safety. The same day, at Gijon, the "pseudo" British *Jenny* entered the port, from where the *Sarastone* and *Tuskar Rock* successfully escaped with thousands of refugees on July 27.

Five days earlier, on July 22, there was another incident involving "Corn Cob" Jones. The *Macgregor* had departed Santander for Paullac with 1,500 refugees, but was intercepted by the *Cervera* within the 3-mile limit. Jones ignored the cruiser's demand to heave-to, underlined by five warning shots, and steamed at full speed to cross the 3-mile limit, where the destroyer HMS *Kempenfelt* was waiting to provide protection. Moreno protested bitterly to the British commander at Jones's failure to stop, stating that for humanitarian reasons he had chosen not to fire upon the steamer, for which Ramsey thanked him. When the *Ploubazlanec*, escorted by the destroyer *Fantasque*, arrived off Santander at dusk on July 23, she was intercepted by patrol boats in international waters 7 miles from the coast. Her master decided to await instructions from the owners, but before they arrived was able to slip into Gijon. The following day, there were mixed fortunes for British ships. The *Backworth* brought out 2,000 refugees from Santander, but as the *African Trader* attempted to enter Gijon, she was intercepted within the 3-mile limit by the *Baleares*. The merchantman ignored orders to heave-to and, encouraged by the destroyer HMS *Escapade*, recrossed the 3-mile limit, where HMS *Royal Oak* was also waiting. The battleship put on a boarding party to ensure she was not carrying contraband, then escorted her to St-Jean, from where she later succeeded in reaching Gijon. On July 27, the British *Mirupanu*, also making for Gijon, was stopped within the 3-mile limit by an auxiliary cruiser and compelled to sail to Ferrol.

The continued threat from the Nationalist blockade meant attempts by the *Marion Moller* to re-enter first Santander, then Gijon, with food and medical supplies on July 27 and 28 were thwarted, although she was later able to reach Gijon. Other ships continued to sail off Santander, awaiting their opportunity. The *Marvia* waited for a fortnight before she succeeded, after ignoring an order to heave-to, while the patience of the Gibraltar-registered *Bobie* and the tanker *Valetta* (later renamed *Arlon*) was ultimately rewarded. The Board of Trade was becoming increasingly worried about merchantmen accidentally creating an incident, and on July 30 issued guidelines defining in detail the 3-mile limit off northern Spain. Their concerns were underlined on August 11 when the British Cape Line steamer *Caper* was captured off the Asturian coast near Cape Vidio by a gunboat and escorted to Corruna for examination.

The *Caper* was a "pseudo," whose only British citizen was the master, Liverpudlian Harry Cossintine. The incident would have a tragic postscript which underlined the concerns of British and French naval officers about the true ownership of ships carrying their ensigns. By August 25, the *Caper* was anchored off Ferrol with six Nationalist sailors on guard. Cossintine later claimed that in the early evening, while in the chart-room below the bridge, he heard a shot. A fight had broken out between the guards and the crew, leading to shooting in which he was wounded. Three of the crew were killed and the remainder arrested, allegedly for trying to overpower the guards, but released after four days. When they returned, they alleged the ship had been plundered, although the British government would later claim there was no evidence of looting. In the House of Lords, Scottish Labour nobleman David Kenworthy Baron Stabolgi (pronounced Strabogie) gave a dramatic account of the fight, claiming three British crewmen had died, but Runciman pointed out the victims were Dutch, Greek, and Russian, which was probably the reason the Foreign Office did not pursue the matter as energetically as they might. The ship was not released until November 13.[118]

Meanwhile, the Nationalist offensive made rapid progress from mid-August, and the destroyer *Díez*, despite having been badly damaged in an air attack, was ordered to join the *Císcar*, three submarines, and a torpedo boat in Gijon, but instead sailed north to Falmouth in Cornwall, where her rabble crew made the British anxious to be rid of her. She departed for Le Havre after 60 of the crew refused to sail, arriving on September 27 and remaining a year for repairs. Most Republican warships assembled at Gijon, although half-a-dozen former Basque minesweepers with refugees were interned at Rochefort together with the gunboats *Bizkaya* and *Gipuzkoa* which had reached Bordeaux on August 28. The submarines *C-2* and *C-4* also departed Gijon for France; the former arrived in Brest on August 26 and requested repairs three days later, while the latter, damaged in an air raid, made a similar request after arriving at Verdon. The Brest naval dockyard was too busy and the boats moved to Saint Nazaire, while a civilian yard was given permission to repair the *C-4*. However, both commanders promptly defected.[119] There were perfunctory attempts by the Republican Navy to harass the blockading forces, but when the *C-6*, still under the Russian Burmitsov, encountered the *Baleares* on August 4, she was damaged by depth charges.[120]

As the Nationalists closed on Santander, thousands sought to escape. On August 19, the USS *Kane* arrived in Santander to pick up largely refugees, mostly Cuban.[121] But the hopes of thousands were crushed on August 11 when Paris announced it would no longer take Spanish refugees, requesting that London inform British shipping companies of the new policy. Both ship-owners and masters ignored the French decree, and 14 ships, mostly British but including three of France-Navigation, brought 22,600 refugees to France during August.[122] Santander and Santona fell on August 25, but there was a poor haul for the Nationalist merchant marine: just two ships (3,482 grt), of which the largest had been laid up since before the war, while the *Aurora y Maruja* was captured as she attempted to take out refugees.[123] On the night of August 24/25, the retired Commander Pursey collected a small party of friends and sailed in a motorboat to a British destroyer.[124]

The most notorious incident in the evacuation involved the Basques. From the end of July, the French Foreign Ministry, through their consul in Santander, was negotiating the evacuation of Basque troops. On August 2, the Basque government chartered four ships to take out 200,000 of their countrymen—the *Seabank* and *Kenfig Pool* at Santander, together with the *Bobie* and *Seven Seas Spray* in Santona—but the rapid Nationalist advance caught them in port.[125] The Italians took Santona and agreed on August 27 with the *Bobie*'s master, French Captain Georges Dupuy, and Brazilian NIC observer Mr Costa e Silva to allow Basque troops to be evacuated.[126] The furious Nationalists immediately repudiated the Santona Agreement, and the following day the Italians forced most of the Basque troops to disembark, although seven stowaways remained when she sailed. Roberts's *Seven Seas Spray* was not allowed to depart, due to her notoriety at Bilbao in April, with ship and crew detained until November; Fifi Roberts would celebrate her 21st birthday playing cricket on the deck.[127] The less notorious *Seabank* and *Kenfig Pool* were allowed to depart for a French port on September 2. In the aftermath of Santander's fall, the French destroyers *Malin* and *Typhon*, together with the sloops *Somme* and *Vauquois*, joined HMS *Resolution* and HMS *Foxhound*, along with the British *Seabank*, just beyond the 3-mile limit, picking up refugees and troops who had fled in every conceivable craft, including rowing boats. On August 28, HMS *Keith*, with the agreement of both sides, evacuated 17 leading Basque figures and their dependents.[128]

End Game at Gijon

Rear Admiral Lachlan McKinnon relieved Ramsey in August as the Nationalists prepared to take Gijon, but retained his predecessor's rules. When Moreno informed him, on September 19, that the British *Margaret-Rose* had picked up an arms consignment in Antwerp and would bring them to Gijon concealed beneath a cargo of beans and lentils, McKinnon relayed the report to London. But the ship's NIC observer had monitored the loading, the report was false, and no action was taken.[129]

On August 11, HMS *Foxhound* was shelled, probably in error, by patrol boats during an engagement between the *Císcar* and the *Júpiter*. An aircraft then dropped two bombs near her, London later warning the Nationalist Navy commander "to be more careful in the future."[130] On August 28, the *Bramhill* was returning to Gijon after taking refugees to Brest, but as she neared the port two patrol boats fired warning shots outside the 3-mile limit. The master ignored them, and the destroyer HMS *Fearless* escorted her to safety. On August 27, Billmeir's *Stanmore*, which had been chartered by France-Navigation, requested the assistance of the French destroyer *Ouragon* to enter Gijon, but the destroyer's commander refused as his mission was only to protect escaping refugees. At the end of the month, the Russians seeking to bring 1,000 Asturian children to Leningrad, chartered France-Navigation's *Ploubazlanec*, which departed Le Havre on September 1, escorted by the sloop *Somme*. As the result of a Nationalist press campaign, the freighter was diverted to Verdon, where the authorities decided it was too dangerous to proceed, Delbos ignoring Russian demands that the freighter be escorted to Gijon.[131] There was good reason for concern, for from the first week of September, the Nationalists deployed not only the usual patrol boats but also the *Cervera*, the *Júpiter*, her sister the *Vulcano*, and the auxiliary cruiser *Ciudad de Palma*. However, they were unable to prevent the Basque patrol boat *Iparreko-Izarra* from breaking out on the night of September 8/9 and sailing to Bordeaux for internment. Yet by the middle of the month, only three merchantmen were standing off Asturian ports.[132]

The ports of Musel and Gijon came under increasing air attack from the Condor Legion's bomber group, K/88, and on August 27 the *African Trader*, *Stanwood*, *Stanbridge*, and *Hilda Moller* were all hit by splinters, with the *African Trader* taking water forward. She, the *Stanwood*, and *Hilda Moller* departed later in the day for La Pallice, accompanied by the destroyers HMS *Fearless* and HMS *Foresight*. The *African Trader*'s pumps worked tirelessly to reach her destination, but she was in such dire straits when she arrived that she was beached. She was later refloated and departed after a month in dry dock. The *Stanbridge* had also been badly damaged and required a fortnight's repairs before she could depart. On August 28, the Germans had another success when they hit the newly arrived *Elcano*, bringing fuel and munitions from Cartagena. With a volunteer crew and a naval reserve officer as her master, she flew the Red Ensign to pass through the Strait, but before she could unload her much-needed cargo she was set ablaze, towed outside the harbor, and run aground to become a constructive total loss, although refloated in October 1938.[133]

The Nationalist offensive began on September 1, initially making slow progress, but the blockade slowly squeezed the port, forcing the *Thorpehall* on September 7 to return to Bayonne.[134] The evening of September 10 saw a strange incident involving Billmeir's *Stanwold*, which HMS *Resolution* observed approaching the 3-mile limit off Ribadesella. The freighter ignored the battleship's warnings and had barely crossed the limit when a torpedo boat came over the horizon at flank speed, overtook her, and fired two warning shots. The merchantman then sailed towards a Nationalist port, her master radioing to the *Resolution*: "I am captured." The battleship's wardroom believed the master had made an arrangement to sell the cargo to the Nationalists, having deliberately allowed his vessel to be captured, but this was very unusual for a Billmeir ship.[135]

The same day, a patrol boat attacked the *Hillfern* 35 miles off the Spanish coast as she sailed to Gijon, but the shells missed and the steamer sailed deeper into international waters. Shortly afterwards, she was strafed by an airplane, which appeared to be aiming for oil drums on her deck, but reached Bayonne undamaged on September 12. The *Stanmore* suffered an air attack on September 15 as she sailed from La Pallice to pick up refugees at Rivadesella. She continued sailing westward along the coast until fire from a coast-defense battery forced her to turn back, arriving in Bordeaux the next day. The following day, the *Stanray*'s attempt to enter Gijon was thwarted by the arrival of the *Vulcano*, but the presence of HMS *Fearless* kept the freighter safe; as the warships exchanged signals, two Republican aircraft bombed the British destroyer in error.[136] Five ships exploited mist in late September to slip into Gijon. Spanish sources stated that, during September, 10 British and French ships brought out 15,000 people, with the *Bramden*, *Stangrove*, and *Stanmore* doing two voyages each, the *Ploubazlanec* carrying 1,100 to safety, and five Spanish vessels saving another 7,500.[137]

With the British naval presence now declining, First Sea Lord Admiral Chatfield wrote to Home Fleet commander Backhouse on September 17: "I shall be very relieved, and I am sure you will also be, when the North coast of Spain is finally cleared up by the Insurgents and you can take away all your ships from there before winter."[138] On October 10, Rear Admiral Thomas Calvert, commander of the 2nd Cruiser Squadron, in the light cruiser HMS *Southampton*, relieved McKinnon. While the Admiralty's rules continued to be applied, there was little enthusiasm among the crews to support what one officer described as "foreign ships with foreign officers and men who bring no credit to the country of their adoption."[139] A hard core of eight merchantmen were willing to challenge the blockade, but only *Stangrove* succeeded and Calvert ensured she was not seized by the *Cervera* when she was intercepted upon departure. The *Stangrove* was luckier than two ships bringing food from Antwerp. On October 3, the *Bobie* was stopped by a Nationalist warship and forced into Ferrol, while on October 5, the *Dover Abbey* (formerly *Yorkbrook*) was stopped 6 miles from the coast, and with no British warship in sight suffered a similar fate.[140]

The Nationalist offensive began to accelerate from October 14, but the following day the Republican Navy delivered its Parthian shot when the submarine *C-6*, still under Burmistrov, launched two torpedoes against the *Júpiter*, although both missed. The Condor Legion made a series of heavy raids on October 19 and 20, and on the latter date badly damaged the submarine, which was scuttled outside the harbour.[141] These raids also sank the *Císcar* on October 19, after she ignored Prieto's orders to break out and sail to Cartagena, as well as the Panamanian *Reina*, which arrived the previous day from Gdynia with the enclave's last weapons consignment.[142] Earlier raids upon Gijon/Port Musel sank the Spanish *Sama* on September 10, a schooner on September 25, and the *Sud* at an unknown date, while the torpedo boat *T-3* was damaged but escaped to Bordeaux carrying Fuentes and his staff, despite lacking charts and having to burn all her timber fittings when she ran out of coal.[143]

The fall of Gijon was now a matter of time, and as the blockade tightened the French *CENS*, carrying iron ore to Bayonne, was captured on October 7 and forced to go to Ribadeao. It was released on October 18 after three French destroyers arrived to reinforce demands for her freedom. Also on October 18, a patrol boat joined by the *Cervera* stopped the *Stangrove*, carrying 600 refugees, just after leaving the port and outside the 3-mile limit, but they were compelled to release their prey by the cruiser HMS *Southampton*, despite Moreno's protests. The following day, Nationalist supporters seized Gijon, while Aviles and Musel were captured by the army as some 9,000 panic-stricken civilians and Republican troops sought to escape in every available vessel, including tugs, barges, and motorboats. A rag-tag fleet of 60 vessels fled across the Cantabrian Sea, while three former Basque minesweepers sailed to Bordeaux with refugees and were interned upon arrival. On October 22, Paris opened negotiations with Salamanca for the evacuation of Republican troops in the French *Petite Terre*, but the Nationalists broke off the talks. Two days later, the French stationed the destroyers *Bourrasque* and *Ouragon*, with the sloop *Aisne*, off Gijon to support refugees.[144]

British and French warships shielded the refugees once they were beyond the 3-mile limit, while some merchantmen remained offshore hoping to dash in on a rescue mission. A patrol boat stopped the *Stanray* on October 27 outside the 3-mile limit off Aviles, but she was freed by a British destroyer. The Royal Navy presence in the region ended on October 30, but not before HMS *Southampton* used her Vickers Walrus flying boat to detect refugee ships. The Walrus helped to save 400 people in the Bay of Biscay on October 26 when it discovered the drifting Spanish fishing boat *Mary Tere*. Her crew and refugee passengers were taken off by a French warship, which then sank her with gunfire.[145] The total number of refugees evacuated from the enclave under the Royal Navy's protection from May to October 1937 was 89,000, of whom 10,000 were saved by British warships, while the French, who withdrew their warships from the coast on November 1, reported they had evacuated some 25,000 between July 16 and October 15.[146] But not everyone was lucky, and from October 20 to October 21 Nationalist warships captured 25 Spanish vessels, mostly fishing boats but also including eight merchantmen, mostly small coastal-trading puffers, totalling 4,646 grt, together with 1,130 refugees. Their haul in Gijon was also sparse: three freighters (3,047 grt) and some fishing vessels, although the *Reina* and four sunken Spanish vessels (4,558 grt) were salvageable.[147]

Many ships remained abroad, with 39 Basque-owned vessels (137,508 grt) in British ports alone, and a further 190, many of them fishing boats, in French ports. In Britain, the Bay of Biscay Shipping Company was established with a share capital of £80,000 ($400,000) as a means of transferring the Basque ships to the British registry, while some 60 ships (192,357 grt) in British and foreign ports came under the control of Strubin and the Mid-Atlantic Steamship Company. The Bilbao-based Naviera Amaya sold three of its fleet—*Margari*, *Mari*, and *Santurce*—to the British Phoenix Shipping Company, with these and the *Redstone*, *Houstone*, and *Widstone* being transferred in 1939 to Charles Strubin & Company. The first two were sunk as blockships in Scapa Flow after the loss of HMS *Royal Oak*, while the *Widstone* was torpedoed and sunk by a U-boat on November 17, 1942.[148] In October, the Republic's Consul in Marseilles vainly tried to transfer the most modern Spanish ships to the French registry. Some Nationalist owners began legal attempts to recover their vessels, while Republican owners operated parts of their fleet to raise revenue for both their owners and the Republic. A few masters and skippers, with their crews, decided to chance their luck and sail to Nationalist ports, and the Russians seized the Basque *Marzo* in Murmansk.[149] Crews were paid by the Mid-Atlantic Company until the British government officially recognized the Nationalists in March 1939, after which the National Union of Seamen and the trades union movement provided welfare, paying more than £614 ($3,070) in March and April 1939, and continued to do so through the early years of World War II until the men were able to find fresh berths.[150]

While the clashes between Nationalist and foreign vessels grabbed the headlines, Major Troncoso waged his secret war in France. Aided by the Italian SIM and French members of The Cowl, his networks monitored ships heading for Republican Spain

A Savoia-Marchetti S.81 Pipistrello (Bat), pictured dropping bombs, was the spearhead of the Italian offensive against Spanish ports. Later, they were confined to night attacks, but were used extensively for daytime maritime reconnaissance. (Aerophoto)

The Heinkel He 59 floatplane, known as Zatapones (Big Boots), was the spearhead of the Condor Legion's anti-shipping operations, attacking shipping both on the high seas and in ports. The latter targets were often approached with engines throttled-back, so the victim's first inkling was the roar of engines, followed by exploding bombs. The seaplanes made at least two torpedo-bomber attacks using Norwegian-made weapons. (EN-Archive)

The Savoia-Marchetti S.79 Sparviero (Sparrowhawk) would replace the S.81 as the spearhead of the Italian offensive against Republican ports. The dorsal gun position led the crew to call these aircraft "The Damned Hunchback" (*gobbo maledetto*). It would be the prime Italian medium and torpedo bomber during World War II. (Aerophoto)

An S.79 pulling away from a blazing Valencia on January 19, 1938. On this occasion no ships were sunk, but on February 10, the Hawks would sink the British *Lucky*. (Aerophoto)

The port of Barcelona seen from an Italian reconnaissance aircraft on January 20, 1938. Weeks later, bombers and seaplanes from Majorca would begin taking a steady toll of merchantmen in and off the port. (Aerophoto)

From March 16–18, the Balearic Falcons attacked Barcelona both to interdict traffic and terrorize civilians. This image was taken on the last day of this operation. (Aerophoto)

Italian bombers fly a victory formation over Palma de Majorca and its cathedral. (Via F. Bortolotti)

A Cant Z.501 Gabbiano (Gull) of Nationalist squadron 2-G-62 pictured on January 26, 1938. These were exported to Spain during the Civil War and were used extensively by the Italian Navy for maritime reconnaissance. (Archivo César O'Donnell)

The Pollensa Bay seaplane base was a prewar naval facility and was used by the Condor Legion's AS/88, with He 59 and He 60 floatplanes, which can be seen both on the water and in the base. It was also the home of the Nationalist squadron 1-E-70, one of whose Whales is being lifted into the water in late 1938. Behind the crane is a Cant Z.506 Airone (Heron) floatplane, which augmented the Nationalist squadron and in one of which Ramón Franco died. Pollensa Bay is still used by seaplane bombers, but these aircraft now drop water on fires. (Archivo César O'Donnell)

Josef Veltjens pictured during the Great War, when he achieved air ace status with 35 victories. Afterwards, he drifted into arms dealing and would work closely with Hitler's deputy, Luftwaffe commander Hermann Goering, even selling arms to the Republic. (Gregory van Wyngarden)

Jack Billmeir was a key figure in trading with the Republic. In addition to using ships of his Stanhope Line, he was closely involved with other ship-owners, notably Greeks, trading with Republican Spain. Contrary to his contemporary reputation, there is no evidence to indicate he was directly involved in arms smuggling. After World War II, he would negotiate compensation from Madrid for the salvage and seizure of British ships, including his own. (The Worshipful Company of Shipwrights)

Admiral Francisco Moreno would play a key role in Nationalist naval operations and be the last blockade commander. He was also involved in sinking the Russian *Komsomolsk* and the Greek *Poli* in controversial circumstances. (Archivo Lucas Molina)

Admiral Miguel Buiza had a distinguished career in the Republican Navy and would lead the fleet to internment in Bizerta in March 1939. (Bibliotecha Nacional de España)

The memorial to Spanish blockade runners set up in Glasgow and inscribed with the names of all the British sailors, both Merchant Navy and Royal Navy, who lost their lives. (Craig Maclean)

Unveiling of the Blockade Runners monument in Glasgow, with sculptor Frank Casey (right) and Mike Arnott, who organized the memorial. (Craig Maclean)

An Italian ground crew load bombs on an S.81. (Aerophoto)

Commander Primo Longobardo, whose submarine *Galileo Ferraris* sank the freighter *Navarra* in February 1937. At the age of 40, he would be the oldest Italian submarine commander to be lost during World War II in July 1942, when shells hit the *Pietro Calvi* after he ordered her to be scuttled.

Franco's brother, Ramón, was the nominal air commander in the Balaerics, but his authority was undermined both by his allies and even Admiral Cervera. He is seen here with Colonel Mario Bernasconi, who commanded Italian squadrons on Majorca. Ramón would be lost on a bombing mission in October 1938, when his seaplane suffered engine failure. (IHCA)

Nationalist naval leader Admiral Juan Cervera Valderrama was the last Naval Chief of Staff under the Spanish monarchy. Denied permission by the Republic to resign his commission, he held minor posts until the uprising and became the Nationalist Navy Chief of Staff. Despite operating on a shoestring, he made the Nationalist Navy a dynamic force which dominated the waters of the western Mediterranean and might have done more but for Franco's restrictions. His disputes with Franco meant he was sidelined after the conflict. He is seen here broadcasting in September 1938. (Bibliotecha Nacional de España)

The first foreign merchantman to be lost during military operations in the Spanish Civil War was the *Gulnes*, owned by Hans Storaas of Bergen. She was built in Stockton in 1888 and was one of the oldest ships in the Norwegian Merchant Fleet in 1936, when she was bombed by Russian-made SBs or Katies. The attack killed five of the crew, including her master, and the ship was so badly damaged that she was sent to the breakers. (Bergens Sjøfartsmuseum)

The trans-Atlantic liner *Uruguay* would spend the war moored in Barcelona as a prison ship before she was bombed and wrecked. (Arxiu fotogràfic. Museu Marítim de Barcelona)

The Republican cruiser *Miguel de Cervantes* was torpedoed in November 1936 by the Italian submarine *Evangelista Torricelli*, commanded by Lieutenant Commander Giuseppe Zarpellon, and was thereafter non-operational for a year. (Juan Carlos Salgado collection)

The Estonian- and later British-owned *Yorkbrook* was the most notorious arms smuggler during the Civil War. Her ignominious career ended in Barcelona, where she had been towed after engine failure, leaving her a sitting duck to bombers in January 1939. (Pärnu Museum)

The symbol of British naval power was the battlecruiser HMS *Hood*, seen here in 1937, and her deployment off Bilbao in April indicated how seriously London considered the Nationalist naval blockade. (Captain Barry Roberts, Chairman, HMS Hood Association)

The Dutch *Parklaan*, acquired by Rotterdam's NV Stoomschip *Hannah* in 1937, was the only Dutch vessel bombed in 1938. It was hit in Barcelona on June 6, killing the First Engineer and injuring the First Officer and the British NIC observer. However, she survived the attack. This photograph was taken after the outbreak of war in 1939 and before May 1940, when she was marked to show she was a neutral vessel. She ended her days as part of the Mulberry Harbour, Goosberry 3, in Normandy. (Collection National Maritime Museum, Amsterdam, The Netherlands)

The Danish steamer *Edith* was bombed and sunk off Majorca by Condor Legion Big Boots on August 12, 1937. There was only one fatality, an Austrian cabin boy called Alfred Kugel, who was mortally wounded. He was one of four boys killed by the bombs of the Nationalists' allies during the Civil War. (M/S Maritime Museum of Denmark)

Billmeir's *Stancroft* was one of four ships sunk twice during the Spanish Civil War. She is shown here in Barcelona after succumbing to bombs on December 28, 1938. (Arxiu fotogràfic. Museu Marítim de Barcelona)

Refloating the *Stancroft* in Barcelona after the war. She was salvaged and became the *Castillo Almansa*, but Billmeir was able to secure compensation after World War II. (Arxiu fotogràfic. Museu Marítim de Barcelona)

The beached British steamer *African Mariner* was fatally damaged at Barcelona on January 22, 1939. (Arxiu fotogràfic. Museu Marítim de Barcelona)

The battleship *Jaime I* moored in Cartagena during the Civil War. An explosion in the aft main turret destroyed her in 1937. (Archivo Casaú)

While sailing on the surface off the Andalusian coast, the Republican submarine *C-3* was torpedoed and sunk by Lieutenant Harald Grosse's *U-34*, returning after an unsuccessful deployment in the western Mediterranean. There were only three survivors, one of them being blown off the conning tower. Grosse would be killed on his first patrol of the Battle of the Atlantic when HMS *Gurkha* depth-charged him in February 1940 in *U-53*. (Archivo Juan L. Coello)

The Nationalist submarine *General Mola*, pictured in Cartagena after the war. She was the former Italian *Torricelli*, and under Lieutenant Commander Rafael Fernández de Bobadilla y Ragel she sank the Spanish *Cabo Palos*, the Dutch *Hannah*, and three schooners. After the war, Bobadilla would be Naval Attaché in London in 1950, then Naval Chief of Staff from 1966. (Archivo Casaú)

The Nationalist submarine *General Sanjurjo*, pictured during the war at the Puerto Sóller naval base. Under Lieutenant Commander Pablo Suances Jáudenes since May 1937, she had sunk the Republican freighters *Ciudad de Barcelona* and *Ciutat de Reus*. However, her sinking of the British *Endymion* on January 31, 1938, with the loss of most of her crew, including the master and his wife, provoked such an outcry that Suances was relieved of his command. The fishing village of Puerto Soller, which was the Nationalists' prime submarine base, is currently a marina and delightful summer resort. (Archivo Casaú)

The heavy cruiser *Canarias* was the Nationalist Navy flagship and developed a formidable reputation as a commerce raider, taking or sinking 34 ships. Designed by British naval architects, she and her sistership, the *Baleares*, were a radical redesign of the County-class heavy cruisers, with a superstructure which resembled the Nelson-class battleships. She was scrapped in 1977. (Archivo César O'Donnell)

At the outbreak of the Spanish Civil War, the *Mar Cantábrico* was one of the most modern freighters in the Spanish merchant marine. While attempting to bring in war materiel from the United States and Mexico, she was captured in April 1937 and converted into an auxiliary cruiser, as shown here. She reverted to her original role after the war and was badly damaged by a fire in September 1963 while carrying sulphur from Port Arthur in Texas to Spain. She was a constructive total loss and scrapped. (Archivo Juan L. Coello)

The loss of the heavy cruiser *Baleares* on the night of March 5/6, 1938, was the greatest disaster suffered by the Nationalist Navy. Torpedoes from the destroyer *Lepanto* hit her forward magazine and boiler room, igniting propellant which threw a sheet of flame high above the forward superstructure, incinerating everyone on the bridge, including Rear Admiral Manuel de Vierna Belando and his staff. The ship did not detonate, but uncontrollable fires eventually caused her to sink with the loss of 788 lives, including one of Admiral Cervera's sons. (Archivo Juan L. Coello)

Although torpedoes from the *Lepanto* sank the *Baleares*, the destroyer was itself damaged by Italian bombs 24 hours later. She was a Churruca-class ship, based on the British Scott class, which saw a great deal of action during the Civil War. In July 1940, during exercises, she ran down the submarine *C-4*, which was lost with all hands. The destroyer was scrapped in 1958. (Josep Branguli)

The Nationalist Navy kept detailed files on merchant ships trading with the Republic, including photographs, such as this one taken of the Abbey Line's *Margam Abbey* as she sailed through the Strait of Gibraltar. Her sister ship, the *Neath Abbey*, made a £4,034 ($20,100) profit on her first commercial voyage to the Republic. This was almost twice her total profit the previous year and explains why so many ship-owners were willing to risk their vessels trading with the Republic. (Guildhall Library, City of London)

The Soviet freighter *Kursk* brought in Igrek 7 to Cartagena on November 3, 1936, with 15 I-16 fighters, six British 60-pounder (127mm) guns, 150 automatic rifles, and 9,000 bolt-action rifles, plus ammunition. Like other Soviet freighters, she was later used for commercial trade. (Bibliotecha Nacional de España)

and tried to sabotage them. The *María Amelia* was bombed in Bayonne in February, with little damage, but a month later the *Valentín Ruiz Senén* was so badly damaged she had to turn back from a voyage to Bilbao. Troncoso also organized defections with ships' masters, and in July succeeded in getting the tanker *Campoamor* to sail into Pasajes, where she promptly ran aground although later refloated. The following month, the freighter *Arichachu* defected and became the *Tivoli* to make two trips carrying Italian war materiel in 1938.[151]

Troncoso's most spectacular operation on September 18 also proved his downfall. He had long harbored ambitions of seizing a Republican warship, having failed to take the *Díez* in March, but then set his sights on the submarine *C-2*, which was interned in St Nazaire's commercial harbour. Troncoso hoped the former commander of *C-4*, Lieutenant Jesús Lasheras Mercadal, could persuade the *C-2*'s commander, Midshipman José Luis Ferrando Talayero, to follow his example and defect. A gang boarded the boat and tied up some of the crew, but a sailor in a guard post opened fire, killing one of the plotters. The police, who had been observing the gang for days, now arrived, but the would-be hijackers drove off. Troncoso went to Brest on a reconnaissance mission, but was arrested on September 30. The plotters were imprisoned until their trial on March 22, 1938, for possessing weapons, which earned them short jail sentences, and Troncoso rejoined the Nationalist Army in a more conventional role. On November 8, the submarine was towed to Saint Nazaire, while a score of the crew were repatriated to Republican Spain to rejoin the Republican Fleet, the boat itself following on June 17, 1938.[152]

Behind the scenes, London was creeping crab-like towards recognition of the Nationalist regime. This began unofficially on November 16 with an exchange of diplomatic agents; Hodgson for Great Britain and Jacobo Fitz-James Stuart y Falcó, 17th Duke of Alba, 10th Duke of Berwick, for the Nationalists, having been their representative in London since 1936. This accelerated the freeing of British ships held in northern Spain, beginning on November 1 with the *Seven Seas Spray* and ending with the *Yorkbrook* on November 20.[153] The end of the war in the north led to the transfer of most of the Nationalist blockade force to the Mediterranean. The Republican Navy formally assumed control of the Basque gunboat *Donostia* interned at La Pallice and sought to rearm the *Gipuzkoa* as a commerce raider, but the French kept her in harbor. Most Republican/Basque sailors disembarked and returned to Spain, the vessels being restored to their original owners after the war ended. The Nationalist blockade helped bring about the destruction of the Republic's northern enclave, despite having very limited resources. While it did not cut the enclave's maritime lifeline, it certainly restricted access, despite the presence of the world's supreme naval power, from whom it won grudging support because the blockading forces themselves sometimes showed considerable restraint.

CHAPTER FOUR

They Called it Piracy!
August 1937–February 1938

In the summer of 1937, rumors of a huge Republican resupply effort alarmed General Franco and led to an Italian naval and air campaign which so blatantly ignored international law that both London and Paris were forced to make a stand.

By the end of July 1937, Franco had thwarted a Republican offensive near Madrid and was preparing to renew the campaign against the northern enclave. However, his Intelligence organization now put a very large spanner in the works, reporting on July 30 that five Soviet merchantmen—believed to be carrying 2,500 tanks and 300 aircraft—had passed through the Bosphorus. They had indeed passed through the Bosphorus, but none were carrying war materiel to Spain. Indeed, the German Embassy in Ankara, using similar sources, reported that during July and August only 10 Spanish and one French ship carried war materiel through the Bosphorus, and their cargoes included only 68 tanks and 30 aircraft, so the German Foreign Ministry was puzzled by Franco's "very strange" claims.[1]

Two major arms shipments did arrive during August in the Spanish merchant marine's largest freighters, the Ybarra Line's 12,589 grt *Cabo Santo Tomé* and *Cabo San Agustin*, ships so important they were armed.[2] The former landed 26 aircraft at Cartagena, while the latter delivered I-37 on August 10, including 50 tanks and 62 fighters. The *Cabo San Agustin*'s master, Captain Rodriguez Balaguer, had a Soviet "advisor," Lieutenant Commander Semyon Slavin. Balaguer was not pleased when the Russians cut holes in the beams at the top of the hold to accommodate the tank turrets, while during the voyage her superstructure was altered to resemble the liner *Habana*, allowing her to arrive unscathed, although the tank crews traveled overland to Spain.[3]

While Franco was also skeptical about the reports, they provided leverage, and on August 3 he passed them to his ambassador in Rome, Pedro García Conde, with the proviso: "But if it is confirmed then we must urgently stop the shipments in the narrow waters south of Italy. This can be achieved either by strengthening the Spanish fleet or intervention by the Italian fleet." He wanted destroyers to intercept the freighters, but suggested they repeat the earlier ruse with submarines of embarking a Spanish officer and flying the Nationalist flag to pretend they were Spanish. Two days later, Franco's brother Nicolás, accompanied by naval staff officer Commander Francisco Regalado, met Mussolini and Ciano and requested a blockade of the Sicilian Channel and the monitoring of North African and Aegean waters using surface combatants and submarines. They also requested a submarine blockade of Republican ports.

The Italian reponse was underwhelming. As Mussolini told German ambassador Ulrich von Hassel, they too believed the threat was exaggerated, and open naval intervention would only increase friction with both France and Great Britain just as he was making progress with rapprochement. The new British Premier, Neville Chamberlain, was clearly responsive, bypassing Eden by sending a letter to Mussolini through ambassador Count Dino Grandi. To him, (Chamberlain,) this was "the Chamberlain touch," but he was described as "alert, business-like, opinionated and self-confident in a very high degree … he conceived himself able to comprehend the whole field of Europe," and for these reasons was willing to bypass the Foreign Office and concealed correspondence to secure the same goal.[4] Because of the apparent progress, Mussolini offered only to deploy a few submarines in the Sicilian Channel. But like a petulant child denied sweets, Franco continued to plead, and like many a harassed parent, Mussolini agreed in principle to intercept ships carrying war materiel in the Sicilian Channel to avoid looking weak.

This would be the most intensive naval blockade since the Great War, and on August 7 messages were transmitted from Rome's Navy Ministry deploying 50 surface combatants, including 41 percent of the destroyer/torpedo boat force. Meanwhile, the auxiliary cruisers *Adriatico* and *Barletta*, posing as the Spanish *Lago* and *Rio* and flying Nationalist colors, would operate from Favignana. Ships deployed from August 8, although only on August 11 did Mussolini inform Franco that he was beginning the blockade. The previous day, Lange, the Naval Attaché in Rome, informed the OKM that the Italians were dispatching submarines to attack Russian transports, with the Italian naval staff requesting all German warships to withdraw west of Gibraltar. He added that the Nationalist Navy planned to increase operations in the western Mediterranean and requested all German merchant ships avoid the Sicilian Channel.[5]

The Sicilian Terror

Between Sicily and Tunisia's Cape Bon is a "choke point" 80 miles wide at its narrowest point, with most shipping using the 55-mile-wide Malta and Sicilian Channels, bounded by the islands of Malta/Gozo and Pantelleria. There are deep waters south of these two islands and north of the island of Lampedusa, with relatively shallower waters 10–30 miles off the African coast. Rear Admiral Riccardo Paladini's Sicilian Naval Command had 10 destroyers and eight torpedo boats, supported by 18 seaplanes, and was reinforced by 17 destroyers, including 13 of Training Command's (Scuola Comando) elderly ships, a new colonial sloop, and Admiral Pietro Barone's 4th Squadron (4a Divisione Navale) with the light cruisers *Luigi Cardona* and *Armando Diaz*. The Submarine Command (Comando Sommergibili) deployed boats from the Messina-based 3rd Squadron (3a Grupo Sommergibili), and in addition to three or four submarinesa dozen surface vessels and six seaplanes were always on station. Ships which evaded the blockade at night would be attacked from the air, while the auxiliary cruisers patrolling off Cape Bon would alert Nationalist warships to potential blockade runners in Tunisian waters. Particular attention was paid to Soviet, Republican, and Panamanian ships, those which failed to display lights or fly a flag, had military loads on their decks, or had been specifically identified as arms smugglers by the Navy Ministry.

On August 9, the Navy Ministry alerted Paladini of the imminent arrival of the Spanish tanker *Campeador*, sailing through the Bosphorus carrying 9,500 tons of gasoline from Constanta in Romania to Valencia. He was ordered to capture her for the Nationalists, but if she sought sanctuary in French North Africa, submarines were to torpedo her. She was sighted southwest of Lampedusa in the early afternoon of August 11 by the destroyer *Saetta* (Lieutenant Commander Giulio Cerrina Feroni), and they exchanged maritime courtesies. Feroni then trailed her, hoping he could sieze the *Canarias* off Cape Bon, and during the afternoon he was joined by the destroyer *Strale*, the pair taking station on the tanker's starboard side at dusk, switching off their lights although they could still clearly be seen.[6]

The *Campeador*'s worried master ran out the lifeboats as he turned towards the Tunisian coast while Feroni sought instructions from Messina, and at 2100 hours Palladini authorized him to sink the tanker. Feroni promptly closed with her and, without warning, launched four torpedoes, of which three hit, thwarting the submarine *Santorre Santarosa*, which was separately moving into an attack position. The tanker burst into flames and sank rapidly 12 miles south of Cape Bon, with the loss of 12 of her crew, including all the men in the engine room. The destroyers sailed off as survivors struggled amid pools of burning fuel, but 35 were rescued by two British ships. Two nights later, the destroyer *Ostro* (Lieutenant Commander Teodorico Capone), patrolling the central Sicilian Channel, encountered the Spanish freighter *Conde de Abasalo* off the island of Linosa, north of Lampedusa. She had called at Malta for an NIC inspection of the commercial cargo she had loaded at a Russian port, but as she was sailing with dimmed lights, Capone put a torpedo into her engine room and she quickly sank. Twenty-three survivors of her 40-man crew were rescued by the British *City of Wellington*, which landed them in Algiers on August 17.

The following evening, Italian recklessness was demonstrated when the destroyer *Freccia* (Captain Ernesto Pacchiarotti) encountered the tanker *Geo. W. McKnight* north of Pantelleria.[7] She was registered to the Panama Transport Company Gmbh, a German subsidiary of the Standard Oil Company (Esso), with an American master and a 38-man German crew from Danzig, while her 8,000 tonnes of oil was destined for the German armed forces. Her Panamanian registration led Pacchiarotti to assume she was heading for Republican Spain, but he made no attempt to check. When the ships were 11 miles north of the Tunisian island of Zembra, just off Cape Bon, he launched five torpedoes without warning. Two hit, and he also fired 54 3-inch (76mm) shells, setting the tanker ablaze and forcing the crew to abandon ship. Pacchiarotti then sailed off, triumphantly claiming to have sunk her. The crew was picked up by the tanker *British Commodore*, which towed her to Tunis, later assisted by the Italian salvage tug *Hercule*. Most of her cargo was transferred to the *British Commodore* while the *McKnight* was repaired and returned to service, and in 1940 she was sold to a British company.[8] Following these attacks and the international outcry, the Deputy Chief of the Naval Staff, Admiral Pini, telephoned Paladini and in the early hours of August 16 they suggested to Admiral Cavagnari a scaling back of the blockade for a couple of days, but were ignored.

On August 17, the Spanish steamer *Aldecoa*, which had brought in several arms shipments and was now sailing from Odessa to Valencia under the Red Ensign, avoided the destroyers *Turbine* and *Pancaldo*, despite the former's threat to torpedo her, and sailed through French territorial waters to Algiers. In response, the Navy Ministry dispatched destroyer patrols every four days on two or three-day missions to sweep the western Mediterrnean down to the Algerian coast, to detect and report blockade runners to the Nationalist Navy, whose cruisers would then capture them. The Nationalists feared the *Aldecoa* was part of a convoy, which every maritime reconnaissance aircraft began to seek, including the Italian Bat bombers for whom this now became a growing role.[9]

The western Mediterranean "sweepers" had a success a fortnight later, on the afternoon of August 30, as the destroyers *Turbine* (Lieutenant Commander Virginio Rusca) and *Ostro* (still under Capone) reached the Algerian coast and were about to reverse course to Palma. Rusca encountered the diesel-powered Russian *Timiryiazev*, carrying 2,834 tonnes of coal, a regular cargo for Soviet ships, from Cardiff to Port Said. The *Turbine*, flying the Italian ensign, circled the collier for 30 minutes, calling up Capone, who soon arrived. Shortly after sunset, they began trailing her through six moonless hours but made no challenge. Just after the watch in the *Timiryiazev* changed, Rusco launched two torpedoes and Capone one, although the latter failed to explode. Rusco's first weapon hit the forward hold and the freighter began to sink, but with the coast barely 5 miles away, Captain A. A. Rindyuk tried to run her ashore, ordering "abandon ship" only when the second torpedo hit. The crew of 26 men and three women scrambled into the boats, although there was a brief panic when one of the female mess attendants could not be found. The *Timiryiazev* slipped beneath the waves 74 miles east of Algiers and her attackers sailed away, an Algerian fishing boat towing the lifeboats to land.

Auxiliary cruisers prowled the waters west of the Sicilian Channel, and on August 31 the *Barletta* (Commander Ernesto Ciurlo) intercepted the British-registered tanker *Burlington* off northern Sicily, after receiving reports that as she sailed through the Strait of Messina her Greek master changed his ensign several times. The *Burlington* was the former French *Nausicaa*, having been acquired in 1937 by J. N. Vassiliov's Greek-owned Finchley Steamship Company registered in Gibraltar, and was under charter to the Republican government. A boarding party, led by a Nationalist officer, seized her because she was carrying 7,700 tonnes of oil from Batum to Cartagena. Ciurlo then escorted her northwards, rendezvousing with the Nationalist auxiliary cruiser *Mallorca*, which took her to Palma, where the cargo was unloaded despite British protests. She was later released and would succumb to German bombs the following year. Between August 15 and August 25, two French ships were stopped and inspected off Tunisia and Sardinia by Nationalist warships, but allowed to proceed.[10]

Paladini's ships had one last success after the Republican *Mar Negro*, carrying 200 vehicles, spares, and barrels of lubricants, sought sanctuary in the Algerian port of Bône on August 25. Nationalist agents worked upon the crew's fears and they decided to defect when she departed on September 1 and set course for Palma. She was met the following day by the *Turbine* and *l'Ostro*, who handed her over to the auxiliary cruiser *Jaime I* off Majorca, the freighter eventually becoming an auxiliary cruiser.

In all, Paladini had tracked 1,070 ships, sinking three (13,205 grt), taking two (11,637 grt), one of which was later released, and damaging one (12,442 grt). None carried war materiel and some were not even sailing to Republican ports, and with such a poor return for so large an investment in resources, the Sicilian blockade was abandoned on September 12. One reason it failed was because ships evaded it during the night or sailed close to the French North African coast, where they could easily seek sanctuary. Two Spanish ships supporting the "Kh" Program certainly succeeded in reaching Spain; the *Darro*, which carried load I-36 with 450 tonnes of aviation POL, and the *Cabo San Agustin*, Russian sources claiming the latter was detected but not stopped due to her disguise.[11]

The Submarine Command's contribution was especially disappointing, despite the deployment of 17 boats from Messina, including five veterans of the earlier offensive, the La Spezia-based 1st Squadron and the Taranto-based 4th Squadron. All returned to base by September 5, claiming to have made 131 attempts to get into attack positions and launching four torpedoes at unidentified vessels, but only the *Satorre Santarosa* came close to success. Frustration made commanders rash, such as Lieutenant Commander Giusseppe Mellina in the *Diaspro*, who launched a torpedo on August 13 at the French *Paramé* 20 miles off Bizerta, sailing from Marseilles to Tripoli. It exploded prematurely 400 meters from the ship, whose shaken crew watched the submarine surface and sail away. The freighter safely reached Tunis, where the master requested a naval escort. When this was refused, the crew called a meeting of all French crews in the port, and it was unanimously agreed they would refuse to sail without escorts.

The Third Submarine Offensive

It was the unrestricted Italian submarine offensive in the Aegean and western Mediterranean which aroused Anglo-French ire. Submarines slipped their moorings from August 5 and headed for their assigned patrol areas (see Table 4.1); seven veterans of the first western Mediterranean campaign returning to the scene of their crimes, four taking station in the Sicilian Channel, while two were in the Aegean south of the Dardanelles. Simultaneously, Rome and Salamanca/Burgos leaked stories to the newspapers of an expansion in the Nationalist Navy and its activities to spread confusion.[12]

Patrols would last up to 18 days, with boats submerged 15 hours a day, but the Navy Ministry eased the earlier restrictions; while night attacks were still preferred against warships and darkened merchantmen, daylight attacks were now permitted upon any steamer on the naval staff's special list of arms smugglers. Gun attacks were also permitted within Spanish territorial waters on ships suspected of having an ASW role. The naval staff expanded the target range on August 11 and 12 by permitting attacks upon all tankers and then all merchantmen heading for Republican ports at night, even if fully lit and where their nationality was uncertain.

Mussolini gleefully anticipated carnage and impotent international protest, not knowing the Royal Navy was aware of his plans. Two months earlier, the British Naval Intelligence Division (NID) had expanded its movements' section under Paymaster Lieutenant Commander Norman Denning, using Comint to track Italian submarines after decrypting Code SM 19/S. There was an early setback when a signal which appeared to order the sinking of any potential blockade runners outside Spanish territorial waters proved to be an inaccurate interpretation, as the Foreign Office was patronizingly happy to point out. Undaunted, Denning improved his interpretation,

Table 4.1. Italian submarine offensive: weekly patrols dispatched by area

Week	Western	Central	Eastern	Total
Aug. 5–8, '37	7	4	2	13
Aug. 9–15, '37	6	1	3	10
Aug. 16–22, '37	2	4	4	10
Aug. 23–29, '37	7	8	3	18
Aug. 30–Sep. 5, '37	2	–	6	8
Total	24	17	18	59

Sources: Bargoni III
Note: Aug. 5–8 is a partial week

and shortly afterwards the NID-detected signals led the Admiralty to alert Dudley Pound on August 12 that the new submarine offensive was imminent.[13]

In the Aegean, the Italians deployed boats from the Taranto-based 4th Squadron, including five veterans of the first offensive, most operating from Leros in the Italian-held Dodecanese Islands. On the morning of August 15, Lieutenant Commander Sergio Lusena in the *Galileo Ferraris*, disguised as *C-3*, operating off the Turkish island of Bozcaada (also known as Tenedos), unsuccessfully attacked a British ship. The following day, he made a surface attack upon the Spanish *Ciudad de Cadiz*, carrying cooking oil and food from Odessa to Barcelona.[14] At 300 yards, Lusena used his two 3.9-inch (100mm) deck guns to fire eight rounds at the steamer, with little effect, so he launched two torpedoes which sank the ship in 40 minutes, giving the 30-man crew adequate time to take to the lifeboats, although four leaped over the side. The lifeboats were recovered by the Russian tanker *Varlaam Avanesov*, whose horrified crew had witnessed the attack. On August 18, Lusena encountered and torpedoed the Spanish *Armuru*, carrying 5,000 tonnes of wheat from Novorossisk. The sinking vessel made for the coast and was beached but was a total loss, although her crew was rescued by a Turkish ship. This and other attacks led the Republican Chargé d'Affaires to request the Turkish Navy's protection, and while Ankara refused to intervene, the old cruiser *Hamidiye* was dispatched to dissuade submarines from operating in Turkish waters.

On September 3, Senior Lieutenant Beppino Manca's *Luigi Settembrini* surfaced 15 miles off Skyros near the Russian *Blagoev*, carrying 4,480 tonnes of asphalt from Maripol to Sète, near Marseilles. He fired a warning shot and took up station on the steamer's port side, breaking out a Nationalist flag. Manca launched a torpedo, which the ship's master, Captain D. F. Kaminsky, avoided by turning towards it, then the submarine sailed to the steamer's starboard side and fired another warning shot. Officers in the conning tower made gestures indicating they wanted the steamer to lower a boat, and Kaminsky collected the ship's papers so he could be rowed over to the submarine. At this point Manca launched heavyweight (21-inch) and lightweight (17.7-inch) torpedoes which hit the ship, but only the lightweight weapon detonated, with fragments mortally wounding the helmsman. Despite his injuries, he and the rest of the crew, including a female mess attendant, took to the boats, the freighter taking 30 minutes to sink as the submarine departed. The lifeboats took 10 hours to row to Kymi on the island of Evia (also known as Euboa), where the crew were taken by a Greek ship to Istanbul and then repatriated to Odessa.

There were other frightening incidents, beginning on August 30 when the master of the French cargo-liner *Theophile Gautier* claimed a submarine pursued him into the Dardanelles, although this is not confirmed by Italian records. On September 5 and 6, the Soviet steamer *Dimitrov* and British tanker *Pegasus*—owned by Hong Kong's Standard Transportation Company—were intercepted by a surfaced submarine, probably Lieutenant Commander Domenico Emiliani's *Pier Capponi*. No action was taken against the steamer, but the tanker stopped after warning shots were fired, although the submarine then withdrew and the *Pegasus* diverted briefly to Alexandria before sailing westwards. The 10 Aegean boats conducted 18 patrols, of which three were abandoned due either to mechanical problems or high seas, with the *Giovanni da Procida* being the last submarine in the whole Italian offensive to return to base. They claimed to have attempted 155 attacks, but for the expenditure of seven torpedoes only three ships (10,464 grt) were sunk, two (7,364 grt) by Lusena.

The largest commitment saw 24 boats, 14 of them veterans, deployed in the western Mediterranean, including the *Berillo* and the *Diaspro*, which transferred from the central Mediterranean in the fourth week of the operations. Two patrols were abandoned due to technical problems, while the *Enrico Tazzoli* had barely arrived on station when she was recalled. Of these boats, 15 were from the 1st Squadron, the others from the 3rd and 4th Squadrons, but here too the results were disappointing, one attack helping to end the whole offensive.

Lieutenant Commander Silvio Garino in *Jalea* had the first success, attacking two destroyers leaving Cartagena on the morning of August 12. Garino hit the *Churruca* amidships, putting out of action three of her four boilers and inflicting a dozen casualties, three fatal. She was towed back to Cartagena, but would take no further part in the war. Attacks upon Republican destroyers were also made by the *Jantina*, *Pietro Calvi*, *Giussepe Finzi*, and *Malachite*, but their prey turned on them and all were depth-charged, with the *Jantina* and *Finzi* damaged, the latter having her attack periscope wrecked.

After the British *Carpio* reported she was attacked by a submarine, possibly the *Iride*, on August 29 off Cape de la Nao, Mellina's *Diaspro* made a surface torpedo attack off Cape Oropesa, near Castellon, upon the recently registered British tanker *Woodford*, formerly the Greek *Iolkos*, most of whose crew were Greek. She was carrying 10,000 tons of oil from Constanta to Valencia and sank after three hours, with the second engineer killed and eight crew injured, her lifeboats being towed to safety by fishing boats. Before her departure, the Nationalists warned her master, Captain Gregorious Dimitrov, she was under observation. However, Rear Admiral James Somerville—the senior British naval officer off the Spanish Mediterranean coast—had warned Bastarreche the ship was British and should not be attacked, and the Spaniard agreed. Somerville later informed Their Lordships the sinking was an act of revenge because on a previous voyage the ship's master had been bribed to deliver his cargo to Palma, then welched on the deal.[15]

There was an unsuccessful attack upon a two-ship coastal convoy, probably by the *Giuseppe Finzi*, on August 26 off Burriana, near Castellon, but evasive maneuvers by the *Sebastián Martin*, a former prison ship, saw her run aground and abandoned, but later refloated, while another Spanish freighter was also attacked.[16] On the evening of September 3, a submarine surfaced near the Soviet collier *Kiev*, whose master met Rindyuk in Cardiff before the *Timiryiazev's* last voyage, and was now sailing in ballast towards the Black Sea. Fortunately, the *Kiev* had just delivered coal to Livorno; after confirming this, the submarine submerged and allowed the collier to complete her voyage. In all, the Italians in the western Mediterranean claimed they attempted 94 attacks, which sank the *Woodford* and damaged a destroyer, two freighters, and a tanker. However, the most serious incident occured on the night of August 31/ September 1, involving the *Iride* under Senior Lieutenant Junio Valerio Borghese, a Fascist son of a prince whose nickname was "The Black Prince" (Principe Nero), although his formal title was Don Junio.

Borghese had unsuccessfully attacked a merchantman on August 29 and was recharging his batteries on the evening of August 31 when lookouts detected an approaching ship, which he identified as a Churruca-class vessel but was actually the similar British destroyer HMS *Havock* (Lieutenant Commander Rafe Courage), which had departed Valencia that evening and was making for Gibraltar. Borghese made a surface attack with a lightweight torpedo which passed astern, but whose wake was spotted by the destroyer's lookouts as the submarine dived. For a decade, British destroyers had been equipped with active sonar systems, and *Havock* had the latest Type 124 version with gyro-stabilized transducer in a retractable dome and a sophisticated chemical-paper range-recording system, although it could not determine depth.[17] Courage switched on his searchlights and began a sonar sweep.[18]

Following an explosion astern, probably the torpedo, Courage turned, and when sonar detected the *Iride*, dropped depth charges. Borghese lost trim and suddenly surfaced some 400 meters off *Havock*'s port bow, but quickly dived. The sonar now gave a different bearing from one reported by the lookouts and contact was lost, but it was regained in the early hours, when Courage dropped more depth charges, without success. HMS *Galatea*, flying Somerville's flag, with HMS *Hereward* and *Hotspur*, were ordered to join *Havock*, then the whole of the 2nd Destroyer Flotilla arrived to join the hunt. During the afternoon, a new contact was reported, but despite more depth charges being dropped there was no success, the search being abandoned at dawn on September 2. Courage's superiors criticized him, Somerville signaling: "Pursue the hunt with the utmost energy and try to make up for your astounding lack of initiative."[19] In his post-action report, flotilla commander Captain Dennis Boyd condemned Courage for his over-reliance upon sonar, despite admitting official instructions stressed the sensor's reliability, indeed they remained enveloped in Admiralty complacency.[20] Afterwards, destroyers were instructed that a submarine detected at short ranges should immediately be depth-charged, while a court of inquiry vindicated Courage, who would remain in *Havock* through the early years of World War II and sink *Iride*'s sister-ship, *Berillo*, in October 1940.

Borghese surfaced after nine hours; Italian accounts say he returned to Naples on September 5, being moored in a remote part of the port, while British consul Hillgarth reported the boat needed repairs in Puerto Soller. British protests, based upon Comint, were especially strong, the outcry leading Ciano on September 4 to order Cavagnari to suspend all naval actions for a month. Ciano feared a forthcoming international conference at Nyon would decide to take action against Italian ships. Rome may also have felt this was a good time to examine progress on Anglo-Italian rapprochement.[21] The Nationalists protested, Franco vainly pleading with Rome to maintain pressure, which, he claimed, would make the campaign decisive within a few weeks. Meanwhile, six months later, on March 12, 1938, Mussolini would lunch with officers of the ships responsible for the "pirate" attacks and would praise their work.[22]

The offensive involved 49 submarines, or 56 percent of the force, and substantial consumption of the fleet's fuel-oil stocks for a pathetically poor return, a mere seven vessels (30,655 grt) being sunk. Another two ships (11,637 grt) were captured, and Rome consoled itself by claiming the flow of arms down the Bosphorus had ceased by September 12. The submarine effort was especially disappointing, for although 59 patrols intercepted 444 ships, uncertainty about the target's nationality meant there were only 24 attacks using 43 torpedoes. The "bag" of four merchantmen (17,451 grt) and a crippled destroyer raised disturbing questions about both crew training and weapon reliability. Yet Ciano wrote on August 31: "The naval blockade is producing striking results. Four Russian steamers sunk, one Greek captured. One Spanish ship chased into port." The offensive certainly fed apprehension among crews, and on August 22 the men of the British tanker *Miriam*, which had loaded a cargo of kerosene for the Republic at Constanta, refused to sail due to fears about sailing through the Aegean.[23]

In an after-action report, Commander Candido Bigliardi blamed the lack of success upon the rules of engagement, pointing out that ships sailing to Republican harbors increasingly used British or French flags—legally or illegally—while those sailing at night with lights did so in Spanish territorial waters.[24] Nevertheless, this was a wake-up call for the Submarine Command, which demanded root-and-branch reform, while submarine design now emphasized smaller conning towers and faster diving times. Improved training and new tactics were also required, and after the offensive concluded the Italian Navy began intensive exercises to improve both, although the new world war demonstrated they were unsuccessful.[25]

Ciano was satisfied with the campaign's results, although not with the Italian Navy as a whole, noting on August 28: "This Spanish enterprise is constantly opposed by a policy of passive resistance on the part of the Navy." He added on September 3: "Full orchestra: French-Russian-British. Motive: Piracy in the Mediterranean. Responsibility: Fascist. The *Duce* is very calm. He looks towards London and does not believe the English will clash with us." But the following day, the *Havock* incident caused his tone to change: "International opinion is turning hostile. Above all in England following the attempt to torpedo the destroyer *Havock*, fortunately not hit. It was the *Iride*. We are in deep trouble." Indeed, the incident was why Italy stopped the submarine offensive.[26] The French naval history makes the unique claim that attacks also ceased because the Turkish authorities were delaying Russian cargoes at Istanbul.[27] In addition to international outrage, the Republican government made a formal protest to the League of Nations on August 21, and the following day its embassies sent formal notes accusing Italian warships of conducting the attacks.

The Nyon Conference

"The blatant nature of these attacks, carried out when Italy was not at war and when nothing was done to disguise the nationality of the pirates, is astonishing, even after thirty-five years," a naval historian wrote in the early 1970s, while Winston Churchill referred to them as "sheer piracy."[28] Only the Republicans and Russians publicly identified the perpetrators, Moscow informing Rome that the attacks violated the September 2, 1933, pact between the two countries, who had agreed not to conduct acts of war against each other in support of a third party. An oil embargo added weight to Moscow's protests, which included delaying exports to Italy and refusing Italian charters, while the Black Sea Merchant Fleet suspended movements through the Strait of Gibraltar and confined trading to Middle or Far Eastern ports. Yet Moscow had to be circumspect, having ordered in September 1935 from the Odero-Terni-Orlando (OTO) yard at Livorno the destroyer leader *Tashkent*, which was launched on December 28, 1937. The need to possess this fine warship meant Moscow reluctantly agreed in 1938 to supply the Italian Navy with oil until the beginning of 1939, the *Tashkent* being handed over in May 1939.[29]

The British government remained well informed, the Admiralty tracking Italian submarines while the Air Ministry accessed Italian Air Force codes. Yet London's initial reaction to the submarine campaign was muted, simply expressing concern, and there was another inconclusive meeting of ministers on August 24.[30] Eden was on vacation, but kept in close touch with the Admiralty, and on August 17, following the first submarine attacks, he requested Chamberlain discuss the issue with foreign ministers, "since the Admiralty had reliable information that Italian submarines had orders to attack oil tankers of any nationality sailing to ports controlled by the Spanish Government."[31] Eden learned the French intended to protect their ships, while Paris was suggesting joint discussions with Italy about the attacks. Chamberlain had no intention of compromising his chances of a rapprochement with Rome, preferring instead to repeat the fiction these were Nationalist Navy activities, further irritating the Republicans, who had separate evidence of Italian complicity. Reluctantly, London publicly warned that the Royal Navy was authorized to respond to submarines attacking British merchantmen, and Paris followed suit. Both governments were seeking an international response, and on August 26 Paris proposed a conference on the issue, a suggestion enthusiastically supported by Eden. The attacks upon the *Woodford* and *Havock* proved the catalyst by stimulating Anglo-French talks, including the international conference.

Despite knowing the truth, the Royal Navy feared compromising the Empire's security by confronting the Italians. The Assistant Chief of the Naval Staff, Rear Admiral John Cunningham, advised the Cabinet against reinforcing the Mediterranean Fleet, the Plans Division under Captain Tom Phillips claiming it would require another six cruisers and 30 destroyers.[32] The Admiralty and Backhouse sought the easy option of granting the Nationalists belligerent rights, the admiral suggesting they "let them get on with the war." While willing to protect British ships, the admirals did not wish to protect the "pseudos," whom Captain William Tait, commander of the heavy cruiser HMS *Shropshire*, referred to as "changelings" of "disreputable appearance." Pound said that defending a "so-called British ship" would be a "travesty of justice." He had never been in favor of turning the other cheek, and since the summer of 1936 sought permission to fire back if his ships were attacked; he now wanted to sink all unidentified submarines, but rejected proposals to reintroduce the wartime convoy systems.[33] On August 18, the Admiralty ordered him to activate submarine-hunting groups and attack any submerged submarine within 5 miles of an attack upon a British ship, with permission to sink "unidentified" submarines in the certain knowledge that Italy could not protest without admitting her actions.[34]

The Admiralty regarded some of Eden's proposals "with skepticsm verging on ridicule," including his suggestion on August 31 that the Mediterranean Fleet sink the *Canarias*, an idea justifiably rejected on the grounds it might lead to war with Italy. Yet Somerville had proposed attacking Italian air bases on Majorca, and an alarmed Pound had to rein him in, noting this would be a declaration of war against the Nationalists.[35] The Admiralty was anxiously already looking eastwards, where full-scale war had erupted between China and Japan, bringing closer the prospect of dispatching the Mediterranean Fleet-based task force.[36] For this reason, Phillips proposed four options: blockading the Nationalist coast, which would require too great a commitment in resources; shelling a Nationalist port, which was "hunnish"; seizing Majorca or a Nationalist port, which would require considerable naval, army, and air resources; or intensified ASW operations. He considered the ASW threat alone would dissuade the attackers, but added: "If this was not so, the sinking of one submarine would settle any further apprehension for British shipping and for Great Britain's honour."[37] The change towards a more assertive policy was due partly to the blatant nature of the attacks, especially upon the *Woodford*, but also because former Secretary of State for War Duff Cooper—who had written on July 23: "I am determined that not another British sailor shall fall in a cause not worth fighting for"—now became more "malleable."[38]

Across the Channel, Vice-Admiral Darlan also sought military solutions. He believed Italian operations from the Balearics showed Italy was flexing its muscles and was becoming a closer partner with Germany. In September, he proposed to Foreign Minister Delbos an Anglo-French invasion of the Republican-held island of Minorca, and if the Italians did not cease reinforcing Majorca, then France should allow arms supplies across the border. London rejected both schemes, and also one for basing an Anglo-French task force at Port Mahon, the Admiralty describing this idea in October as unnecessary and provocative.[39]

Chamberlain was absent from the Cabinet meeting on September 2 which learned the Italians had 15 boats at sea, and even Deputy Foreign Secretary Edgar Wood, the Earl of Halifax, took a bellicose view, wanting to reinforce the Mediterranean and sink all unidentified submarines. To impliment this policy, the Cabinet ordered the Admiralty to send four more destroyers to the Mediterreanean, despite the admirals claiming this would merely provide more targets![40] The meeting also proposed that the conference on the issue in Switzerland should be at nearby Nyon rather than the League of Nations' headquarters in Geneva, because of Italian sensitivities over League sanctions during the Abyssinia Crisis.

The conference, scheduled for September 10, would "study measures which may be taken to end the current state of insecurity in the Mediterranean and to strengthen the rules of international law with regard to maritime navigation." From September 6, Delbos sought to hammer out a joint Anglo-French approach, proposing the conference include both Spanish sides and the Russians. The British believed it should be confined to Mediterrean powers together with the Soviet Union, Romania, and Bulgaria, but excluding the combatants, and Paris reluctantly agreed. The British Cabinet approved the Nyon Conference plan on September 8, although Chamberlain watered down some wording about the submarine attacks. Eden and First Sea Lord Chatfield were aware from Comint that the Italian blockade had ceased, but the indiscretion of Britain's ambassador in Berlin, the egotistic Sir Neville Henderson, led German Foreign Minister Neurath to telegraph the Rome embassy on September 12: "Please inform Ciano personally that it appears from a statement made to me by the British Ambassador here that the British have intercepted and deciphered radio messages of Italian submarines operating in the Mediterranean."[41]

The threat from submarines was Eden's priority, while the French also wanted to stop surface ships and aircraft threats. The British believed it was easier to tackle "anonymous" submarines, but that engaging easily identified warships and aircraft would lead to a confrontation with Italy, and possibly Germany. The British were even willing to accept a Soviet naval presence in the northern Aegean and were surprised by the strength of opposition expressed by Turkey, Greece, and Yugoslavia, which forced London to deploy extra destroyers into those waters. The Soviet delegation, led by Foreign Minister Litvinov, was accompanied by Black Sea Fleet commander Admiral Petr Smirnov-Svetlovsky, who accepted the conditions because his forces were incapable of operating beyond the Bosphorus.[42] Italy petulantly refused to attend, because on September 8 Moscow continued to accuse Italy of being behind the attacks. Rome would discuss the issue only at the Non-Intervention Committee in London, a view Chamberlain naturally supported, and with Italy boycotting the Nyon Conference, Germany also stayed away out of solidarity, as did pro-Italian Albania.[43]

The absence of Mussolini, the Pirate King, meant the conference quickly agreed a series of safe routes throughout the Mediterranean, each patrolled and protected by ships from one navy, but use of the routes was advisory rather than compulsory. Britain and France shared responsibility for the western and central Mediterranean and the Aegean, the latter with the regional navies, and participants' warships could engage submarines either attacking non-Spanish ships or detected close to where a ship had been sunk. Submarines would be banned from these waters, unless transiting them on the surface and accompanied by a warship, but regional powers' boats were allowed to train in specified areas. As a sop to Italian pride, Rome was given responsibility for preventing attacks in the Tyrrhenian Sea.[44]

Nyon restored the close relations between the British and French navies after the strains of the Abyssinia Crisis and the Anglo-German Naval Treaty until the summer of 1940.[45] The French even agreed, privately, that the British could base ships and aircraft in their territory, and their destroyer deployment exceeded their conference commitments by mobilizing reserve ships. Chatfield was delighted by this new *entente cordiale*, as was Eden, who wrote to Churchill on September 14: "[W]e have emphasized that co-operation between Britain and France can be effective ... I must say that they [the French] could not have co-operated more sincerely, and we have been surprised at the extent of naval co-operation which they have been ready to offer."[46] After the agreement was signed on September 14, Eden met the Press and, thanks to decrypted signals, confidently told them: "If there's another [submarine] attack, I will eat my hat."[47]

The Nationalist naval staff predictably reacted angrily: "These conditions are deplorable, but real; and in the face of reality, we must work with discretion and cunning to maintain the blockade of the Red Coast which is fundamental for victory."[48] They complained that the agreement aided the delivery of "contraband" and were especially vexed that one of the safe passages ran west of Majorca and could be used by ships trading with the Republic. Their cheeky request for the withdrawal of British destroyers to avoid confusion with Republican vessels was quickly rejected.[49] Franco refused to change course and confirmed the blockade would continue with a total ban on any vessel sailing at night, while those sailing during the day in territorial waters would be warned to turn back or sunk if they did not obey. Nationalist surface vessels were ordered to abide by the rules of the Treaty of London, for while the naval staff wished to retain a submarine option, they recognized the need to be more circumspect and restricted to the vicinity of Spanish territorial waters.[50]

After Nyon

Action against surface ships proved a thornier issue, with Chatfield preparing three options to respond to surface ship and air attacks. The French accepted his proposals that warships fire upon aircraft which were attacking merchant ships, but a suggestion for dealing with "inhumane" surface warship attacks was hotly debated. Despite obvious Italian indifference to survivors of surface ship attack, the Admiralty argued these were not "inhumane" actions, and suggested the mere existance of the Nyon Agreement would end them. The French strongly disagreed, and eventually the British accepted that warships be instructed "to intervene to the limits of their power in the case in which a surface ship carried out inhumane attacks." This was incorporated into the Supplementary Agreement signed on September 17 and warmly welcomed by the Republic. In response to an upsurge in the Italian bombing campaign against Republican ports, Delbos suggested to Eden that the two powers occupy Majorca, but wiser heads prevailed and the idea was quietly dropped.

Following the Mediterranean Fleet's rowing regatta at Moudros, on the Greek island of Lemnos, the two navies began Nyon patrols on September 20. HMS *Hood*, now under Admiral "ABC" Cunningham, and three destroyers covered the central Mediterranean from Malta, supported by a squadron of Scapa flying boats which had flown ASW missions during the Abyssinia Crisis.[51] Pound assembled 18 destroyers, including nine Home Fleet reinforcements, for the western Mediterranean, operating from Gibraltar, Algiers, and Oran, with the destroyer-tender HMS *Woolwich* at the latter base. They were supported by the battleship HMS *Barham* and light cruiser HMS *Despatch*, based in Barcelona, Pound regarding the extra workload as "a godsend to the navy" by restoring efficiency to that of the late 1920s.[52]

The RAF dispatched two squadrons with a dozen Short Singapore flying boats to Arzeu, near Oran, supported by the submarine-tender HMS *Cyclops*, and until they arrived the carrier HMS *Glorious* flew stop-gap patrols using a dozen Osprey and Nimrod biplane fighters. However, the threat of submarines restricted the carrier's deployment.[53] The RAF augmented two French seaplane squadrons in Algeria, reinforced by the seaplane-tender *Commandant Teste* at Bougie, a total of 36 aircraft, while four flying boat squadrons (16 aircraft) at Bizerta covered the central Mediterranean.[54] The French also deployed the heavy cruiser *Dupleix*, 30 destroyers and torpedo boats, two sloops, and 10 extra flying boats. During November and December, 1,673 ships sailed through French zones, with escorts for 172, while a report noted 563 ships were encountered in their zones in February 1938 and 622 the following month, although the figures slowly declined through the year.[55] Early September saw a flurry of activity in North Africa: a French flying boat spotted an unidentified submarine on September 3, leading to a major air sweep involving seven sorties a day for a week, while Italian aircraft flying into French territorial waters off Algeria ignored warning shots by air-defense guns, two seaplanes flying over Algiers on September 9.[56]

In the Aegean, Pound had the capital ships HMS *Repulse* and HMS *Malaya*, with eight Fairey IIIF floatplanes from HMS *Glorious*, and four destroyers, which were deployed until the end of the year.[57] Ankara was initially suspicious about the British request to use Turkish harbors, with British negotiations headed by Captain

John Godfrey, commander of *Repulse*. President Kemal Atatürk smoothed the way and relations between the two countries improved, which would later benefit London during World War II.[58]

Nyon sent Mussolini into a violent rage, but he was mollified by belated Anglo-French efforts to integrate Italy into the patrol system. Ciano observed on September 3 that the negotiations turned his country "from suspicious pirates to the policemen of the Mediterranean."[59] The change was driven by Rome's limited success at sea and renewed opportunities to achieve an Anglo-Italian rapprochement. When British and French envoys opened negotiations on September 13, the slippery Italian count attempted to sabotage the Nyon Agreement by pushing for "safe routes" to Italian territories in the Aegean and Libya. The following day, he optimistically noted: "As things stand, Nyon will fall into place."[60] Ciano was prepared to be conciliatory when he received a copy of the supplementary agreement on September 18, but Mussolini was "extremely uncompromising," yet three days later, having secured the concessions he wanted, Ciano crowed: "It is a great victory. From accused torpedoers to Mediterranean policemen, with the exclusion of the Russians, whose ships have been sunk."[61]

Staff talks were held in Paris from September 27, with the Russians demanding a route which avoided the Italian Navy, whose warships were denied access to the territorial waters of Greece and Turkey. At the first meeting, the Italian delegation, relieved that the agreement referred only to "inhumane acts," readily accepted the Franco-British route through the Mediterranean, only to U-turn and demand control of part of it after being berated by Mussolini. Then there was a row between French Premier Camille Chautemps and his Foreign Minister, Delbos, over whether to side with the Russians or the Italians. Chautemps overruled the minister, after discussing the matter with the British, and opted to support Rome, which was given the Tyrrhenean Sea. The Russians then demanded a free route from the Black Sea to Port Said, and an amended agreement was signed on September 30, the Soviet Black Sea Merchant Fleet receiving a list of 13 routes on October 3 to resume Mediterranean voyages.

Final arrangements made for the revised Nyon Agreement were discussed at Bizerta on HMS *Warspite* on October 30 by Pound, Vice-Admiral Jean-Pierre Esteva—the current commander of Alsud—and Italian 2nd Fleet commander Bernotti. Italian attempts to gain access to foreign territorial waters, especially French, were rebuffed and the revised zones were confirmed, taking effect from November 10.[62] The Italian Navy now patrolled using the light cruisers *Bande Nere* and *Da Barbiano*, 12 destroyers, 20 torpedo boats, the auxiliary light cruisers *Barletta* and *Adriatico*, and five seaplane squadrons. The Italian element was little changed until the end of the Spanish Civil War, although command passed from Admiral Bernotti to former Deputy Chief of the Naval Staff Pini on February 15, 1938.

The end of the Italian submarine attacks led to pressure within Whitehall from both the Admiralty and the Air Ministry to reduce their activities, with Pound claiming the ASW patrols increased the strain upon men and ships. To reduce maintenance requirements, destroyers operated on only one boiler, and over time they abandoned a constant sonar watch to reduce strain on operators and equipment.[63] In the short term, it proved politically inexpedient to delay reducing patrols until after the Italians had begun staging theirs, and air attacks upon British ships meant Their Lordships were forced to continue supporting the Nyon Agreement while pressing the Foreign Office for permission to ease the operational burden. Only on November 10 did the Admiralty inform Pound that he could substantially reduce the number of ASW patrols, which he began the following month, with the Home Fleet destroyers returning in January 1938. Pound could still call upon them if there was an upsurge in submarine activity, but the flying boats departed Arzeu on December 17.[64]

The Nyon Agreement provided an excuse to reduce, then abandon, the Naval Patrol, leaving no means of even nominally enforcing compliance of the Non-Intervention Agreement. In protest at the NIC's ineffectiveness, the Russians ceased making payments on October 7.[65] Finally, on New Year's Day 1938, the Admiralty authorized Pound to conduct only the minimum number of ASW patrols. The torpedoing of a British ship off Valencia early in 1938 saw them briefly restored to their old level until the end of March, but even when reduced, Pound was told to ensure they were "adequate."[66]

Pirates in the Air

The air threat was the most difficult aspect of the Italian blockade for the Nyon Conference to address. As early as August 5, Gull flying boats from Sardinia spotted ships north of the Tunisian island of La Galite, and the Majorca-based 225th Land Bomber Group (225a Gruppo BT) "Balearic Bats" (*Pipistrelli dell Baleari*) sent the lumbering bombers to intercept them off Algeria, only to be thwarted by fog. The ships reached Oran, but later three rushed northwards through the night to reach Republican ports, while two transferred their cargoes to French merchantmen which took them to Spain.[67]

On August 6, Bats attacked the tanker *British Corporal* 30 miles west of Algiers as she carried benzine to Britain from Persia (now Iran). One bombed her, causing a fire which forced the crew to abandon the bridge as the ship sailed on at full speed. Then, as the crew swung out lifeboats, two Bats strafed her, but when the bombers departed the crew was able to sail to Algiers. Bats bombed and strafed the CNM's *Djebel Amour* 30 miles north-east of Algiers, her second air attack in six months, but without injuries. They then bombed the Greek *K. Ktistakis*, sailing to Hamburg from Algiers, 18 miles west of Algiers, the bombers defiantly flying through Algerian air space before turning north. Other Bats accidentally bombed the Italian *Mongioia* in passage from Palermo to Seville to load a cargo of marble for the United States, one explosion lifting her out of the water and inflicting considerable damage upon the hull and the engine room. The engine was shaken off its mounting. Her master, Captain Solieri, was killed and the Dutch NIC observer, who had been bombed earlier on another ship, was wounded. Nevertheless, the ship, escorted by the liner *Conte de Savoia*, reached Algiers.

On August 11, aircraft forced the Yugoslav *Plavnik*, en route to Oran, to heave-to and she was later captured by the *Canarias*. At noon, a Gull intercepted the *Edith* of the Danish line J. Lauritzen 30 miles south of Barcelona, as she sailed to Valencia from Marseilles with a cargo of meat, but the aircraft evidently saw her NIC pennant and flew off. Four hours later, a Boot flown by Sub-Lieutenant Hans Reefe arrived and tried by signal lamp to order her to sail to Palma. However, bright sunlight and the aircraft's speed meant the crew could not read the message, so the master heaved-to and ran out her lifeboats while raising signal flags to show he had stopped. The Germans in turn did not see the flags; believing the ship intended to dash to Barcelona, Reefe dropped three bombs, which hit the ship and wounded Austrian cabin boy Alfred Kugel. The crew piled into the lifeboats and rowed away, although the observer remained aboard, as Reefe came around again to drop more bombs, which started fires. Reefe flew off and the crew reboarded the ship to fight the flames, but eventually had to abandon her, which was fortunate as one of Reefe's colleagues appeared, dropped another half-a-dozen bombs, and the *Edith* sank that night. The crew was rescued by fishermen the following morning and taken to Villanueva, Kugel dying in hospital to become the first of four foreign ships boys to die in the Civil War.[68]

On August 20, Bats dropped bombs near the Greek-owned, British-registered tanker *Romford* (formerly the Greek *Ionia*) 20 miles off Barcelona as she sailed in ballast to Constanta. The ship, which had a Greek master, was undamaged, but sailed to Marseilles for inspection before continuing toward the Black Sea, only to be intercepted by the *Canarias* and taken to Ceuta.[69] Three days later, the British *Noemjulia*, carrying iron ore and phosphates from Marseilles to Barcelona, and with two NIC observers aboard, was attacked by two aircraft, probably Condor Legion Boots, near Port Vendres.[70] She was owned by the Noemjulia Steamship Company and managed by W. G. Walton, but none of the 23 crew were British and her master, Captain Glinsky, was a Russian who had joined her two days earlier after seven years on the beach. Her reputation was such that before the Civil War, Parliamentary questions were twice raised about her activities, while in September 1939 she failed in an attempt to smuggle Jewish refugees into Palestine.[71] Their bombs missed and the ship reached Port Vendres. On August 24, Bats attacked two ships anchored off Puerto Rosas, but fighters shot down one of them. The next day, a Nationalist aircraft attacked the Greek *Jona* 20 miles off Barcelona without damaging her, although she too was later intercepted by the *Canarias* and forced to put into Ceuta. On September 1, the Greek *Tsepo*, carrying general cargo from

Marseilles to Barcelona, was bombed just after her air escort departed and she had picked up the pilot. A bomb hit the deck, killing the pilot and injuring a sailor, and the badly damaged ship had to be run aground to prevent it sinking.[72] In the early evening of September 21, a Bat bombed the French liner *Koutoubia*, sailing from Corsica to Morocco with 700 passengers, without effect, and three British destroyers responded to her calls for assistance.[73]

After this incident, the air blockade of the western Mediterranean was scaled down, but the Germans were accidentally caught in Republican retaliation. Between August 2 and 7, 13 Heinkel He 111E bomber reinforcements were flying to Spain and staging through Majorca, supported by a radio detachment which arrived on July 23, but two were damaged in a Katie raid.[74]

The Tightening Blockade

Franco and Cervera were resolute in their determination to interdict the Republican sea-lanes. The cruisers *Canarias* and *Baleares* remained the keel of the Nationalist fleet, but they were suffering from continuous use and were prime targets for the enemy. In August, the *Baleares* surprised a three-ship Republican convoy protected by five destroyers which engaged the cruiser, allowing their charges to escape, although three destroyers were damaged.[75]

On September 7, four Republican freighters, including the *Aldecoa*, arrived off Algiers carrying food and some vehicles, loaded in Soviet Black Sea ports, although the Nationalists alleged they all had war materiel. They were to rendezvous with a task force, including the cruisers *Libertad* and *Méndez Núñez*—the former flying the flag of Fleet Commander Lieutenant Commander Miguel Buiza—and seven destroyers, which sortied from Cartagena. By chance, in the mid-morning just north of Algeria's Cape Cherchell, they encountered the *Baleares* under Captan Manuel de Vierna Belando as she sailed to Cadiz for minor repairs. The *Libertad*'s higher speed put her ahead of the other cruiser, so Buiza and Vierna fought a series of duels, with the Republicans landing a couple of hits while the Nationalist ship's guns suffered technical problems. When the destroyers came up, Vierna broke off the engagement, but the unescorted merchantmen panicked and sailed into Algerian waters, where the *Aldecoa* and *Antonio de Satrústegui* ran aground. The others put into Oran and later sailed separately to Republican ports, followed by the two refloated vessels.[76] On September 13, the day after Italy ended its Sicilian blockade, the *Aldecoa* and *Antonio* departed Algiers shielded by Buiza's task force, but the arrival of Nationalist cruisers saw them flee to Cherchel. Shells fired at them landedg near the British tanker *Harpa*, sailing from Port Said to La Goulette, the port of Tunis.[77]

Three days later, Nationalist Comint detected the departure from Barcelona of the *Jaime II* and *J. J. Sister*, with four destroyers, carrying weapons and munitions to strengthen the Minorca garrison. The flotilla sailed northwards along the Catalan coast before turning east. During the evening, the *Canarias* came up from the south and, off the Catalan town of Calella, intercepted the convoy. Their escort made repeated torpedo attacks, but because their commander, Lieutenant Commander Frederico Monreal y Pilón, had orders to preserve his ships, he abandoned the merchantmen, which surrendered.[78] The poor performance of the Republican Navy led to Buiza being relieved by Lieutenant Commander (later Admiral) Luis González de Ubieta y González del Campillo on October 25, while former Northern Fleet commander Admiral Fuentes became Navy chief of staff and Lieutenant Commander Horacio Pérez Pérez Fleet chief of staff. Surprisingly, Monreal retained his command until Christmas 1938.[79]

Not every Republican ship was taken so easily. On October 12, the Nationalist gunboats *Eduardo Dato* and *Antonio Cánovas del Castillo* intercepted the *Cabo Santo Tomé*, under Captain Rafael Indaren, 45 miles off the Algerian coast between Cape de Garde and Cape Rosa. She was carrying aircraft and 1,800 tons of war materiel from Odessa to Valencia, posing as the British P&O Line's *Corfu*, with temporary wooden structures altering her appearance to confuse the gunboats. After firing a warning shot, the *Cánovas* sent a boarding party, but the freighter carried a concealed armament of four 3-inch (75mm) and four 45mm guns, which it now revealed, holing the *Cánovas* on the waterline and forcing her to withdraw for emergency repairs. The *Dato* and merchantman duelled at point-blank range, but with the freighter quickly set ablaze, Indaren made for the coast. Only when the freighter entered French territorial waters did the gunboat cease fire, watching as she ran aground and the crew took to the lifeboats. Shortly afterwards, the ship, one of the largest freighters in Republican service, exploded and sank in deep water.[80]

Nationalist warships continued to harass foreign merchantmen in the western Mediterranean, and on September 10 the *Canarias* again intercepted the *Romford*, forcing her to unload oil destined for the Republic in Palma. The complexities of the situation were illustrated on December 27, when the *Canarias* and *Cervera* intercepted the French *Yolande*, which as the *Jalisco* had earlier carried Mexican arms to Bilbao. She was acquired in 1937 by R. Gardella of Marseilles and was carrying 500 tonnes of tobacco and 400 tonnes of beans from Marseilles to Barcelona, as well as a Norwegian observer, but the Nationalists were convinced she was again shipping arms. The master radioed for help and the destroyer *Vauquelin* arrived, while Alsud commander Admiral Richard began negotiations with Moreno. Paris ordered him to escort the steamer to Port Vendres, and Richard gave his word of honor the ship would be inspected when she arrived. When it was clear she had no war materiel, she departed for Barcelona on January 2, escorted by the destroyer *Gerfaut*, but during the night evaded her escort. The incident led to an agreement between Moreno and Richard that the French would inspect any ship the Nationalists suspected of carrying war materiel.[81]

December also saw incidents in the Strait of Gibraltar, where three ships, including the French *Sydney* and *François*, were forced into Ceuta on December 17 and December 21, they and their cargoes being seized. That year, the Nationalists seized seven ships as prizes, the first being the Greek *Gardelaki* in March, yet the selection seemed random. While the Russian *Schors* was intercepted on December 23 and inspected, she was allowed to proceed.[82] The Oslo-registered *Alix*, meanwhile, sailing from Almeria to London with a cargo of oranges, was forced into Ceuta in February 1938 and seized, being renamed the *Malaga*; while sailing to Gijon in ballast, she ran aground at Cape Quejo on May 31 and sank.[83]

Destroyers were prominent on the rebels' "wish-list," which the Nationalist Higher Naval Council's two-day meeting from July 22 put at a cruiser, four destroyers, and a doubling of the submarine force to four boats. The *Canarias* and *Baleares* also required dedicated gunfire directors and control equipment, while it was decided to repair the damaged light cruiser *República* in Cadiz naval base and return her to full commission. The Nationalist ambassador in Rome, García Conde, and Nicolás Franco both pressed for destroyers and submarines, arguing they would reduce the burden on Italy's shoulders.[84]

Admiral Cavagnari was unenthusiastic, and Ciano noted in his diary on August 28: "I stopped the legalistic opposition of our navy with a telephone call to Cavagnari giving him a rocket [*un gran cicchetto*]. The Duce approved. This Spanish enterprise is hampered by the constant opposition from the navy of passive resistance."[85] On September 1, Mussolini agreed in principle to the transfer of the 26-year-old Italian light cruiser *Taranto*—the former German SMS *Strassburg*, whose 1936 refit saw two boilers removed, reducing her speed from 27.5 to 18 knots—but financial terms could not be agreed. Rome wanted 50 million lira, the equivalent of $3.65 million in contemporary exchange rates, which the Nationalists thought excessive, but they did agree to pay 40 million lira ($2.92 million) for the transfer of the old destroyers *Aquila*, *Falco*, *Guglielmo Pepe*, and Alessandro Poerio—rated as Sloops (Avisos)—as well as two submarines.[86]

Their appearance was changed at the Castellammare naval dockyard and the Spezia naval arsenal to resemble the Spanish Velasco class in a token attempt to avoid diplomatic protests at the flagrant violation of the Non-Intervention Agreement. The first two, under their new names *Ceuta* and *Melilla*, sailed for the Balearics on October 12–13, and on October 23 intercepted the French *Procida*, south of Marseilles, sailing from Saint Louis, Rhône to Sète. They briefly forced her to sail towards Majorca, before their commanders changed their minds and allowed her to complete her voyage. The *Huesca* and *Teruel* followed in November and December, but after nearly a quarter-of-a-century's service, they were showing their age and suffered mechanical problems; the speed of the first pair was reduced from 36.5 to 29 knots, and 30 knots to 26 knots for the second pair. The Spanish found their turbines especially difficult to operate, a problem compounded by a shortage of experienced engineers. For two months, each ship had to retain an Italian training cadre of an officer and NCO electrician, engineer, radio operators, and gunner until sufficient Spanish personnel were ready. Often described as "scrap iron" (*chatarra*), they still provided a useful addition to the Nationalist Navy, especially for escort work.

The destroyers' arrival marked a major reorganization of Nationalist naval forces on October 10, when Moreno replaced Bastarreche to become Head of Blockade Forces in the Mediterranean (Jefe de las Fuerzas de Bloqueo en el Mediterráneo), which included the Strait. He had the Italian destroyers, two Hispano-Italian submarines, two minelayers, seven auxiliary cruisers, four gunboats, 10 auxiliary patrol boats, and six minesweepers, this force being supported by some 25 seaplanes, but his relations with Cervera were sometimes strained. The cruisers formed the Cruiser Division (División de Cruceros), activated on October 30. Underpinning this force was the Italian Navy, which on New Year's Day 1938 reorganized the five destroyers based in Palma into the 6th Naval Division (6a Divisione Navale), under Rear Admiral Marenco Moriondo, to shield the flow of supply ships from Italy and provide intelligence and meteorological data for air attacks upon Republican ports. They also allowed the Nationalist Navy to focus upon offensive operations.[87]

The reorganization briefly raised hopes in Salamanca and Burgos that it might help to bring about a rapid end of the war, but Anglo-French naval forces remained determined to ensure normal trading. Moreno tried to rein-in his naval forces, but on December 6 Burgos declared they were establishing a close blockade of the eastern coast, despite the fact they lacked the ships to enforce this along a coastline of more than 700 miles. On December 22, the Nationalists announced they reserved the right to stop on the high seas any vessel they suspected of carrying "contraband," without defining just what that was. Five days later, they announced that safe areas in harbours such as Barcelona and Valencia, where neutral ships had previously anchored, would no longer be recognized, except for visiting warships. The existence of such safe anchorages had been one excuse for the Admiralty not to try escorting ships in territorial waters, although there some sympathy within the Royal Navy for the Nationalist position, with the strong belief that many "British" ships trading with Republican ports were carrying war materiel.[88]

The Submarines Return

Spanish submarines continued operations throughout the Italian campaign, and on August 29 the *Sanjurjo*'s guns damaged the Spanish *Ciutat de Reus*, but the boat then departed for an Italian refit with her sister ship. To maintain the submarine threat now the Italian campaign had ceased, Franco successfully sought four boats from Mussolini on September 15. Aware of Franco's chronic shortage of trained submariners, Il Duce stipulated they would be "legionary submarines," nominally part of the Nationalist Navy but with Italian crews and a Spanish commander.

Their rules of engagement, agreed only on October 2, were to attack "any warship or merchant ship unequivocally recognized as Red Spanish" or specific foreign vessels sailing within Spanish territorial waters, but American, British, French, or Japanese ships were off limits. The veteran boats selected were the Archimede-class cruisers *Galileo Galilei* (Senior Lieutenant Alfredo Criscuolo) and *Galileo Ferraris* (Lieutenant Commander Sergio Lusena) and the Perla-class coastal boats *Iride* (Senior Lieutenant Junio Valerio Borghese) and *Onice* (Senior Lieutenant Mario Ricci). The cruisers, given the cover-names *General Mola II* and *General Sanjurjo II*, departed Maddalena on September 20, with the Perlas, now named *Gonzales Lopez* and *Aguilar Tablada*, following three days later.[89] All were based until February 1938 at the small fishing port, now a delightful summer resort, of Puerto Soller, operating alongside the former Italian destroyers.[90]

Italy's proxy submarine campaign saw 13 patrols between October 8 and February 4, but the rules of engagement meant only Ricci's last patrol made a claim for a steamer on the night of November 7/8. Attacks by Criscuolo and Borghese from January 19–22 all failed. As compensation, the crews certainly lived well; on a 10-day patrol, a Perla crew of 45 consumed 71.5 kgs of fresh meat, 95 cans of processed meat, 240 sausages, 99 cans of seafood, 492 eggs, 222 kgs of pasta, rice, and vegetables, 12.5 kgs of cheese, and 1,000 citrus fruits, washed down with 64 liters of table wine, 88 bottles of wine, 10 bottles of brandy, and 12 bottles of champagne, as well as 10 kgs of coffee.[91]

Unwelcome attention on the offensive occurred when the destroyer HMS *Basilisk*, patrolling off the Valencia coastline, reported being attacked off Cape Sant'Antonio on the night of October 3/4 and responding with depth charges. However, the ship, which had the older Type 119 sonar with fixed dome and a mechanical range indicator, was not rated as an ASW platform; a Board of Enquiry determined the "attack" was probably due to self-generated noise. Indeed, the first patrol by the Puerto Soller boats began only on October 8. The incident generated considerable press attention, which undermined Admiralty efforts to reduce the scale of Nyon patrols.[92] From October 18, Spanish crews joined the *General Mola II* and *General Sanjurjo II*, and they embarked in the other boats from January 27.

On November 15, the Admiralty learned details of new plans for a submarine campaign in the western Mediterrean, spurred by the imminent return of the *Mola* and *Sanjurjo*. Between December and March they made five patrols off Cartagena, Valencia, Alicante, and Cape Creus with greater success, despite limited torpedo stocks, because they were not inhibited by Rome's rules of engagement on "neutral" ships. On the morning of January 11, the *Mola*, still under Bobadilla, torpedoed the Dutch *Hannah* just forward of the bridge as she carried wheat and beans from Antwerp to Valencia. She began to list to starboard and the 32 crew abandoned her, rowing to Javea, but the ship did not sink. That afternoon, the master and some of her crew rowed out in a bid to beach her, but she had taken on too much water and went down by the head 6 miles off Cape Sant'Antonio.[93]

Luensa made two unsuccessful attacks, including one upon the *Lake Geneva* on January 15, 3½ miles southwest of Valencia, with a torpedo passing wide, and after a British protest the Nationalists expressed regret.[94] Several days later, he attacked the Limerick Steamship Company's *Clonlara* on the afternoon of January 19 as she sailed from Valencia to Buriana. Her observers spotted the trail of a torpedo 10 miles north of Castellon, then a conning tower broaching the surface, but the ship was able to reach Burriana safely.[95]

Then, on January 31, a dozen miles south of Cape Tinosa, the *Sanjurjo* (Suances) attacked the Gibraltar-registered Verano Line's *Endymion* as she carried 1,700 tons of coal from Newport to Cartagena, her first trip to a Republican port. She was 12 miles off the route recommended by the Nyon Agreement, and when the torpedo hit her forward hold she was obviously lost. The Gibraltar-born master and part-owner, Captain Adolphus Verano, was joined on the bridge by his 28-year-old wife, Laura, as the crew rushed to their muster stations, but the ship sank like a stone within four minutes, sweeping away the Veranos, the Swedish NIC observer, and eight Welsh, Gibraltarian, and Spanish crew. Four survivors included the First Mate and the First Engineer, who had replaced the master's brother; they were left in the water to be picked up by Republican coastguard cutters and landed in Cartagena.[96]

The *Endymion* was lost in the Royal Navy's Nyon patrol zone, although the nearest British destroyer was 38 miles away. Her loss provoked strong reactions from the British public and government, who blamed Mussolini, and eight destroyers were sent to hunt the submarine. A Parliamentary statement by Duff Cooper described the attacker as "a pirate," but also noted that the ship had no radio, although Verano had apparently tried to fit one before he departed.[97] Pound, who was trying to improve relations with Moreno in Majorca, strongly protested, as did other countries, and both submarines were recalled. To molify the international community, Suances—who had commanded the *Sanjurjo* since she was commissioned in May 1937—was relieved of his command on April 12 and replaced by Lieutenant Commander Melchor Ordóñez Mapelli, who remained with the boat until July 1940.

Their Lordships decided not to rock the boat, especially after building up close relations with the Nationalists in Majorca, although Eden publicly stated that from now on the Royal Navy would attack any submerged submarine in its area. Nevertheless, despite his post-Nyon boast, Eden did not place his famed homburg hat on a plate and reach for the ketchup! The attacks did, however, fuel his disquiet at the rapprochement with Italy, and he resigned as Foreign Secretary in protest on February 20, to be replaced by Lord Halifax. Meanwhile, to strengthen the rapprochement, Mussolini decided to withdraw his boats from Puerto Soller.[98] Franco now recognized the submarine campaign was undermining Nationalist diplomacy, especially with London, and despite Cervera's protests, he ordered an indefinite pause in their operations. The decisions also benefitted the Admiralty, which had to reinforce the ASW force after the *Endymion*'s loss, but from May 1938 the absence of submarine attacks provided the excuse to reduce these patrols, which were permanently suspended in August and formally abandoned during the Munich Crisis in September.[99] Nationalist submarine patrols were resumed and they prowled the Mediterranean coast throughout 1938 and early 1939, but without success. On April 14, a surfaced submarine watched the French *El Mansour* off Barcelona before diving, while unsuccessful attacks by the *Mola* on the *Arlon* and *Neath Abbey* were reported in May and June.[100]

The Shadow of the Jackboot

While the submarine threat sank into the depths, the aerial threat soared as both the Germans and Italians intensified operations during the latter half of 1937. After the Spanish air services merged, Cervera was dissatisfied with his air support, especially reconnaissance, although on July 15, Nationalist air chief Kindelán demanded more dynamic air operations against warships, sea-lanes, and ports, leading Rámon Franco to provide Bastarreche with a naval pilot in August as both technical advisor and aviation coordinator.[101] Franco blamed the "disgraceful shortage of materiel" for the failure to cut enemy maritime traffic and wanted the Italians to bomb the ports and warships, while the German and Spanish seaplanes roamed the sea-lanes, augmented by Majorca-based Bats. Better information was reflected in improved performances from the Condor Legion's Boots during the final quarter of 1937.

The Boots were increasingly used for bombing ports, striking like stilettos deftly wielded by assassins. Usually operating in pairs, they would circle ports for one or two hours, seeking prey; once they had selected a target, they would turn towards it, throttle-back or even switch-off the engines and glide down. The 250-kg bombs and incendiaries would be released from heights of 250 meters (820 feet), and often as low as 50 meters (160 feet), then the pilot would throttle up and the seaplane would pull away, with gunners strafing the target.[102]

From the end of September, the Boots harassed merchant shipping. On October 5, a seaplane 33 miles northwest of the Balearics intercepted France-Navigation's *Cassidaigne*, sailing from Sète to Oran with a cargo of casks, and by signal lamp ordered her to Palma, warships arriving to enforce the demand. When the freighter arrived, the Nationalist authorities tried to persuade the master to land his cargo, but he refused and was freed through the intervention of the French Consul, supported by his Danish colleague, his ship being met as she departed by the destroyer *Le Fantasque*.[103] Two days later, a seaplane attacked the Italian *Ettore* off North Africa but she escaped damage.

There was a tense incident on the morning of October 8 when a seaplane intercepted the London-based MacAndrews & Company's *Cervantes* 8 miles off

Tarragona. The aircraft ignored her NIC pennant and used a signal lamp to order her to Palma, underlining the demand by strafing and bombing in front of her. The ship was in ballast after unloading food, radios, and crates from Antwerp at the Cartagena arsenal, and refused to comply, so another Boot arrived carrying a torpedo just after noon. This seaplane attacked just as HMS *Firedrake* arrived, the torpedo passing astern of the freighter, which then changed course to Valencia, where she arrived the next morning. When the British consul, Hillgarth, complained to Bastarreche, he was told the attacker had been a German who had carried a torpedo without orders and been arrested.[104]

This was probably a face-saving sop to the British, for the Boots now intensified their efforts. After the unsuccessful bombing of the British *Marvia* north of the Balearics on October 21, two seaplanes attacked CNP's *Oued-Mellah* three days later as she was carrying grain from Casablanca to Port Vendres. Two bombs hit the ship, which began to sink, the shaken but uninjured crew taking to the lifeboats and being picked up by the destroyer *Milan*, which watched the freighter slip beneath the waves. The following day, seaplanes attacked the Minorcan port of Fornells, which was a staging post for Air France's Marseilles–Algiers seaplane service. This service apparently continued throughout the war, with a French destroyer patrolling off the port in support, but the attack set ablaze the 60 grt support boat *Chasseur 91*, which then sank.[105] Condor Legion attacks on the high seas worried Raeder, who feared the diplomatic consequences, and on November 6 he requested the seaplanes confine their operations to Spanish territorial waters and Spanish ships, but was ignored.[106]

The end of the month saw the sinking of the *Jean Weems* of the Greek-owned Thameside Line. She had recently emerged from dry dock in Marseilles, following repairs after being hit on September 15/16 during a raid upon Valencia which injured her master, Captain Eversett. After loading wheat, condensed milk, and cow hides, she departed for Barcelona flying the NIC pennant with Swedish and Latvian observers. Despite this, in the early morning of October 30, a Boot approached her north of Barcelona and, with signal lamp, ordered her to stop and her 26-man British crew to abandon ship. They obeyed, and from the lifeboats saw the seaplane drop bombs which set the ship ablaze, causing her to sink 15 minutes later. The lifeboats rowed towards the Catalonian coast, which they reached after seven hours. The pilot was reportedly Spanish and claimed his attack had taken place inside Spanish territorial waters.

By November, the tour of AS/88 squadron commander Captain Günther Klünder was almost over, but on November 4 a seaplane ordered the crew of the *La Corse*, sailing from Barcelona to Marseilles, to abandon ship. However, after a fruitless bombing attack the arrival of two French destroyers allowed the crew to reboard and sail to Marseilles. Moreno claimed she was on a black list and had been attacked in territorial waters, and denied reports the *Lézardrieux* was straffed on November 29. The bizzare nature of the situation in the western Mediterranean was highlighted three days later when a Boot force-landed 60 miles south of Formentera. She was discovered by HMS *Basilisk*, which stood by for 24 hours until the *Velasco* arrived to tow the aircraft to nearby Ibiza. Velardi informed Rome: "I must put it on record that the conduct of the British destroyer could not have been better."[107] From November 19, Pollensa Bay became the Nationalists' prime seaplane base, but the problems of putting so many eggs in one basket were demonstrated on February 12 when a severe storm wrecked almost all of them.[108] Kindelán assigned AS/88 a new role on November 27, interdicting communications between Barcelona and Sagunto and also acting as train-busters.[109] However, not all seaplane attacks were by the Germans, for on November 13 a Spanish Whale strafed the *Comandante Dorise* 19 miles off Cadiz.[110]

Germany's allies decried the Boots' operations, and many postwar accounts credited Nationalist seaplanes with their successes.[111] In a message to Rome on January 30, Italian air liaison officer Lieutenant Colonel Carlo Drago complained that AS/88 "works too little work alternating with long periods of inactivity."[112] He was speaking too soon, for on December 1, Klünder was relieved by Captain Martin Harlinghausen, nicknamed "Iron Gustav."[113] During his 12-month tenure, Harlinghausen would reinvigorate the squadron, and it was a sign of the times on New Year's Day 1938 when a bombing attack upon the French *Guarija*, sailing from Marseilles to New York, forced her to run aground.

On February 4, a Boot intercepted the British *Alcira*, carrying coal from Immingham near Hull to Barcelona just 20 miles southeast of the port. Although she flew the NIC pennant and carried an observer, the seaplane fired tracers across her bow and signaled that the 21-man British crew had just five minutes to abandon ship. Even as the boats were being lowered, the seaplane began her bomb run; one bomb hit the engine room, bursting the boiler, with debris raining down to burn one crew member. The vessel sank within five minutes, the crew being rescued by Catalan fishermen. A Nationalist inquiry stated that the German pilot thought the ship was the *Aldecoa* and blamed the master for refusing an order to sail to Palma. However, relations between Harlinghausen, Moreno, and Cervera were tense, leading Moreno to order Harlinghausen not to attack any British or French ship, no matter where they encountered them. Rear Admiral Wilhelm Marschall, commanding German naval forces off Spain, protested to the OKM and to Cervera, saying there was evidence that ships from these nations were bringing "contraband" to Republican ports and warning that the Spanish demands would encourage other freighters to fly the Red Ensign and the *Tricoleur*.[114]

Harlinghausen decided to turn a blind eye, and on February 22 his men attacked the French *Prada* off Valencia, causing slight damage and injuring a crewman, the attack being broken off with the appearance of the French destroyer *Epervier*. The following night, Boots attacked the British *Shetland* anchored in the Valencia Roads, badly damaging the forecastle and holing the hull, but after repairs she was able to continue. Then on February 25, the Bramhall Line's *Bramden* was bombed in Sagunto, with bomb splinters injuring three men, including the radio operator. The British *Shetland* was also damaged, sailing to Valencia for repairs.[115] During the early hours of February 28, a Boot bombed the *Stanwell*, which had just arrived in Tarragona with 8,000 tonnes of Welsh coal, setting her ablaze and killing two of the stokers and a Danish observer, while six other men were injured, four seriously. Her master ordered "abandon ship," but the fire was extinguished after destroying the crew accommodation, the shaken men being housed ashore and demanding repatriation.

The Deadly Hawks

General Velardi's bomber force continued its stuttering bombing campaign into early September, but the Bats were increasingly diverted to maritime reconnaissance. However, the second half of the year saw an intensification of the bombing campaign, with 10 raids on Catalonian ports during August and September. There were 18 raids in the last quarter of the year, rising to 22 for the first two months of 1938.[116] Reinforcements made this possible, with Velardi receiving two Hawk squadrons of the 12th Fast Bomber Wing (12a Stormo BV), the Green Mice (Sorci Verdi), on September 27, one flown by Sergeant Bruno Mussolini, Il Duce's son and the country's youngest pilot.[117] They flew 93 sorties between October 1 and November 25 before being transferred to the mainland, but would soon be replaced.

These attacks were rather like a wildly swung cutlass, with Hawks approaching ports at high altitude of 4,000–5,000 meters (13,000–16,000 feet) to bomb installations such as quays and warehouses, hitting ships being collateral damage. After the Hawks were withdrawn, the Bats continued night attacks. Indeed, just before the Green Mice arrived, they damaged a destroyer and two British ships, while a dawn raid by three Bats upon Tarragona on September 23 inflicted minor damage upon two British ships, including the *Hamsterley*, with several crewmen suffering post-traumatic stress.

On November 24, Kindelán requested Velardi increase the scale of attacks upon the port facilities and industries of Valencia and Barcelona in anticipation of a major Nationalist offensive around Madrid.[118] The following day, Mussolini ordered replacement Hawk squadrons to Majorca, and on November 30 elements of the 28th Fast Bomber Group (28a Gruppo BV) arrived with a dozen bombers.[119] They flew their first mission against Barcelona on December 7, and a week later Mussolini informed CTV commander General Mario Berti that further reinforcements would be sent "to terrorise the Red rear and specifically urban centres." This ignored Franco's directive of December 4 informing his brother only military targets were to be attacked.[120] From October 1–25, the Italians flew 119 sorties against Spanish targets, 21 by Bats, with missions involving up to 10 bombers in the daytime and six at night. In a surge of optimism, Rome asked Velardi if his airfields could accommodate up to 50 bombers and 24 fighters, while the French Navy, having detected the reinforcements, grew more concerned about the strategic threat from the Balearics.[121]

While nominally under Moreno and Ramón Franco, the Italians flew their own course, but the German attitude sometimes seemed supercilious, generating friction between the allies. On November 7, Moreno informed Cervera he was restricting Italian and German attacks to the mainland due to strong protests from the French. An unsympathetic Cervera responded that Moreno should inform the British and French his mission was to harass ships in enemy ports, and on November 19 urged him to act more energetically against maritime traffic. Time and again, in response to British protests, Moreno would apologize, promise to prevent further attacks, but claim the Germans and Italians were ignoring his orders. Until late in 1937, neutral shipping was allocated safe zones within Republican ports, which the Nationalists reluctantly recognized, but Cervera sought to abolish them. On November 26, Moreno informed Somerville of his commander's intentions. Somerville requested a delay so he could inform the Admiralty and allow shipping companies to assess the decision. Moreno was sympathetic, informig Cervera that nothing would be gained by rousing British public opinion and urging that the neutral zones be maintained for warships. Nevertheless, Cervera ignored him, and the following day he announced the abolition of the safe zones.[122]

On the night of December 14/15, the Republicans attacked at Teruel, leading to a bloody two-month-long battle of attrition, which added urgency to port attacks.[123] Italian Chief of the Air Staff General Giuseppe Valle celebrated the start of 1938 by flying a 2,000-kilometer night round-trip in a Hawk from Guidonia, over the Tyrrhenian Sea and Gulf of Lyon to Barcelona, and dropping 800 kgs of bombs. Within a fortnight, Majorca was reinforced by the headquarters of the 8th Fast Bomber Wing (8° Stormo BV) and its 27th Bomber Group arrived, the wing calling itself the Balearic Falcons (Falchi delle Baleari). A relative lull during December saw Nationalist cruisers shell Burriana on December 30, showering the British *Bramhill* with fragments, but she was able to sail to Marseilles. The reinforcements may explain why the Italians reneged on an agreement to provide their allies with a dozen Hawks; when the group commander, Major José Gomá Orduña, arrived in Palma to collect them on November 9, he received only half the bombers. Kindelán's poor compensation was a couple of Gulls.[124]

A mission against Tarragona on January 16 inflicted minor damage upon the *Seabank Spray* (formerly *Joyce Llewellyn*), while four days later a bomb hit the forward end of the British *Thorpeness*, which was unloading coal, killing four of the all-British crew and wounding another seven, mostly from Grimsby. Her master, Captain Edward Roberts, who observed this was the third attack in 18 days, reported that when air raid sirens began to wail, his crew started to make for quayside shelters.

But bombs fell almost immediately, killing two crew on the quayside and two others walking down the gangway, two of the dead being identifiable only from pieces of their clothing. Roberts later commented: "The whole area was an absolute shambles. You cannot have any idea of the terror of it."[125] A raid upon Valencia on January 26 saw 125 killed and 208 wounded, the dead including Captain Arnold Crone, master of the British *Dover Abbey*, which was loading oranges.

By January 15, Velardi had 27 Sparrowhawks and 11 Bats, although only 18 of the former were serviceable, compared with all of the latter. They were now attacking strategic targets, including ports, almost on a daily basis, with 110 sorties—20 by Bats—between February 1 and March 8. Their only success appears to have been on February 10, when the Gibraltar-registered *Lucky* failed to live up to her name, being sunk in Valencia. The reinforcements increased both sortie rates and bomb tonnage (Table 4.2). Yet this did not translate into more bangs for their buck, for an embarrassed Velardi had to admit to Legionary Air chief Bernasconi on December 14 that some bombs failed to detonate, asking for checks on the fillings for fear of deterioration. Despite Italians efforts to conceal their embarrassment, Rámon Franco informed Kindelán on January 16 that most of the bombs dropped on Barcelona the previous day had failed to explode. The following day, Velardi blamed the problem on failures of delayed-action fuzes and asked Rome how Franco had learned about it. Rome swiftly batted the problem back, pointing out on January 28 that bombers on the Spanish mainland had no problems and asking that Balearic crews ensure safety catches were switched off once bombs were loaded. Bomb consumption was considerable. Velardi informed Rome on January 17 he had a stock of 657 tonnes of bombs, and on February 8 he was told that the *Aniene* would be arriving with another 396 tonnes.[126]

The strategic bombing issue was controversial, with the Italians eager to practice the theories of their countryman General Guilio Douhet, who believed wars could be won by air power alone, destroying enemy industry and infrastructure and terrorizing the civilian population. They ignored Nationalist attempts to confine bombing to military targets and thwarted their efforts to strengthen the Spanish

Table 4.2. The Italian bombing offensive from Majorca, August 1937–January 1938

Month	Sorties	Bomb tonnage (kg)
August 1937	39	28,200
September 1937	18	18,290
October 1937	100	91,790
November 1937	18	20,320
December 1937	138	75,040
January 1938	276	184,780

Source: UKNA HW 21/3 and 21/4

bomber force. On January 10, Ramón Franco, reviewing operations since the publication of Directive 318 six months earlier, noted that attacks upon the ports had great potential to complement the naval blockade, especially Harlinghausen's operations. He recommended reducing the Italian presence to a single squadron and adding 10 Spanish squadrons of Hawks, together with a combined torpedo-bomber/night-bomber group. When asked about this proposal, Kindelán claimed Ramón Franco was a Freemason whom he did not trust, a man with "no moral sense," and possibly even a Communist! On February 15, General Valle advised Bernasconi to follow Nationalist wishes and avoid attacking ports or hitting city centers. However, three days later Franco ordered his brother to resume attacks against coastal military targets, and that same day the Italians began striking inland communications. Curiously, Kindelán's Italian liaison officer, Drago, noted the Germans were worried about international indignation over bombing of urban areas, fearing being tarred with the same brush and that it might undermine support within Nationalist Spain.[127]

The air offensive did not go unchallenged, with Katies making retaliatory attacks upon Majorca. One on August 7 destroyed a Bat and damaged two more, together with two refueling Condor Legion Heinkel He 111s. Two raids on October 7 saw 9 tonnes dropped upon Palma, with one bomb falling 300 yards from the cruiser HMS *Delhi*. On December 7, 24 Katies struck Palma and Puerto Soller, dropping 14.4 tonnes of bombs that slightly damaged two Bats and killed 10 civilians, but losing one bomber, although the defenses claimed seven.[128]

They were also active at sea, being responsible for three incidents involving French ships in early 1938, two of them off Cape Béar. On January 11, the sloop *Suippe* was strafed by two French-built Dewoitine fighters, while on January 24 bombs were aimed at the destroyer *La Poursuivante*, both almost certainly being cases of mistaken identity. On February 18, aircraft seeking an enemy task force mistakenly made high-altitude attacks off Port Vendres upon the liner *El Mansour*, sailing to Algiers with 100–200 passengers, and the destroyer *La Cordeliere*, neither ship being hit. Then on March 3, Katies bombed in error the French destroyers *Tartu* and *Chevalier Paul* north of Barcelona, with the bombs falling 50 meters from the latter.

Neither Friend nor Foe

The Royal Navy and the Marine Nationale sought a *modis vivandi* with the Nationalist Navy, despite a profound chasm between the two sides. To the Spanish, the conflict was a crusade, and they could not comprehend why navies who had ruthlessly blockaded the Central Powers during the Great War opposed their operation.[129] Relations with the French were such that when the *Cervera* encountered the French destroyer *Milan* on February 18, she pointed her guns towards the French vessel which, in turn, turned her torpedo tubes towards the cruiser.[130] While the British and French had little sympathy for the Republic, and only contempt for its navy, with no granting of belligerent rights their duty was to ensure legitimate trading. While they, and their nations, waxed indignant at the sinking of ships, they were all too well aware of the "pseudo" problem.

As neither London nor Paris recognized the Nationalist regime, protests were conveyed through the Nationalist Navy to "the responsible officer" in Majorca, first Bastarreche and then Moreno.[131] At one point this was the role of Battlecruiser Squadron commander "ABC" Cunningham, using Palma as his forward base, allowing him to observe Italian squadrons heading westwards to bomb British ships. He noted: "It was the Flag Officer's rather difficult and unsavoury task to see that British shipping was not unnecessarily molested, particularly outside Spanish territorial waters."[132]

Somerville, on the other hand, had an easy professional relationship with both Bastarreche and Moreno, remaining friends with the former until Somerville's death in 1949. "Whilst I read out to him some terrific raspberry [reprimand] we sit on the foredeck of his yacht and drink beer. It's the only place in Palma where you can get decent beer."[133] Yet Somerville could sometimes deliver a serious message, and following air attacks on August 24, 1937, he threatened to take offensive action against the Majorca air bases, only for an alarmed Pound to countermand him.[134] Even when Bastarreche became commander of the Cadiz naval base (Comandante General del Departamento Marítimo de Cádiz), Somerville continued consulting him. On October 29, he reported to Pound that "Admiral Bastarteche" had promised to inform the Mediterranean Fleet when Nationalist submarines were on patrol. For his part, Bastarreche kept Cervera in the loop, with his promises sanctioned by the Nationalist Navy commander.[135]

Moreno claimed to Cervera on November 30 that he also had a warm relationship with Admiral Cunningham and Vice-Admiral Charles Kennedy-Purvis, commander of 1st Cruiser Squadron, who both seemed sympathetic to the Nationalist cause. However, Cunningham, who flew his flag on HMS *Hood*, referred to him as "Admiral Morena" and wrote: "He was a weak man with little real control over the Italian and few Spanish aircraft supposed to be acting under his orders." He claimed Moreno went to sea to avoid meeting him. In turn, Moreno's sons noted that Cunningham "showed signs of a lack of understanding and sympathy towards the Nationalist cause."[136] For his part, Moreno, after consulting the British and French, sought guidelines for air attacks upon the ports to reduce friction with the two major powers, but without undermining the Nationalist war effort.[137] On November 7, however, he wrote to Cervera claiming the Nyon Agreement had facilitated the trade in "contraband," with British and French warships virtually escorting the "smugglers" to their destination. He identified the British "pseudos" as the core of the problem and demanded an increase in the scale of air attacks upon ports.[138]

The relationship between Bastarreche and Somerville gave Cervera insights into British thinking, which he laid out in a memo to Franco on September 22, aiming to reduce potential friction. He proposed neutral vessels carry prominent markings, as they had done in the Great War, and sail no closer than 10 miles from the coast. He wished to abandon granting safe zones for neutral ships within Republican ports, because "smugglers" exploited them. The Nationalists also needed guarantees the Red Ensign would not be abused and that the Royal Navy would take responsibility for ensuring no British ship carried arms.[139] While the markings idea was not accepted, Somerville did agree on September 29 that the Royal Navy would stop and inspect any vessels which the Nationalists suspected of carrying war materiel. This was similar to the agreement Ramsey had made in the north that was adopted by the French a few months later.[140]

The agreements were compromised by poor Nationalist intelligence, as the *African Mariner* illustrated in mid-November. She was intercepted by the destroyer HMS *Greyhound* while sailing from Odessa and Novorossisk to Barcelona, following a Nationalist claim she was an arms smuggler. She was diverted to Malta, where a thorough inspection established she was carrying salt fish, wheat, and sulphate of ammonia, allowing her to complete her voyage. A similar report about the British *Euphorbia* saw Pound deploy three cruisers and 10 destroyers to intercept her, HMS *Galatea* succeeding on November 21, but when inspected in Gibraltar she was found to be carrying manganese ore and cotton from Odessa, Poti, and Istanbul to Gydnia. A few days later, when the Nationalists asked Somerville to pass on a request for the Royal Navy to stop war materiel being transported across the North Sea and through the Channel, he responded sharply that British warships could not be expected to conduct "expensive wild goose chases." The British continued to honor the arrangement in the Strait with ships flying the Red Ensign, although it became embarrassingly obvious this was a waste of time. The *Sunion* was forced into Gibraltar by a Nationalist patrol boat on January 18, but when inspected was found to be carrying only coal. A few days later, the auxiliary cruiser *Mallorca*, having been specifically informed that the *Partridge Hill* was carrying weapons, forced it to sail to Gibraltar, where an inspection discovered she was carrying steel ingots and trucks, which she was allowed to deliver to Barcelona.

While the admirals might be seeking a working relationship, the sailors were less diplomatic, especially those of HMS *Hood*. During runs ashore, and when the sailors were in their cups, they would insult Nationalist sailors with the Republican clenched fist salute. The inevitable response was a series of brawls, which a Spanish source wrongly claims led to a British fatality.[141]

If the Royal Navy seemed quite relaxed, the Marine Nationale was becoming ever more concerned about the situation in their back yard.[142] Italy's sale of destroyers and membership of the Anti-Comintern Pact with Germany and Japan from October 1937, fed Darlan's fears that in a major conflict Britain and France would face both the Pact signatories and Nationalist Spain. The naval staff felt the threat was further justification for accelerating construction of the naval base at Mers-el-Kebir, near Oran, and even the conquest of Spanish Morocco. Defense Minister Daladier underlined the strategic importance of the Mediterranean, noting at the November 3 meeting of the National Defense Permanent Committee (Comité Permanent de la Défense Nationale, CPDN) that it linked the European powers with their empires. In December, Daladier commented: "France must remain ready to pursue, as a matter of priority, the defeat of Italy."[143] He reluctantly accepted the naval staff's view that an aggressive policy should be pursued in the western Mediterranean, aiming to destroy the Italian fleet and occupy Libya, Spanish Morocco, and the Balearics, before focusing upon Germany. By contrast, the French Army regarded Germany as the prime enemy and sought an alliance with Rome. Vice-Admiral Darlan, who would push through a three-year naval rearmament program in March 1938, observed: "If we continue to sleep our country will be incapable of pursuing a strong foreign policy. We will lose our friends and our alliances."[144]

Eve of a Breakthrough

Meanwhile, the Nationalist blockade tightened, and by the end of 1937 had captured 106 Republican merchantmen, sunk 28, and recovered 70, giving them 400,000 tons of shipping.[145] During the last quarter of 1937 alone, they stopped 53 ships, none carrying war materiel, but few were British or French due to the vigilance of their warships.[146] A Foreign Office report claimed that in October 1937, only 68 ships (53 British, 11 French, three Irish, and one Dutch) visited Republican ports, while 174 visited Nationalist ones, including 70 German, 35 British, 25 Danish, 10 Dutch, and 14 Italian.[147]

Italian assessments of traffic (Tables 4.3 and 4.4) between the Black Sea and eastern Spain also showed a marked decline in numbers. By the end of the year, the Republic's Official Management of the Merchant Marine (Gerencia Oficial de la Marina Mercante, GOMBE) reluctantly decided it was now too risky for its ships to voyage directly between the Black Sea and the Iberian Peninsula. Most of this lucrative trade was left to foreign vessels, and those Spanish ships which did pick up cargoes in Black Sea ports headed for French North Africa to transfer their cargoes to foreign vessels, which then made the hazardous high-speed dash across the Mediterranean. Billmeir's *Stanbrook*, for example, after delivering a cargo from Odessa at the beginning of March, then delivered a Spanish ship's cargo loaded in Bône. Spanish ships were largely confined to the less-exposed waters down the coast from French ports.

British ships were prominent (see Table 4.3). In January 1938, Nationalist intelligence reported that of 75 British ships going to Republican ports, 15 had food, 26 had coal, eight had POL, 10 had cotton, and the remainder carried various cargoes. The following month, 46 of the 84 British ships sailing to Republican ports went to Barcelona, and 30 of the British ships carried coal, but their crews were feeling the strain.[148] After the *Celtic Star* picked up a cargo of Argentinian meat in

Table 4.3. Foreign ships sailing to Republican ports

Month	Total	British
January 1938	120	75
February 1938	122	84

Source: González, 361–64

Table 4.4. Italian assessment of ships sailing to Republican ports from Black Sea ports, second half of 1937

Period	Ships							
	Russian	Republican	British	Greek	Panamanian	French	Other	Total
August–September	8	3	10	–	2	–	–	23
October	4	1	12	3	1	1	1	23
November	3	–	15	2	2	–	–	22
December	–	–	17	–	–	2	–	19
Total	15	4	54	5	5	3	1	87

Source: Rapalino, Appendix VI.

December, her 57-man crew learned their destination was a Republican port, leading to 26 of them walking off the ship when she stopped at Gibraltar.[149] Two months later, when the crew of Billmeir's *Stanmount* learned in Valencia they would be sailing to Odessa, they went on strike, demanding a 50 percent increase in danger pay. The master, Captain John Roberts, was able to sail for Malta, where the crew members were paid off and repatriated to Great Britain at their own expense, to be replaced by Maltese sailors.[150]

The blockade severely reduced military aid sent directly to Republican ports, with only a score of shipments between August 1, 1937, and February 28, 1938, and only four after September; increasingly, they were shipped to western France. France-Navigation's *Ploubazlanec*, for example, landed Polish and Paraguayan weapons at Bordeaux on September 30, where they were ostensibly impounded but actually crossed the border the following month. Such cross-border traffic of "impounded" supplies depended upon the political persuasion of the government and the judicious use of bribes.[151] By December, the Republic and the Soviet Union reluctantly recognized it was almost impossible to break the Nationalist blockade, and even the formidable *Cabo San Agustin* had to land arms shipment I-40 in Marseilles on February 1. The "Kh" delivery program was now restricted to Murmansk and Bordeaux, usually in France-Navigation ships, starting with I-38 in the *Guilvinec*, which departed on December 14 and arrived on December 25. Soviet weapons deliveries were reduced following the outbreak of the Sino-Japanese War, with the Soviet Union's strategic priority now being China. The Republic's ambassador to

Moscow, Marcelino Pascua Martínez, made anguished appeals to Defense Commissar Voroshilov, but Republican funds were dwindling, Stalin's purges were in full swing, and few officials wished to attract the attention of "Uncle Joe" and the NKVD.[152] Yet by the spring of 1938, the Republic was in dire need after events at Teruel, as it became apparent that the Nationalists were preparing to strike eastwards.[153]

The Nationalist Navy continued tightening the blockade during the first two months of 1938. France-Navigation was obviously on their blacklist, and on January 17 its *Lézardrieux*, sailing from Bastia in Corsica, ostensibly to Oran but actually to Valencia, was intercepted north of the Balearics by a destroyer and ordered to Palma. The destroyer *Chevalier Paul* intervened and allowed her to proceed. Meanwhile, the Nationalist minelayer *Vulcano* stopped the Russian *Syryanin*, carrying 3,193 tons of rye and wheat to Marseille, when only 60 miles south of her destination. She was forced into Majorca, where her cargo was unloaded and the crew was jailed, the female mess attendant being held in a separate cell until her hunger strike led to her rejoining her shipmates. After 26 days, the cargo was reloaded and the ship allowed to complete her voyage. That same day, it was the turn of the American tanker *Nantucket Chief*, registered to the Nantucket Chief Steamship Company in Port Arthur. She was carrying gasoline and kerosene from Russia to Barcelona, but was captured by a Nationalist warship and forced into Palma. Pressure from Washington meant she was released on February 1 and sailed to Gibraltar, but without her cargo.[154]

The first two months of 1938 saw several foreign vessels harassed by Moreno's ships, leading to intervention by French warships. In the early hours of January 24, a Nationalist ship captured the French *Prado*, owned by Cottaropoulos and Theophylactos, 8 miles off Palamos while sailing from Marseilles to Barcelona with a cargo of food. Ordered to follow, she radioed for help and the destroyer *Albatros* arrived to force her release. On February 18, warships followed the French *El Mansour* after she departed Port Vendres for Algiers with 150 passengers and fired a warning shot, but she radioed for help and the destroyer *La Palme* forced the Spanish to back down before escorting the merchantman to her destination.

Within the Strait, between August 1937 and February 1938, at least 50 vessels were stopped on suspicion of trading with the enemy and forced into Ceuta for inspections. Usually, they were allowed to proceed, but in the second half of 1937 the Panamanian *Janu* and the Greek *Nagos* and *Gardelaki* were all seized for carrying contraband and requisitioned by the Spanish merchant marine. In January, the Estonian *Juss* and *Pomaron*, carrying coal to Barcelona and Valencia respectively, were seized and their cargoes confiscated. The Nationalists were especially suspicious of Russian ships. On November 26, the freighters *Tsurupa* and *Cheluskinets*, towing the tugs *Chkalov* and *Belyakov* from the Baltic to the Black Sea merchant fleets, were forced into Ceuta but allowed to proceed after inspection. The same fate was suffered by five Soviet merchantmen between December 23 and February 15.

On January 22, the Nationalist cruisers took some respite from escorting convoys to bombard Valencia, the seat of the Republican government, leading to the air attack which damaged the *Cervera*. On January 28, all three cruisers sortied together to cover mine-laying off Valencia by the auxiliary cruisers *Lazaro* and *Puchol*. After refueling at Palma, they returned to patrol the Republican coast during February.[155] The cruisers supported destroyers and gunboats escorting supply ships from Italy to Palma, where auxiliary cruisers and minor vessels took over for the last section to Ceuta and Cadiz.

CHAPTER FIVE

Bats, Boots and Hawks: March 1938–April 1939

In March 1938, the Spanish Civil War entered its final phase with a Nationalist offensive into Aragon south of the Ebro. The defenders were unable to prevent the enemy reaching the sea at the fishing village of Vinaroz on April 15, splitting the Republic in twain, before striking into Catalonia and then towards Valencia, taking Castellon on June 14. In response, the new French government under Blum opened the frontier on March 17 and a great reservoir of arms and munitions flowed south until June 12, boosting Republican resistance. Forces in Catalonia would use the new supplies to launch an offensive across the Ebro on July 25, obliging Franco to abandon the advance upon Valencia.[1] During this period, the Nationalists and their Fascist allies used air power to strangle the Republic, sinking 68 merchantmen (150,854 grt), 31 of them (81,660 grt) from neutral countries; some 85 foreign seamen became casualties, 68 of them fatal, in the bloodiest and most destructive phase in the interdiction of the Republic's sea-lanes.

The Loss of the *Baleares*

However, there was an evil omen at sea for the Nationalist offensive. On March 5, the Cruiser Division under Admiral Vierna—flying his flag in the *Baleares*—sortied from Palma to cover the movement of two supply ships. They were unaware that a Republican task force under Ubieta, with the cruisers *Libertad* and *Méndez Núñez*, plus five destroyers, had sortied to cover a planned MTB attack upon Palma which was abandoned due to heavy seas. That evening, the two task forces accidentally encountered, then lost, each other before blundering into each other again around midnight on March 6/7, some 70 miles off Cape Palos.[2]

Vierna deployed his ships with searchlights and signal lamps, which alerted Ubieta, who used shortwave radio to dispatch his destroyers on a torpedo attack. As they approached, Vierna fired a star shell, silhouetting his ship, and the torpedoes were launched. These were detected by the *Baleares*'s newly installed sonar, but Vierna was unable to prevent two from the *Lepanto* striking the forward magazine and boiler room. Ignited propellant sent a sheet of flame 1,200 metres into the air, incinerating gun and bridge crews, then starting fires throughout the superstructure. Nevertheless, there was no catastrophic explosion, allowing the doomed cruiser to remain afloat for another three hours.[3] Damage control was compromised by the loss of power, and with few emergency lights installed, fires provided the only illumination in the ship, which was listing to port and sinking by the head. The crew had been swelled by dockyard staff and a dozen cadets, but the two task forces withdrew, leaving them to their fate, many unable to swim and with few life rafts.

Fortunately, the British destroyers HMS *Boreas* and *Kempenfelt* saw the pyrotechnics and began a rescue mission; life rafts were thrown, boats lowered, and scrambling nets deployed, but there remained many wounded on the stricken cruiser's deck. The *Kempenfelt* attempted to come alongside, but just as the second attempt was close to success it became clear the cruiser was going down and the destroyer hastily backed off.[4] The destroyers picked up 469 survivors, with *Kempenfelt*'s medical staff treating 130, many with burns, and the Nationalists later sent London a note of thanks. But 788 crew perished, including Vierna and his staff, with one of Cervera's sons as well as a German sonar technician, Jürgen Jensen. More Spanish sailors were lost in this one incident than during the whole of the 1898 war with the United States. The transfer of survivors to the *Kempenfelt* was briefly delayed when nine Katies attacked, mistaking the British vessels for the enemy, bomb splinters wounding five of *Boreas*'s crew, one mortally.

This was Franco's worst nightmare, and afterwards he renewed his plea to Rome for the cruiser *Taranto*.[5] But Ciano feared the diplomatic consequences of breaching the Non-Intervention Agreement, which might threaten the long-sought rapprochement with Britain. Mussolini promised "a more detailed study of the matter" as a face-saving gesture, and agreed to intensify air attacks on ports. On March 7, in retaliation for the sinking of the *Baleares*, a dozen Hawks dropped 7.5 tonnes of bombs on Cartagena, damaging the *Libertad* and *Lepanto*, but this aerial campaign backfired, increasing pressure to end the bombing and renewing British demands for the withdrawal of air squadrons from Majorca.[6]

Ciano's caution was also influenced by events in Austria, whose annexation (Anschluss) by Hitler on March 12 left Rome distinctly uneasy. Early 1938 saw a surge of U-boat activity, with five boats passing through the Strait on training missions while calling at Moroccan ports, followed by the battleship *Scheer* in May. On March 19, Pound was ordered not to attack submerged submarines west of 5° West, but the Germany Navy had already informed its Foreign Ministry on February 7 that it was confining operations to the Atlantic basin.[7] During the crisis, Chatfield visited Gibraltar and met Backhouse and Cunningham, respectively scheduled to be First Sea Lord and Deputy Chief of the Naval Staff, to discuss the European naval situation.[8] The U-boat surge worried the Royal Navy, but in Paris the crisis—and Mussolini's weak response—eroded opposition to the navy's Mediterranean-First strategy, with even French Army chief General Maurice Gamelin agreeing the Germans and Italians were working together. Darlan would inform his fellow chiefs of staff later in March that the navy would soon be strong enough to oppose an Italian landing in Tunisia, fight a decisive battle in those waters, and interdict Italian supply lines to Libya.[9]

Still Trading with the Republic

By the beginning of 1938, the Nationalists' 18-month blockade had largely achieved its primary aim; few arms and little ammunition reached Republican ports, while weapons shipments could be delivered only to western France. Worse still for the Republic, almost all the Spanish gold had been spent, although Moscow granted the Republic a $70 million loan in March.

Nationalist intelligence indicated the importance of maritime traffic in propping up the Republic by calculating that during 1938 there were 1,443 ship movements into Republican ports—including 1,033 British, 156 French, 83 Panamanian, and 18 Russian—importing 4 million tonnes, 451,000 tonnes in March alone and 406,500 tonnes in July. Their claim that 241 ships brought in war materiel was exaggerated, but they admitted 473 brought in foodstuffs, 343 coal, and 172 POL, departing with fruit and minerals which provided much-needed foreign currency.[10] The monthly pattern during the Nationalist offensives and the early weeks of the Ebro campaign is shown in Table 5.1. During this period, much of this traffic was with Black Sea ports, as shown in Table 5.2, bringing grain, raw materials, and POL, with Moscow providing 700,000 tonnes worth $34 million during 1938.[11] With merchant traffic reportedly coordinated from Paris by a committee chaired by the ambassador, Angel Osorio y Gallardo, with much of the loading activity based in Antwerp, much of this trade was in British-registered hulls. They carried 81 percent of the coal trade: Valencia ordered 70,000 tonnes of British coal, this trade being very profitable at £4 ($20) a tonne for Barcelona.[12] French and Spanish vessels tended to come from neighbouring France, notably Marseilles, while transhipments continued in North African ports.[13]

Table 5.1. Ship movements into Republican ports, mid-1938

Month	Total ships	British ships
April	124	85
May	120	84
June	115	79
July	138	88
August	152	103

Source: González, 362–62

Table 5.2. Italian assessment of ships sailing to Republican ports from Black Sea ports, 1938

Period	Ships							
	Russian	Republican	British	Greek	Panamanian	French	Other	Total
January	2	–	13	6	–	–	1	22
February	2	–	10	8	3	–	–	23
March	2	–	17	4	–	1	–	24
April	2	–	10	3	2	2	2	21
May	2	–	12	4	–	1	–	19
June–July	2	–	15	–	1	1	–	19
Total	12	–	77	25	6	5	3	128

Source: Rapalino, Appendix VI

The Hawks Swoop

It was the Italians who spearheaded the interdiction of Republican sea-lanes, with Mussolini demanding a continuous and methodical assault upon the busiest ports, especially Barcelona and Valencia.[14] The Ebro loosely marked a boundary from mid-April until July, with Balearic-based bombers striking to the north while the Legionary Air Force on the mainland bombed to the south. When the Legionary Air Force concentrated upon supporting the battle of the Ebro during the second half of the year, the Balearic bombers carried the burden of interdicting the sea-lanes, with 84 attacks upon ports.[15]

The Falcons' wing flew 494 sorties between mid-March and mid-April and dropped 409 tonnes of bombs, while the Bats flew 114 bombing and 174 maritime reconnaissance sorties between May and December. The Falcons would later claim to have flown 206 missions during 1938 and sunk 150,000 tons of shipping.[16] On June 4, Italian headquarters in Spain proudly informed Rome that in the previous four months 150 ships had been attacked, with 22 British ships sunk and 52 damaged, inflicting 200 casualties upon the crews, 50 of them fatal.[17] The Majorcan bombers maintained the pressure during the second half of the year, with Hawks flying 261 sorties in September and dropping 240 tonnes of bombs, while in November and December Hawks and Bats flew 217 sorties (149.5 tonnes) and 165 sorties (131 tonnes) respectively.[18]

The Majorca force remained under Velardi until June, then General Adriano Monti until December 1938, and General Giuseppe Manceratini until the end of the war. It averaged 35 bombers, of which around 20 were serviceable, flying 24 missions during the first quarter and 47 in the second in daily formations of half-a-dozen Hawks, with night attacks by two or three Bats.[19] They were supported by the *Aniene*, which delivered 425 tonnes of bombs, 30 tonnes of lubricants, and 49 cases

Table 5.3. Merchant ships over 100 grt sunk in ports, March–July 1938

Month	Valencia		Other		Total	
	Spanish	Foreign	Spanish	Foreign	Spanish	Foreign
March	–	–	2 (3,249)	–	2 (3,249)	–
April	–	–	3 (3,564)	–	3 (3,564)	–
May	2 (1,187)	3 (6,741)	1 (1,508)	–	3 (2,695)	3 (6,741)
June	3 (5,830)	6 (20,298)	4 (1,976)	5 (19,084)	7 (7,806)	11 (39,382)
July	2 (6,971)	–	2 (1,545)	1 (1,451)	4 (8,516)	1(1,451)
Total	7 (13,988)	9 (27,039)	12 (11,842)	6 (20,535)	19 (25,830)	15 (47,574)

of spares on March 31 and 350 tonnes of bombs on June 5.[20] The Condor Legion's mainland-based Heinkels also had some success, sinking a couple of ships, and on April 17 flew 59 sorties and dropped 82.5 tonnes of bombs upon the Cartagena naval base in Operation *Neptune* (Unternehmen *Neptun*), but with little effect.[21] The bombers faced weak air defenses, with only a handful of obsolete fighters and guns. A French report noted that Barcelona had nine batteries (27 guns); four of 75mm, two of 105mm, and three of 20mm Orelikon, together with 22 searchlights. Cartagena, meanwhile, had 20 guns of 76–105mm calibre, two batteries of 20mm Oerlikon, and 18 searchlights, and Valencia had four batteries with a dozen 76mm and 20mm Oerlikon and a dozen searchlights.[22]

The high-speed approach of the Hawks made their daylight attacks especially deadly as they gave the defenders little time to warn the population, with the result that the sirens were still wailing as bombs fell to cut down crews and dock workers racing for air-raid shelters. Between March and December, dozens of ships were also showered with splinters which left holes in the hull and superstructure, sometimes making living spaces uninhabitable, reducing lifeboats to matchwood, and cutting steam pipes to auxiliary machinery such as the derricks. Threats to foreign vessels fueled the loudest protests but it was the Spanish merchant marine which suffered worst numerically, with 19 (25,830 grt) sunk from March to July (see Table 5.3) alone, compared with 15 (47,574 grt) foreign vessels although their tonnage losses were greater. Repairs made the vessels seaworthy, but once they reached a foreign port they often required a spell in dry dock. This led to a doleful stream of stories in the press of sunken ships and dead or injured crewmen, many of them foreigners, but the situation is best reflected in studying incidents rather than repeating the mournful list of death and destruction.

Barcelona was a prime target throughout the year, but especially in the second half when there might be two raids in the daytime and one at night to undermine Republican operations. From March 15–18, the bombers' campaign had a secondary objective of terrorizing the civilian population, at the behest of Mussolini and Ciano, who wanted to test Douhet's theories, ignoring Spanish demands they strike only military targets. There were only 47 sorties, but they inflicted 1,900 casualties, 670 of them fatal, arousing a storm of international protest which caused even Bernasconi to question the concept and forced Rome on March 19 reluctantly to order Velardi to strike only military targets.

After a brief delay, Mussolini ordered a resumption on April 6, with Ciano commenting: "Franco doesn't want air raids on cities, but in this case the game is worth the candle."[23] A British Comint summary on April 23 noted: "As the Italian air force in Palma, is now known to have instructions not to inform Spanish Authorities of any activity carried out contrary to General Franco's wishes, these reports from Spanish air force headquarters in Palma can no longer be relied upon to give a complete account of all activity of aircraft based on Majorca."[24] Velardi and Monti kept Rome fully informed, but after hearing from Kindelán that Italian bombers were dropping their loads in the sea, Bernasconi radioed Palma on April 24: "Please … verify this report and above all warn and instruct all personnel that the objectives and results of raids should be kept absolutely secret. This is to prevent Spanish Air Force Headquarters Salamanca from getting official reports of air activity which differ from those that you send to me." Velardi replied that he had photo evidence of bombs having hit targets.[25] On June 29, the British intercepted a Nationalist Air Force report indicating the Italians were no longer withholding information, "and so it would be reasonable to suppose the attacks on Spanish Ports and shipping therein are being carried out with the approval of General Franco."[26]

Despite everything, the attacks upon Barcelona had limited success in the first half of the year, although they injured the *Euphorbia*'s master, Captain Thomas Hilton, and First Mate on May 15. Then on June 20 they damaged the American National Bulk Carriers freighter *Wisconsin*, the company normally being associated with tankers and owned by reclusive billionaire Daniel K. Ludwig, who lived in a Manhattan penthouse. Under the 39-year-old Yankee master Captain Hiram Taft, who had served in both the U.S. Navy and the U.S. merchant marine, she appears to have been the only American-registered ship involved in trading with the Republic. Raids on Barcelona intensified with the Ebro campaign, 15 during October alone, but with limited effect upon shipping.[27] The *Stancroft*, unloading zinc spelter from Montreal, was sunk on October 13; although she was later salvaged, she was sunk a second time while moored under repair on December 27, to be salvaged by the Nationalists. On October 19, the *African Explorer* and *Lake Hallwil* were both badly damaged.[28] Italian bombers also struck other Catalonian ports, with victims including the Spanish *Vicente de Roda* at Palamos on May 9.[29] A raid upon Vallcarca, south of Barcelona, on August 17 hit the *Stanbrook* while loading cement and her forward hold began to fill, while a follow-up raid that afternoon sank her, although she was quickly salvaged, repaired in Barcelona, and returned to service.

South of the Ebro, Valencia was the prime Italian target. Nearly a dozen foreign, largely British, ships were bombed there by early April, leading their masters to send a protest letter to the Foreign Office claiming they were deliberately being attacked despite the fact their nationality was clearly visible and there were no military targets nearby. It was the first of a series of futile protests which fell on deaf ears. On May 7, a bomb blew out the forecastle of the Newbegin Line's *Greatend*, injuring two men and causing a fire which lasted nine hours. Her master, Captain Frederick Fleet from West Hartlepool, telegraphed the owners: "Consider attacks, besides barbarous and inhuman, are now absolutely deliberate against British steamers."[30] Further raids caused the ship to be abandoned, and a hit on the stern sank her on May 28. The crew was repatriated, but the Republican authorities refused to allow the Italian NIC observer to land; when brought ashore by one of the *Thorpeness* boats, he was arrested, and released only after a demand from the British government.[31]

A raid on May 30 set ablaze the French *El Djem*, owned by Cottaropoulos, which had arrived from Barcelona carrying a general cargo from Porte-la-Nouvelle.[32] She was towed out of the harbor and beached as a total loss, while her 34 survivors, furious at the absence of naval protection, abused the crew of the *Indomptable* who came to repatriate them on June 2.[33] During these raids, the *Stanbury's* cook was mortally wounded, and as men from the West Hartlepool-registered *Thurston* ran to the air-raid shelter, one of them, James Montgomery, was critically wounded, as was the boatswain, Robert Jackson, who still rescued him. Newcastle-born Jackson had served in Q-ships as a signalman during the Great War, and reportedly assumed command and sank a U-boat when his commander was killed.[34]

Another protest telegram was sent to the Foreign Office by masters of British ships on May 9: "If British merchant ships [are] allowed [to] trade [with] Spain under non-intervention agreement, neutral zones should be allotted [in] every harbour for discharging and loading legitimate cargoes." They added: "Attacks now ruthless and absolutely deliberate against British ships ... Earnestly desire you take immediate action."[35] Yet during his visit to Valencia on May 27, Vice-Admiral Hugh Binney, commander of the 1st Battle Squadron, said he observed 10 ships flying British flags and more from other nationalities. He reported: "I interviewed several Masters and their general attitude is that they realise the risk they run and consider their recompense well worth it."[36]

Two months later, Captain Henry Mant of the *Farnham* admitted: "We go through at our own risk and we get good wages. There is only a small percentage of the British merchant service engaged in the trade to Spain, and I would not like to think that there is a danger of us going to war because of them. On the three occasions I was bombed, sufficient warning was given to get the crew ashore and a non-intervention observer was the only man killed in the raids ... Shipping should be protected and British rights should be upheld, but if there is a possibility of war, I should not like it to be caused by the few ships going to Spain." Captain L. J. Llewelyn of the *Stanhope*—an experienced seaman who had been trading with Spain for 21 years, carrying cargoes for both sides during the Civil War, having gone to sea at the beginning of the century and twice been torpedoed during the Great War—said: "We have heard a lot about trading with Spain and the profits that are to be made out of it. But I would like to say that seamen do not trade with Spain for profit. I have resigned my ship because I saw the weakness of the British government and at the present time I am out of a job." He suggested the British should bomb the Nationalists to deter them from attacking unarmed merchantmen.[37]

Between June 4 and June 15, the Italians claimed to have dropped 1,000 tonnes of bombs on Valencia.[38] On June 6, the Barry Line's *St Winifred*, which had brought in food, was hit twice, leaving five dead, including the messroom and cabin boys. Towed to Marseilles, she was declared a total loss but was repaired to become the Italian *Capo Vita*, only to be torpedoed by a British submarine on March 9, 1941. The line's managing director, Richard Street, was so sickened by the incident that he ceased trading with Spain. On June 27, the British tanker *Arlon*, which had spent two days unloading a 7,000-tonne cargo of high-octane aviation gasoline—obtained at St Louis, Rhôna (also known as Port-Saint-Louis-du-Rhôn), a suburb of Marseilles—was unloading the last 100 tonnes in her tanks and was due to depart in 30 minutes. But the Hawks struck first, setting her ablaze, killing a Romanian crew member and forcing the authorities to tow her outside the harbor, where she sank off Nazaret beach, a mile to the south. A July 27 raid sank for the second time the Spanish *Kardin* (the former *Cabo Creux*), while the following day bomb splinters struck "Potato" Jones's *Kellwyn* (formerly the *Marie Llewellyn*), killing the Danish observer and a Chinese cook.

The Italians also struck other ports south of the Ebro, notably Alicante, where on June 4 the Pallas Oil and Trading Company tanker *Maryad* was hit and set ablaze. Three crewmen were injured, including the NIC observer, while the second engineer went over the side and drowned. The blaze took a week to control, and three months of emergency repairs followed before she was towed to Marseilles by the Panamanian-registered, French-owned salvage tug the *Authorpe* on October 1, the 22 survivors having been taken to Valencia by the *Dover Abbey*.[39] The ship's misfortune followed her to Marseilles, where sources state that four or five shipyard workers were killed by a blast on December 9 while working in one of the oil tanks. Three weeks later, on June 27, the Alpha Steam Ship Company freighter *Farnham*, which had arrived from Antwerp with sugar, was hit amidships, burst into flames, and later sank. Three men were killed, while the NIC observer was listed as missing, believed dead.

"Iron Gustav" Attacks

The Condor Legion's "Iron Gustav" Harlinghausen had less success, flying around 30–35 sorties a week, half on maritime reconnaissance, with some attacks interdicting

Republican land communications. His attacks sometimes attracted unwelcome publicity. An early morning attack upon Tarragona on March 15 set ablaze Captain D. E. Jones's *Stanwell*, delivering Welsh coal, causing 11 casualties, three fatal, including the Danish NIC observer. Before she departed a fortnight later, she was hit again by the Italians.[40]

In the early hours of May 25, seaplanes attacked the darkened British Westcliffe Line's *Thorpehall*, anchored in the roads awaiting a berth in Valencia's inner harbour after arriving from Marseilles with 3,000 tonnes of wheat. The Boots swooped to put a bomb into the aft hold, but the crew had time to take to the lifeboats before she sank. It was a sign of the economic times that five men—including the cook—were Hull fishermen unable to find berths in trawlers, one of them, Robert Kingston, being a former skipper who signed on as a seaman.[41] London sent a vigorous protest note to the Nationalists, demanding the Burgos government punish those responsible and cease bombing British ships, but Franco rejected this on June 2.[42]

Just before midnight on June 6, a Boot bombed and badly damaged the Hull-registered tanker *English Tanker*, formerly part of the Mid-Atlantic fleet but now operated by Townsend Brothers and under charter to CAMPSA. The vessel was finished off by a second attack shortly after midnight. Another seaplane bombed and sank the Westcliffe Line freighter *Thorpehaven*, which had just arrived from Marseilles with a cargo of wheat, the blast blowing the funnel overboard.[43] Hours later, in Denia, bombs hit the Le Havre-registered freighter *Brisbane*, carrying 4,000 tonnes of sulphate of ammonia fertilizer, causing eight casualties, including the master, of whom five were killed, including the British observer. Later attacks finished her off.

There were two successive successes in Valencia on June 21 and 22. In the first, the crew of the Westcliffe Line's *Thorpeness*, moored in the outer harbor after arriving with 6,500 tonnes of wheat from Marseilles, suddenly heard the roar of engines and the explosion of bombs which hit a hold and the engine room. Captain W. R. Kermode, from Douglas, Isle of Man, who had assumed his first command only a few days earlier, later said: "I knew immediately that the ship was finished." The port-side lifeboat was destroyed, but 25 of the crew and the French observer got away in the starboard boat under the second officer. The remaining crew leapt overboard in panic, some with lifebelts, and the ship sank within 10 minutes, the third ship lost by the line. A port authority motorboat, alerted by the second officer, rescued the remaining men, but Kermode was in the water for three hours until rescued by a boat from the African & Continental freighter *Sunion*, which had arrived in ballast from Oran and was anchored only a mile away. Kermode borrowed some clothes and was taken ashore.[44] The following morning, the *Sunion* was herself hit by incendiary bombs forward and amidships, wrecking the bridge and setting her ablaze. The 32-man crew and her German observer escaped injury and were taken off when it became clear the ship was lost.

The loss of the Welsh-owned *Dellwyn* on July 25 provoked a particular political storm. She had arrived in Gandia from Oran with a cargo of coal and was sunk in the early hours, but with the crew in air-raid shelters there were no casualties. However, anchored half-a-mile off her port side was the destroyer HMS *Hero*, supporting the British Consul, and her perceived lack of action infuriated the British public. The government pointed out that the Royal Navy could not interfere if ships were attacked within Spanish territorial waters, but such arguments fell on deaf ears.[45] On the night of August 7/8, Harlinghausen's men bombed and set ablaze in Palamos harbor the Swiss-owned, British-registered *Lake Lugano*, carrying medical supplies from Antwerp, one crewman being injured. She was towed out and beached, but the next day was strafed and bombed again, the latter splitting her in two. Her master, Captain Thompson, told the press: "I do not object to the bombing, which is all in the game, but the machinegunning of the crew is barbarous and unwarranted. They used the ship for target practice."[46]

After a two-month lull, the Grimsby-registered former trawler *Margaret Rose*, acting as a salvage tug, was hit in Almeria, beached, salvaged, and towed to Marseilles for repairs. At the end of the month, Boots sank the Famagusta-registered *Eleni*, owned by the Inter-Levant Steamship Company and carrying 874 tonnes of general cargo, at Aguilas. In the early hours of December 5, Billmeir's *Stanwell*, moored in Tarragona with 8,000 tons of Welsh coal, was badly damaged and suffered eight casualties, with two dead, including the Danish observer. With their accommodation destroyed, the crew refused to embark and demanded repatriation home; she would return to service after repairs and served the Stanhope Line until becoming a Mulberry harbor block ship off Omaha Beach in July 1944 after the Normandy landings.

Harlinghausen also harassed ships at sea, and during the early hours of March 17 attacked the French *Navarinon*, formerly Billmeir's *Stancliffe*, sailing from Porte-la-Nouvelle to Barcelona. The ship was set ablaze, but her master managed to run her aground near Cape Creus. She was owned by Cottaropoulos, with Strubin as her London agent, but was then sold to Jean Milonas, a Paris-based Greek who renamed her *Lena*—registered in Greece—and towed her to Barcelona for repairs. Hoswever, she was bombed and sunk in January 1939, becoming one of four merchantmen in the Spanish Civil War to be sunk twice![47]

The tanker *Nausicaa*, which as the *Burlington* was captured by the Nationalists in August 1937, was now attacked 20 miles south of Minorca on June 4. She had been sold to M. K. Veniselos of Piraeus, who registered her in Panama under her original name, and was carrying 7,800 tons of crude oil from Maracaibo to Port-de-Bou. She was set ablaze and sank the next day, but the 30-man crew were rescued by the Italian *Securitas* and taken to Genoa. Just over a fortnight later, in the mid-afternoon of July 21, 25 miles southeast of Palamos, a Boot intercepted the Danish *Bodil*, owned like the ill-fated *Edith* by the Lauritzen Line, while carrying coal from Gdynia to Porte-la-Nouvelle and Nice. The seaplane circled several times and her master heaved-to, anticipating it would land and examine his papers. The seaplane made a vain attempt to communicate with a signal lamp, but the Danes could not understand the message. The freighter was then strafed, injuring one man while the crew hastily took to the boats. Once they had pulled away, the seaplane bombed the steamer, which rolled over and sank within a minute. Twenty minutes later, the cruiser HMS *Shropshire*, which had been 14 miles away when she heard the bombs exploding, arrived to pick up the survivors and carry them to Marseilles. Nationalist historians falsely claim the ship was carrying aircraft.[48]

Three days later, the Norwegian Wilhelmsen Line's brand-new motorship *Tirranna*, sailing from the Far East to Oslo, was bombed and strafed by a seaplane west of Tangiers. Incendiaries caused fires which were quickly extinguished, but one of her officers was killed and the master slightly injured. French and British warships escorted her to the Strait, and when she arrived in Antwerp a Nationalist representative boarded to exress regret for the attack, but denied it was by a Nationalist aircraft. The master, diplomatically, stated he had not been able to say which side attacked him.[49]

There was a curious incident on October 13 involving Captain James Simpson's collier *Lucky*, returning in ballast to Port-de-Bou, having delivered coal to Port Mahon on Minorca. She had no radio, so the seaplane used a signal lamp to order her to Pollensa Bay, Majorca, where she was boarded by a German officer. After meeting the observer, he allowed her to proceed, claiming she had been mistaken for a Russian, but as Simpson pointed out, the light signal was in English.[50] Pollensa Bay remained the home of AS/88 and the Nationalist seaplane squadron, whose Gulls were reinforced in August by four Cant Z.506 Heron (*Airone*) triple-engined seaplanes, which flew their first mission on October 6, dropping bags of bread on Alicante as a propaganda gesture. One, piloted by Rámon Franco, was lost on October 28 during a bombing mission to Valencia after suffering engine problems.[51] He was succeeded by the seaplane squadron commander, Lieutenant Colonel Fernando Sartorius y Díaz de Mendoza, Count of San Luis San Luis. The squadron had 11 seaplanes, having scrapped their ancient Dornier Whales, by the end of the year augmenting the eight German He 59s.[52]

Seaplanes from there attacked three British and French ships in the western Mediterranean in November, mostly without effect. Following these attacks, Lord Halifax wrote to the Admiralty seeking the return of the flying boat squadrons deployed in Oran a year earlier.[53] On December 29, a Heron bombed and strafed the Greek-owned, British-registered *Marionga*, carrying coal from Oran to Barcelona, 20 miles off Cape Sant'Antonio, forcing the 30-man British crew to take to the lifeboats. Although the ship was undamaged, the crew awaited the arrival of the French destroyer *Siroco* before reboarding.[54] Republican Katies damaged the Trieste-registered Italian freighter *Etruria* on June 4 and attacked two French destroyers off Catalonia on August 9, without effect, but an attack on Nationalist warships off Majorca on November 20 claimed several hits.[55]

The potential threat from sabotage also continued, with three curious incidents involving tankers at the end of the year. On November 4, the *Stanburgh* was loading gasoline in the French port of Étang de Thau, southwest of Montpelier, when an explosion started a fire, which also destroyed five trucks on the quayside; the ship was towed out of the harbor and beached. She burned all night and, although subsequently refloated, was a constructive total loss and was scrapped. Whether this was an accident or sabotage was never established, but a fortnight later the Republican tanker *Torras Ybages* also caught fire in the same port, while on December 10 in Marseilles, the British tanker *Maryad* suffered fire damage.[56]

Assessing the Attacks

The Italians were delighted with the effects of the aerial offensive, especially in the first half of the year.[57] Velardi reported on July 5: "The effectiveness of the aerial bombardments of the Levant ports was daily shown by the increasing protests from elements of the Left." One of his intelligence reports noted: "The Reds' situation is very serious as only nine of the 31 steamers are available to supply them because the others have been sunk." He concluded: "If the intense bombardment of steamers in Red ports had continued for another month there would have been no possibility of resistance."[58]

The opening of the French frontier by Blum's government, and maintained by Daladier's, ensured some 25,000 tonnes of military aid crossed the border until British pressure forced the reluctant French to close it again on June 12. Still, it meant little war materiel was sent by sea. The closure was also influenced by the desire for rapprochement with Italy, together with industrial demand for Spanish pyrites from Nationalist-held territory.[59] To prevent the shipping of war materiel down the coast, Kindelán informed Ramón Franco on March 22 that attacks upon Port-de-Bou should be intensified, although the Germans did not make the first raid until March 30.[60] Yet the supplies which crossed the frontier sustained and encouraged the Republican resistance, as the Nationalist Foreign Ministry ruefully admitted to the Germans.[61]

But as Kindelán informed Velardi on May 31: "The incessant and effective bombings on the main Red harbors have increased the daily difficulties of transport for these ports. This fact is due mainly to the demoralization of the crews."[62] He claimed seven British ships in Marseilles were refusing to sail to Republican ports, while the disruption of supplies was confirmed by a U.S. air attaché who visited Valencia in June 1938 and noted that all the warehouses and quays had been damaged, while berths were blocked by wrecks.[63] The constant need to seek air-raid shelters delayed unloading, sometimes for up to a week, forcing ships awaiting cargoes to remain in port for two or three weeks at a time, their crews sleeping ashore.[64] In mid-March, it took a fortnight to unload the Abbey Line's *Neath Abbey* when she arrived in Valencia, while the raids on Barcelona delayed the departure of the *Margam Abbey*, meaning her insurance expired, costing £2,735 ($12,854) to renew. Despite the Mid-Atlantic Shipping Company paying £333 ($1,565) for the delay, the voyage made a profit of only £202 ($950), and for economic reasons the line reduced its Spanish activity from three ships to one.[65] The insurance problem was aggravated on June 20 when Lloyd's of London raised insurance rates by 25 percent for ships using Republican ports. The strain on NIC observers was also great and there was a steady stream of resignations, posing serious concern about maintaining the system, but the majority continued to risk both life and limb.[66]

Italian headquarters in Spain claimed on August 15 that the percentage of British ships serving Republican ports in July had dropped from 70 to 63.[67] By September, the number of ships entering Republican ports halved, and such were the perceived dangers that 40,000 tonnes of imports were trans-shipped from Oran, adding to the Republic's expenses. Yet during the second half of December, 140 vessels brought 446,000 tonnes of supplies into Republican ports.[68]

In June, Moreno assured foreign navies he had forbidden attacks upon their ships and that aircrew were ordered to identify their targets, while the Nationalists did attempt to restrain their allies. On June 9, Kindelán informed Rámon Franco that while his brother had authorized the bombing of "Red" ports, the bombers were to avoid civilian casualties or damaging foreign warships, passenger, or prison ships to prevent enemy propaganda. But Franco appears to have been ambiguous on the issue; while on June 20 Kindelán ordered Velardi to cease nocturnal raids to avoid hitting neutral shipping, six days later he was claiming it was essential to avoid hitting British and French ships on the high seas and, as far as possible, in ports. The following day, he suspended attacks on ports for four days, yet on June 22 he thanked Velardi for attacks upon the ports, which if maintained for a month, he said, would end "Red" resistance.[69] To avoid the odium, the Germans requested the Nationalists to deny that German bombers had struck Valencia in June.[70]

Britain and France made numerous futile protests about the Italian bombing campaign. British ambassador Eric Drummond, the Earl of Perth, warned Ciano several times that attacking British ships undermined attempts at a rapprochement. Yet it remained Chamberlain's priority to drive a wedge between Rome and Berlin, while Mussolini in turn sought to divide London and Paris. Chamberlain vainly hoped to shield British shipping through diplomatic pressure, implementing non-intervention, and warnings to Franco. On April 16, rapprochement appeared to have achieved success with the Easter Agreement, which recognized the Italian occupation of Abyssinia in return for Mussolini's promise to withdraw his forces from Spain when the war ended. Both parties hoped this triumph of appeasement would help to achieve their goals, but the bombing undermined this aim.[71]

The Royal Navy was skeptical about the Easter Agreement and as Cunningham observed: "Nobody was prepared to trust anything Mussolini said or signed ... As our merchant ships were being bombed almost daily by Italian bombers in and outside the Spanish ports it was not easy to work up cordiality."[72] Nevertheless, the fleet was ordered to prepare for the visit of an Italian squadron to Malta at the end of June, Admiral Arturo Riccardi arriving with the battleships *Conte di Cavour* and *Giulio Cesare*, together with four destroyers. Pound, who liked fast cars, took his guest for a drive around the island that left the Italian very shaken.[73] A few weeks later, the Mediterranean Fleet held its annual sailing regatta at Navarino Bay (now Pylos), allowing Pound to brief Cunningham, who would replace him in June 1939.[74]

In late June, the bombing created a crisis for rapprochement. The Republican government threatened reprisals against Majorcan bases, only back-tracking under strong British and French pressure on June 25, but Rome took no chances. On July 1, the Italian Air Force Operations Division ordered planning for a retaliatory mission against Barcelona using some 150 aircraft, employing "violence and great intensity." The Republican threat was renewed, and on July 6 Kindelán informed Rámon Franco that in this event, reinforcements would be sent to Majorca for an 80-bomber attack upon Barcelona.[75] On June 27, ambassador Grandi telephoned from London and warned Ciano the attacks had aroused British public opinion and put Chamberlain's government under considerable pressure, facing 17 Parliamentary questions the following day. On June 28, Lord Perth requested an end to the campaign, noting that 22 British ships had been attacked between mid-April and mid-June, with half sunk or badly damaged. However, Ciano claimed Rome had no infuence and noted that Mussolini seemed "very calm" and refused to put pressure upon Franco. Franco's only public concession, on June 27, was to propose making Almeria a safe haven, with strict controls for commercial traffic, but Barcelona rejected this because only 14 percent of ships trading with the Republic could use the harbour at any one time, and supplies could not reach Catalonia.[76]

Parliamentary anger at the government's supine response to attacks upon the Red Ensign saw an increasingly bellicose Opposition. During a debate on June 23, former wartime premier David Lloyd George proposed bombing Majorca and Labour leader Clement Attlee suggested blockading the island, while Sir William Brass asked if the merchantmen could carry the "pom-pom" light antiaircraft guns to defend themselves.[77] With a safe majority, the Conservative government rejected all these ideas, Chamberlain pointing out that the Royal Navy could not intervene within Spanish territorial waters, but was doing so on the high seas. He said it was the shipowners' responsibility whether or not they entered Republican ports, and his comments on "King" Billmeir bordered on the anti-semitic. Having said the installation of "pom-poms" was a matter for the owners, he rhetorically asked Parliament whether or not it wished to arm British ships so the owners could get big profits? He did, however, accept William Wedgewood Benn's suggestion that he meet two Cardiff-based masters of bombed ships, Lewis Llewellyn of the *Stanhope* and D. E. Jones of the *Stanwell*.

The Opposition case was weakened by the absence of practical solutions, for few MPs were briefed on the issue. Even the Labour Party's major critic, Philip Noel-Baker, a Quaker and League of Nations supporter, later admitted he simply relayed telephoned complaints from ship-owners.[78] He commented: "Of course, no-one suggested that Britain go to war to stop … attacks on British shipping. It was wholly unnecessary to do so. Action much short of war would have been entirely efficacious e.g. the supply of arms to the Republican government, or the withdrawal of British Ambassadors in Rome & Berlin or even a debate in the League Council and a British Naval escort for the ships which were engaged on their 'lawful occasions.'"[79] The sinking of the *Dellwyn* added fuel to the fire, with talk of blockading the Balearics, bombing Italian airfields, and even sinking one Nationalist ship for every British ship sunk, but once again it came to nothing.

To justify the attacks, the Nationalists published a list on June 12 of 200 British ships they claimed had carried war materiel since January 1, 1937, but it demonstrated instead the inadequacy of their intelligence, confirmed by postwar examination of records. Some ships were not on any shipping register while there were wild claims about the Bright Navigation Company's *Muneric*, the Gothic Steamship Company's *Gothic*, Angel Sons' *Bramden*, and the Abbey Line's *Neath Abbey*. Ship-owners such as Claude Angel and Edward Newbegin indignantly dismissed the claims, accurately claiming that foreign-owned vessels were responsible for transporting war materiel to Republican Spain.[80] These included France-Navigation ships which brought into French ports arms shipments I-51 to I-53 between June and August, as well as carrying POL to the Republic.[81]

The Royal Navy vigilantly ensured British ships complied with the Carriage of Munitions to Spain Act, as was demonstrated with Billmeir's *Stancroft* when she arrived in Valencia from Barcelona. Her German NIC observer, Captain Hintze, informed the commander of HMS *Hyperion* that she was carrying munitions, and a boarding party on May 9 compelled her to sail to Gibraltar, where 17 boxes of spent cartridge and shell cases, nine aero-engines, and other "contraband" were discovered. Her master, Captain Stanley Scott, was charged with contravening the act, but the remainder of the cargo was reloaded and she returned to Valencia under Captain S. L. Spence.

Scott was defended by Labour Hammersmith North MP Dennis Pritt, a Communist sympathizer who in 1931 defended Ho Chi Minh against a French attempt to extradite him from Hong Kong. Pritt successfully argued that the transport of war materiel between Spanish ports did not contravene the act, and Scott was found not guilty, but this was overturned by Gibraltar's Supreme Court following an appeal by the Crown. The strain of the trial caused Scott to suffer a fatal heart attack before its judgement, and with him died the case.[82]

In the furore, British and French ASW patrols steadily declined, although the French deployed 16 destroyers and torpedo boats, most drawn from the Atlantic Fleet, allowing the Mediterranean Fleet to conduct intensive exercises to improve training at all levels. To counter air attacks, the French reinforced patrols, but from May the numbers of ships assigned to protect merchantmen was steadily reduced. On June 17, Pound proposed abandoning ASW patrols from the Strait to Majorca, and four days later the Admiralty agreed, warning him to keep this secret. From March 1938 to the end of the war, the Royal Navy continued to protect British ships trading with Republican Spain.[83]

Woe unto the Greeks

For much of the Civil War, Greece and Greek ship-owners supplied military aid to both sides, rather like Great Britain during the American Civil War.[84] Athens was happy to accept at face value war materiel end-user certificates, and regarded violations of the Non-Intervention Agreement as the ship-owner's responsibility, but the Nationalists took their revenge as they gained the upper hand.[85]

The NIC was also frustrated, and on June 29, 1937, secretary Francis Hemming complained to the Greek ambassador in London, Charalambos Simopoulos, that some Greek ships were retaining their NIC pennants for illegal use. The NIC noted that from April 19 to November 24, 1937, 34 Greek ships had complied with its provisions, while nine sailed to Spanish ports without observers, this figure rising to 19 by June 1938. In fairness, the Greek Foreign Ministry was also ignored by the Merchant Shipping Secretariat, and matters were not eased by ship-owners playing shell games. A day after the *Laris* arrived in Marseilles on May 23 with 400 tonnes of "heavy cargo," supposedly for Vera Cruz in Mexico, a favorite end-user certificate destination, she was renamed the *Shepo* and registered in Panama, giving the master the excuse to reject the Greek Consul's efforts to inspect his papers. One of the most complex arrangements involved the *Jaron*, which was owned by Paris-based Georgios Kokotos, who bought her from France-Navigation. In September 1937, she picked up a SEPEWE cargo worth £1.5 million ($7.5 million) in Gdynia and departed with two masters, John Williams and Nicolas Vassilakis, allowing her to switch British and Greek ensigns at will. During the voyage to a port in western France, she was sold to A. G. Papadakis, based in London and Galati in Romania, and renamed the *Vena*.[86]

However, Nationalist naval intelligence was very well informed about Greek arms shipments to its foes, and the exasperation of Burgos at Athens's "double game" led to growing pressure from the spring of 1938, beginning with Nationalist harbors banning Greek crews from coming ashore.[87] Control of the Strait allowed the Nationalists to turn the screws. Greek ships sailing past Gibraltar had been stopped for inspection since the uprising, and in the last quarter of 1937 alone eight were inspected but allowed to proceed. Before 1938, only the *Gardelaki* had been seized, in March 1937, but now they began harassing Greek vessels which were not sailing to Republican ports.[88]

On May 27, the Nationalist Foreign Ministry protested to the Greek diplomatic agent, Admiral Argyropoulos, about six Greek ships transporting war materiel to "Marxist Spain." Argyropoulos wrote to Metaxas, warning that Nationalist wrath was growing, and they had rhetorically asked him: "What harm have we done to Greece that she should kill us with their ammunition?" The previous month, Nationalist commerce raiders had begun hunting ships which supplied their foes, and in a three-month campaign ranging into the Sicilian Channel seized the *Hellinikon Vounos*, *Nagos*, and *Victoria*, the latter, at 6,600 grt, being the Nationalist Navy's largest foreign prize. Their cargoes were seized and the ships pressed into service, while during the year another 18 shared their fate. Simopoulos observed on June 10 that the Nationalists now seemed to regard anything transported to the Republic as contraband.[89] The Greek Foreign Ministry protested to Burgos about the harassment of their ships and "arbitrary arrests," and said that even though Greek ships were carrying war materiel to the Republic, this did not legitimize the Nationalists' actions.

Lloyd's of London were quickly involved, London brokers Lambert Bros informing ship-owners Rethymnis & Kulukundis on June 17 that war risk premiums would be twice as much for Greek ships as for others, although it was also extended to Panamanian and Russian vessels. Ambassador Simopoulos warned Metaxas that these new premiums threatened the whole Greek merchant marine, while the alarmed Greek Shipowners Association, EEE, believed it was a ploy by their British competitors. They sent Metaxas a lengthy memorandum on August 26 which said 100 ships were laid up due to increased premiums. They warned that the merchant marine was being driven out of export markets and losing charters for cargoes from the Soviet Union to French ports. They also claimed the Nationalists had privately informed underwriters they would capture or sink all Greek-registered vessels.[90] The Merchant Shipping Secretariat warned masters on August 17 that the Nationalists were fully informed about the activities of the Greek ships, the only way to protect themselves being to avoid charters to Oran and Marseilles and cargoes destined anywhere in Spain.

The Nationalists suggested to Argyropoulos on September 14 that Greeks might avoid harassment either by ending voyages to Republican ports or providing Burgos with full details of voyages through the Strait. To emphasize their "proposals," their Strait patrols compelled nine Greek vessels sailing from Soviet Black Sea ports into Ceuta for inspection, then seized the cargo of the *Garoufalia*, despite the papers showing it was for a Dutch customer, ignoring Dutch government protests. The Greek shipping community in London described this as "silent persecution," while the EEE argued owners were not always aware of the ultimate destination of cargoes loaded in French ports, but their protests fell on deaf ears. Worse still, Lloyd's warned Simopoulos that with the cargoes of Greek ships now facing higher risks they might not be insured at all.

A postwar blacklist of 400 ships banned from Spanish ports included 53 (13 percent) Greek, and by the end of the war 60 Greek-registered vessels had been forced into Nationalist ports. To avoid this fate, some EEE members accepted humiliation and provided the Nationalists with details of voyages, which ensured their freedom to pass through the Strait. The doom of the Republic eased the problem for Athens, for fewer ships were finding voyages profitable and many began looking at the profits trading with China.[91]

The Fruits of Success

Somerville succinctly summarized the naval situation in mid-1938: "The Nationalist navy has almost complete command of the sea, but seems to do singularly little with it."[92] The loss of the *Baleares* was a major problem, but, as Franco informed Mussolini on March 20, it also highlighted the need to strengthen the Nationalist fleet to escort convoys from Italy.[93] The old light cruiser *Navarra* (formerly *República*) joined the fleet in July, while the salvaged Republican destroyer *Císcar* was comissioned just before the end of the war, but in the late summer the *Cervera* had to be withdrawn for a long-overdue refit. Franco again pressed for the sale of the *Taranto*, as well requesting another two destroyers, but the cruiser would remain under the Italian ensign until scuttled in September 1943.[94] As a sop, Mussolini agreed to increase Italian monitoring of Republican maritime traffic, which led the Nationalist Navy to capture several ships in the Sicilian Channel.[95]

The Nationalists retained a tight grip on the Strait, and although Germany's CaptainCiliax encouraged Moreno to greater efforts, fewer ships were stopped in those waters by March because of Franco banning interfering with British and French shipping.[96] The exceptions were ships on the blacklist, such as those of Stanhope and France-Navigation, and only Anglo-French naval intervention saved them. The Nationalists improved the efficiency of their blockade in June by creating 14 boarding vessels, which rotated the task using 10 dedicated teams. In September, the numbers in each team were reduced, possibly reflecting a manpower shortage permanently embarked in the boarding vessels.[97] Soviet ships were harassed as much as those of the Greeks, with six (19,600 grt) seized in 1938 and pressed into Nationalist service, including the *Komsomol*'s sister ship, the *Max Hölz*, while another 10 had their papers inspected.

During the summer, Cervera's headquarters moved to Burgos to improve strategic and diplomatic coordination.[98] The capture of Vinaroz and then Castellon gave the Nationalists new supply bases for their forces, but they could not be used for the blockade as Republican bombers were a frequent threat, sinking schooners at Benicarlo on May 3 and in Vinaroz on September 1.[99] Supplies and 6,000 reinforcements were routed into the captured ports via Palma, and extensive use was made of captured "Castillo" freighters such as the *Castillo Mombeltrán*, the former *Hellinikon Vounos*.[100]

The Republican fleet remained passive, despite the recommissioning of the *Miguel de Cervantes* and the arrival of the repaired submarines *C-2* and *C-4* from France during the third week of June. The destroyer *Jose Luis Diez* reluctantly departed Le Havre on August 20, 1938, and headed south, topping her bunkers from the captured merchantman *El Saturnino* before sailing towards the Strait and sinking two Nationalist trawlers off Huelva. She made two attempts to break through the Strait, on August 26 and December 29, but was damaged each time and driven into Gibraltar, where she remained until the end of the war. The spring defeats saw Prieto lose his Defence portfolio to Premier Negrín, who replaced Fuentes with former submariner Lieutenant Commander Prado, who would in turn be relieved by Buiza in January 1939. But the fleet made no attempt to support the embattled Ebro front.[101]

The Italian Navy continued to escort supply ships from Italy. From New Year's Day 1938, pairs of Navigatori and Sauro-class destroyers stationed in Palma, Malaga, and Tangiers became the 6th Naval Division (6a Divisione Navale), under Rear Admiral Moriondo in the destroyer leader *Quatro*. The original vessels were replaced by Mirabello and Turbine-class ships. Moriondo was relieved by Rear Admiral Paolo Maroni on July 1, but a month later the *Quatro* suffered a boiler explosion in Pollenca, with 35 crew becoming casualties, seven of them fatal. The old vessel was scrapped and replaced by the destroyer *Emanuele Pessagno*, flying the flag of Rear Admiral Alberto Lais, until the division was disbanded in September.[102]

The Munich Crisis

Germany's threat to attack Czechoslovakia over alleged mistreatment of the German minority in the Sudentenland brought the threat of a European war over Czechoslovakia in the fall of 1938 and drove Spain off the front pages, leading to a key meeting in Munich in what came to be called the Munich Crisis. Britain, France, and Germany all mobilized for war, with Hitler threatening to annex the largely German-speaking western region of Czechoslovakia, but Chamberlain and Daladier capitulated and signed the infamous Munich Agreement on September 30, whereby the Sudetenland was ceded to Germany. The prospect of war offered the Republicans the brief hope of fighting on the Allied side and snatching victory from the jaws of defeat, while Franco, recognizing his own isolation, notified the Germans on September 26 he would be neutral. Rome learned of this only from the German ambassador, Hans-Georg Mackensen, infuriating Ciano, who instructed Chief of the Air Staff General Valle to begin planning the withdrawal of the mainland air squadrons, but leaving the troops.[103]

From mid-August, the OKM recalled the *Scheer*, three torpedo boats, and six U-boats to the homeland, although the *Deutschland* visited Ceuta from September 20 and three supply ships were moored in Spain's Atlantic ports as covert support for operations against Allied sea-lanes. When the crisis abated, the German naval presence off Spain was reduced to a pocket battleship and a couple of U-boats, but during July and August, 13 Special Ships delivered 2,200 men and 6,900 tonnes, compared with a monthly average between January and June of four ships, 460 men, 2,000 tonnes, a rate restored from September.[104]

Nationalist concerns about the security of Spanish Morocco during the crisis led to 10,000 troops being rushed across the Strait in auxiliary cruisers and minelayers.[105] The threat was real, as on September 5 the French Navy dispatched seaplane-tender *Commandant Teste* and four submarines to Oran and Casablanca. When France mobilized on September 23, the Navy Ministry ordered preparations for operations against Germany and Italy, reinforcing the fleet with Vice-Admiral Esteva's DSM vessels, the admiral being appointed commander of the Mediterranean Fleet on September 28. Soon after the Munich Agreement, he proposed to the ministry a reduction of the patrols between the Balearics and Spanish coast, but wished to maintain the Nyon ASW patrols to ensure "unidentified submarines" did not harass traffic.[106] The Royal Navy mobilized on September 28 and concentrated in Alexandria and the eastern Mediterranean. Pound fretted at his lack of supplies and resources, noting that he had only 23 destroyers to meet a wartime requirement for 40, and required another two light cruisers, 11 destroyers, and 14 submarines.[107]

In seeking a joint naval strategy, Daladier argued that the bombing of Barcelona, the Nationalist offensives, and Italy's refusal to condemn the Anschluss all demonstrated Germany and Italy were growing closer. Chamberlain reluctantly agreed, but Britain's Committee of Imperial Defense demanded that talks be confined to attaché level, with a Germany-first approach. A furious Darlan had no option but to accept, although the Royal Navy's weakness meant the French would ultimately dictate Mediterranean naval strategy and be responsible for the western waters. After the crisis passed, Darlan successfully pressed for a more aggressive French Navy strategy in the Mediterranean, while recognizing the country faced a dual threat from Germany and Italy.[108]

Rome was also considering its strategic options, and the Palma-based 6th Naval Division was deactivated. After the Munich Agreement, however, destroyers returned to Palma, augmented in early 1939 by the light cruiser *Luigi de Savoia Duca degli Abruzzi*, while seven Taranto and Naples-based destroyers and torpedo boats continued to escort supply ships.[109] As late as June 26, the Italian General Staff's Operations Division drew up Plan V (Piano V) for an amphibious assault by two divisions north of Valencia to take the Republican capital. The plan reflected CTV commander General Mario Berti's frustration at Franco's refusal to take his advice, but was eventually cancelled because Franco feared it would encourage British and French intervention.[110]

The response to Plan V and the growing crisis in Europe helped to reshape Mussolini's Spanish commitment. To strengthen his forces in metropolitan Italy and improve relations with London, Mussolini decided on August 22 to reduce the size of the CTV. Franco objected, but following prolonged discussions between Burgos and Rome it was agreed to withdraw 10,151 men who had 28 months' overseas service.

The move, enthusiastically supported by the British Foreign Office and the NIC, was quickly implemented. Four of the Region-class liners—*Sardegna, Liguria, Calabria,* and *Piemonte*—sailed to Cadiz and departed with the troops on October 5, escorted by a 2nd Fleet task force under fleet commander Admiral Pini, flying his flag in the heavy cruiser *Trieste*, and with eight destroyers. They arrived in Naples to a heroes' reception on October 20, being met by King Victor Emmanuel and Ciano.[111]

Into the North Sea

The Munich Crisis delayed implementation of a Nationalist plan for a foray into the North Sea, where the SIPM had identified 37 Spanish merchantmen trading for the Republic. Only after the easing of international tensions did the auxiliary cruisers *Ciudad de Alicante* and *Ciudad de Valencia* sortie on September 29, but they were driven back by bad weather—like the Armada of 1588—and a month passed before they reached Emden in northwest Germany. Their orders were to interdict trade in the Skagerrak–Rhine–British Isles triangle, but British and French ships were off limits. The two-month campaign saw the *Ciudad de Alicante* make three sorties and the *Ciudad de Valencia* four, with the former capturing the *Río Miera* on October 30, outside the British 3-mile limit, when she emerged from the Humber.[112]

Three days later, the *Cantabria*, a vessel with a bloody history, was intercepted by the *Ciudad de Valencia* off the Norfolk coast. Originally the prison ship *Alfonso Perez* in Santander, where 276 prisoners were massacred on December 27, 1936, she was renamed and reverted to her freighter role. Her first voyage was to Cardiff, arriving with iron ore on June 1, and she later made trans-Atlantic voyages and trips to Narvik in Norway. On November 2, under Captain Manuel Argüelles, she was sailing in ballast from Gravesend on a charter from Mid-Atlantic to Sunderland and then to Leningrad. Argüelles had on board his wife and two children, together with the wife and three children of another officer.

Realizing he was being shadowed, Argüelles made for the coast, but in the early afternoon the cruiser fired a shot across the *Cantabria's* bows and ordered "Heave-to or I fire." British fishing vessels reacted by sailing towards the cruiser with blaring sirens, causing her to withdraw, but when they departed she returned with guns blazing. Shells destroyed the bridge and disabled the engines, killing one member of the crew, injuring two, and setting the ship ablaze. Watched by appalled British and Norwegian merchantmen, the cruiser circled the listing ship and opened fire with machine guns.

The crew took to the boats, but the captain, his family, and a steward remained aboard, fearing capture. Responding to the *Cantabria's* distress call, the *Pattersonian* under Captain Blackmore arrived and steered across the bow of the cruiser to pick up 11 men from one lifeboat, but the cruiser captured the other, which contained 20 men. The Cromer lifeboat *H. F. Bailey* now arrived, with 62-year-old coxswain Henry Blogg at the helm, recovering from an operation for appendicitis. Argüelles signaled them with a torch to come alongside, allowing everyone to abandon ship, although the lifeboat's stanchions were damaged when the freighter suddenly heeled over and sank. The lifeboat took them to Cromer, while the remainder of the crew was landed in Great Yarmouth.[113]

The loss of the *Cantabria* and the capture of the *Rio Miera* sent ripples across the North Sea. While seeking sanctuary in Norwegian waters, the *Guernica* ran aground and was lost, the *Cabo Quintres* had a narrow escape when pursued by the *Ciudad de Valencia*—but managed to take refuge in Bergen, where she remained for the duration—and three more merchantmen decided to lay up in British and Norwegian waters.

A fortnight after the *Cantabria* was sunk, Danish police broke up a German Naval Intelligence network run by Horst von Pflug-Hartnung, nominally a correspondent for the *Berliner Börsen Zeitung* but a friend of Abwehr chief Canaris who had established his seven-man cell in 1932. He and other German "journalists," together with three Danes, were found with radio transmitters and numerous official charts, and were apparently monitoring the activities of the *Cantabria* and other vessels. Pflug-Hartnung was jailed for 18 months, but pressure from Berlin meant he was soon released and worked for German Naval Intelligence throughout World War II.

Running the Final Gauntlet

In preparation for the Nationalist offensive into Catalonia, the Hawks concentrated upon Barcelona from December 20, while bad weather grounded the Bats for almost the whole month.[114] Franco considered a supporting amphibious assault, but the Nationalist Navy lacked the resources and planning was abandoned, which was unfortunate as the land offensive, which began on December 23, quickly stalled until early January.

As the offensive's pace increased, and the Nationalists closed on Barcelona, the city attracted a quarter of the Balearic Falcons' 47 attacks in January, with another 29 in February.[115] The Condor Legion's Heinkels joined the feeding frenzy on January 21, flying 131 sorties against the city, including three by Junkers 87 dive-bombers, or Stukas, developed by the Condor Legion's new commander, Major General Wolfram von Richthofen, a cousin of German World War I ace Manfred von Richthofen (the "Red Baron"). These attacks sank eight merchantmen, five of them foreign.[116] The attacks also saw a steady stream of fatal casualties: the second mate and a Greek mess boy of the *Thorpebay* on January 3, and six days later the chief engineer of the *Alresford*. After the latter's funeral, the captains of British ships in Barcelona sent a telegram to Chamberlain, who was in Rome, demanding full government protection for men and ships conducting legitimate trade. The National Union of Seamen also sent the Premier a telegram demanding he press the Italians to use their influence to cease attacks upon British shipping.[117]

On January 22, the infamous arms smuggler *Yorkbrook* was sunk after being towed into Barcelona when her engines failed. The *African Mariner*, unloading frozen meat and wheat, was hit in a series of raid which killed four Greek crewmen, although she did not sink until January 24, by which time the Spanish liners/prison ships *Argentina* and *Uruguay* had also been sunk. Two days later, the day the Nationalists entered the city, the British tanker *Miocene*, which had brought in a cargo of benzine from Porte-la-Nouvelle, was also sunk, together with another infamous arms smuggler, the Marseilles-registered *Yolande*, formerly the Mexican *Jalisco*.[118]

These raids spurred the departure from Barcelona of every foreign ship which could raise steam on January 24, although an Admiralty tug had to escort two of Billmeir's ships to Port Vendres following aerial harassment. The victorious Nationalists found the silence of the tomb had fallen on what had been a bustling port, with 32 wrecked ships (57,000 grt) in the harbor. The Nationalists based patrol boats and minesweepers there, and during February Italian ships made five trips to Barcelona, bringing in 3,230 tonnes of much-needed food for the civilian population, three in the former auxiliary cruiser *Barletta*.[119] Catalonia's smaller ports were also attacked, and on January 14, as the Nationalists closed in on Tarragona, Stukas flew their first dedicated missions against shipping, claiming the Spanish coaster *Barcino* and some smaller vessels, while Boots sank three schooners between January 25 and February 8.[120]

The aerial onslaught—which damaged at least 17 British ships in the first two months of 1939—the shortage of destinations, and the Republic's declining fortunes meant there was a steady decline in ship movements into Republican ports (see Table 5.4) during the last months of the war. While the Nationalists dubiously claimed that 13 vessels brought in war materiel, they admitted 156 brought in either food or coal.[121] Significantly, after the fall of Barcelona, Alfred Pope, whose *Seven Seas Spray* broke the Bilbao blockade and who boasted: "General Franco is not going to keep a single one of our ships from going about its lawful occasions," ceased trading with Spain and shortly afterwards sold all his shipping interests.[122]

With the loss of Barcelona, Valencia remained the prime destination, attracting 11 raids by the Balearic Falcons during January and nine in February.[123] On the afternoon of January 27, the Falcons hit the Irish former Limerick Line freighter and former Q-ship *Foynes*, which was now owned by Mid-Atlantic.[124] She had arrived

Table 5.4. Shipping movements into Republican ports, 1939

Month	Total	British	French	Greek
January	119	91	12	2
February	66	52	6	3
March	39	24	13	1

Source: González, 400

from Marseilles a week earlier and was loading a cargo of oranges when she was hit, the crew being repatriated to Marseilles in HMS *Hostile*.[125] When the Nationalists occupied Valencia, they found 35 wrecks (23,000 grt), most of them sunk in 1939.

There were also attacks on the high seas, such as on February 6, when Billmeier's *Stangrove*, carrying mercury, sulphur, nitrate potash, and nitrate ammonia from Valencia to Port de la Selva, was bombed and strafed. The master, Captain William Richards, ordered the crew into the lifeboat, but he remained; when the aircraft flew off, the crew reboarded, although owing to rough seas a lifeboat was wrecked. The following day, a Nationalist destroyer arrived and forced her to sail to Barcelona, where several of the 15-man crew—five of them British—and the NIC observer were jailed. She was then sailed to Palma, Majorca, where the Nationalists agreed to release her due to a British protest and the absence of war materiel in her holds. However, during a gale on February 23 she parted her moorings and was driven ashore in the inner harbor; the crew discovered Captain Richards, who had refused to leave the ship, dead in his cabin. A surveyor doubted she was salvagable, but the Nationalists did so and she became the *Castillo del Oro*.[126]

It was poetic justice on the afternoon of January 20 when the Italian-operated *Aniene*, the backbone of the Italian air offensive, was attacked by Katies south of Ibiza while sailing from Palma to the mainland, escorted by the Italian torpedo boat *Orsa*. Near misses holed the freighter, setting two cases ablaze, but she returned to Palma, escorted by the Italian destroyer *Usodimare*, and her cargo was transferred to the *Castillo de Soller*. The *Aniene* was repaired in Italy and made two more voyages.[127]

The Republic's Last Days

When Soviet Defense Commissar Voroshilov asked about new Republican arms supplies on February 16, Stalin replied: "The question is no longer important."[128] With London recognizing the Nationalist government on February 27, many Republicans grew rightfully concerned about their future, including the Minorca garrison, where the Royal Navy helped to broker a deal. Britain's Majorcan consul, Hillgarth, learned that garrison commander Admiral Ubieta was willing to surrender the island and informed the Foreign Office, which was anxious to ensure it would not become an Italian base.

To act as a neutral forum, the Admiralty assigned HMS *Devonshire* under Captain Gerard Muirhead-Gould, the Scottish laird of Bredisholm and former head of British Naval Intelligence in Germany between 1933 and 1936. The *Devonshire* dropped anchor in Port Mahon on the morning of February 7, carrying the Balearics' air commander, Sartorius, a former naval colleague of Ubieta, who was rowed out to the British cruiser. The negotiations were compromised by Italian air raids personally led by General Manceratini, but negotiations continued after Palma guaranteed they would not be repeated.[129]

The next morning, the handover of the island was agreed, provided those most at risk of the Nationalists' wrath would be evacuated. On February 9, news got out and hundreds of people rushed to the docks. Muirhead-Gould embarked 425 of them, filling three sackloads of pistols in the process, and before dawn on February 10 he sailed to Marseilles. That afternoon, four auxiliary cruisers, a destroyer, and a minelayer landed a division of Nationalist troops, and from February 12 three destroyers and some small surface combatant vessels arrived to use the base facilities. Moreno apologized to Hillgarth for the Italian bombing and formally requested the Italian Air Force withdraw from Majorca.

The Republic faced either surrender or continuing a hopeless struggle, but the leaders could not decide when they met at the Los Llanos air base on February 26. Buiza warned that because of poor air defenses, the fleet might have to leave Cartagena.[130] He then joined Colonel Segismundo Casado López in planning a coup against Negrín to negotiate an end to the conflict, but when he informed warship commanders of his intentions on March 2, many opted for outright surrender. To secure his position, Negrín decided on a military reshuffle, including appointing the Communist Colonel Francisco Galán Rodríguez as Cartagena's commander on March 4. Nevertheless, Casado launched his uprising that night. In Cartagena, Buiza arrested Galan, but loyal forces held some 15-inch coast defense batteries and helped Negrín's troops to suppress the rebellion, leaving the fleet uncertain as to its future.

This uncertainty, and a Balearic Falcons raid which damaged two destroyers, confirmed Buiza's belief that the base was no longer secure, so he sortied with the cruisers *Libertad*, *Cervantes*, and *Méndez Núñez*, eight destroyers, and the submarine *C-2*, which promptly defected to Majorca. When it became clear on the morning of March 6 that the rebellion had been crushed, Buiza headed for the Mers-el-Kebir base, but the French promptly ordered him to Bizerta, where he arrived on March 11. By now Paris too had recognized the Burgos government, and on March 26 Moreno sailed into Bizerta in the destroyer *Císcar* to assume command of the fleet. When he led it back to Spain on April 2, only 2,278 of the fleet's 4,300 men opted to return to Spain, many of the remainder—including five ship commanders—being used for forced labour or joining the French Foreign Legion. Delays in returning both the Republican fleet and the Basque fishing fleet were said to have compromised Paris's appointment as the new ambassador of Marshal Philippe Pétain, who had led French forces during the Rif War.[131]

Learning of Buiza's departure, Rome concluded that he intended to join the Soviet Black Sea Fleet. To prevent this, on March 6, the Italian Naval Staff ordered extensive air and surface surveillance of the western Mediterranean and the Sicilian Channel, using eight destroyers and four torpedo boats suported by seaplanes. The Sicilian screen was reinforced the following morning by the light cruiser *Giovanni delle Bande Nere*, supported by 17 destroyers and torpedo boats from Sicily Naval Command under Iachino's Training Division (Divisione Scuola). They were supported by the Balearic Falcons and part of the 1st Fleet (1a Squadra), the heavy cruisers *Fiume*, *Pola*, *Zara*, and *Gorizia*. They were later joined by the battleships *Cavour* and *Caesare* and eight destroyers under Riccardi, whose orders were to force Buiza to enter Augusta, engaging them only if they resisted. However, after trailing Buiza to Bizerta, the Italians stood down.

With only a vague idea of the kaleidoscopic situation in Cartagena, Franco demanded that troops be sent to support the rebels. Cervera ordered Moreno to embark troops at Castellon and land them in Cartagena, with 3,000 in the auxiliary cruisers *Mar Cantabrico* and *Mar Negro* and three minelayers, covered by the *Canarias* and two destroyers. Another 4,000 embarked in the slow old freighters *Castillo de Olite* and *Castillo de Peñafiel* and the former Russian vessels *Postishev* and *Smidovich*, whose radios the Nationalists had been removed![132]

Four 15-inch (381mm) and 16 6-inch (152mm) guns defended the base and engaged Moreno as he approached on the morning of March 6, one 15-inch shell narrowly missing the *Canarias*. His task force remained offshore, unable to warn the follow-up force, and as the *Castillo de Olite* approached the coast, defense guns began firing. A 15-inch shell hit her, detonating ammunition and splitting her in two, leaving only 700 survivors of the 1,923 troops to be picked up by fishing boats.[133] Delayed by air attacks, the *Castillo de Peñafiel* did not arrive until the early afternoon and was shelled, together with the Dutch merchantman *Aurora*, as they approached Cartagena. Only the Spanish vessel was damaged, but managed to reach Ibiza, while a destroyer warned off the other two transports.

On March 8, the Nationalists ordered all ships carrying cargo to "Red" ports to enter "White" ports and warned they would deploy submarines to enforce the new diktat.[134] Seeing the way the wind was blowing, most ship-owners refused to risk their vessels. There were relatively few air attacks upon ports during March; the Falcons made only four, sinking a Spanish schooner in Cartagena. The *African Explorer* appears to have been the last British ship damaged during an attack by mainland-based bombers on March 19, but she was able to sail for repairs to Oran, where she arrived on March 21. The absurdity of the situation facing foreign navies was highlighted on March 22 when a Boot, hunting foreign merchantmen, force-landed at sea north of Ibiza. The frozen crew were picked up by a British destroyer, which took them to Palma and warmed up the airmen with whisky, ensuring they were in brighter spirits when they disembarked.[135]

On the evening of March 10, the *Bellwyn* and *Stangate* were intercepted off Cape Sant'Antonio as they sailed from Valencia to pick up oranges at Almeria. The *Bellwyn* radioed for help as the unidentified warship tried to jam her radio, but her master refused to submit. After an hour the warship gave up and went after Billmeier's *Stangate*, forcing it to sail towards Palma, then HMS *Intrepid* and *Impulsive* arrived in response to *Bellwyn*'s "Mayday" and at her request went after the *Stangate*. They quickly found her, forced the Spanish to back down, and escorted the freighter to Gibraltar.[136] However, on March 17 she was again stopped by the auxiliary cruiser *Mar Negro* off the Spanish coast and compelled to sail to Palma, where she remained until after the war, the last foreign ship taken by the Nationalist Navy. The radio of the *Stanhope*, sailing from Gandia to Gibraltar, was also jammed when a Nationalist warship intercepted her on March 16 and ordered her to Palma, but part of the message was intercepted by the heavy cruiser HMS *Sussex*, which freed the merchantman in what was the last intervention of its kind.[137]

The final weeks of the Spanish Civil War saw thousands trying to flee by sea, and Negrín would later claim that Casado's uprising and the fleet's departure wrecked his plans to evacuate 40,00–50,000 people. When London recognized Burgos, Chamberlain announced the Royal Navy would not prevent Spanish warships stopping merchantmen departing with refugees. However, on February 16 the Foreign Office informed the British consul in Valencia, Mr Abingdon Godden, that he could make arrangements to evacuate the desperate Republicans. Even without this official sanction, British warships and merchantmen were already helping thousands to flee as the Republic began to collapse. One of the first was the *Stancor* with 200 refugees, which departed Valencia on the night of March 14/15 to be met at the 3-mile-limit by HMS *Devonshire* and escorted to safety.[138]

As Nationalist forces surged forward, meeting little resistance, thousands of desperate people fled to Alicante, seeking passage. The French Communist Party arranged for 380 of their Spanish comrades to escape in France-Navigation's *Lézardrieux*, but it was British ships which bore the brunt of the evacuation, with four departing on March 30. They included Billmeir's *Stanbrook*, which was due to load tobacco, oranges, and saffron, but her master, Captain Archibald Dickson, was stunned to see thousands of people crowding the port and decided to embark as many as possible. He departed with 2,683 of them, who were in the crew's accommodation, on decks, in the holds, and even in the lifeboats. The freighters departed low in the water and without lights to avoid interception. The other ships had 2,743 refugees between them, of which about half were on the *African Trader*, and all sailed to Oran in a two-day voyage with limited food and water and sanitary facilities which were quickly overwhelmed. The latter problem provided the French authorities the excuse for refusing to allow passengers to disembark, ostensibly because they might cause epidemics; even to moor his ship, Dickson had to threaten to ram the quayside.[139] A Spanish Socialist politician, Rodolfo Llopis Ferrándiz, managed to persuade the authorities to allow the women and children to disembark, but the men remained aboard for up to three months. The French authorities offered no warm embrace when they did disembark, with refugees put into "reception centers," which were actually forced-labor camps, matters improving only with the arrival of the Allies in North Africa in the fall of 1942.

The Foreign Office authorized some refugees to embark in Royal Navy ships. On the morning of March 29, the destroyer HMS *Nubian* entered Gandia to find

200 refugees, including army commander General José Miaja Menant. As they embarked, some troops also forced their way aboard, although they were later persuaded to disembark at Alicante. Some 190 people, including a sick Casado, embarked in HMS *Galatea*, which departed on March 29, the general later being transferred to the hospital ship HMHS *Maine*. Meanwhile, the last cities of Republican Spain fell; Madrid on March 27, followed respectively by Valencia, Alicante, and Almeria on March 29, 30, and 31. Franco announced the end of the Civil War after a thousand days on April 1. On March 29, the *Atlantic Guide* sailed into Valencia, unaware of its fall, to pick up refugees, undaunted even by a strafing aircraft. Even more remarkably, in the chaos she was able to embark refugees and depart. On April 20, the NIC dissolved itself, having not met since July.[140]

Yet the seas were not safe, with drifting mines remaining a hazard. One had sunk the French *Artois*, owned by Marseille Maritime or Societé de Navigation Côtière, in the Alboran Sea 35 miles southeast of Gibraltar on August 14, 1938, as she carried general cargo from Marseilles to Casablanca. The 14-man crew had time to take to the boats and were soon picked up by the German *Theresa L. M. Russ*. The line, owned by an E. Huret of Rouen, had three small coasters which often operated between Marseilles and Barcelona. On February 25, 1939, the Greek *Loulis*, sailing from Port Vendres to Gandia, was lost following an explosion off Cape Creus. The saddest loss, however, was on March 8. The French freighter *Saint Prosper*, owned by Société Naval de l'Ouest, was sailing in ballast from Algiers to Marseilles with 300 tonnes of crude oil in drums. She encountered a storm and her master, Captain Jules Langlois, decided to ride it out off Puerto Rosas, but she struck a drifting mine and split in two, taking down all 27 of the crew, the last foreign seafarers lost in the conflict.[141]

CHAPTER SIX

The Flotsam of History

For a brief six months, sailors did business in Great Waters facing only natural hazards. In June 1939, France-Navigation's *Ploubazlanec*, which once delivered Soviet war materiel to western France but was now carrying wheat and general cargo from Tunis to Cueta, ran aground near Cape Bon, and although towed off, sank on June 27. Months later, the Soviet Union signed a Non-Aggression Pact with Germany, and in 1940 the French government seized the line's assets.

The German and Italian expeditionary forces returned home in triumph, the Germans the first to depart in six KdF liners, including the fleet flagship *Robert Ley*, which arrived in Vigo on May 23. Meanwhile, two of Veltjens's Special Ships, which had brought in 700 tonnes of food and medicines, departed for Hamburg on the night of May 25/26 with war materiel, including some of the latest combat aircraft.[1] The liners departed with 5,000 men the following day, escorted by the *Graf Spee*, flying Marschall's flag, the *Scheer*, six destroyers, and torpedo boats, arriving in the Elbe on May 31 to be greeted by Goering in his yacht.[2] During the conflict, AS/88 flew 850 sorties, lost seven seaplanes, and claimed to have sunk 30 ships (90,000 grt).[3]

On the day the Condor Legion returned to Germany, 20,390 Italian troops departed from Cadiz in nine "Region" liners which had brought the CTV three years earlier. They were escorted by the cruisers *Gorizia* and *d'Aosta*, with 10 destroyers, and arrived in Naples on June 6. The 5,000 airmen followed shortly after in the *Sardegna* and *Piemonte* from Alicante, departing on the morning of June 18 and reaching Naples on June 28. The last bombers flew out of Majorca by the end of May.[4] The Italian Navy sharpened its blade five days after the Spanish Civil War ended when the battleships *Cesare* and *Cavour*, six cruisers, and 23 destroyers and torpedo boats participated in the invasion of Albania, supporting landings by troops in nine transports.[5]

The Butcher's Bill

In supporting the Nationalist cause, Italian historians claimed that 140 Italian warships conducted 870 "special missions," although an official report of May 27,

1939, stated that 89 surface vessels conducted 677 missions, with 91 patrols by 58 submarines. Another source says there were 114 patrols by 92 boats.[6] In 40 attacks, they sank six merchantmen (19,022 grt), while Spanish submarines also sank six (16,643 grt). Their campaign demonstrated the limitations of the Italian submarine arm. During the forthcoming global conflict, it would sink in the Mediterranean, its home waters, only 15 merchantmen, including three fishing vessels, totalling 39,337 grt in 64 attacks.[7] Italian airmen were a scourge to merchant fleets. From November 1937 to March 1939, the Majorca-based Falcons Wing flew 639 sorties, dropping 1,293 tonnes of bombs, with 70 raids on Valencia and 51 on Barcelona. They exaggerated in claiming to have sunk 40 steamers and a sailing vessel, as well as setting ablaze a tanker and a cargo ship for a total of 132,000 grt, while damaging two cruisers, six destroyers, and 50 steamers, all for the loss of just three bombers.[8]

Shipping losses are difficult to calculate, with Spanish sources giving postwar figures (see Table 6.5) ranging from 52 ships (129,000 grt) to 106 (191,555 grt), sometimes excluding sailing vessels and fishing boats, but including auxiliary warships. In the eastern ports, the Nationalists discovered a total of 93 wrecks (132,800 grt) of merchant and naval vessels. A Russian source gave more detailed figures, claiming the Republic lost 99 ships (172,893 grt) to enemy action, including 63 steamers, 19 sailing vessels, and 13 fishing vessels. In addition, 14 vessels (22,115 grt) were lost to natural causes, including seven steamers and two dredgers. It is claimed the Nationalists lost six vessels (4,253 grt) to enemy action, including two fishing boats, while nine (8,208 grt) were lost to natural causes, including three sailing vessels.[9]

There are questions on the Spanish methodology illustrated by Alcofar, Marina IV, and VI, in which some of the ships named cannot be traced, such as the "800 grt *Arroutado*," the "300 grt *Campico*," the "*Tesar Pelsaven*," and the "*Cap Luis*," while some claimed sunk in Barcelona and Valencia are not shown in the same author's wreck diagrams in *La Aviacion Legionaria en la Guerra Española*. There are also inaccuracies in displacement figures, such as the 66 grt schooner *Antonio Matutes*, which Alcofar gives as 400 grt, while the 96 grt tug *Dalmatic* is shown as 195 grt, the figures being contradicted by González Echegaray's *La Marina Mercante y el Tráfico Marítimo en la Guerra Civil*.[10]

A careful examination of losses of vessels over 100 grt (see Tables 6.6 and 6.7, as well as the Appendix) suggests the Nationalists and their allies sank, beached, or

Table 6.5. Nationalist claims for ships sunk

Method	Republican (grt)	Foreign (grt)	Total (grt)
Aircraft	35 (89,950)/39 (79,251)	30 (79,358)/28 (72,213)	65 (169,308)/67 (151,464)
Ships	13 (18,408)	14 (54,172)	27 (72,580)
Total	48 (108,358)/52 (97,659)	44 (133,530)/42 (126,385)	92 (241,888)/94 (224,044)

Source: Alcofar, Aviación, 259; Cervera, 422; Mattesini II, 167–68

Table 6.6. Republican ships lost to enemy action

Cause	Steamers	Fishing	Sailing	Miscellaneous	Total
Air	40 (102,827)	7 (1,532)	12 (2,015)	7 (3,325)	66 (109,699)
Surface Ship	11 (52,252)	9 (1,286)	–	–	20 (53,538)
Submarine	6 (33,359)	1 (112)	3 (449)	–	10 (33,920)
Mine	–	–	1 (426)	–	1 (426)
Miscellaneous	3 (5,171)	–	–	–	3 (5,171)
Total	60 (193,609)	17 (2,930)	16 (2,890)	7 (3,325)	100 (202,754)

Note: Figures in parenthesis are grt displacements

Table 6.7. Foreign ships lost to enemy action

Cause	Steamers	Sailing	Miscellaneous	Total
Air	35 (89,705)	2 (389)	2 (622)	39 (90,716)
Surface Ship	4 (11,505)	–	–	4 (11,505)
Submarine	4 (14,704)	–	–	4 (14,704)
Mine	4 (7,242)	–	–	4 (7,242)
Total	47 (123,156)	2 (389)	2 (622)	51 (124,167)

made constructive total losses of 145 (306,734 grt), including 123 (303,089 grt) merchantmen, 17 (2,985 grt) of them sailing vessels, 14 fishing boats (2,541 grt), together with dredgers, yachts, and salvage vessels.[11] While international attention focused upon neutral vessels sunk, including 23 British ships (73,188 grt), 59 percent of the merchant ships lost were registered in Spain. These statistics do not include ships sunk twice and exclude the British *Stanburgh* on November 4, 1938, and *Ulumus* on January 18, 1939, both of which Lloyd's attributed to an accident. Nor do they include the alleged sinking of the French schooner *Belle Hirondelle* off Las Palmas on May 2, 1937, which is not confirmed by French sources.[12] The Republicans sank three Nationalist merchantmen (4,067 grt), the Norwegian *Gulnes* (1,196 grt), and three fishing boats (322 grt) to enemy action. The war also threatened several thousand men, women, and children—sometimes in error, sometimes deliberately, and occasionally through negligence. There were some 400 casualties in foreign-registered vessels of men, women, and boys, of which 171 were fatal, although this may be an underestimate, while dozens of Spanish seamen perished or were injured, together with 187 passengers in the *Ciudad de Barcelona*.

According to Cervera, the blockade stopped 538 foreign ships, of which 98 had their cargoes seized, while 23 were pressed into Nationalist service.[13] He also claimed his ships seized 202 Republican vessels (262,599 grt), although an Italian source stated that 227 Spanish ships (257,577 grt) was the real figure.[14] Some indication of the harassment suffered is shown in Table 6.8, in which "Incidents" refers to vessels which

Table 6.8. Impact of the Spanish Civil War upon merchant marines

Nationality	Incidents		Ships seized		Ships sunk		Total
	Nationalist	Republican	Nationalist	Republican	Nationalist	Republican	
American	6	1	–	–	–	–	7
Argentinian	2	1	–	–	–	–	3
Belgian	1	–	–	–	–	–	1
Danish	36	–	1	–	2	–	39
Dutch	8	–	–	–	1	–	9
British	260	8	–	–	24	–	292
Estonian	7	–	2	–	–	–	9
Finnish	3	–	–	–	–	–	3
French	57	2	7	–	4	–	70
German	–	9	–	–	–	–	9
Greek	60	–	5	–	4	–	69
Italian	–	5	–	–	–	–	5
Lithuanian	1	–	1	–	–	–	2
Lebanese	1	–	–	–	–	–	1
Mexican	1	–	–	–	–	–	1
Norwegian	45	3	2	–	–	–	50
Panamanian	5	–	5	–	5	–	15
Portuguese	–	1	–	–	–	–	1
Romanian	1	–	–	–	–	–	1
Soviet	125	–	7	–	3	–	135
Swedish	9	1	–	–	–	–	10
Yugoslav	1	–	–	–	–	–	1
Total	629	31	30	–	43	–	733

were stopped for an inspection of their papers or attacked, either on the high seas or in harbor.[15] This shows there were more than 730 incidents, 702 involving Nationalist forces, with 43 ships sunk, although these figures exclude those lost to mines.

Aftermath

Britain and France sought to assess the naval lessons of the Spanish conflict, during which the British Chiefs of Staff Committee issued six reports, including COS #685 of February 17, 1938, which noted 81 air attacks upon merchant ships, of which six had been sunk and 29 damaged, a 15.6 percent success rate. While the paper drew no conclusions, the Royal Navy strove to improve its Antiair Warfare capabilities and was procuring light air defense guns for merchantmen.[16] The Royal Navy's actions have frequently been criticized. Edwards comments: "For it is now clear that the response of the British government to naval problems contributed positively to Franco's ultimate victory ... the Admiralty under Sir Samuel Hoare was consistently and emphatically anti-Republican."[17] But this ignores the Royal Navy's problems, which forced the Admiralty reluctantly to accept in February 1939 that it could no longer fight simultaneously in Europe and Asia, with First Sea Lord Backhouse deciding to abandon the Far Eastern task force strategic concept despite this exposing most of the Empire.[18]

Darlan's attitude towards Italy further hardened and he shocked his fellow chiefs of staff in January 1939 by announcing plans to interdict Italian communications with Libya and to bombard their naval bases, while the British would help neutralize the Dodecanese Islands. These plans were opposed because they compromised the Germany-first strategy, but Darlan believed a short-term offensive against Italy was compatible with this concept.[19] As London and Paris drew nearer to military alliance in early 1939, the CPDN met on March 9 and hammered out a compromise in which there would be no attacks upon the Italian mainland, but if Rome attacked their African colonials there would be an offensive against Libya.[20]

In September 1939, the long-feared European war erupted and spread over the globe, with many ships and brave crews being sucked to the bottom in the maelstrom, as illustrated by the fate of the Stanhope Line. It began the war with 17 ships (45,282 grt), but lost a dozen to enemy action or accidents, while three were sold. Of the lost ships, submarines sank nine, including the *Stanbrook*, which had carried to safety so many refugees from Alicante. She was torpedoed in the North Sea on November 18, 1939, and sank like a stone, carrying Captain Dickson and 19 crew to the bottom. To replace the lost 41,128 grt, Billmeir bought 18 vessels (105, 315 grt), but seven of these (36,336 grt) would be lost during the war, leaving him with 13 ships (73,133 grt).[21]

The Stanhope Line alone lost 233 men. It has not been possible to determine the fate of most of the merchant seamen mentioned in these pages, but "Potato" Jones (of the *Marie Llewellyn/Kellwyn*) survived the war and would die aged 92 in 1965.[22] Yankee blockade runner Hiram Taft returned home on the liner *Europa* in April 1939, after the *Wisconsin* was sold to a Norwegian shipping line, Rederi A/S, as the *Nidarland*. He remained with the U.S. merchant marine during the Battle of the Atlantic and emerged unscathed, unlike the *Nidarland*, which was torpedoed and sunk on November 9, 1942, while on passage from Buenos Aires to Baltimore with a cargo including silver ingots. After the war, Taft came ashore and in 1953 became secretary and treasurer of the United Merchant Marine Officers' Association. A couple of years later, he became a Wall Street analyst and continued in this unusual career path until his death in Brooklyn in 1971.[23]

Juan Cervera was promoted to admiral in May, but retired in August 1939 and died in 1952. The Moreno brothers did well; Francisco became base commander first of Cartagena and later Ferrol, where he died in 1945, while Salvador was Navy Minister from August 1939 until 1945 and a major opponent of Spain entering the war on the Axis side, then as Navy Minister again from 1951–57 he helped rebuild the service before dying in 1966. The two submarine commanders, Boadilla and Suances, both had distinguished postwar careers, rising to admiral. Boadilla was Naval Attaché in London in 1950 and Naval Chief of Staff from 1966, dying in 1979, eight years before Suances. Buiza became an officer in the French Foreign Legion and settled in North Africa, but with Algerian independence he moved to Marseilles in 1962, where he died a year later. After being interned in France, Ubieta emigrated to Mexico in 1940; he became the master of a merchantman but went down with his ship off Columbia in 1950.

Of the British admirals, Chatfield retired in August 1938 and died in 1967, while Backhouse died in July 1939, to be succeeded by Pound, who remained until 1943 and died on Trafalgar Day, October 21, 1943. Somerville was invalided out with suspected tuberculosis in 1939, but returned to help develop naval radar then head the troubleshooting Force H. After two years as Commander in Chief of the Eastern Fleet, in October 1944 he became head of the British naval delegation in Washington, D.C., where he surprised everyone by establishing good relations with the U.S. Navy's abrasive, Anglophobic Chief of Naval Operations, Admiral Ernest J. King. Blake returned to the colors in April 1940 to become Assistant Chief of the Naval Staff, and later was the liaison officer with the U.S. Navy in Europe.[24] In May 1941, he had the melancholy duty of determining the circumstances in which his old command, HMS *Hood*, was lost. After the war, he was the Parliamentary official "Black Rod" until 1949, in a role which every year saw the Commons ceremonially slam the door in his face! He died in 1968, five years after Cunningham, whose distinguished career peaked with his signal of September 11, 1943: "Be pleased to inform their Lordships that the Italian battle fleet now lies at anchor under the guns of the fortress of Malta." Kennedy-Purvis, who commanded the 1st Cruiser Squadron, became Commander in Chief of the America and West Indies Station, and played a major role in the 1941 destroyers-for-bases deal, later being made a Commander of the Legion of Merit. He became Deputy First Sea Lord and died just after the war.

Of the junior officers, Clifford Caslon remained in destroyers until November 1944, when he commanded a battleship, and after postwar service he died in 1973. *Havock*'s commander, Rafe Courage, died in 1960. A heart condition denied Muirhead-Gould wartime command at sea, but he headed a board examining the loss of HMS *Royal Oak* in October 1939. Although he officially retired in July 1941, from February 1940 until September 1944 he was Naval Officer in Command at Sydney Harbor. He was not popular, especially when in June 1942 he refused to believe midget submarines were attacking and delayed alerting the harbor defenses. He died shortly after becoming Flag Officer Western Germany at the war's end. Bryan Scurfield, of HMS *Hunter*, served with distinction in destroyers but was captured in June 1942, being fatally wounded in 1945 while in a column of prisoners as it was strafed by Allied fighters.

Darlan became the French Navy's commander in chief at the outbreak of World War II and later a minister in the Vichy French government. In November 1942, as Vichy armed forces commander in chief, he ordered the defenders of Algeria and Morocco to cease fire after the *Torch* landings, but was assassinated the following month. Esteva, who commanded the Mediterranean Fleet from September 1938, was jailed after the war for loyally serving the Vichy regime. He was pardoned in 1950, but died just a few months later. Of the DSM commanders, Gensoul would be confronted by Somerville at Mers-el-Kebir in July 1940, with tragic consequences for the almost 1,300 French sailors who died when the British sank the battleship *Bretagne* and badly damaged several other French warships to prevent them being seized by the Germans. Until he died in 1973, Gensoul never publicly commented on these events. Muselier was one of the few officers who would rally to the Free French, but had an acrimonious relationship with De Gaulle, who once freed him from a British prison. He retired in 1946 and died in 1965.

There were mixed fortunes for the Germans involved in the Spanish Civil War. Hermann Boehm commanded forces in Norway until 1943 and lived until 1972. He was relieved by Otto Ciliax, who died in 1964, and whose "Channel Dash" in February 1942—when the *Scharnhorst, Gneisenau, Prinz Eugen*, and several other German warships were allowed to leave Brest and steam through the Channel to their home bases in Germany—helped to undermine Pound's reputation. Rolf Carls was on the shortlist to replace Raeder in 1943 as head of the Kriegsmarine, but when Dönitz was selected instead he resigned his commission to avoid friction, being killed in an air raid in 1945. Fischel was involved in planning for the invasion of Britain, Operation *Sealion*, and retired in November 1944, but was captured by the Russians and died in a PoW camp in 1950. Wilhelm Marschall would be Fleet Commander during the Norwegian campaign of 1940, but disputes with his superiors meant he spent most of the war in shore postings. He lived on until 1976. Of the U-boat commanders, Harald Grosse was lost in February 1940, while Kurt Freiwald had a distinguished career and would become a rear admiral in the West German Navy, living on until 1975. Veltjens continued commercial work for Goering after rejoining the Luftwaffe and died in an air crash in 1943, although his shipping line survived until the end of World War II.

Italian Navy Chief of Staff Cavagnari was dismissed for a series of setbacks in 1940 and died in 1966. Iachino led the Italian fleet in several clashes with the Royal Navy during World War II, including the battle of Cape Matapan, but he remained on the active list until 1954 and died in 1976. The 2nd Fleet commander,

Pini, spent most of World War II on administrative duties, refusing to collaborate with the Germans after their 1943 occupation but resuming his career in 1944. A well-known historian, he would write a dozen books before his death in 1959. Paladini, whose ships terrorized the Sicilian Channel in 1937, would succeed Pini until invalided out in 1940, but remained commander of the Naval Academy until his death in 1943. Submarine Fleet commander Antonio Legnani died in a car accident in October 1943; of his subordinates, only Criscuolo and Longobardo commanded boats during World War II, the latter being the oldest Italian submarine commander lost in the war in 1942. Moccagatta died in 1941 during a special forces raid upon Malta. Borghese also served in Italy's special forces, collaborating with the Germans, but after the war he became the blackshirts' "black sheep," was expelled, and died in Spain in 1974. Margottini, who played a key role in the defence of Majorca in 1936, was mortally wounded in a clash with the Royal Navy in the Sicilian Channel in October 1940.

Of the civilians involved in the Spanish Civil War, Samuel Hoare became ambassador to Spain from 1940–44, despite loathing Franco, and by funding sympathetic monarchist senior army officers he helped prevent Spain joining the Axis. He pursued a variety of interests after the war until his death in 1959. After three decades working in the City of London, Charles Strubin went home to Basel in 1948; he died there three years later after founding a shortlived shipping line. After World War II, Jack Billmeir participated in negotiations on behalf of Lloyd's underwriters with the Spanish government to secure compensation for ships which the Nationalists had salvaged. The man whose ships had once been banned from Spain, and claimed a cargo of oranges from Spain contained a time bomb, succeeded in regaining £90,000, for which the Salvage Association gave him a grandfather clock. He would live through the rapid decline of the British merchant fleet due to the end of the Empire and the failure, unlike the Greeks and Danes, to participate in the postwar maritime business and technological revolutions. In February 1952, Billmeir put the Stanhope Steamship Co into voluntary liquidation and his management company, J. A. Billmeir and Co, followed in March 1953. He re-formed the line, but when he died in 1963, he had only three ships, which were quickly sold. Alan Hillgarth became naval attaché in Madrid at the outbreak of World War II and was heavily involved in espionage, including Operation *Mincemeat*, "The Man Who Never Was," the successful ploy to make the Axis forces believe the Allis were set to move into the Balkans in the summer of 1943 rather than invade Sicily. After the war, Hillgarth became a recluse in Ireland, where he died in 1978.

Thorkill Rieber, who had literally fueled Franco, ignored American neutrality after the outbreak of World War II to channel oil to Germany. In June 1940, with other U.S.-based pro-German business leaders, he threw a banquet to celebrate the German conquest of Western Europe in the Waldorf Astoria Hotel, New York, attended by a German spy. British Intelligence alerted the press, and the ensuing scandal forced him off the Texaco Board. After the war, Rieber played a major role in negotiations with the Iranian oil industry. He died in 1968. Daniel Ludwig, who owned the sole American blockade runner, would go on to revolutionize merchant shipping finances and pioneered the construction of supertankers after World War II. He died in 1992.

Lest We Forget

The events of World War II inevitably overshadowed the effect of the Spanish Civil War upon foreign navies and merchant ships, and it was not until after General Franco's death that there was any attempt to commemorate their actions. The first was in Alicante, where a bust of Captain Dickson was unveiled, while in 2019—after a 15-year struggle by the Glasgow branch of the National Union of Rail, Maritime and Transport Workers, supported by the International Brigades' Memorial Trust—a memorial to The Blockade Runners to Spain, sculpted by Frank Casey, was unveiled on the Clyde walkway in Glasgow next to the Jamaica Street bridge. The memorial lists all the British ships lost, together with the names of 43 Royal Navy and Merchant Navy men killed, as well as the nearly 50 badly injured.

Sadly, and as usual, the lesson of history has been that no-one learns the lessons of history. Shipping is still subject to attack in conventional conflicts, as the 1980–88 Iran-Iraq War demonstrated, and other harassment, such as state-sponsored action from Iran's Revolutionary Guards or China's paramilitary forces, as well as from pirates operating off poorly policed, or lawless, shores. Only if navies are willing to "wave the cutlass," like happened at Nyon in 1937 or as Washington did against Iran in the Persian Gulf in 1987, is there any hope of safety from harassment. But now, as then, few are willing to do so for fear of poking the shark of international protest.

Appendix

War casualties over 100 grt in the Spanish Civil War

Name	Date of attack	GRT (type)	Flag	Cause	Location
African Mariner	Jan. 24, '39	6,581	Great Britain	Air	Barcelona
Alcira	Feb. 4, '38	1,387	Great Britain	Air	Off Barcelona
Alicante	Jan. '39	3,878	Spain	Air	Barcelona
Almeria	Nov. 7, '38	564 (dredger)	Spain	Air	Almeria
Alonso	Unknown	252 (dredger)	Spain	Air	San Esteban de Pravia
Alvarez Feijoo	Sep. 14, '36	112 (fishing boat)	Spain (N)	Submarine	Gran Sol
Amalia	Feb. 4, '37	108 (fishing boat)	Spain	Warship	Off Malaga
Ambos	Jan. '39	342	Spain	Air	Barcelona
Amparo	Unknown	772	Spain	Air	Valencia
Andra	Apr. 4, '37	1,384	Panama	Warship	Off Castro Urdiales
Andutz-Mendi	Jan. '39	1,601	Spain	Air	Barcelona
Asunción de las Peñas	Jan. '39	120 (sailing ship)	Spain	Air	Barcelona
Argentina	Jan. 23, '39	10,137	Spain	Air	Barcelona
Arlon	Jun. 27, '38	4,903	Great Britain	Air	Valencia
Armuru	Aug. 14, '37	2,762	Spain	Submarine	Aegean
Arriluce	Aug. 19, '36	2,127	Spain	Warship	Cape Negro
Artabro	Feb. 7, '37	770	Spain	Scuttled	Malaga
Artois	Aug. 14, '38	439	France	Mined	Straits
Authorpe	Jan. 6, '39	274 (salvage tug)	Panama	Air	Alicante
Azelma	Jan. 25, '39	177 (sailing ship)	France	Air	San Feliu de Guixois
Barcino	Jan. 14, '39	504	Spain	Air	Tarragona
Betis	Jul. 10, '38	1,011	Spain	Air	Tarragona
Blagoev	Sep. 3, '37	3,100	Soviet Union	Submarine	Aegean
Bodil	Jul. 21, '38	844	Denmark	Air	Off Palamos
Brisbane	Jun. 8, '38	4,004	France	Air	Denia
Cabañal	May 30, '38	124 (sailing ship)	Spain	Air	Valencia
Cabo Cullera	Mar. 15, '38	2,246	Spain	Air	Tarragona
Cabo Palos	Jun. 26, '37	6,342	Spain	Submarine	Cape Santa Pola

(Continued)

Name	Date of attack	GRT (type)	Flag	Cause	Location
Cabo Santo Tomé	Oct. 10, '37	12,598	Spain	Warship	Cape Rosas
Cabo Tres Forcas	Feb. 27, '38	2,265	Spain	Air	San Feliu de Guixois
Cala Esperanza	Nov. 25, '37	426 (sailing ship)	Spain	Mine	off Castellon
Cala Milo	Sep. 1, '38	229 (sailing ship)	Spain (N)	Air (R)	Vinaroz
Cala Morlanda	May 3, '38	293 (sailing ship)	Spain (N)	Air (R)	Benicarlo
Cala Murta	Feb. 6/7, '39	152 (sailing ship)	Spain	Air	La Selva
Cala Portals	Jun. 7, '38	129 (sailing ship)	Spain	Air	Gandia
Campeador	Aug. 12, '37	7,932	Spain	Warship	Cape Bone
Campomanes	Aug. 15, '38	6,276	Spain	Air	Valencia
Camprodón	Jun. 14, '38	1,080	Spain	Air	Valencia
Cantabria	Nov. 2, '38	5,649	Spain	Warship	North Sea
Cap Bear	Jun. 15, '38	212 (sailing ship)	France	Air	Valencia
Carol Pi	Feb. 8, '39	197 (sailing ship)	Spain	Air	La Selva
Castillo Olite	Mar. 7, '39	3,545	Spain (N)	Gunfire	Cartagena
Ceferino Varela	May 24, '37	103 (fishing boat)	Spain	Warship	Cantabrian coast
Ciudad de Barcelona	May 30, '37	3,946	Spain	Submarine	Off Malgrat
Ciudad de Cádiz	Aug. 15, '37	4,602	Spain	Submarine	Aegean
Ciutat de Reus	Aug. 30, '37	943	Spain	Submarine	Gulf of Lyon
Con	Aug. 26, '38	107 (fishing boat)	Spain (N)	Warship	Moroccan coast
Conde de Abasolo	Aug. 13, '37	3,122	Spain	Warship	Sicilian Strait
Consulado de Bilbao	Apr. 25, '37	950 Dredger	Spain	Air	Bilbao
Delfín	Jan. 30, '37	1,253	Spain	Air	Nerja, Malaga
Dellwyn	Jul. 27, '38	1,451	Great Britain	Air	Gandia
Edith	Aug. 12, '37	1,566	Denmark	Air	Off Balearics
El Djem	May 30, '38	1,999	France	Air	Off El Grao, Valencia
El Gaitero	Oct. '37	180 (fishing boat)	Spain	Air	Gijon
Elcano	Aug. 28, '37	5,199	Spain	Air	Gijon
Eleni	Nov. 30, '38	1,138	Cyprus	Air	Aguilas
Endymion	Jan. 31, '38	887	Great Britain	Submarine	Cape Tiñoso
English Tanker	Jun. 7, '38	5,387	Great Britain	Air	Alicante
España 3	Jun. 8, '37	2,188	Spain	Air	Barcelona
Farnham	Jun. 27, '38	4,793	Great Britain	Air	Alicante
Foynes	Jan. 27, '39	822	Ireland	Air	Valencia
Fernando Poo	Oct. 15, '36	6,914	Spain	Warship	Bata, Spanish Guinea
Francisco	Late 1938	201 (fishing boat)	Spain	Air	Tarragona
Frutero	Jun. 1, '38	341 (fishing boat)	Spain	Air (N)	Castellon

(Continued)

(*Continued*)

Name	Date of attack	GRT (type)	Flag	Cause	Location
Gandia	Jun. 8, '38	??? (dredger)	Spain	Air	Gandia
Gaulois	Jun. 15, '38	500	France	Air	Valencia
Gonzalito	Mar. 20, '37	129 (fishing boat)	Spain	Warship	Cantabrian coast
Granada	May 30, '37	234 (sailing ship)	Spain	Submarine	Cape Palos
Greatend	May 28, '38	1,495	Great Britain	Air	Valencia
Gulnes	Dec. 7, '36	1,196	Norway	Air (R)	Seville. CTL
Guecho	Sep. 30, '37	3,276	Spain	Air	Valencia
Hannah	Jan. 11, '38	3,730	Netherlands	Submarine	Cape San Antonio
Isadora	Jun. 10, '38	1,212	Great Britain	Air	Castellon
Isla de Menorca	Mar. 14, '38	1,003	Spain	Air	Cambrils
Isobel Matute	Unknown	155 (sailing ship)	Spain	Air	Barcelona
Jaime Girona	Oct. 21, '37	2,434	Spanish	Air	Gijon
Jean Weems	Oct. 30, '37	2,455	Great Britain	Air	Cape San Antonio
José Antonio	Oct. 31, '37	4,397	Spain	Air	Luarca
Joven Pura	Mar. '39	137 (sailing ship)	Spain	Air	Cartagena
Kakau	Jul. 27, '38	169 (fishing boat)	Spain	Air	Valencia
Kardin (Cabo Creux)	May 28, '37 (i) Jul. 27, '38 (ii)	3,717	Spain	Air	Valencia
Kirikis	Feb. '39	368 (fishing boat)	Spain	Air	Valencia
Komsomol	Dec. 14, '36	5,109	Soviet Union	Warship	Cape Palos
Konstan	Aug. 27, '36	1,857	Spain	Warship	Cantabrian coast
La Guardia	Jun. 15, '38	667	Spain	Air	Sagunto
Lake Lugano	Aug. 8, '38	2,120	Great Britain	Air	Palamos
Legazpi	May 19, '37	4,349	Spain	Air	Benicasim
Loukia	Mar. 4, '37	2,143	Greece	Mine	Cape San Sebastian
Loulis	Feb. 25, '39	330	Greece	Mine	Off Cape Creux
Lucky	Feb. 10, '38	1,235	Great Britain	Air	Valencia
Mahón	Jan. 1, '39	913	Spain	Air	Barcelona
Manuel	Nov. 11, '36	976	Spain	Warship	Off Rosas
Mar Caspio	Mar. 29, '37	3,080	Spain	Warship	La Boucau
Margaret Rose	Nov. 6, '38	348 (salvage tug)	Great Britain	Air	Almeria
María	Jan. '39	339	Spain	Air	Barcelona
María Hevia	May 24, '37	103 (fishing boat)	Spain	Warship	Cantabrian coast

(*Continued*)

Name	Date of attack	GRT (type)	Flag	Cause	Location
Mendo	Jun. 15, '38	289 (sailing ship)	Spain	Air	Valencia
Miocene	Jan. 24, '39	2,153	Great Britain	Air	Barcelona
Morisca	Apr. 15, '38	209	Spain	Air	Vallcarca
Naranco	Feb. '37	856	Spain	unknown	Malaga
Nausicaa	May 27, '38	5,005	Panama	Air	Off Minorca
Navarra	Feb. 8, '37	1,693	Spain	Submarine	Off Torredembarra
Navarinon/Lena	Mar. 17, '38 (i) Jan. '39 (ii)	1,735	France/ Greece	Air	Beached near Cape Gros; refloated, then Barcelona
Nere-Ametza	Unknown	450 (yacht)	Spain	Air	Barcelona
Noemjulia	Aug. 15, '38	2,499	Great Britain	Air	Alicante
Oued Mellah	Oct. 24, '37	2,413	France	Air	Off Balearics
Pailebote N.254	Jun. 4, '37	110 (sailing ship)	Spain	Submarine	Off Villajoyosa
Pascual Flores	Jun. 7, '38	169 (sailing ship)	Spain	Air	Castellon
Paulita	Feb. '39	125 (sailing ship)	Spain	Air	Valencia
Pedro (i)	Unknown	143 (fishing boat)	Spain	Air	Valencia
Pedro (ii)	Jul. 22, '37	322 (fishing boat)	Spain	Warship	Off Rosas
Penthames	May 31, '38	3,995	Great Britain	Air	Valencia
Poeta Arolas	Jul. 12, '38	3,254	Spain	Air	Valencia
Poli	Apr. 2, '37	2,861	Greece	Warship	San Antioco
Rápido	Jun. 4, '37	105 (sailing ship)	Spain	Submarine	Cape San Antonio
Reina	Oct. 19, '37	1,436	Panama	Air	Gijon
Remedios	Jun. 14, '38	4,461	Spain	Air	Valencia
Rosa V.	Unknown	375 (yacht)	Spain	Air	Barcelona
Rosita	Oct. '37	144	Spain	Air	Gijon
Sac 4	Nov. 17, '36	2,382	Spain	Warship	Off Palamos
Sac 5	Apr. 15, '38	2,520	Spain	Air	San Feliu de Guixois
Sac 7	Apr. 30, '38	835	Spain	Air	Barcelona
Sagunto	Unknown	962	Spain	Air	Valencia
Saint Prosper	Mar. 8, '39	4,330	France	Mine	Western Mediterranean
Salvador	Jan. '39	130 (fishing boat)	Spain	Air	Barcelona
Sama	Oct. 10, '37	735	Spain	Air	Musel
San Antonio	Mar. 4, '37	110 (fishing boat)	Spain	Warship	Cartagena
San Fausto	Aug. 26, '38	103 (fishing boat)	Spain (N)	Warship	Moroccan coast

(Continued)

(Continued)

Name	Date of attack	GRT (type)	Flag	Cause	Location
San Luis	Unknown	125 (sailing ship)	Spain	Air	Huelva
Sebastián Martín	May 30, '38	1,063	Spain	Air	Valencia
Siete Hermanos	Oct. 12, '36	201 (fishing boat)	Spain	Warship	Cape Rosa
Sotón	Oct. 21, '37	1,375	Spain	Air	Musel
St Winifred	Jun. 6, '38	6,775	Great Britain	Air	Valencia
Stanbrook	Aug. 17, '38	1,383	Great Britain	Air	Vallcarca
Stancroft	Oct. 13, '38 (i) Dec. 28, '38 (ii)	1,407	Great Britain	Air	Barcelona
Sud	Sep. '37	2,949	Spain	Air	Musel
Sunion	Jun. 22, '38	3,110	Great Britain	Air	Valencia
Teide	Dec. 10, '37	5,570	Spanish	Warship	Off Cape Huertas
Thorpehall	May 25, '38	1,251	Great Britain	Air	Valencia
Thorpehaven	Jun. 7, '38	3,688	Great Britain	Air	Alicante
Thorpeness	Jun. 22, '38	4,798	Great Britain	Air	Valencia
Timiryazev	Aug. 30, '37	2,151	Soviet Union	Warship	Off Tigzirt, Algeria
Urola	Unknown	3,675	Spain	Air	Valencia
Uruguay	Jan. 25, '39	10,348	Spain	Air	Barcelona
Valencia	Unknown	734 (dredger)	Spain	Air	Valencia
Vicente	Jul. 25, '38	534	Spain	Air	Gandia
Vicente La Roda	May 9, '38	1,508	Spain	Air	Palamos
Villa de Madrid	Jan. 21, '39	6,871	Spain	Air	Barcelona
Villamanrique	Nov. 23, '37	1,537	Spain	Air	San Feliu de Guixois
Woodford	Sep. 1, '37	6,987	Great Britain	Submarine	Columbretes Islands
Yolande	Jan. 26, '39	1,733	France	Air	Barcelona
Yorkbrook	Jan. 22, '39	1,236	Great Britain	Air	Barcelona

Notes: CTL is Constructive Total Losss. N are Nationalist ships and R refers to Republican air attacks.
Sources: Alcofar Nassaes, La Aviacion Legionaria en la Guerra Espanola, Appendix VI; Belgian Shiplover No 95 (Septembre/Octobre 1963), 383–94; Foreign Ships Sunk website; González, 411–41; O'Donnell; Mattesini, Il blocco aeronavale italiano nella Guerra di Spagna; Morenos III, 1977, 2109; Revista Historia Naval Ano 11 (1993) #43, 55–84; K. B. Strelbitskiy, Spain in 1936–1939 Years. Civil War at Sea website

Endnotes

Chapter 1

1   Spanish men formally include both parents' family name but informally tend to drop the maternal name, hence Moreno rather than Moreno Fernández. This style will be used throughout this work.

2   The Spanish Navy from 1898 to 1936, see Alpert, *The Spanish Civil War at Sea*, 4–20, hereafter Alpert; Cerezo, *Armada Española, Siglo XX*, Vols 1–2; English, *The Spanish Civil War at Sea*, 15–17, 25–26, hereafter English; Gretton, *The Forgotten Factor* manuscript, 6–27, hereafter Gretton. For warships, see *Jane's Fighting Ships* of various dates.

3   Alpert, 6. In March 1934, the *Dédalo* became the first naval vessel to land and fly-off a rotary-wing aircraft, an autogyro. She was decommissioned shortly afterwards and struck off the list in April 1936. The first *España* was lost in 1923.

4   After the uprising in July 1936, six British SECN workers continued working at Ferrol and three at Cartagena. Gretton, 20.

5   Vickers also provided most of the coast defense artillery.

6   Submarines, see Viscasillas's article, "Centenario del Arma Submarina."

7   Leguina & Núñez, *Ramón Franco, el hermano olvidado del dictador*, 172–73.

8   Thomas, *The Spanish Civil War*, 58n5, hereafter Thomas.

9   Alpert, 8–9.

10 Alpert, 15.

11 The plot and the Navy, see Alpert, 14–18; English, 18; Thomas, 212n2.

12 The rising and initial naval operations, see Alpert, 23–33, 40–50; English, 32–44; Kersh, *Influence of Naval Power on the Course of the Spanish Civil War*, 7–8, hereafter Kersh; Thomas, 242–43, 331–32; Mattesini, "Il blocco navale italiano nerra Guerra di Spagna," Part I, 8, hereafter Mattesini I; Moreno de Alborán y de Reyna, Fernando and Salvador, *La Guerra Silenciosa y Silenciada* Volume 1, 119–493, hereafter Morenos.

13 Lachadenède, *La Marine Francaise et la Guerre Civile d'Espagne*, 376, hereafter Lachadenède.

14 Heaton, *Spanish Civil War Blockade Runners*, 27, hereafter Heaton.

15 The two navies, see Alpert, 33–39, 46–47, 60–71, 107; English, 35, 42; Kersh, 8–9.

16 Buiza, a very professional officer with considerable charisma, was promoted to admiral and became Fleet commander in late August 1936.

17 For operations to the end of the year, see Alpert, 81–84; Admiral Cervera, *Memorias de Guerra*, 85–126, hereafter Cervera; English, 52, 60, 63; Gretton, 21–27; Heaton, 21–22; Lachadenède 376–78; Moreno, *La Guerra en el mar*, 110–14, 126–35, hereafter Francisco Moreno; Cerezo Martínez, "La estrategia naval en la guerra española," 9–14, hereafter Cerezo; Morenos I, 528–48; Morenos II, 778–832, 871–919, 934–41.

18 In HMS *Hood*, the Royal Navy's largest ship, fresh water for washing was restricted to one hour a day, with seamen allocated an 8-liter (4½-pint) bucket. Article, Osborne, "A Memoir" Part 2, hereafter Osborne.

19 Tangier was restored to Morocco in 1956. For the international naval response, see Bargoni, *La Participation naval italiana en la Guerra civil espanola*, 89–92, 134–41, hereafter Bargoni; Bargoni, "L'impegno della Regia Marina in difsa della neutralità della zona internazionale di Tangier," hereafter Bargoni, *Tangier*; Frank, "Multinational Naval Cooperation in the Spanish Civil War," 85, hereafter Frank, "Cooperation"; Morenos I, 709–13; Macintyre, *Fighting Admiral*, 36–37, hereafter Macintyre.

20 Gretton, "The Royal Navy in the Spanish Civil War, Part 1," 13, hereafter Gretton I.

21 These attacks, see Heaton, 17–19; Lachadenède, 82, 385–86; Gretton I, 13–14; *Liverpool Journal of Commerce and Shipping Telegraph*, July 21 and 22, 1936, herefter *LJOC*.

22 Bargoni, *Tangier*; Frank, "Cooperation," 85.

23 Tanner, "German Naval Intervention in the Spanish Civil War," 69–70, hereafter Tanner.

24 The Victory Convoy, see Morenos I, 643–709; Gretton I, 14.

25 Air operations in August 1936, see Alpert, 48–59; see Proctor, *Hitler's Luftwaffe in the Spanish Civil War*, 28–31, hereafter Proctor; Ries & Ring, *The Legion Condor*, 12–17, hereafter Ries/Ring; Saiz Cidoncha, *Aviación Republicana* Volume 1, 205, hereafter Saiz 1 etc.

26 Hermann, *Eagle's Wings*, 33–36, hereafter Hermann. Meredith, *Phoenix* Volume 2, 520–21, hereafter Meredith; Ries/Ring, 17.

27 Tanner, 56–57.

28 "The Cruise to the North," see Alpert, 78–80; English, 52–55; Morenos I, 582–84; Morenos II, 773–78, 838–63.

29 English, 59–61; Heaton, 1. Aleksandr Rozin website, "Soviet sailors in the Spanish Civil War, Troubled Waters," hereafter Rozin.

30 The Majorca operation, see Alcofar Nassaes, *La Aviación Legionaria en la Guerra Española*, 100–11, hereafter Alcofar, *Aviación*; Alpert, 59, 102; Bargoni, 102–13; English, 58–59; Frank, "Cooperation," 92–93; Macintyre, 37–38; Morenos I, 734–54; Saiz 1, 344–45; Thomas, 381–84.

31 Hillgarth, see Day, *Franco's Friends*, and Hart-Davis, *Man of War*. UKNA ADM 196/122/23. Hillgarth had been a midshipman under Cunningham in the Dardanelles campaign and is described by him as "a very live wire" (186). He was also praised by Captain C. Tait, commander of HMS *Shropshire*, in a letter to Mediterranean Fleet commander Admiral Alfred Dudley Pound of July 26, 1937. Halpern, *The Mediterranean Fleet*, 273, hereafter Halpern.

32 Cunningham would be one of the most distinguished Royal Navy commanders in World War II.

33 Brodhurst, 96; Macintyre, 28–30, 31, 34, 41.

34 Frank, "Cooperation," 85–86; Macintyre, 37–38. Carls and Somerville had been on opposite sides in the Dardanelles in 1915–16.

35 Gretton I, 16.

36 Alcofar, *Aviación*, 111–12; González Echegaray, *La Marine Mercante y el Tráfico Marítimo en la Guerra Civil*, 299, hereafter González.

37 Documents of German Foreign Policy, 173–74, hereafter DGFP.

38 The Abyssinia Crisis and the Royal Navy, see Gibbs, *Grand Strategy*, 187–89, 198–202, 217–22, hereafter Gibbs. Abyssinia was not formally recognized as Ethiopia until 1948.

39 Kennedy, *Rise and Fall of British Naval Mastery*, 268, 273, hereafter Kennedy. See also Roskill, *Naval Policy Between the Wars*, hereafter Roskill.

40 The decline in political support for the Royal Navy, see Kennedy, 270–74.

41 Barnett, *The Collapse of British Power*, 297, but see Boyd, *The Royal Navy in Eastern Waters*, 18, hereafter Boyd.

42 The treaties, see Goldstein and Maurer, *The Washington Conference, 1921–22*, also Maurer and Bell, *At the Crossroads between Peace and War*. For their impact, see Boyd, 4–16; Kennedy, 274–78.

43 Gretton, 13–14; Halpern, 206, 375–77; Kennedy, 289; Marder, *From the Dardanelles to Oran*, 82–83, hereafter Marder.

44 Kennedy, 278; Salerno, "The French Navy and the Appeasement of Italy," 69, hereafter Salerno.

45 Gretton, 14; Pratt, *East of Malta, West of Suez*, 17, hereafter Pratt.

46 Political attitudes to naval matters, see Edwards, *The British Government and the Spanish Civil War*, 101–2, 104–5, hereafter Edwards; Kennedy, 286.

47 Marder, 85.

48 For the Abyssinia Crisis and Mediterranean Fleet, see Gibbs, 189–98, 202–17; Gretton, 28; Halpern, 63–75; Marder, 64–93; Pratt, 15–28; Salerno, 70–71. The Royal Navy order of battle from 1936–39, see Royal Navy Organisation and Ship Deployment website.

49 Boyd, 38; Brodhurst, *Churchill's Anchor*, 92, 96, hereafter Brodhurst; Marder, 80.

50 Marder, 85.

51 LJOC February 8, 1937. See article, Young, "Aircraft Attacks or Gunfire against Warships."

52 Gretton, 9; Halpern, 102; Marder, 66n4. The QF Two-Pounder "pom-pom" was a short-range weapon later superceded by the 40mm Bofors.

53 Marder, 86–87.

54 I would like to thank Dr Norman Friedmann for his advice in drafting this paragraph.

55 Gibbs, 190–91; Gretton, 14; Marder, 99.

56 Chatfield, see Marder, 75–76; Pratt, 22; Roskill, 48–49. Also Chatfield, *The Navy and Defence*.

57 Marder, 65.

58 Fisher died in June 1937.

59 Brodhurst, 94–106; Marder, 80. Pound's full name was Alfred Dudley Pickman Rogers Pound, Dudley Pickman Rogers reflecting his American mother's maiden name and Salem-based family.

60 Marder, 95–97.

61 Marder, 88–90; Salerno, 71.

62 The 1935 agreement, see Gretton, 8; Maiolo, *The Royal Navy and Nazi Germany, 1933–39*, hereafter Maiolo; Tanner, 47–50.

63 Kennedy, 289–90, 292.

64 Alpert, 55; Young, *An Uncertain Idea of France*, 40–41.

65 Marder, 96. James's nickname was due to his appearance in the famous commercial painting "Bubbles."

66 Brodhurst, 93; Marder, 98; Pratt, 37; Roskill, 373.

67 Marder, 101n82.

68 Lachadenède, 88.

69 Berlin was selected in 1931 over Barcelona.

70 Frank, "Cooperation," Table 1.

71 For humanitarian operations, the most detailed account is Frank's "Cooperation." See also Alpert, 53–54; Bargoni, 56–70, 92–101; Edwards, 105–6; Gretton, 29–52; Gretton I, 13–14; Halpern, 191–206; Kersh, 13–15; Lachadenède, 3–12; Macintyre, 36, 40; Mattesini I, 8–9; Roskill, 373–75; Tanner, 31–36, 57–61, 98–128. Ship List website.

72 Chatfield, 92; Gretton I, 13–14.

73 The SFIR was a state-controlled syndicate created in 1932 in response to the Depression and widespread unemployment in the Italian merchant marine. Rome combined most of the major shipping companies into syndicates, but a rapid recovery meant that in 1937 this syndicate repaid the Government bonds which had supported it and became the commercial company Italia Società Anonima di Navigazione (ISAN).

74 The German Navy in Spain, see DGFP, 26; Huan, "La Kriegsmarine y la guerra de España," 17–20, hereafter Huan; Tanner, 47–63.

75 This is based upon the Wells website, United States Ships Participating in the Spanish Civil War.

76 It is unclear when the squadron was deactivated. U.S. Navy records state it was October 22, 1940, but other sources suggest the year should be 1939. Lackey had been Commander, U.S. Naval Forces in Europe in 1926–27 and hosted King Alfonso. Upon his return in 1927, he returned the heroic aviator Charles A. Lindbergh and *The Spirit of St Louis* to the United States.

77 For Argentinian and Mexican ships, see Morenos I, 631–33.

78 Howson, *Arms for Spain*, 103, hereafter Howson.

79 For these incidents, see Lachadenède, 67–75. For relations with the Spanish navies, see Lachadenède, 81–85, 169–76, 273–85, 327–31.

80 Frank, "Cooperation," 83; Tanner, 150–52.

81 Gretton, 48–49; Gretton I, 15.

82 Alpert, 94–95.

83 Thomas, 618–19.

84 UKNA FO 371/205/33. See also Cable, *The Royal Navy and the Siege of Bilbao*, 91–92, hereafter Cable; Edwards, 106.

85 The Republican blockade, see Edwards, 106–8; Gretton, 48.

86 Alpert, 89.

87 Thomas, 387.

88 At the time of the uprising, 27 German merchantmen were in Spanish ports. DGFP, 47–48; Huan, 18.

89 The Nationalist blockade and interdiction of traffic in the Strait to mid-1937, see Alcofar Nassaes, *Las Fuerzas Navales en la Guerra Civil Española*, 96–99, hereafter Alcofar, *Fuerzas*; Alpert, 55–59, 105–22; Cervera, 50–54; González, 257; Gretton I, 14–15; Heaton, 19–33, 56–71; Howson, 194–95; Lachadenède, 29–79, 97–101; Mattesini I, 118–21; Tanner, 65–81.

90 Seized cargoes, see Gretton, 62; Heaton, 28–32; Morenos III, 1747–48.

91 Dutch activity, see Cervera, 245–46; Heaton, 31, 56; *Jaarboek van de Koninklijke Marine 1936–1937*, 125–27, and *1937–1938*, 126–27; Münching, "Een herinnering aan veertig jaar geleden."

92 Cervera, 246.

93 Heaton, 27.

94 Alpert, 108. From September 1936, the Nationalists, like the Netherlands, had twin capitals, with Franco's military headquarters in Salamanca and the administration in Burgos, but from 1938, Burgos became the de facto capital.

95 Alpert, 108.

96 Cervera, 51–52.

97 These incidents, see Alpert, 110–11; Cervera, 107–8; Heaton, 31–32.

98 Lachadenède, 84n3.

99 It should be noted that Soviet arms were delivered only to Alicante and Cartagena during 1936.

100 Granting the Nationalists belligerent rights, see Gretton, 127–32; Edwards, 109; Roskill, 375–77.

101 Edwards, 109.

102 Spanish trade, see Edwards, Table 4; Thomas, 335 Appendix 2, and online article by Betrán & Huberman, Against the Grain, esp. 47, 52, 60, 62.

103 Constants never traded with the Republic, but their *Hermitage* was involved in trade with Nationalist ports. Heaton, 16, 26. See also website Short Histories of some Cardiff area Shipping Companies.

104 Heaton, 26.

105 The Spanish merchant marine, see González, 83–191; *Lloyd's Register of Shipping 1936*; Statistical Notes on the 1936–37 edition of *Lloyd's Shipping Register*, 2–4, hereafter Lloyd's, Statistics; Thomas, Appendix 1.

106 Alpert, 88–89; González, 32.

107 Spain's merchant fleet and the uprising, see González, 67–73; Heaton, 98.

108 Legal interventions, see González, 157, 164–65, 182.

109 González, 171.

110 Spanish ships under German and Italian control, see Bargoni, 65–168; González, 43–45; De Toro, "L'intervento navale tedesco nella guerra civile spagnola Parte I," 81, hereafter Toro I.

111 González, 231–33. Heaton, 106–7.

112 Data extracted from González and *Lloyd's Shipping Register*. Information on Nationalist scrapping decisions from González, 127, 235, 233n1.

113 Alpert, 129–30; Heaton, 69–71; González, 119, 156, 165, 177, 181.

114 Alcofar Nassaes, *La Marina Italiana en la Guerra de España*, 250, hereafter Alcofar, *Marina*.

115 For the British lines using Nationalist ports, see González, 254–55. Information on Norwegian activity was kindly provided by Mr Svein Aage Knudsen in an email of May 1, 2023.

116 González, 347.

117 Heaton, 26–27.

118 Half of CTE's 14 ships were laid up throughout the conflict, including four in Port Mahon; González, 84–88.

119 Based on ship entries in González especially, 325–26, 379. For both sides' administrative arrangements, see González, 40–57, 63–79. The decline is illustrated in Cerezo's graph, 19.

120 González, 95, 99; Heaton, 22.

121 González, 58–60.

122 González, 237–39. Five of these ships were sunk during World War II while flying the Hammer and Sickle. See also Axis History Forum, Spanish Civil War, Russians seize Spanish ships, July 27, 2022, and Ironmachine response of July 31; Rozin, "Spanish Ships remaining in the USSR."

123 González, 133–34.

124 Cervera, 422.

125 Kennedy, 268–79.

126 Lloyd's Statistics.

127 *Lloyd's Shipping Register*, Returns of Ships Totally Lost, Condemned &c. 1936 etc. Hereafter *Lloyd's Lost*.

128 The author would like to thank Mr Tony Selman, Chairman of The Radio Officers' Association, for information from May 25, 2022. The *Lake Champlin* became the Japanese oil transport *Choran Maru* and survived the war.

129 Kennedy, 272–73.

130 For the life of a Boy Sailor in HMS *Hood* in this period, see Osborne, Parts 1–3. Between July 1936 and March 1939, 37 Ship's Boys died of illness or accidents in naval schools, ships, and bases together with three midshipmen. Osborne commented that in 15 years' service, he never saw a Royal Navy doctor use a stethoscope. Royal Navy Casualties website. Osborne Part 1.

131 McGee, *They Shall Not Grow Old*; British Merchant Navy Sea Schools website. HMS *Hood* website. Tyne & Wear Museums website.

132 *Lascar* is a word of Persian origin.

133 House of Commons record, Hansard, Volume 311, debate of May 4, 1936, hereafter HOC. Lascar recruitment expanded due to manpower shortages during World War II.

134 Seamen's conditions, see Dyer and Edwards, *Death and Donkeys' Breakfasts*; Edwards, *The Quiet Heroes*; Hurd, *Britain's Merchant Navy*; Lane, *The Merchant Seaman's War*; Linskey, *No Longer Required*; and Peppit, *The Crew*.

135 Macintyre, 42–45.

136 The author would like to express his gratitude to Thanasis D. Sfikas, who was kind enough to send translations of two chapters from his study of Greece in the Spanish Civil War, *I Ellada Kai o Ispanikos Empulios*. Chapter 3, 135–74, covers arms exports, and Chapter 4, 174–221, the Greek merchant marine; hereafter Sfikas 3 & 4. This is augmented by Harlafatis, *A History of Greek-Owned Shipping*, 189–223, hereafter Harlafatis. See also Rozin, "Greek deliveries."

137 Harlafatis, 226–29.

138 Harlafatis, 189–202, 206, 211; Lloyd's Statistics.

139 Harlafatis, 194–97.

140 Cervera, 422.

141 Gretton, 124; Heaton, 67–68; Edwards, 113.

142 Catepodis may have been involved with an arms-smuggling *Sylvia*.

143 British-based shipping lines trading with the Republic, see Alcofar, *Marina*, 245; González, 315–23; Gretton, 121–26; Heaton, 53–54, 63–64, 67; *Lloyd's Shipping Register*; Sfikas 4. Rozin, "Auxiliary cruisers of nationalists in the North Sea and Transport ships of war."

144 Heaton, *Jack Billmeir*, 36, hereafter Heaton, *Billmeir*.

145 Shipslist website, Stanhope Line.

146 Marder, 88–90. The 1st Fleet was renamed the Mediterranean Fleet on October 30, while the 2nd Fleet became the Atlantic Fleet on August 15. Lachadenède, Annex In1. Mouget was succeeded on October 30, 1936, by Vice-Admiral Jean-Marie Abrial and died in April 1937. Lachadenède, 55.

147 The French Navy reaction, see Lachadenède, 15–18; Frank, "Cooperation," 93–94; Gretton, 67–68. Durand-Viel retired in March 1937.

148 Lachadenède, 63.

149 Non-intervention, see Eden, *The Eden Memoirs* Volume I, 452–67, hereafter Eden. Padelford, "The International Non-Intervention Agreement and the Spanish Civil War," esp. 578–79.

150 Roskill, 375.

151 DGFP, 50; Frank, "Cooperation," 93–95.

152 Hooton, *Spain in Arms*, 72, and 79n169, hereafter Hooton. Tierney, *FDR and the Spanish Civil War*, 68, hereafter Tierney.

153 Edwards, 40–63, Appendices D and E; Gretton, 93–97; Howson, 114–19.

154 Eden, 463.

155 Eden, 489–91; Edwards, 111; Roskill, 375–76.

156 Salerno, 66–67.

157 The naval inspection element, see Alpert, 167–69; Alpert, *A New International History of the Spanish Civil War*, 116, hereafter Alpert, *International*; Bargoni, "La seconda campagna sottomarina," 78–79, hereafter Bargoni II; Eden, 489–91; Edwards, 53–56; Frank, "Misperception and Incidents at Sea," hereafter Frank, "Misperception"; Gretton, 136–38; Heaton, 31, 69; Huan, 32; Inglis, "Danza de la Muerte," 55–56, hereafter Inglis; Lachadenède, 105–31, 163–68; Mattesini I, 118–21; Salgado, 60; Tanner, 202–12, 236–50; De Toro, "L'intervento navale tedesco nella guerra civile spagnola Parte II," 88–90, hereafter Toro II.

158 Howson, 51–56, 85–87.

159 Edwards, 60.

160 Cunningham, *A Sailor's Odyssey*, 185, hereafter Cunningham.

161 Tanner, 52n20. UKNA ADM 116/3519. Proceedings HMS *Hasty*.

162 Toro I, 84.

163 Lachadenède, 390.

164 Frank, "Cooperation," 95.

165 This passage is based upon Blanco Nuñez, *Participacion de la marina de Guerra portuguesa*; Salgado, "Portugal and the Spanish Civil War at Sea." See also DGFP, 53, 78; Tanner, 73.

Chapter 2

1 German maritime support, see Alcofar, *Marina*, Appendix IV; Alcofar, Navales, Appendix VII; Alpert, 91–93, 105–6; González, 249–53; Meredith, 516–19, 531–32; Tanner, 74–88, 167–81, 305–6; Salas Larrazábal, *Intervención Extranjera en la Guerra de España*, Annex 27, hereafter Salas, *Intervención*; Toro I, 74, 76–79.

2 Data from *Lloyd's Shipping Register*; Salas, *Intervención*, Annex 27.

3 Special Ships, see Jung, "Der Einsatz der deutschen Handelsshiffahrt wahrend des Spanienkrieges," hereafter Jung. See also Huan, 26; Mattesini I, 76–78; Meredith, 532; Salas, *Intervención*, Annex 27; Tanner, 234–35; Toro I, 78, 80.

4 Meredith, 532; Toro I, 79.

5 Mattesini I, 25–31. Ciano's father, Costanzo, a former naval officer, reorganized the Italian mercantile marine in the 1920s.

6 Mattesini I, 22.

7 Tanner, 172; Manrique & Molina, *Las Armas de la Guerra Civil Española*, 528, hereafter Manrique/Molina.

8 Huan, 22–23; Tanner, 72–81.

9 Tanner, 234, 234n8.

10 Edwards, Tables 8 and 10.

11 Tanner, 83–84.

12 DGFP, 34, 40; Jung, 324–26.

13 For Veltjens, see Veltjens, *Seppl, A Step Ahead of Politics*, hereafter Veltjens. For the *Allegro*, see Rozon website, *Gold for trash*; Werner website, *The truth about the Allegro Affair*. In June 1937, the *Yorkbrook* was owned by Strubin, managed by Claude Angel, the broker was Billmeir, and the ship was chartered by the Mid-Atlantic Line. Gretton, 121.

14 Jung, 328; Toro I, 80.

15 Toro I, 86.

16 Italian shipping activity, see Alcofar, *Fuerzas*, Appendix VII; Alcofar, *Marina*, 129–33, Appendix IV; Bargoni, 123–25, 170–73, 246–71, 390–423, 436–66; González, 256–58; Mattesini I, 79–80; Rapalino, *La Regia Marina in Spagna*, 202–3, Appendices 2 & 3, hereafter Rapalino; Salas, *Intervención*, 265, Annex 28.

17 The Italian merchant marine, see Cherini website, *La Marina Mercantile 1818–1975*, and Miles Forum, *La Guerra Civile Spagnola, La Marina Mercantile nella Guerra di Spagna*.

18 The most detailed data is in Bargoni and Rapalino. Chemical munitions, Manrique/Molina, 528.

19 Alpert, 101–2.

20 Mattesini I, 95.

21 Mattesini, "Il blocco navale italiano nerra Guerra di Spagna," Part II, 170, hereafter Mattesini II; Francisco Moreno, 287.

22 This is based upon Bargoni, 258–63, 396–423, 465–66.

23 Bargoni, 421–22.

24 Alpert, 106.

25 Gretton, 55.

26 Heaton, 15, 24. Details and names of victims from Foreign Ships Sunk website. The attack is mentioned by neither González nor in Saiz, Volume 1. See Forside-Sjøhistorie website for details.

27 Howson, 103.

28 Heaton, 21. Heaton's claim of a second shipment in the *Manuel Arnus* is incorrect.

29 Mexican arms shipments, see Howson, 103. Cárdenas was Mexico's War Minister from 1942–45, when his country entered World War II.

30 The Bilbao-registered ship was later renamed *Itxas-Alde*. González, 166.

31 Polish arms exports, see Ciechanowski, *Podwójna gra* (Annex 1 details arms to Spain), hereafter Ciechanowski; Howson, 106–10. Also articles by Deszczyński, "Polski eksport sprzętu wojskowego w okresie międzywojennym," and Kabaciński, "Wojsko Polskie wobec wojny domowej w Hiszpanii."

32 Ciechanowski, 638–39.

33 The author would again like to express his gratitude to Thanasis D. Sfikas for information on Greek shipping.

34 France-Navigation, see Grisoni and Hertzog, *Les Brigades de la Mer*, hereafter Grisoni/Hertzog. Also Alpert, 169–70; González, 316–21; Howson, 235–36; Rozin, "Supply of weapons to the Spanish Republic" and "Jaron Epic"; Spanish Civil War and the Seafarers and Dockers website, France-Navigation.

35 West, *Mask*, 108ff.

36 The company's constitution is in Grisoni/Hertzog, Appendix 1.

37 Grisoni/Hertzog, 113n5. See Appendices III and IV for official reports on arms shipments.

38 Rapalino, Appendix VII; Rozin, "Humanitarian Aid from the USSR" and "Troubled Waters." See also DGFP, 100, 120, 126.

39 Frank, "Logistic Supply and Commerce War in the Spanish Civil War," 165, hereafter Frank, *Logistic*.

40 For decision-making, see Kowalsky, *Stalin and the Spanish Civil War*, Chapter 9, "Operation X," Section 1, "The Initiation of Operation X," hereafter Kowalsky, with references to the down-loaded chapters. Rozin, "Decision to assist Spain." The Cyrillic letter which resembles the Latin "X" is pronounced "Kh" in Russian. Uristkii was arrested in November 1937 and executed in August 1938. Slutskii, who was responsible for recruiting the infamous Cambridge Five spy ring, was poisoned in February 1938.

41 Spain held the world's fourth largest gold reserve. On January 27, 1937, the Spanish *Tramontana* arrived in Marseilles with more than 22.5 tonnes of gold worth $25.3 million and a case of jewels worth FF6 million or $12.85 million. Heaton, 27–28.

42 The transport of gold, see website Soviet shipping in the Spanish Civil War, 8, hereafter SovShip; Kowalsky, Chapter 11, "The Spanish Gold and Financing Soviet Military Aid." Rozin, "Transportation of Spanish Gold to the USSR."

43 Howson provides the best general account of arms supplies to the Republic, but should be read with comments from Spanish historians. The SB was called Katiuska by both the Russians and the Spanish, the latter after a character in an operetta. Saiz, Vol 1, 346nII. See also DGFP, 129–30; Martínez, "Los Katiuskas."

44 Russian maritime activities, see Alpert, 116–23; González, 275–77; Howson, 125–35, Appendix 3; Kowalsky, Chapter 9-II, *The Logistics of Delivery*; Monakov and Ribalkin, "Los marinos de la flota soviéta y la asistencia a la España republicana"; SovShip, 1–10; Thomas, 448–50; Rozin, "Supply organization," "Second series of deliveries," "Third series of deliveries," "Fourth series of deliveries," and "Completion of deliveries in the South."

45 Edwards, Table 20.

46 SovShip, 1–3.

47 *Lloyd's Shipping Register*; SovShip, 4–6.

48 The agreement, see Eden, 471–73.

49 Kowalsky, Chapter 9-II.

50 SovShip, 7–9.

51 The Soviet merchant fleet, see Lloyd's Statistics.

52 Howson, 132–35; Kowalsky, Chapter 9-II.

53 González, 336, 339; Rozin, "Spies buy weapons for the Republic."

54 Heaton, 23.

55 Manrique/Molina, 529.

56 Howson, 294.

57 Kowalsky, Chapter 9-II.

58 Howson, 144n1, 150n1.

59 This and subsequent paragraphs are based upon Sfikas 3 & 4 together with Sfikas, *Greek attitudes to the Spanish Civil War*, augmented by Howson, 198–99, Inglis, 61–72, and the websites Greek Shipping Miracle 1930–1939, Rozin, "Greek deliveries"; Ships List; Stanhope Line. All errors of interpretation are my responsibility.

60 The Mavroleon family, and especially Basil, were well-known ship-brokers in the Baltic Exchange. There were two ships named *Kimon*; one of 1,200 grt and the other of 454 grt. In 1938, the *Nepheligeretis* was renamed the *Hermes*, then *Suzy*, then *Ionanna*.

61 Sfikas 4.

62 Inglis, 63.

63 Inglis, 71.

64 Inglis, 62, 72.

65 Inglis, 64–68.

66 The *Bramhall* is often referred to as the *Bramhill*.

67 British ships and arms shipments, see Alpert, 111–12; González, 281, 368; Gretton, 84; *Lloyd's Shipping Register*; UKNA ADM 116/4084.

68 Lloyd's Statistics, Table 4.

69 The United States had the world's largest tanker fleet with 388 hulls (2,489,725 grt). Lloyd's Statistics, Table 4.

70 Rieber and Texaco, see Estapé, "Los Kennedy en la Guerra de España"; González, 259–60, 300; Howson, 73–74.

71 Tierney, 68.

72 Lloyd's Statistics, Table 4.

73 Edwards, 67; Howson, 74. For Norwegian tankers, I have been greatly aided by Mr Svein Aage Knudsen, who most generously helped me, notably in emails of May 1 and May 2, 2023.

74 Howson, 73–74.

75 Gretton, 62; Morenos III, 747–48.

76 The Republican oil trade, see González, 259–60, 330–39; Rapalino, Appendix VII. Rozin, "Fuel the blood of war."

77 The *Komsomol* and *Poli* incidents, see Alpert, 123–25; Cervera, 182; Francisco Moreno, 129–30; González, 235, 339–40; González Echegaray, "Las pérdidas soviéticas," 25–26, hereafter González, "Pérdidas"; English, 63; Francisco Moreno, 129–31; Heaton, 24, 56, 74; Kowalsky, Chapter 9-II nn88–90; Mattesini I, 33–34, 38; Morenos II, 912–17; Morenos III, 1604, 1607; Morenos, "El Hunimiento del Komsomol"; Sfikas 4; SovShip, 13–22; Infiesta, "Más Datos sobre el Huniemento del Komsomol"; *Lloyd's Shipping Casualties*, hereafter *Lloyd's Lost*; SovShip claims Mezentsev scuttled the freighter because she carried concealed war materiel. The Infiesta article led to a weak rebuttal by Morenos's sons.

78 Heaton, 24.

79 Faldella would be the chief of staff of 6th Army defending Sicily in 1943.

80 Frank, *Logistic*, 169. Orlov was arrested in July 1937 and executed in July 1938, while his successor, Mikhail Viktorov, was arrested at the end of 1937 and shot in August 1938.

81 See SovShip, 13–22. Mezentsev, who died in 1976, ended his career as Deputy Navy Minister.

82 Cervera, 422. The Spanish included in British vessels those of the Irish Free State, or Ireland, from December 1937.

83   Edwards, 99–100, Tables 6, 7.

84   Kitroeff, "The Greek Seamen's Movement 1940–1944," 76.

85   Heaton, *The Abbey Line*, 95, hereafter Heaton, *Abbey*.

86   Heaton, *Abbey*, 95–96. For further details of the Abbey Line's activities and financial returns, see Heaton, 84–89.

87   Heaton, 26; Heaton, *Abbey*, 96; Heaton, *Billmeir*, 19.

88   See Heaton, 84–89, and Heaton, *Abbey*, 95–96. Rozin, "Spanish Trade."

89   For Strubin, see González, 280, 316; websites trafina_history-e and Strübin_Charles-ausland-SwissShips.

90   Heaton, 16.

91   *Lloyd's Shipping Register*.

92   González, 280; Heaton, 53–54, 67. See Chapter 3.

93   Billmeir, see Heaton, 54–55, and Heaton, *Billmeir*, 19–43; Higgins's article "The House that Jack Built"; Newall Dunn Cuttings Folder, Bill Meir, in Guildhall Library.

94   Heaton, *Billmeir*, 19–29; Gretton, 123.

95   Newall Dunn Cuttings Folder.

96   Heaton, *Billmeir*, 36; Gretton, 123; Mattesini II, 126. LJOC July 15, 1938.

97   *Country Life* magazine on May 12, 2011.

98   Claims that Billmeir was Commodore of the Royal Southampton Yacht Club, in González, 278, Heaton, *Billmeir*, 61, and Howson, 89, were denied by Membership Secretary Ms Maggie Puleston in her kind response on May 30, 2022, to the author's inquiry. She noted: "The name means nothing to us at all."

99   For information about Billmeir and the guild I am very grateful to Lieutenant Colonel Richard Cole-Mackintosh the Chief Executive Officer in an email on October 5, 2022.

100 González, 370–72.

101 European companies, see González, 317–18, 339, 370. Foreign ships sunk website.

102 The GC&CS priorities at this time were Italy, Japan, the Soviet Union, and the United States.

103 This passage is based upon Kahn, *Seizing the Enigma*, 99–102, hereafter Kahn. For air force and some maritime intercepts, see UKNA HW 21/1–4.

104 For Italian Comint, see Santoni, *Ultra intelligence e machine enigma nella guerra di Spagna*, esp. 26–29, 133–207, 208–62. Christos's Military and Intelligence Corner website, Italian codebreakers of FII; Poggiaroni website, Naval Intelligence Operations of the Servizio Informazioni Segrete; Axis History Forum website, Spanish Civil War, subject Italian comint, SIM leaders and activities in France, correspondence from January 22, 2022.

105 German and Italian intelligence actvities monitoring shipping, see Alcofar, *Marina*, 123–24; Alpert, 98–101; Mattesini I, 34; Tanner, 154–58, 269–70.

106 Hermann, 33.

107 Alcofar, *Marina*, 123–24; Cervera, 223; Morenos II, 871.

108 Kahn, 106.

109 See Pasqualini, *Carte Segrete dell'Intelligence Italiana*, 294–99.

110 Sfikas 4.

111 Alpert, 109.

112 The Espinosa network, see Morenos III, 1794–96; Red Espinosa website. Soler and López-Brea, *Soldados sin rostro*, 92–93, 233–34. The author was unable to examine this work and the references come from the Red Espinoa website.

113 The formal name of The Cowl was Secret Committee of Revolutionary Action, or Comité Secret d'Action Révolutionnaire. French security authorities infiltrated the movement and rolled it up in November 1937.

114 González, 127, 187; Mattesini I, 115–18.

115 Details of Left-Wing sabotage are from the Soviet Empire website, summarized in Axis History Forum website, Spanish Civil War, Chronology of Spanish Republican Naval Actions + Comintern (Wollweber) sabotages. Correspondence from January 13, 2023. Also, *Lloyd's Lost*. After the war, Wollweber became East German Security Minister until he fell out of favor with his superiors and died in obscurity in 1967.

116 Details of these discussions and the consequences are in Alcofar, *Marina*, 101–3; Alpert, 102; Mattesini I, 23–48; Rapalino Appendix VI, Thomas Appendix 4.

117 Submarine deployment, see Alcofar, *Marina*, 106–8; Mattesini I, 51–54, 84–91.

118 Sonar, called Asdic by the British, originally referred to an active underwater sensor, but since all navies used a passive sensor based upon hydrophones, the generic term sonar will be used to refer to both sensors.

119 See discussion on Axis History Forum website, World War 2 in Africa & the Mediterranean, Italian submarine strategy, from January 15, 2023.

120 The term "sacred ego" (*sacro egoism*) was coined to define Italy's approach in entering the Great War. For international law and submarine operations, see Grunawalt, "Submarine Warfare," esp. 307–13.

121 The first Italian submarine campaign, see Alcofar, *Marina*, 106–15, 136–40, Appendix 3; Alpert, 102–6; Bargoni, 151–65, 222–43; Bargoni, "La prima campagna sottomarina," 78–86, hereafter Bargoni I; English, 62; Heaton, 26–28; Mattesini I, 54–56, 80–84, 94–107; Morenos II, 893–903, 920–23; Morenos III, 1499–503, 1534–37, 1577–83; Rapalino, 169–80, which includes examples of commanders' complaints; Recalde, *Los submarinos italianos*, 28–52; Tanner, 261–65.

122 Tanner, 139.

123 These discussions, see Mattesini I, 69–76; Tanner, 261–65.

124 The German attitudes to the Italian submarine campaign, see Tanner, 262–63.

125 UKNA HW 21/1 AS/0094.

126 Rapalino, 170.

127 Rapalino, 179.

128 González, 111.

129 "Ursula" was apparently named by Dönitz after his daughter. For U-boat operations, see Alpert, 98–101; Bendert, "La Operación 'Ursula'"; Frank, "Misperception," 42; Huan, 23, 26–28; Mattesini I, 58–64; Morenos II, 939–41; Tanner, 225–27, 258–60; Toro II, 85–87; U-boat website, Vega, "Operation Ursula," and Feldgrau website, *Pre–1939 U-boat missions?*

130 Alcofar, *Marina*, 106–8; Mattesini I, 51–54.

131 Verdiá was killed in an air attack upon Malaga a fortnight later.

132 Iachino was the navy's youngest rear admiral. Fischel would command German naval forces off Spain until March 19, 1937, and then from May 14–June 22 and September 8–October 7, 1937, and February 8–March 18, 1938, while remaining Commander of Armoured Ships until September 8, 1938.

133 These meetings, see Alcofar, *Marina*, 122–23; Alpert, 106–7; Alpert, *International*, 94; Bargoni, 173–89; Mattesini I, 84–91.

134 Spanish sources are unclear as to when they were given names.

135 For the second submarine campaign, see Alcofar, *Marina*, 279, 300–1; Bargoni, 300–2, 314–31, 344–56, 373–86. See also Alpert, 200–1; English, 67–68; González, 96, 110–11, 121, 132, 167, 180, 235, 339–40, 436; Heaton, 57–58, 70–71; Lachadenède, 400–1; *Lloyd's Lost*; Mattesini I, 129–32; Morenos III, 1679–81, 1733–39, 1775–77; Recalde, 54–71, 73–89.

136 González, 132, says this attack was on May 30.

137 The minelaying campaign, see Alpert, 171–72, 200–1; Bargoni I, 273–76; Cervera, 86, 164; Edwards, 113; English, 137–38; Francisco Moreno, 147–48, 248–49; González, 336–39; Gretton, 139; Heaton, 30, 70; Huan, 25; Lachadenède, 383–85; *Lloyd's Lost*; Manrique/Molina, 376; Mattesini I, 114–15, 121; Morenos III, 1569–679; Tanner, 142–50.

138 Cervera, 86.

139 Tanner, 142, calls her the *August Schultz*. The Germans later supplied some EMD weapons with a 150-kg charge. The Nationalists later received former Dutch Vickers H Mk II, Swedish Motola 1930, and 100 pear-shaped Carbonite mines.

140 Tanner, 142.

141 LJOC February 26, 1937.

142 The three men who suffered the longer sentences had them halved on appeal. Aylen, who spent his whole career with Union Castle, retired in June 1939 and died, aged 88, in February 1963. Data courtesy of Marian Gray through the British Merchant Navy website. Hereafter Marian Gray BMN web.

143 Lachadenède, 384.

144 This account is based upon the inquiry held in Gibraltar on May 17 which is in UKNA ADM 116/3521 and ignores Republican Navy assistance. See also Alpert, 171; Morenos III, 1677–79.

145 Scurfield was promoted to commander on June 30, 1937. Seven of the destroyer's crew received gallantry awards. For Royal Navy casualties, see Royal Navy Casualties website.

146 Morenos III, 2144–45.

147 The *Belle Hirondelle*, see González, 433, which is not confirmed by any other source, including Lachadenède's official account of French activity.

148 Saiz 1, 407; Saiz 2, 468.

149 Attacks upon ships, see Edwards, 134; Heaton, 28, 31; Lachadenède, 58–62, 380–86; Morenos III, 1819–21; Saiz 1, 468–73. Press Bureau of Spanish Embassy, "List of Ships," hereafter "Spanish Ship List." UKNA ADM 116/3534 and ADM 116/4084.

150 Lachadenède, 56.

151 Salerno, 73–74, 76.

152 The *Djebel Antar* was sold to J. A. Billmeir and Company later in the year and renamed *Helendra*, but did not trade with the Spanish Republic, and in January 1938 was sold. For the French reaction, see Lachadenède, 57–58.

153 The attack on the *Jaime I*, see Alcofar, *Aviación*, 195–96.

154 The *Cala Mayor* was raised but again sunk by Republican bombers at Vinaroz in May 1938.

155 The *Barletta* and *Deutschland* incidents, see Alcofar, *Marina*, 177–83; Alpert, 172–77; Bargoni, *Participación*, 288–92; DGFP, 296–99; Edwards, 58; English, 138–42; Frank, "Misperception," 31–41; Garcia Martinez, *Katiuskas*, 49; Heaton, 57; Huan, 24, 34, 36–39; Lachadenède, 120–21; Mattesini I, 122–25; Morenos III, 1703–13; Saiz 2, 468–73; Tänner, 213–19, 223–25; Toro II, 89–90. See also from Axis History website, Spanish Civil Web section on the subject Panzerschiff Deutschland, 1937, from September 22, 2012, and Wells website.

156 Proskurov would later head the GRU then the Long-Range Bomber Force, but was executed in October 1941, a scapegoat for the German surprise attack upon the Soviet Union. The other pilot was Captain Anton Progrorin.

157 Claims by Alpert, 172, and Mattesini I, 121, that the *Deutschland* incident was linked to delivery I–28, of 31 Katie bombers by the *Cabo San Tomé* on May Day, are wrong. I–28 consisted of R-Z ground-attack aircraft and no Katies were delivered until May 31 and June 21 (I–33/34), in the *Artea Mendi* and *Aldecoa* respectively.

158 Germany and the Naval Patrol, see DGFP, 298, 306–32, 348–52.

159 Frank, "Misperception," 41ff, is the best account of this incident, which has similarities with the Gulf of Tonkin incident in 1964. Tanner, 244–47, claims there was a hit. See also Huan, 39–42; Gretton, 176–79; Morenos III, 1718–22. The author would like to thank Dr Norman Friedmann for his technical advice in a message of January 23, 2023.

160 Tanner, 245.

161 Halpern, 266–67.

162 The Abwehr was making frequent reports of the presence of "Red" and even of Russian boats; indeed, it later confidently reported that "one or perhaps two Russian submarines fired the torpedoes against *Leipzig.*" In December 1937, an OKM intelligence officer commented upon another Abwehr submarine report: "This account appears to be a complete fantasy." Tanner, 244n22.

163 Tanner, 243.

164 See DGFP, 354–85, 414–20; Edwards, 59–63; Mattesini I, 127.

165 For the missions, see Alcofar, *Marina*, 102; Alpert, 97–98; Bargoni, 113–22, 147–49, 194–97, 243–46; Huan, 29; Mattesini I, 91–94; Tanner, 194; Toro II, 87–88. Meyer-Döhner remained Naval Attaché until the end of World War II. Ferretti was relieved at the end of 1938 by Rear Admiral Enrico Accorretti.

166 Fascist naval supplies from Bargoni, 132–34, Annex 6; Manrique/Molina, 210–11, 376, 378–81; Mattesini I, 32–33; Mortera Pérez, *La artillería naval en la Guerra Civil Española*, Appendix IV, hereafter Mortera. For Favignana, see Alcofar, *Marina*, 297–98; Bargoni, 297–98; Cervera, 86; González, 333, 336.

167 Alpert, 106–7; Mattesini I, 50; Tanner, 142–43.

168 Nelson's ships were based there and it was where Admiral Cuthbert Collingwood, his friend who commanded the Mediterranean Fleet after Trafalgar, spent his final years, his home now a hotel. The U.S. Navy was also based there in the 1830s and 1840s, and left a small cemetery on the northern shore of the bay.

169 English, 63; Mattesini I, 22. Santafé, Palma de Mallorca website.

170 For the base, see Alcofar, *Marina*, 219–22; Bargoni, 219, 303–4; Mattesini I, 32–33. On November 7, there were 3,150 tonnes of fuel oil in Palma. UKNA HW 21/1 AS/0056.

171 Eden, 475; Lachadenède, 48, 63–64; Tanner, 200.

172 For the impact of the agreement, see Playfair, *The Mediterranean and Middle East*, Volume 1, 7–9, hereafter Playfair. See also Mattesini I, 95–97; Tanner, 276. UKNA HW 21/2 for the period December 1936–June 1937, FO 371/22641.

173 For the Malaga campaign and its maritime aspects, see Alcofar, *Marina*, 135–36; Alpert, 126–33; Bargoni, 204–9; Cervera, 67–74; English, 65–66; González, 100–1, 119, 169; Heaton, 26–28; Mattesini I, 107–10; Morenos III, 1453–530, 1629; Rapalino, 204–6; Thomas, 480–83.

174 For these operations, see Bargoni, 209–11; Heaton, 70; Mattesini I, 110–14.

175 For the Nationalist Navy to mid-1937, see Alpert, 69–71, 194–97; English, 48–49, 63–69; Francisco Moreno, 137–45, 160–88; Gretton, 59–60; Mattesini I, 49–50; Morenos III, 1553–77, 1583–601, 1637–69. For the fleet's strategic dilemmas, see Frank, "Un peso muerto o una fuerza frustrada?"

176 Cerezo, 15.

177 Gretton, 54.

178 Alpert, 200; English, 70–71. Soviet Empire website, Spanish Republican Navy during the Civil War.

179 For the Republican Fleet to mid-1937, see Alpert, 60–69, 112–22, 133–44, 187–94, 201–6, Appendix II; Cerezo, 14–21; English, 61–71, 100–1; Gretton, 60–61; Heaton, 22; Mattesini I, 33–34; Morenos III, 1589–93, 1620–23, 1669–74, 1729–87; Saiz 2, 446–48.

180 While many of their Red Army colleagues were purged upon returning to the Soviet Union, the sailors appear to have escaped this fate.

181 For this subject, see the three articles in Frank, "Submarinos republicanos españoles bajo mando soviéto"; Infiesta, "La marina soviéta en la guerra de España," 84–85; Monakov/Ribalkin, 71.

182 Similar causes probably accounted for many of the 15 U-boats lost to unknown causes on their first North Atlantic patrol from November 1942 to February 1945. U-boat website, Fates/losses/cause.htm.

183 Monakov/Ribalkin, 68.

184 The French Navy ordered eight, which were completed after the German Occupation of 1940, some as air-sea rescue boats, the design being the basis of some French Navy postwar patrol boats. For this information the author would like to thank Mr Philip Simons of the World Ship Society in a message of March 21, 2021.

185 Mortera, Appendix IV.

186 For aircraft, see Gardner, "Ramón Franco," 101–2, hereafter Gardner; Howson, *Aircraft of the Spanish Civil War*, 177–78, hereafter Howson, *Air*; Morenos II, 941–44.

187 For the interdiction of these sea-lanes, see Alcofar, *Aviación*, 223–27, 224n6; González, 112, 132; Heaton, 28, 30–31, 33, 56–57, 69: Morenos III, 1623–24; Mattesini I, 127–28, 166; Ries/Ring, 49–50, call the ship *Nuria*; Richardson, "The Development of Airpower Concepts and Air Combat Techniques in the Spanish Civil War," 17, 19, hereafter Richardson. The torpedoes were imported from Norway, but AS/88 abandoned their use in August. Ries/Ring, 83.

188 Mattesini I, 50.

189 For air attacks in 1936, see Alpert, 121–22; Frank, "Cooperation," 83; Morenos II, 903–6.

190 Mattesini I, 120.

191 Ramón Franco, see Gardner, esp. 85–86.

192 Gardner, 98; Morenos III, 1669.

193 For the Italian air force in the Balearics to July 1937, see Alcofar, *Aviación*, Appendices III, IV; González, 112, 132; Heaton, 57, 70; Howson, *Air*, 228, 275; Mattesini II, 98–104. UKNA HW 21/2 AS/0062, 0115, 0126, 0143, 0150, 0155, 0182, 0190 and 0196.

194 Alcofar, *Marina*, 297; Bargoni, 297; Mattesini I, 127–28, UKNA HW 21/2 AS/0190 and 0194.

195 Heaton, 70; Lachadenède, 400; Reis/Ring, 830; Sfikas 4.

196 *Northern Daily Mail*, May 25, 1937.

197 A claim in the official Spanish account that the Irish-registered *Foynes* was sunk in Alicante on June 27 is inaccurate; she was actually sunk in Valencia in January 1939. González, 429. I would like to thank Dr Matthew Potter, the Curator of Limerick Museum, for cross-checking Cork and Limerick journals. Details of her loss in January 1939 are given in the Scott article, "Limerick Steam," 30, while the online copy of the 1938 *Lloyd's Shipping Register* held by the Surveyors' Office, Middlesbrough, has a printed note that she was "Sunk in port by aircraft 1.39."

198 Lachadenède, 400–1.

199 For these discussions, see Richardson.

200 Francisco Moreno, 211–13; Morenos III, 2004–5, 2039–41; O'Donnell, "Las Pérdidas de Buques Mercantes Republicanos Causadas por Hidroaviones de la Legión Cóndor," 62, hereafter O'Donnell. Salvador Moreno was relieved as commander of the *Canarias* on August 27. Francisco Moreno, 191n1.

Chapter 3

1 Hooton, 69.

2 English, 45.

3 Tanner, 63–65.

4 Saville's name is sometimes shown as Savile. His name is not on any of the 1936 lists of British serving and retired officers.

5 For this incident, see Alpert, 75–76; Heaton, 19; Ribelles, *La Marina Real Británica y la Guerra civil in Asturias*, 140, hereafter Ribelles. *Daily News*, Perth, Australia, August 10, 1936. UKNA FO 371/20533 W9093, 9086. Letter from W. A. Goodman to British Ambassador Sir Henry Chilton, August 13, 1936.

6 Nationalist sources say the 4-inch guns were used, while the Foreign Office reports said it was a 6-inch shell, but a hit, or even a near miss, with them would have sunk the diminutive craft.

7 Alpert, 74; English 49; Thomas 384.

8 For Republican submarine operations, see Alpert, 75–77; English, 52–53; Heaton, 20.

9 Lachadenède, 385–86.

10 For the Basque Navy and operations to March 1937, see Alpert, 146–47; English, 95–96; Heaton, 22–29; Website Activities of the Basque Auxiliary Navy.

11 Edwards, 112; González, 313.

12 For the Nationalist Navy to March 1937, see Alpert, 31–32; English, 48; Morenos II, 953–1026. Castro died in January 1939.

13 Gretton I, 12–13.

14 Based on ship entries in González, esp. 325–26.

15 For commercial traffic in northern ports, August 1936 to March 1937, see González, 113, 144, 165, 268–69, 272; Morenos II, 981–82, 1020–24; Ribelles, 101–9; Salas, *Intervención*, Annex 20.

16 For merchant shipping losses in this chapter, see González, 141–42, 411–41; Heaton, 20. *Lloyd's Lost*; "Spanish Ship List"; Strelbitskiy website.

17 Sota y Aznar, see González, 114–22; Naviera Aznar-Auñamendi Eusko Entziklopedia and Shipslist websites.

18 Wells website.

19 English, 94–95; Heaton, 19.

20 Salas, *Intervención*, Annex 20. The British imported some 60,000 tons of Basque iron ore annually for foundries in South Wales and Tyneside/Wearside, according to official trade statistics.

21 For the voyage of the *Andriev*, see Rozin, "Soviet sailors in the Spanish Civil War – Supply of the Northern Front."

22 For ams shipments, see Alpert, 142; González, 310–12; English, 96–97; Howson, 261, 264.

23 UKNA ADM 116/4084; Website SS-Douglas.

24 For French ships stopped, see Lachadenède, Annex 5, and for Soviet ships, see Rozin, "Northern Front." González, 315–25, provides much information about the foreign shipping companies, totalling some fifty vessels trading with the enclave.

25 For the *Palos* incident, see Alpert, 93–96; DGFP, 201–3; English, 96–97; González, 188; Gretton 108–10; Heaton, 24–25; Morenos II, 992–96; Tanner, 93–96; Thomas, 572, 577. Activities of the Basque Navy website.

26 Alpert, 94–95.

27 Heaton, 25, 27. Spanish sources wrongly claim the *Blackhill*'s sister ship, *Bramhill*, delivered four French guns to Bilbao in January.

28 For the harassment of merchantmen in the first quarter of 1937, see Alpert, 125, 142; Cable, 45–46; Cerezo, 18, 20; Cervera, 125–72, 191–98; Edwards, 114–17; English, 98; González, 123–24; González, "Pérdidas," 27, 29; Gretton, 57–58; Heaton, 26, 31, 33; Lachadenède, Annex 5, 380, 385–86; Ribelles, 101–9. Rozin, "Northern Front." Nelogov website, Soviet Merchant Marine. Civil War in Spain.

29 On December 31, the Americans informed Berlin there was no legal impediment to Cuse assembling war materiel. DGFP, 198.

30   For the *Mar Cantábrico*, see Alpert, 140–42; English, 97–99; Francisco Moreno, 150–58; Heaton, 29–30; Howson, 172–91; Lachadenède, 378–80; Morenos II, 1034–39, 1039–69; Thomas, 575–76, 614. The cargo is listed in Axis History Forum, Spanish Civil War, Aircraft captured aboard the Republican ship Mar Cantabr (*sic*), response by Ironmachine on September 27, 2013. Websites Aberdeen Ships: Vendaval and Activities of the Basque Navy.

31   The *Yorkbrook* was previously Estonian, registered to Usalduhing Jakobson ja Ko, with Charles Strubin acting as manager.

32   Lachadenède, 38–39.

33   Francisco Moreno, 154–55, confirmed receiving the Comint data.

34   She would return to the mercantile marine after the war but became a constructive total loss after a fire in September 1962.

35   Alpert, 148–50; English, 100–1.

36   For this campaign, see Hooton, 87–101.

37   González, 437.

38   Morenos II, 1,114–15.

39   Cable, 58.

40   Cable, 44–45.

41   Cable, 45, quoting UKNA FO 371/21351.

42   Cable, 45–46. UKNA ADM 116/3512.

43   González, 436.

44   For the *Thorpehall* incident, see Cable, 46–53; Morenos II, 1100–1. UKNA ADM 116/3514. The ship is sometimes called the *Thorpehill*.

45   Some British accounts refer to Moreno as Moreu.

46   Lachadenède, 48–49.

47   Gretton I, 12.

48   Pursey had served on HMS *Hood* and played a part in the Invergordon Mutiny. Roskill, 378. He would later become a Labour Party MP and was succeeded in 1970 by John Prescott, later Deputy Prime Minister under Tony Blair.

49   Wells website, United States ships … Mining of Shipping Lanes and Harbors.

50   Tanner, 145.

51   For British decision-making on the blockade, see Alpert, 150–53; Alpert, *International*, 40–42; Cable, 53–76, 87–91; Cervera, 170; Eden, 498–500; Edwards, 113; Gretton II, 98–99; Heaton, 34–36, 41–42; Roskill, 377–80; Thomas, 618–21. UKNA ADM 116/3512 and 3514, CAB 23/88/5. HOC Vol 322 Cols 1029–142.

52   When Baldwin was replaced by Neville Chamberlain at the end of May, Hoare moved to the Home Office, where he became one of the most liberal Home Secretaries (Secretary for the Interior). He was replaced by the womanizing former Secretary of State for War (Army Minister) Alfred Duff Cooper, usually known as Duff. He should not be confused with the First Sea Lord, Chatfield. Despite the title, the First Sea Lord is rarely a member of the nobility, although for expanding the Royal Navy, Chatfield was made the First Baron Chatfield by King George VI on June 11.

53   Cable, 56. Runciman lost his position when Chamberlain became Premier, but was ennobled and had the unique achievement of sitting with his father, also Walter, in the House of Lords. Walter Senior founded the Hall Line, which merged with Ellerman in 1901 to become Ellerman-Hall, which had 46 ships in 1936. The report by Walter Junior following a visit to Czechoslovakia laid the foundation for the infamous Munich Agreement in 1938.

54   Morenos II, 1131n240.

55   Heaton, 36.

56 UKNA FO 371/21352.
57 Cable, 70.
58 Cervera, 136; Morenos II, 1090–92.
59 Cable, 72.
60 Cable, 62–63.
61 For Troncoso's intervention and its impact, see Cable 62–66. UKNA ADM 116/3512.
62 Information from HMS Hood Association.
63 Aberdeen Ships Verdaval website.
64 Cable, 72.
65 Lachadenède, Annex 5.
66 On the same day, his old command, the *Bramhill*, departed Valencia carrying food to Bilbao.
67 Heaton, 41–42.
68 Cable, 74.
69 Heaton, 46. Pope sold the ship in 1939; she was renamed the *Jeanne M* and sunk by a U-boat on December 2, 1940, while sailing from Cardiff to Lisbon with coal. The author would like to thank Marian Gray BMN web, for details of the dockers, William and Beatrice, who died in 1967 and 1962 respectively.
70 For events from April–June, see Cable, 75–76, 87–91; Gretton, 214–50; Heaton, 46; Morenos II, 1027–151, 1153–211; Ribelles, 114–33. UKNA ADM116/3514.
71 Pridham had commanded the battlecruiser in her previous commission. HMS Hood Association.
72 Many thanks to Mr Paul Bevand, Vice-President of the HMS Hood Association, for identifying Terry.
73 Prance died in February 1946 when Indian rioters threw him out of a window. Thanks to Marian Gray BMN web for this information.
74 According to the *Daily Express* of April 24, which had a reporter on board the *Hamsterley*, when *Firedrake* signaled *Hamsterly* to proceed, Still bellowed through his megaphone to the *Stanbrook*: "Come on, my lads! Follow me into Bilbao!"
75 Ramsey should not be confused with Admiral Bertram Ramsay, who at that time was inactive, having briefly been chief of staff to his friend Backhouse, with whom he had quarreled.
76 Letter to author from Captain Dick, March 6, 1978.
77 The *Backworth* departed Bilbao in early May carrying iron ore, together with 600 women and children.
78 Gretton, 171.
79 Morenos II, 1149.
80 Heaton, 51.
81 Morenos II, 1132. For other Spanish accounts of these incidents, see Cervera, 139–40. He claimed (on 138) that during this incident the British signaled: "We do not recognize its blockade and we will not permit the intervention of ships on the high seas."
82 Huan, 29.
83 For the loss of *España*, see Alpert, 163–64; Cervera, 140–41; Heaton, 51; Howson, *Air*, 158–60; Morenos II, 1131–37; Saiz 2, 446–48. Axis History Forum, Spanish Civil War, Loss of the Battleship España entry from February 2, 2022, especially Ironmachine's comments.
84 Tyne & Wear Archives and Museums website.
85 Edwards, 117.
86 Gretton, 171; González, 235.
87 Cable, 118; González, 236; HOC May 4, 1937, Volume 323 cc.946–53.
88 Leborde was a nobleman, nicknamed "Count Jean," a pioneer of naval aviation who commanded France's first carrier. In November 1942, he ordered the scuttling of the French fleet at Toulon.

89 For the evacuation of Bilbao, see Cable, 8–14, 105–19; Cervera, 135; González, 328–29; Heaton, 51–52; Lachadenède, 108–10, Annex 10; Morenos II, 1153–211; Roskill, 381.

90 I have relied more upon Cable's detailed description of these events, 8–14, than Heaton's, 51. See also Lachadenède, 423.

91 Lachadenède, 432–33.

92 Edwards, 101; Roskill, 380–81.

93 The *Habana* would take Basque refugees to both Pallice and Southampton before finally sailing to Bordeaux, where she remained moored until the end of the war. The yacht was requisitioned as HMS *Warrior II* in 1939 and lost to a Stuka attack in July 1940. González, 235.

94 Heaton, 52.

95 Heaton, 30–31.

96 Oden'hal would head the French naval mission to London at the beginning of the war.

97 Lachadenède, 424–25. See also Cable, 118. In July 1940, Godfroy's task force, Force X, was compelled to surrender to the British in Alexandria.

98 Lachadenède, 425–26. He calls Ceretti "Ceruti."

99 Heaton, 52; Lachadenède, 481.

100 LJOC July 3, 1937.

101 Cervera, 172; González, 298n1; Lachadenède, 426.

102 Lachadenède, 432–33.

103 Cervera, 170; González, 301.

104 González, 294–95, 347.

105 Alpert, *International*, 94–99, 157–59; DGFP, 412–13.

106 DGFP, 565; Edwards, 96; Thomas, 736–37.

107 Edwards, 95–97; Heaton, 64–65.

108 HOC May 4, 1937, Volume 323 cc 946–53.

109 For this campaign, see Hooton, 102–9. See also Ribelles, 144.

110 For French refugee operations, see Lachadenède, Annex 10.

111 For the Santander blockade, see Alpert, 164–65; Gretton II, 100–2; Heaton, 64–65; Ribelles, 143–93; Lachadenède, Annex 10; Martínez, *El final del frente norte*, 26–28; Morenos II, 1213–92; Activities of the Basque Navy and Tyne & Wear Museums websites.

112 González, 434; Lachadenède, 427n1.

113 Gretton II, 101.

114 Lachadenède, 427–28.

115 For Glanely, see biography in Museum of Wales website, William James Tatem, 1st Baron Glanely 1868–1942. He was killed while on holiday during an air raid on Weston-Super-Mare on June 24, 1942.

116 González, 424; Gretton I, 13.

117 Ribelles, 149.

118 Heaton, 67. House of Lords debate, December 13, 1938, Volume 111 cc 502–43. For details of this incident, thanks to Hugh of BMN web.

119 For Spanish ships sailing to French ports, see Lachadenède, 483–85.

120 Other sources say this incident was on August 24.

121 Ribelles, 173–74.

122 Heaton, 65; González, 328; Lachadenède, 432–33; Morenos II, 1285, 1291–92; Ribelles, Table IV.

123 González, 297n1, 298n1.

124 Roskill, 381.

125 Lachadenède, 429.

126 The *Bobie* was registered in Gibraltar and owned by Mr W. H. McEwen, a relative of Alfred Pope's partner, Thomas McEwen. Despite flying the Red Ensign, her crew was Greek. Heaton, 67; Ribelles, 147.

127 See Lonsdale's web article, "The blockade-running British women at the forefront of Basque evacuations."

128 Lachadenède, 430.

129 Alpert, 183.

130 LJOC August 13, 1937.

131 Lachadenède, 431–32.

132 Ribelles, 198–99.

133 González, 130.

134 For this offensive, see Hooton, 109–14.

135 For events off Gijon, see Alpert, 165–66; Gretton, 245; Gretton II, 102–3; Heaton, 65–67; Heaton, *Billmeir*, 126; Lachadenède, Annex 10; Morenos II, 1293–383; Ribelles, 195–236. Gretton, 126, believed "from reliable evidence" that the *Stanwold* allowed herself to be captured in the north in 1937.

136 Lachadenède, 431.

137 Morenos II, 1379.

138 Roskill, 382.

139 Gretton II, 102.

140 The Spanish List shows this as two incidents, with the ship listed under both names. Of the *Dover Abbey*'s 20-man crew, her master and one other were British. Heaton, 67.

141 Saiz 1, 569.

142 González, 424–25. The destroyer was salvaged in March and joined the Nationalist fleet. The *Reina* was salvaged in June 1938.

143 Fuentes would die in Paris in 1975.

144 Heaton, 67; Lachadenède, 432; Morenos II, 1381.

145 González, 421; Morenos, 1381; *Lloyd's Lost* 1937, which gives the date as October 29.

146 Gretton, 254; Lachadenède, 432–33; Ribelles, 236.

147 González, 297n1, 298n1; Morenos II, 1381.

148 Sales and disposals from González, 234–35, 233n1.

149 González, 315, 297n1; Morenos II, 1383, Annex III, 1437–38, Annex I.

150 Details in the Trades Union Congress archives, Spanish Seamen in British Ports 1939–1940 and 1939–1942, 292/946/25b, and in particular 292/946/25b/3.

151 For nationalist special operations, see Alpert, 165–66; González, 127, 131, 154, 177, 187; Lachadenède, 481; D. W. Pike, *Conjecture, Propaganda and Deceit and the Spanish Civil War* (Stanford, 1970), 129. Moreno website, "Historia del intento de secuestro del submarino republicano C2," provides the greatest detail. Lachadenède calls the tanker the *Campo Amour*.

152 Lachadenède, 484.

153 Alpert, 184; Heaton, 67.

Chapter 4

1 For the background, see Alpert, 177; DGFP, 432–33; Mattesini II, 39–43; Mills, "The Nyon Conference," hereafter Mills. None of the Russian vessels listed in González, 276–77, carried an *Igrek*.

2 Many of the larger Republican ships received 12.7mm machine guns and some carried depth charges. Website Rozin, "The Fourth Series of Deliveries."

3 See Rozin, "Completion of deliveries to the South."

4   Churchill, *The Second World War* Volume 1, 199; Eden, 473–86, 505–17, 535–38.

5   Bargoni, 297, 300; Tanner, 269.

6   For Paladini's attacks, see Alpert, 142; Bargoni, 331–36, 339, 343–44; Howson, 195; González, 105, 131–39; Heaton, 72–73; Lachadenède, 136, 400; *Lloyd's Lost*; Mattesini II, 46–56; SovShip, 12; Rozin website, "Blockade of the Tunisian Strait: The outrages continue."

7   This is how the ship's name is recorded in Lloyd's Shipping Register, and not *George W. McKnight*.

8   Heaton, 72. Lachadenède, 400, claims she was part of a 12-ship convoy which dispersed as it approached Sicily. Although damaged by a U-boat in May 1945, she survived the war, to be broken up in 1954. See the U-boat website, entry https://uboat.net/allies/merchants/ship/1594. html.

9   UKNA HW 21/3 AS/0230.

10   Lachadenède, Annex 8.

11   Rozin, "Second campaign of the Italian Fleet."

12   For the submarine campaign I have relied largely upon Bargoni, 314–31, 343–56, 373–86, Annexes 4 and 5, rather than Mattesini II, 51–54, 63–65. See also Alcofar, *Marina*, 193–210; Alpert, 178–80; González, 96, 139; González, "Pérdidas," 29–30; Gretton III, 204–6; Heaton, 73; Lachadenède, 133–49, 185–259; Recalde, 95–109, 145–47. Rozin, *Robbery in the Aegean Sea*.

13   Kahn, 99–102; Roskill, 388–89. See also Frank, *Logistic*, 185n40. Later Italian submarine signals may be found in UKNA HW18.

14   Predictably, González, 96, claims she was carrying unidentified "war material." Rozin, "Robbery in the Aegean Sea." Lusena replaced Commander Primo Longobardo, who had sunk the *Navarra* earlier in the year.

15   Alpert, 179; González, 73, 432; Gretton III, 204–5. UKNA ADM 116/3917. Apart from Greeks there was a British NIC observer, a Hungarian radio operator, and a Romanian cook. Gretton, 216.

16   González, 180.

17   The Type 124 would be the standard sonar for destroyers and frigates throughout World War II.

18   For the *Havock* incident and the Nyon Agreement, see Alpert, 178–79; Bargoni, 356–60; Bargoni II, 84; Brodhurst, 97–98; Gretton, 193–96; Gretton III, 205; Somerville, 40; Mattesini II, 59–61; Morenos III, 1819–21; UKNA ADM 116/3534. Somerville was promoted to vice-admiral on September 11. For the effect upon sonar performance of sea conditions in the Mediterranean, see Marder, 70.

19   Brodhurst, 97.

20   Roskill, 384.

21   DGFP, 456.

22   Ciano, *Dairy 1937–1943*, 88, hereafter Ciano.

23   For the effects of the blockade, see Mattesini II, 57–62. Rozin, "Robbery in the Aegean Sea."

24   Mattesini II, 146.

25   Mattesini II, 165.

26   Ciano, 1, 4–5.

27   Lachadenède, 136.

28   Churchill, 220; Gretton III, 204.

29   She would distinguish herself during the Siege of Sevastapol in 1941–42. Rozin, "Soviet note to Italy and Nyon Conference."

30   For the Nyon Conference, its background, and aftermath, see Alcofar, *Marina*, 210–43; Alpert, 178–83; Bargoni, 362–73; Cervera, 231–42; Churchill, 220–23; Ciano, 6–10; Cortada, "Ships, Diplomacy and the Spanish Civil War"; Eden, 461, 467, 518–32; Edwards, 117–25; Gretton,

204–21, 234–41; Gretton III, 312–15; Gretton, "The Nyon Conference"; Halpern, 311–31; Heaton, 69, 74; Lachadenède, Annexes 9 and 13; Lammers, "The Nyon Arrangements of 1937"; Mattesini II, 59–74; Mills; Morenos III, 1835–49; Roskill, 383–87; Salerno, 76; Sfikas 4; Tanner, 273–300. UKNA ADM 116/3520, 3522 & 3525. Rozin, "Soviet note to Italy and Nyon Conference."

31 Eden, 516.
32 Phillips was lost on HMS *Prince of Wales* in December 1941.
33 Brodhurst, 97.
34 Gretton III, 205; Halpern, 187–89. Edwards, 117–23; Gretton, 205–7; Roskill, 383–85.
35 Edwards, 119; Halpern, 187–89.
36 Edwards, 120.
37 Gretton III, 205–6.
38 Edwards, 101, 119.
39 Lachadenède, 261–70; Salerno, 75–56, 79.
40 Gretton III, 205.
41 DGFP, 443.
42 Smirnov-Svetlovsky became First Deputy Commisar of the Navy on December 31, but was arrested on March 26, 1939, and executed a year later. Axis History Forum website, Soviet Union, entry Admiral Petr Ivanovich Smirnov-Svetlovsky of March 9, 2022.
43 Edwards, 126.
44 The Nyons zones and routes are shown in Lachadenède, Maps 7 and 8.
45 Gretton, 226.
46 Churchill, 221; Lachadenède, 261–70.
47 Eden, 532.
48 Morenos III, 1835–36.
49 Gretton III, 208.
50 Cervera, 235–38.
51 Rawlings, *Coastal, Support and Special Squadrons of the RAF*, 130–31, hereafter Rawlings. Blake had suffered two heart attacks during the summer, which shocked his friend Pound, and appointed Cunningham as a temporary measure, this becoming permanent when Blake was forced to retire on medical grounds. Cunningham then established a close relationship with Pound. Brodhurst, 95–96; Cunningham, 181, 187.
52 For British deployments, see Brodhurst, 98–99; Gretton, 230–32; Gretton III, 208; Rawlings, 139–43; Roskill, 385–87. Royal Navy organization and Deployment website.
53 Gretton III, 207–8. The carrier's sister ship, HMS *Courageous*, was lost to a U-boat in 1939.
54 For the French, see Lachadenède, 232–34, 315–18. Website Aeronavale, l'almanache année 1937.
55 Lachadenède, 212, 236.
56 Lachadenède, 402–3.
57 Halpern, 205, 371.
58 Gretton III, 208–9. Godfrey would be Director of Naval Intelligence from 1939–42 and a controversial commander of the Royal Indian Navy until 1946. James Bond's creator, Ian Fleming, served under Godfrey, whose wife and daughter were both involved in the British decryption center at Bletchley Park, and he was reportedly the model for Bond's boss, "M."
59 Ciano, 12.
60 Op cit.
61 Ciano, 14–15.
62 For the conference, see Cunningham, 186.

63 UKNA ADM 116/3678.

64 For the wind-down, see Alpert, 184; Halpern, 353–55; Gretton III, 208–10; UKNA ADM 116/3533.

65 UKNA FO 371/22641.

66 Roskill, 387.

67 For attacks by aircraft supporting the Italian blockade, see Bargoni, "Il dispositivo di blocco del Canale di Sicilia," 86–87, hereafter Bargoni III; González, 132; Gretton III, 204; Heaton, 71–73; Mattesini II, 39–51. See also LJOC at various dates.

68 This account incorporates details from the Danish official inquiry, a copy of which was kindly provided by Mr Jannik Hartrup, Curator, Maritime Museum of Denmark. See also Morenos III, 1813–14.

69 Gretton, 62; Mattesini II, 44, identifies her as the *Ilford*.

70 According to LJOC August 24, 1938, this ship had been bombed earlier, on August 6.

71 Gretton, 198; Halpern, 279–82.

72 According to LJOC of September 2, she was carrying ammunition.

73 The *Koutoubia* had picked up survivors from the Republican destroyers sunk off Tangiers in September 1936.

74 Howson, *Air*, 183. UKNA HW 12/3 AS/0216, 0221, 0223, 0227.

75 For the Nationalist fleet in this period, see Alpert, 184, 202–04; Cervera, 223–30; Francisco Moreno, 191–210; González, 109–10; Gretton, 255; English, 71–74, 108–9; Heaton, 74–75; Lachadenède, 402–3; Morenos III, 1859–67, 1873–81, 1907–8, 1919–59, 2123–47. Cerezo, 14–23. Rozin, "The outrages continue and Nationalists attack convoys."

76 An account of this clash is in UKNA ADM 116/3678. Gretton, 62–64.

77 LJOC September 14, 1937.

78 English, 74; Gretton, 64–65; Morenos III, 1922–32. Monreal's predecessor, Lieutenant Commander Vicente Ramírez de Togores, had been relieved in July as a scapegoat for failure in a clash with the *Baleares*. Alpert, 202.

79 For the Republican fleet, see Cerezo, 14–23; Gretton, 255; Morenos III, 1973–74, 2102–4, 2159–61.

80 English, 108–9; Gretton, 261–62. A list published in *Enciclopedia de la Aviación Militar Española* suggests the ship carried six aircraft, 50 tanks, 75 guns, 2,100 tonnes of small arms, 500 tonnes of munitions, and more than 2,700 tonnes of food. González, 109, wrongly claimed she had four 152mm and three 45mm guns. Axis History Forum, Spanish Civil War, Cabo San Tome Details response from Ironmachine, February 21, 2022.

81 Cervera, 248, claims the *Yolande*, *Sydney*, and *Francois* were actually Greek and carrying war materiel. Francisco Moreno, 227–31; Lachadenède suggests the *Yolande* was carrying war materiel, which she jettisoned before she entered Port Vendres.

82 Heaton, 75; González, 433–34; González, "Pérdidas," 30–36; Lachadenède, 438–39.

83 Heaton, 75.

84 For the Nationalist acquisition of Italian warships, see Alpert, 197–200; Bargoni, 360–62; Cervera, 181–88, 199–212; Ciano, 3; English, 107–8; Mattesini II, 77–79; Morenos III, 1962–64.

85 Ciano, 6.

86 Bargoni, 309–13, 360–62.

87 Mattesini II, 85–91.

88 For the Nationalists' reorganized blockade organization and operations, see Alpert, 196–97; Cervera, 228; Francico Moreno, 211–14; Halpern, 352; Mattesini II, 85–91; Morenos III, 1985–97, 2049–107. UKNA ADM 116/3525.

89 Alternate designations were *L–1* to *L–4*. Morenos III, 2099.

90 For Nationalist submarine operations from August 1937 to March 1938, see Alcofar, *Marina*, 280; Alpert, 199–200, 207–8; Bargoni, 300–2, 373–86; Cervera, 237–38, 247–48; Ciano, 8; González, 384–85; Heaton, 74–76; Lachadenède, 440; Mattesini II, 74–85; Morenos III, 1909–10, 2064–65, 2099–101; Recalde, 53–71, 90–119, 145–83. UKNA ADM 116/3532. For the Puerto Soller base, see Racalde, 54–71.

91 Recalde, 172.

92 For the *Basilisk* incident, see Bargon I, 389–91; Gretton II, 209; Halpern, 203, 330–31; Morenos III, 1967–73; Recalde, 150–51.

93 Details on the loss of the *Hannah* from website Stichting Maritiem-Historische Databank. See also Recaldes, 173.

94 LJOC January 16, 1938.

95 The Irish ship is called *Clouroa* in Mattesini II, 82.

96 This account greatly benefits from details in the *Gibraltar Chronicle and Official Gazette* of February 2–4, 1938, kindly provided by Mr Gerard Wood of the Gibraltar National Archives. Cervera, 247–48, claims a "Gibraltar merchant" had offered the ship to the Nationalists as a troop transport for £1,500 ($7,500) a voyage. His account of her sinking is full of self-righteous indignation and implies, wrongly, the ship was carrying weapons.

97 See HOC February 2, 1938, Volume 331, cc 232–234.

98 DGFP, 578–79, 599.

99 Tanner, 242–43.

100 For Nationalist submarine operations in 1938 and early 1939, see González, 384–85; Gretton, 267; Lachadenède, 441; Morenos IV–I, 2276–81, 2333–35, 2569–77, 2745–50.

101 O'Donnell, 64–65.

102 For seaplane air operations from August 1937 to February 1938, see Alpert, 183–84, 208–9; González, 112, 440; Gretton, 258–59; Heaton, 74, 76–77; Howson, *Air*, 176–77; Lachadenède, 436–41; Mattesini II, 104–5; Morenos III, 2001–2, 2026–28, 2067–68; O'Donnell, 67–68; Tanner 311, 314–18. Rozin, "The outrages continue and Soviet note to Italy, Nyon Conference." LJOC at various dates. UKNA ADM 116/3532. Armee de l'Air Archive 2B79/1, *Étude sur l'offensive menée en 1938*, states that the Republicans called the He 59 "The Duck" (*El Pato*).

103 Heaton, 74; Lachadenède, 436.

104 Details from UKNA ADM 116/3532. See Gretton, 298.

105 Lachadenède, 437. ADM 116/3532. This vessel is frequently described as a French Navy sub-chaser. See González, 433.

106 Tanner, 321.

107 UKNA HW21/3 AS/0289.

108 UKNA HW21/3 AS/0312, 0370.

109 Ries/Ring, 135–38, 157, 179. UKNA HW 21/4 AS/0301.

110 Lachadenède, 438.

111 See Alcofar, *Aviación*, 255–56, 370; Mattesini II, 104–5, 230, 270; Salas, *La Guerra de España desde el aire*, 449, hereafter Salas, *Air*.

112 Mattesini II, 109. Drago distinguish himself as a wartime torpedo-bomber commander.

113 See Hooton, *Phoenix Triumphant*, 138, and website Axis Biographical Research, Luftwaffe, Generalleutnant Martin Harlinghausen and Luftwaffe Officer Career Summaries G-K section. Klünder was killed on September 5, 1939, when his transport was shot down by friendly fire from the *Scheer*.

114 Tanner, 321–22.

115 LJOC February 24, 1938.

116 For the Italian bombing campaign, see Alcofar, *Aviación*, 223–28, Appendix III; Alcofar, *Marina*, 243–48; Caliaro, *Savoia-Marchetti S.79 Sparviero*, 106–7, hereafter Caliaro; Heaton, 75; Lachadenède, 435; Mattesini II, 89, 99–101, 103–4, 106–9; Morenos III, 2003–4, 2011–12, 2065–69; Saiz 1, 602–6, 661–72.

117 Ciano, 10. For Sparrowhawk operations, see Caliaro, 103–16. The dorsal structure on the bomber earned it the crews' nickname of "'The Damned Hunchback" (*Il Gobbo Maledetto*), or simply "'The Hunchback" (*Il Gobbo*). UKNA HW21/3 AS/0267, 0269. Bruno, who had served in Abyssinia, would die in an air crash in August 1941.

118 See Hooton, 149–50.

119 UKNA HW21/4 AS/0307, 0329, 0330.

120 Mattesini II, 100–1.

121 Salerno, 75–76. UKNA HW21/3 AS/0276.

122 Morenos III, 2071.

123 For this battle, see Hooton, 157–73.

124 Morenos III, 2003–4; UKNA HW 21/3 AS/0289.

125 LJOC January 22, 1938.

126 UKNA HW 21/4 AS/0312, 0349, 0352, 0354, 0368.

127 Mattesini II, 104–23; Morenos III, 2003–4, 2018–28.

128 For Republican air activity, see Howson, *Air*, 272–76; Lachadenède, 439–41; Massot, *Els bombardeigs de Mallorca*, 122–71; Recalde, 140–41; Saiz 2, 662–63. LJOC February 19, 1938. UKNA ADM 116/3532, HW 21/3 AS/0223 and AS/0272, HW 21/4 AS/0309.

129 The Spanish viewpoint is in Cervera, 243–45; Morenos III, 2069–72.

130 Lachadenède, 441.

131 Morenos III, 2069.

132 Cunningham, 185–86.

133 Macintyre, 39. See also Francisco Moreno, 225–34; Macintyre, 38–39.

134 Halpern, 277–79.

135 See Cervera, 243–44; Macintyre, 39. UKNA ADM 116/3678.

136 Cervera, 243; Cunningham, 186–87; Morenos III, 2069–70.

137 Morenos III, 2012.

138 Morenos III, 2070.

139 Cervera, 244.

140 For the impact of the Anglo-Spanish arrangement, see Alpert, 211–12; Cervera, 247; Halpern, 356, 364; Heaton, 74–75; Morenos III, 2070–71. UKNA ADM 116/3892.

141 Morenos III, 2069n45. The Royal Navy Casualties website shows no such fatality.

142 For the French Navy, see Lachadenède, 261–70, 295–303; Salerno, 76–79.

143 Salerno, 79.

144 Salerno, 77.

145 Alpert, 185; Cerezo Vol IV, 46, and Appendix 7.

146 For the effects of the blockade in the first quarter of 1938, see Alpert, 106, 207; González, 441; Heaton, 72–75; Lachadenède, 439–41; *Lloyd's Lost*; Francisco Moreno, 237–45; Morenos IV, Appendix III. Rozin, "Capture and confiscation of Soviet steamships." LJOC January 15 and February 23, 1938.

147 Edwards, Table 18, 126.

148 González, 361–64. These figures included Irish vessels.

149 LJOC December 9, 1937.

150 Heaton, 77; Heaton, *Billmeir*, 31.

151 Heaton, 77; Howson, 297; Kowalsky, Chapter 9, II. Rozin, "The fifth series of deliveries."

152 Rozin, "Completion of deliveries."

153 For the preparations, see Hooton, 174–75.

154 As the *Gulflight*, she was the first American ship torpedoed by a U-boat in May 1915, with the loss of three lives, one of them a Spanish seaman, while the British believed she was refuelling U-boats! In April 1938, she was renamed *Refast* under the Gibraltar-based Refast Line and was sunk by a U-boat in January 1942 (U-boat.net website, https://uboat.net/allies/merchant/ship/1295.html).

155 English, 110.

Chapter 5

1 For the Aragon, Catalonia, and Levante offensives, see Hooton, 174–83, 183–88, 191–99. For the opening of the border, see Hooton, 188; Howson, 239–40.

2 For the loss of the *Baleares*, see Alpert, 212–16; Cervera, 279–89; English, 110–16; Francisco Moreno, 254–64; Fullana et al., "El crucero 'Baleares'"; García Domingo, "Recompensas Republicanas por el hundimiento del Baleares"; Gretton, 272–79; Peñalva Acedo, "El combate de Cabo de Palos." The only survivor of Vierna's staff was Lieutenant Manuel Cervera, grandson of Admiral Pascual Cervera y Topete, the Spanish commander in the battle of Santiago de Cuba in 1898. I am grateful to Ironmachine for this information in the Axis History Forum, Spanish Civil War, *Sinking of the cruiser Baleares – A mystery*. Entries March 22–24, 2023.

3 Magazine explosions sank half-a-dozen capital ships between 1916 and 1943, including HMS *Hood* in May 1941. Before the cruiser departed, the propellant was reported to be deteriorating. The author is grateful for the advice of Dr Norman Friedmann.

4 Heaton, 76; Gretton III, 210–11. Details of the rescue effort are shown in Somerville's report to Moreno, a copy of which is an annex in Fullana.

5 Mattesini II, 86–91, 109, 111.

6 Ciano, 72; Mattesini II, 86–91.

7 Halpern, 382, 410; Roskill, 387–88; DGFP, 581.

8 Cunningham, 188.

9 Salerno, 79–80.

10 González, 386–87.

11 Rozin, "The Fifth Series of Deliveries."

12 Data from González, 361–63.

13 Heaton, *Billmeir*, 31.

14 The background to the Balearic air campaign in the first half of 1938 is shown in Alcofar, *Aviación*, Appendix VII; Ciano, March 20, 91; Morenos III, 2004–5, 2039–41, 2004n39; Morenos IV–I, 2276–81, 2337–42; Mattesini II, 104–23nn116, 117, 119.

15 Alcofar, *Aviación*, Appendix IV. For the Ebro campaign, see Hooton, 209–24.

16 Howson, *Air*, 272–73; Mattesini II, 144.

17 Mattesini II, 141.

18 Mattesini II, 145; Alcofar, *Aviación*, Appendix VII.

19 For the Italian aerial campaign from March–June, see Alpert, 209–11; González, 180–81, 376–77, 429–37; Heaton, 78–83, 91–94; Heaton, *Billmeir*, 31–32, 34–35; Lachadenède, 441–44; Moreno III, 2337–41, and Morenos IV–I, 2276–81, 2337–42, 2390–91; Mattesini II, 114–28, 132–35; Puchol and Manuel Rodríguez Aguilar, "El hundimiento del vapor *Eleni*"; *Lloyd's Lost*; "Spanish Ship List." LJOC March 9, April 6, May 8, 11, and 27, June 16, 21, 23, and 27, and July 3 and 19, 1938. UKNA ADM 116/3532.

20 Alcofar, *Aviación*, Appendix IV; Bargoni, 438–39; Morenos III, 2004n39. UKNA HW21/5 AS/0414 and AS/0472.

21 Arias Ramos, *La Legion Cóndor*, 246; González, 383; Ries/Ring, 195; Mattesini II, 129; Saiz 1, 719–21.

22 Armée de l'Air File 2B79/1. See also Saiz 2, 602, 688, 672 f/n.

23 Ciano, 98.

24 UKNA HW21/5 AS/0432.

25 UKNA HW21/5 AS/0437.

26 UKNA HW 21/5 AS/0490.

27 For Italian attacks from August–December 1938, see González, 384–85, 429–30; DGFP, 617–25; Heaton, 96–101; Heaton, *Billmeir*, 37–39; Lachadenède, 444–45; Mattesini II, 141–47; Morenos IV–I, 2392–93, 2517–18, 2595–96, 2658–61; O'Donnell, 76–77; Tanner, 322; *Lloyd's Lost*; "Spanish Ship List"; LJOC, August 15, November 4, 14, and 27, December 10 and 23, 1938, and January 1 and 21, 1939. Armee de l'Air Archives, 2B78 Dossier 1 Annex III Chart of attacks on Barcelona September 4–October 21, 1938.UKNA ADM 116/3532, ADM 116/4084.

28 The latter is often incorrectly called the *Lake Hallwell*, *Lake Hallwill*, or even *Lake Vollvill*. Her master, Captain Thompson, had commanded the *Lake Lugano* when she was sunk.

29 She sank in 1938, not 1937 as Garcia, 425.

30 LJOC May 11, 1938.

31 LJOC May 27, 1938. The Nationalists would later salvage the *Greatend*.

32 *Lloyd's Lost*, but according to Lachadenède, 441, 443, she was carrying 1,200 tonnes of fuel oil.

33 Lachadenède, 443.

34 *Northern Daily Mail*, May 31, 1938. Information kindly provided by Museum of Hartlepool.

35 LJOC May 10, 1938.

36 UKNA ADM 116/3532.

37 Both in LJOC July 19, 1938.

38 Caliaro, 107.

39 The *Authorpe* was owned by Enterprise Jean Negri et Fils, and although listed as a trawler was acting as a salvage vessel.

40 For AS/88 operations, see Alpert, 209–11; Heaton, 77–78, 91–92; González, 429–37; Lachadenède, 442–44; Mattesini II, 127; Morenos IV–I, 2278–81, 2337–42, 2390–91; O'Donnell, 69–71; Tanner, 320–21; *Lloyd's Lost*; Sfikas 4; "List of Ships." LJOC June 16 and July 17, 19, and 30, 1938 UKNA ADM 116/3532.

41 Heaton, 82. *Hull Daily Mail*, May 26, 1938, and *Yorkshire Post*, June 6, 1938.

42 Mattesini II, 127. He wrongly claims the Italians sank this ship, but the Balearic squadrons struck Alicante that day.

43 Mattesini II, 127, 133, claims Hawks sank both ships.

44 O'Donnell, 74, claims the *Thorpeness* was sunk by a torpedo, but the crew's account makes it clear she was hit by bombs.

45 The *Dellwyn* was later salvaged and served under the Spanish flag.

46 LJOC August 15, 1938.

47 The others were the Spanish *Kardin* and *Cala Mayor*, and the British *Stancroft*. She was later salvaged for Spanish service. González, 435, wrongly claims the *Navarinon* was a victim of the *Mola*, but O'Donnell, 68, clearly describes the attack "on a 1,000-ton ship" but gives the date as March 18. She is sometimes referred to as the British *Clifford*. Lachadenède, 441, erroneously claims she had picked up 15 Nieuport fighters at La Nouvelle.

48 The author would like to thank Mr Jørgen Dieckmann Rasmussen, head of the City of Esbjerg's archives, for a copy of the official report into the loss of the *Bodil*.

49 In 1940, the *Tirranna* was captured by the German raider *Atlantis* and sent to France loaded with loot, only to be sunk by a British submarine.

50 UKNA ADM 116/4084. This *Lucky* should not be confused with the Gibraltar-registered vessel sunk in Valencia on February 10, 1938.

51 Gardner, 103.

52 Howson, *Air*, 72–73; Mattesini II, 145; Morenos IV–II, 2658. An intercepted Italian message suggests the first Spanish Heron bombing mission was about October 22, when 1.6 tonnes of bombs were dropped on Valencia. UKNA HW 21/7 AS0601.

53 Halpern, 387, 465–66.

54 UKNA ADM 116/2532. She had been owned by C. M. Prios and registered on the Greek island of Chios until November 28, and was now owned by Neill and Pondellis.

55 Garcia Martinez, "Los Katiuskas," 55.

56 For these incidents, see González, 384–85; Heaton, 98; Lachadenède, 473; *Lloyd's Lost*.

57 The effects of the air offensive are shown in Heaton, 79, 83, 94; González, 361–62, 386–87; Mattesini II, 133; Morenos IV–I, 2340–41.

58 Mattesini II, 134–35.

59 See Hooton, 188. See also Alpert, *International*, 160–67; Kowalsky, Chapter 9-IIn55.

60 UKNA HW21/5 AS/0423.

61 DGFP, 644–46, 653.

62 Velardi's report of June 4. Mattesini II, 126–27.

63 Richardson article.

64 Heaton, 94.

65 Heaton, *Abbey*, 99–100.

66 Salgada, 60.

67 Mattesini II, 140.

68 González, 361–64.

69 Mattesini II, 132–35.

70 DGFP, 700–1.

71 For the political and diplomatic background, see Alpert, 209–11; DGFP, 704–5; Mattesini II, 128–30, 135–38.

72 Brodhurst, 94.

73 Cunningham, 190; Brodhurst, 94. By the time of the visit, the British had decided Malta would not be used as a naval base in the event of war with Italy.

74 Cunningham, 191.

75 González, 383; Mattesini II, 131–32.

76 DGFP, 702.

77 HOC Volume 337, cc1343–403. The "pom-pom" would have been effective against the Boot, but not Italian bombers.

78 Letter of August 15, 1972, to author.

79 Op cit. The last three words of the typed letter were written in his own hand.

80 See González, 368–74, 377–79; Heaton, 94–96.

81 Howson, 300.

82 For the *Stancroft*, see Alpert, 170; Heaton, 79–80; Heaton, *Billmeir*, 33–34; Tanner, 242–43, who describes the ship as "a notorious gun runner … illegally flying the British flag." Heaton does not mention the appeal. Pritt would be expelled from the Labour Party in 1940 for supporting the Soviet invasion of Finland, but as an Independent Labour member held his seat until 1950. I would again like to express my thanks to Marian Gray BMN web for their help.

83 Gretton III, 211; Halpern, 383, 420; Lachadenède, 232–34, 261–70, 315–18.

84 This passage is based upon Sfikas 4.

85 Inglis, 67.

86   For the *Jaron*, see also Rozin, "Jaron Epic."

87   Inglis, 73.

88   Morenos III, 2111–12.

89   See González, 435–36; Inglis, 74–76; Lachadenède, 237, 443; Mattesini II, 92–93; Morenos III, 2135. The *Hellinikon Vounos* carried 140 trucks, which boosted the Nationalist Army.

90   LJOC August 26, 1938.

91   González, 377–79; Inglis, 76. Rozin, "Greek deliveries."

92   UKNA ADM 116/3678, Med 684/S.10/12 Report on situation July 28, 1938.

93   Mattesini II, 92, 153–54.

94   Mattesini II, 86–91, 109, 111.

95   For Nationalist naval operations from March–December 1938, see Cerezo, 21–23; Cervera, 323–50; English, 118, 123; Francisco Moreno, 267–75; Gretton, 281–85; Mattesini II, 92; Morenos IV–I, 2241–85, 2327–58, 2371–87, 2419–511, 2551–95, 2625–28. The Destroyer Flotilla was under former Rome attaché Génova.

96   For the blockade, see González, 367–68, 379–80; González, "Pérdidas," 38, 40–42; Heaton, 78, 92; Lachadenède, 237–38, 474–75; Mattesini II, 92–93, 147–54; Morenos IV–I, 2289–315, 2319–23, 2358–67; "Spanish Ship List"; Tanner, 158–60.

97   The British also created boarding vessels to inspect ships at the beginning of World War II.

98   Gretton, 270.

99   González gives two dates for the loss of the *Cala Milo*; September 1 on 414 and September 14 in a caption facing 288.

100 For traffic into Vinaroz and Castellon, see Cervera, 323; González, 351–53; Morenos IV–I, 2330–33, 2387–89, 2511–13, 2657–58, 2752–54, 2822–24; Saiz 1, 721–22, and Saiz 3, 825–27.

101 For Republican naval operations from March 1938 to January 1939, see Alpert, 216–24; Cerezo, 21–23; English, 118–23; Francisco Moreno, 267–75; Gretton, 281–85; Lachadenède, 483–85; Morenos IV–I, 2281–84, 2348–402, 2411–56, 2520–32, 2754–62.

102 Mattesini II, 85–91.

103 Mattesini II, 96, 98.

104 Salas, *Intervención*, Annex 6; Toro II, 94.

105 Morenos IV–I, 2489.

106 Lachadenède, 240–41.

107 Halpern, 381–87, 428–31, 436–40, 443–60; Roskill, 15; Playfair, 17–20. Royal Navy Organization website.

108 Salerno, 80–86.

109 Mattesini II, 85–91.

110 Mattesini II, 149n146.

111 Mattesini II, 151–53.

112 For North Sea operations and their aftermath, see Alpert, 211–12; Cervera, 341–43; Coni, "A Tale of Two Ships"; González, 148–49, 175–76, 181, 189, 382; Heaton, 98; Lachadenède, 474; Morenos II, 1385–438. UKNA ADM 116/3892. The *Ciudad de Valencia* is often referred to as the *Nadir*, which was a cover name.

113 Blogg was one of the most distinguished lifeboat coxswains, winning numerous medals, including the George Cross (the civilian equivalent of the Victoria Cross), and retired in 1947 having rescued 873 people. Argüelles and his family emigrated to Mexico, but when the Henry Blogg lifeboat museum was opened in 2006, the Argüelles children were guests of honor.

114 The Catalonia campaign is in Hooton, 231–38. See also Morenos IV–I, 2599–618.

115 Alcofar, *Aviación*, Appendix VII; Mattesini II, 145–46n139.

116 For the air raids in January and February 1939, see Alcofar, *Aviación*, 252–53, 254–55; Arias Ramos, *La Legion Cóndor*, 265; Cervera, 351–59; Heaton, 101–3, 107; Heaton, *Billmeir*, 40; *Lloyd's Lost*; Mattesini II, 145–47; Morenos IV–I, 2681–708, 2722–26, 2763–66; O'Donnell, 78; Ries/Ring, 207, 211–12. LJOC January 4, 16, 23, and 25, February 3, 5, and 25, and March 21, 1939. UKNA ADM 116/3532.

117 LJOC January 11, 1939.

118 The *Yorkbrook* and *African Mariner* were later salvaged for Spanish use. The *Miocene* was owned by Lotco, a subsidiary of Messrs Angel, Son and Company.

119 Bargoni, 462–63.

120 Gonzáles, 413. Axis History Forum, Spanish Civil War, section Junkers 87 and the Spanish Civil War, entry by "Tigre," March 18, 2018.

121 González, 400.

122 Heaton, 107.

123 Alcofar, *Aviación*, Appendix VII; González, 398–99.

124 She was commissioned as HMS *Privett* in November 1916 and sank *U–85* on March 7, 1917, and has been credited with sinking *U–34* near Gibraltar on November 9, 1918, although this is disputed. She was sold to the Limerick line in 1919. See websites Channel Island Shipping Page 42 and U-boats, The U-boat War in World War One. See also Scott, "Limerick Steam."

125 See the *Cork Examiner*, January 28, 1939; *Limerick Leader*, January 30, 1939, also Scott's article "Limerick Steam." The author would again like to thank the Limerick Museum's Dr Potter for providing extracts from local newspapers on the loss of the *Foynes*, which was later salvaged for Spanish service.

126 For this incident, see Garcia, 431; Heaton, 102–3; Heaton, *Billmeir*, 41; LJOC February 25 and March 21, 1939.

127 Mattesini II, 153.

128 Howson, 244.

129 For the surrender of Minorca, see Alcofar, *Aviación*, 253–55; Alpert, 226–34; Cervera, 359–66; English, 124; Francisco Moreno, 278–79; Gretton, 286–91; Gretton III, 211–13; Halpern, 476–89; Mattesini II, 154–58; Morenos IV–I, 2775–822, 2831–38. UKNA ADM 116/3896.

130 For events in March 1939, see Alcofar, *Aviación*, Appendix VII; Alpert, 228–38; Ramos, 268; English, 125–29; Francisco Moreno, 249, 280–82; González, "Pérdidas," 29; Gretton, 286–91, 310; Halpern, 502, 504; Heaton, 103–5; Lachadenède, 475; Mattesini II, 154–58; Morenos IV–II, 2869–926, 2929–3082, 3119–58, 3190–218. LJOC March 11, 18, and 20, 1939. UKNA ADM 116/3896.

131 DGFP, 877–79.

132 For this operation, see Alpert, 231–33; English, 126–29; González, *Perdidas*, 27, 29; Gómez Vizcaíno, "Los acontecimientos de marzo de 1939 en Cartagena"; Morenos IV–II, 2869–926, 2929–3082. For other Nationalist naval operations, see Morenos IV–I, 2708–34, 2750–52.

133 Gómez Vizcaíno, 84.

134 Heaton, *Billmeir*, 41–42.

135 Ries/Ring, 221–22.

136 Heaton, *Billmeir*, 43.

137 Heaton, *Billmeir*, 43–44.

138 For the last days of the Republic, see Hooton, 239–40.

139 For the *Stanbrook* and Spanish refugees, see Heaton, 105. Websites Stanbrook – The Spanish Civil War and Valencia University, Stanbrook, and The Stanbrook Story by David Ebsworth.

140 English, 143.

141 González, 376–77, 434–35.

Chapter 6

1   Ring/Ring, 226.
2   Jung, 326–27; Toro I, 87.
3   Huan, 43.
4   Bargoni, 466–71.
5   Playfair, 24.
6   Alcofar, *Marina*, 250; Bargoni, Annexes 6 and 7.
7   Mattesini II, 164.
8   Mattesini II, 146.
9   Soviet fleet website.
10 For these claims, see Alcofar, *Aviación*, 256, 259; Cervera, 422; Francisco Moreno, 289–90; Mattesini II, 167–68n157, 159, 160; Rapalino, Appendix V; Lloyd's Shipping Register. Soviet Fleet website.
11 Data based upon González, 411–41, and Lloyd's Shipping Register, Returns of Ships Totally Lost, Condemned &c. 1936–1939. Displacements normally based upon Lloyd's Shipping Register, Steam Ships 1936 or 1939.
12 González, 432–33.
13 Cervera, 422.
14 Mattesini II, 159.
15 Lachadenède, Annex 24. Based upon Garcia Duran, *Les interventions étrangères dans la mer* (Colloque de Barcelona, September 1981).
16 Roskill, 390–91.
17 Edwards, 101.
18 Kennedy, 292–93.
19 Salerno, 87.
20 Salerno, 88–89.
21 See Heaton, *Billmeir*, 45–51. Ships List website, Stanhope Line and U-boat.net/allies/merchants/ship/Stanbrook. The former *Seven Seas Spray* was lost to a U-boat in 1941.
22 Heaton, 107.
23 Once again, I would like to thank Dr Joshua Smith and his amazing staff of the American Merchant Marine Museum, together with Ms Sheila M. Sova, National Vice-President of the American Merchant Marine Veterans' Association, for this information.
24 Information from HMS Hood Association.

Bibliography

Books

Alcofar Nassaes, José Luis. *Las Fuerzas Navales en la Guerra Civil Española.* Barcelona: Dopesa, 1971.

Alcofar Nassaes, José Luis. *La Marina Italiana en la Guerra de España.* Barcelona: Editorial Euros, 1975.

Alcofar Nassaes, José Luis. *La Aviación Legionaria en la Guerra Española.* Barcelona: Editorial Euros, 1975.

Alpert, Michael. *The Spanish Civil War at Sea: Dark and Dangerous Waters.* Barnsley: Pen & Sword Military, 2021.

Alpert, Michael. *A New International History of the Spanish Civil War.* Basingstoke: Palgrave Macmillan, 2004.

Arias Ramos, Raúl. *La Legion Cóndor en la Guerra Civil: El apoyo militar alemán a Franco.* Madrid: Esfera de los Libros, 2003.

Bargoni, Franco, trans. José Manuel Veiga Garcia. *La Participación Naval Italiana en la Guerra Civil Española.* Madrid: Instituto de Historia y Cultura Naval, 1995.

Barnett, Correlli. *The Collapse of British Power.* London: Sutton Publishing, 1984.

Boyd, Andrew. *The Royal Navy in Eastern Waters: Linchpin of victory 1935–1942.* Barnsley: Seaforth Publishing, 2017.

Brodhurst, Robin. *Churchill's Anchor: The Biography of Admiral of the Fleet Sir Dudley Pound OM, GCB, GCVO.* Barnsley: Pen & Sword Maritime, 2015.

Cable, James. *The Royal Navy & the Siege of Bilbao.* Cambridge: Cambridge University Press, 1979.

Caliaro, Luigino, *Savoia-Marchetti S.79 Sparviero. From Airliner and Record-Breaker to Bomber and Torpedo Bomber 1934–1947.* Manchester: Crecy Publishing, 2022.

Cerezo Martínez, Ricardo. *Armada Española, Siglo XX.* Madrid: Poniente, 1983.

Cervera Valderrama, Juan, Marquis de Casa-Cervera. *Memorias de Guerra: Mi labor en el Estado Mayor de la Armada afecto al Cuartel General del Generalísimo durante la Guerra de Liberación Nacional, 1936–1939.* Madrid: Editora Nacional, 1968.

Chatfield, Lord (Admiral Sir A. Ernle). *The Navy and Defence.* London: William Heinemann, 1942.

Churchill, Winston S. *The Second World War, Volume 1: The Gathering Storm.* London: Cassel & Co Ltd, 1949.

Ciano, Count Galeazzo. *Dairy 1937–1943: The complete unabridged diaries of Count Galeazzo Ciano, Italian Minister for Foreign Affairs, 1936–1943.* London: Phoenix, 2002.

Ciechanowski, Jan Stanislaw. *Podwójna gra: Rzeczpospolita Polska wobec hiszpanskiej wojny domowej.* Warsaw: Fundacja Historia I Kultura, 2014.

Cunningham, Viscount of Hyndhope. *A Sailor's Odyssey: The Autobiography of Admiral of the Fleet Viscount Cunningham of Hyndhope.* London: Hutchinson and Co Publishers Ltd, 1951.

Day, Peter. *Franco's Friends: How British Intelligence Helped Bring Franco to Power in Spain.* London: Biteback Publishing, 2011.

Departement van Defensie. *Jaarboek van de Koninklijke Marine 1936–1937.* Den Haag: Algemeene Landsdrukkerij, 1938.

Departement van Defensie. *Jaarboek van de Koninklijke Marine 1937–1938.* Den Haag: Algemeene Landsdrukkerij, 1939.

Dyer, Jim, and Bernard Edwards. *Death and Donkey's Breakfasts: The War beyond Lundy.* Newport: D & E Books, 1988.

Eden, Sir Anthony (Lord Avon). *The Eden Memoirs Volume 1: Facing the Dictators.* London: Cassell, 1962.

Edwards, Bernard. *The Quiet Heroes: British Merchant Seamen at War.* Barnsley: Pen & Sword Maritime, 2010.

Edwards, Jill. *The British Government and the Spanish Civil War, 1936–1939.* London: Macmillan, 1979.

Elleman, Bruce A., and S. C. M. Paine, eds. *Commerce Raiding: Historical case studies 1755–2009.* Newport, Rhode Island: Naval War College Press, Center for Naval Warfare Studies, 2013.

English, Adrian J. *The Spanish Civil War at Sea.* Nottingham: Partizan Press, 2013.

German Foreign Ministry. *From the archives of the German Foreign Ministry 1918–1945. Series D (1937–1945) Vol III: Germany and the Spanish Civil War 1936–1939.* London: HMSO, 1951.

Gibbs, N. H. *Grand Strategy. Volume 1. Rearmament Policy.* London: HMSO, 1976.

Goldstein, Erik, and John H. Maurer, eds. *The Washington Conference, 1921–22: Naval Rivalry, East Asian Stability and the Road to Pearl Harbor.* London: Taylor & Francis, 1994.

González Echegaray, R. *La Marina Mercante y el Tráfico Marítimo en la Guerra Civil.* Madrid: Libreria Editorial San Martín, 1977.

Gretton, Admiral Sir Peter. *El Factor Olvidado: La marina Británica y la Guerra Civil Española.* Madrid: Editorial San Martin, 1984.

Gretton, Admiral Sir Peter. *The Forgotten Factor: The Naval Aspects of the Spanish Civil War.* Caird Library Greenwich, Manuscript (undated).

Grisoni, Dominique, and Gilles Hertzog., *Les Brigades de la Mer.* Paris: Bernard Grasset, 1979.

Halpern, Paul G., ed. *The Mediterranean Fleet 1930–1939.* London: Routledge/Taylor, 2016.

Harlafatis, Gelina. *A History of Greek-Owned Shipping: The Making of an International Tramp Fleet, 1830 to the Present Day.* London: Routledge, 1996.

Hart-Davis, Duff. *Man of War: The Secret Life of Captain Alan Hillgarth, Officer, Adventurer, Agent.* London: Century Publishing, 2012.

Heaton, Paul, *Abbey Line: History of a Cardiff Shipping Venture.* Newport: The Starling Press, 1983.

Heaton, Paul. *Jack Billmeier, Merchant Shipowner.* Newport: The Starling Press, 1989.

Heaton, Paul. *Spanish Civil War Blockade Runners.* Abergavenny: P. M. Heaton Publishing, 2006.

Hermann, Hajo, trans. Peter Hinchliffe. *Eagle's Wings: The Autobiography of a Luftwaffe Pilot.* Shrewsbury: Airlife Publishing, 1991.

Hooton, E. R. *Phoenix Triumphant: The Rise and Rise of the Luftwaffe.* London: Arms and Armour Press, 1994.

Hooton, E. R. *Spain in Arms: A Military History of the Spanish Civil War.* Havertown and Oxford: Casemate Publishers, 2019.

Howson, Gerald. *Aircraft of the Spanish Civil War 1936–1939.* London: Putnam, 1990.

Howson, Gerald. *Arms for Spain: The Untold Story of the Spanish Civil War.* London: St Martin's Press, 1999.

Hurd, Sir Archibald, ed. *Britain's Merchant Navy.* London: Odhams Press, 1943.

Jane, Fred T. *Jane's Fighting Ships 1898.* London: Brown and Company, 1898.

Jane, Fred T. *Jane's Fighting Ships 1915.* London: Sampson, Low Marston, 1915.

Kahn, David. *Seizing the Enigma: The Race to Break the German U-Boat Codes, 1939–1943.* New York: Barnes & Noble, 1998.

Kennedy, Paul M. *The Rise and Fall of British Naval Mastery.* London: Allan Lane, 1976.

Kersh, Commander John M. *Influence of Naval Power on the Course of the Spanish Civil War, 1936–1939.* Carlisle Barracks: U.S. Army War College, 2001.

Kowalsky, Daniel. *Stalin and the Spanish Civil War.* New York: Columbia University Press 2004, downloaded from www.Gutenberg-e.org/kod01.

Lachadenède, René de, Vice-amiral d'Escadre. *La Marine Francaise et la Guerre Civile d'Espagne.* Paris: Service Historique de la Marine, 1993.

Lane, Tony. *The Merchant Seamen's War.* Manchester: Manchester University Press, 1990.

Leguina, Joaquín, and Asunción Núñez. *Ramón Franco, el hermano olvidado del dictador.* Madrid: Editcones Temas de Hoy, 2002.

Linskey, Bill. *No Longer Required.* London: Pisces Press, 1999.

Lloyd's Insurers. *Lloyd's Register of Shipping 1936 Volume II.* London: Lloyd's Printing, 1936.

Lloyd's Insurers. *Lloyd's Register of Shipping 1937 Volume II.* London: Lloyd's Printing, 1937.

Lloyd's Insurers. *Lloyd's Register of Shipping 1938 Volume II.* London: Lloyd's Printing, 1938.

Lloyd's Insurers. *Lloyd's Register of Shipping 1939 Volume II.* London: Lloyd's Printing, 1939.

Maiolo, Joseph. *The Royal Navy and Nazi Germany, 1933–39. A Study in Appeasement and the Origins of the Second World War.* London: Macmillan Press, 1998.

Marder, Arthur J. *From the Dardanelles to Oran: Studies of the Royal Navy in War and Peace 1915–1940.* London: Oxford University Press, 1974.

Maurer, John, and Christopher Bell, eds. *At the Crossroads between Peace and War: The London Naval Conference in 1930.* Annapolis: Naval Institute Press, 2014.

McGee, Billy (William). *They Shall Not Grow Old.* Self-published, 2021.

Macintyre, Donald G. F. W. *Fighting Admiral: The Life of Admiral of the Fleet Sir James Somerville.* London: Evans Brothers, 1961.

McMurtie, Francis E. *Jane's Fighting Ships 1936.* London: Sampson, Low Marston, 1936.

McMurtie, Francis E. *Jane's Fighting Ships 1937.* London: Sampson, Low Marston, 1937.

Manrique García, José María, and Franco Lucas Molina. *Las Armas de la Guerra Civil Española: El primo studio global y sistemático del armament empleado por ambos contendientes.* Madrid: Esfera de los Libros, 2006.

Massot i Muntaner, Josep. *Els bombardeigs de Mallorca Durant la Guerra civil.* Barcelona: Publicacions de l'Abadia de Montserrat, 1998.

Meredith, Richard. *Phoenix: A Complete History of the Luftwaffe 1918–1945, Volume 2: The Genesis of Air Power 1935–1937.* Warwick: Helion, 2017.

Moreno, Francisco. *La Guerra en el Mar: Hombres, barcos y honra. Basado en las memorias del Almirante Francisco Moreno.* Barcelona: Editorial Ahr, 1959.

Moreno de Alborán y de Reyna, Fernando and Salvador. *La Guerra Silenciosa y Silenciada: Historia de la campana naval durante la Guerra de 1936–1939.* Madrid: Lormo, 1998.

Mortera Pérez, Artemio. *La artillería naval en la Guerra Civil Española, 1936/1939.* Gijon: Fundación Alvargonzález, 2007.

Padelford, Norman Judson. *International Law and Diplomacy in the Spanish Civil Strife.* New York: Macmillan, 1939.

Parks, Dr Oscar, and Maurice Prendergast. *Jane's Fighting Ships 1919.* London: Sampson, Low Marston, 1919.

Parks, Dr Oscar, with Francis E. McMurtie. *Jane's Fighting Ships 1925.* London: Sampson, Low Marston, 1925.

Parks, Dr Oscar. *Jane's Fighting Ships 1931.* London: Sampson, Low Marston, 1931.

Pasqualini, Maria Gabriella. *Carte Segrete dell'Intelligence Italiana: Il S.I.M. in archive Stranieri.* Rome: Ministero della Difesa, 2014.

Peppit, Tom. *The Crew. A Portrait of Merchant Seamen at the End of the Tramp Steamer Era.* Ware: Chaffcutter Books, 2000.

Playfair, Maj Gen I. S. O. *The Mediterranean and Middle East Volume 1.* London: HMSO, 1954.

Pratt, Lawrence R. *East of Malta, West of Suez: Britain's Mediterranean Crisis 1936–1939.* Cambridge: Cambridge University Press, 1975.

Proctor, Raymond L. *Hitler's Luftwaffe in the Spanish Civil War.* Westpoint: Greenwood Press, 1983.

Rapalino, Patrizio. *La Regia Marina in Spagna 1936–1939.* Milan: Mursia, 2007.

Rawlings, John D. R. *Coastal, Support and Special Squadrons of the RAF and their Aircraft.* London: Jane's Publishing Company, 1982.

Recalde Canals, Ignacio. *Los Submarinos Italianos de Mallorca y el Bloqueo Clandestino a la República (1936–1939).* Palma: Objeto perdido, 2011.

Ribelles de la Vega, Silvia. *La Marina Real Británica y la Guerra Civil en Asturias (1936–1937): Politica, estrategia y labor humanitarian.* Oviedo: Real Instituto de Estudios Asturianos, 2008.

Ries, Karl, and Hans Ring. *Legion Condor: A History of the Luftwaffe in the Spanish Civil War 1936–1939.* West Chester: Schiffer Military History, 1992.

Roskill, S. W. *Naval Policy Between the Wars Volume 2: The Period of Reluctant Rearmament, 1930–1939.* Barnsley: Seaforth Publishing, 2016.

Saiz Cidoncha, Carlos. *Aviación Republicana: Historia de las Fuerzas Aéreas de la Republica Española (1931–1939).* Madrid: Almena Ediciones, 2006.

Salas Larrazábal, Jesús. *Intervención Extranjera en la Guerra de España.* Madrid: Editora Nacional, 1974.

Salas Larrazábal, Jesús. *La Guerra de España desde el aire.* Barcelona: Ediciones Ariel, 1972.

Santoni, Alberto. *ULTRA intelligence e machine Enigma nella Guerra di Spagna, 1936–1939.* Milan: Mursia, 2010.

Sfikas, Thanasis D., *I Ellada Kai o Ispanikos Empulios: Ideologia, Oikonimia, Diplomatica.* Thessalonika: Stachy Publications, 2000.

Soler, Jose Ramónand Francisco Javier López-Brea. *Soldados sin rostro. Los servicios de información, espionaje y criptografía en la Guerra Civil Española.* Barcelona: Inédita Eds, 2008.

Thomas, Hugh. *The Spanish Civil War.* London: Penguin Books, 1990.

Tierney, Dominic. *FDR and the Spanish Civil War: Neutrality and Commitment in the Struggle that Divided America.* Durham, NC: Duke University Press, 2007.

Veltjens, Klaus. *Seppl: A Step Ahead of Politics.* Scott's Valley: CreateSpace Independent Publishing Platform, 2009.

West, Nigel. *Mask: MI5's Penetration of the Communist Party of Great Britain.* London: Routledge, 2012.

Young, Robert J. *An Uncertain Idea of France: Essays and Reminiscence on the Third Republic.* New York: Peter Lang Publishing, 2005.

Articles and Theses

Bargoni, Franco. "Il dispositivo di blocco del Canale di Sicilia con navi di superficie contro it traffico marittimo di rifornimento alle forze del Governo Spagnolo Repubblicano, Agosto-Settembre 1937." *Revista Italiana Difesa,* May 1985: 84–92.

Bargoni, Franco. "L'impegno della Regia Marina in difsa della neutralità della zona internazionale di Tangier." *Revista Italiana Difesa* October 1984 (10/84): 78–86.

Bargoni, Franco. "La prima campagna sottomarina e le azioni contra Costa in appoggio all'avanzata deife truppe nazionaliste e dei legionari italiani su Malaga. Novembre 1936 – Febbraio 1937." *Revista Italiana Difesa,* March 1985 (3/85): 78–86

Bargoni, Franco. "La seconda campagna sottomarina contro il traffico marittimo di rifornimento alle forze del governo spagnolo repubblicano Agosto-Settembre 1937." *Revista Italiana Difesa,* April 1985 (4/85): 77–86.

Bendert, Harald. "La Operación 'Ursula' y el Hundimiento del C-3." *Revista de Historia Naval* XVII (1999) #67: 77–80.

Blanco Nuñez, Jose María. "Participación de la marina de Guerra portuguesa en la Guerra civil Española." *Revisión de la Guerra civil española*: 1051–63.

Cerezo Martínez, Ricardo. "La estrategia naval en la guerra Española." *Revista de Historia Naval* Ano II (1984) # 6: 5–24.

Coni, Nicholas. "A tale of two ships: The Spanish Civil War reached the British coast." *International Journal of Maritime History* Volume 26 #1 (February 2014): 44–63.

Cortada, James W. "Ships, Diplomacy and the Spanish Civil War: Nyon Conference, September 1937." *Politico* Vol 37 #4 (December 1972): 673 ff. Instituto di scienze politiche, Università di Pavia, Italy.

Deszczyński, Marek Piotr. "Polski eksport sprzętu wojskowego w okresie międzywojennym: (zarys problematyki)." *Przegląd Historyczny* 85/1–2 (1994): 75–113.

Estapé, Fabián. "Los Kennedy en la Guerra de España." *Historia y Vida* #81.

Frank, Willard C. "Logistic Supply and Commerce War in the Spanish Civil War 1936–1939." In Elleman and Paine, *Commerce Raiding*: 165–86

Frank, Willard C. "Misperception and Incidents at Sea: The Deutschland and Leipzig Crises, 1937." *Naval War College Review*, Vol XLIII #2 (Spring 1990): 31–46.

Frank, Willard C. "Multinational Naval Cooperation in the Spanish Civil War, 1936." *Naval War College Review*, Vol XLVII #2 (Spring 1993): 72–101.

Frank, Willard C. "Submarinos republicanos españoles bajo mando sovíeto (I)." *Revista de Historia Naval* Ano XVII (1999) #64: 7–34.

Frank, Willard C. "Submarinos republicanos españoles bajo mando sovíeto (II)." *Revista de Historia Naval* Ano XVIII (2000) #69: 37–55.

Frank, Willard C. "Submarinos republicanos españoles bajo mando sovíeto (III)." *Revista de Historia Naval* Ano XVIII (2000) #70: 25–46.

Frank, Willard C. "Un peso muerto o una fuerza frustrada? Las dificultades estratégicas de la Marina Republicana durante la Guerra Civil, 1936–1939." *Revista de Historia Naval* Ano XXVII (2009) #105: 7–38.

García Domingo, Enrique. "Recompensas Republicanas por el hundimiento del Baleares." *Revista de Historia Naval*, XV (1997) No 59: 67–73.

Garcia Martinez, "Los Katiuskas." *Air Enthusiast*, 32 (December 1986–April 1987): 45–55.

Gardner, Philip Harold. "Ramon Franco: El caballero del aire, 1896–1938." Thesis. (ProQuest Dissertations Publishing, 1998).

Gómez Vizcaíno, Juan Antonio. "Los acontecimientos de marzo de 1939 en Cartagena. El hundimiento del Castillo de Olite, la mayor tragedia naval de la Guerra Civil." *Revista de Historia Naval*, Ano XXVII (2009) #106: 73–86.

González Echegaray, Rafael. "Las pérdidas soviéticas en la Guerra de España." *Revista de Historia Naval* Ano II (1984) #7: 25–42.

Gretton, Admiral Sir Peter. "The Royal Navy in the Spanish Civil War of 1936–39, Part 1." *Naval Review*, Vol LXII #1 (January 1974): 8–17.

Gretton, Admiral Sir Peter. "The Royal Navy in the Spanish Civil War of 1936–39, Part 2." *Naval Review*, Vol LXII #2 (April 1974): 96–103.

Gretton, Admiral Sir Peter. "The Royal Navy in the Spanish Civil War of 1936–39, Part 3." *Naval Review*, Vol LXII #3 (July 1974): 203–12.

Gretton, Peter. "The Nyon Conference – The Naval Aspect." *The English Historical Review* Volume 90 (January 1975): 103–12.

Grunawalt, Richard J., ed. "Submarine Warfare: With Emphasis on the 1936 London Protocol." *International Law Studies* Volume 70 Levie on the Law of War: 293–337.

Higgins, Katherine. "The House that Jack Built." *Sunday Express Magazine* (August 20, 1985): 40–41.

Huan, Claude. "La Kriegsmarine y la guerra de España." *Revista de Historia Naval* Ano IV (1986) #14: 17–45.

Infiesta Pérez, José Luis. "La marina soviéta en la guerra de España." *Revista de Historia Naval* Ano XIII (1995) #48: 48–91.

Infiesta Pérez, José Luis. "Más Datos sobre el Huniemento del Komsomol." *Revista de Historia Naval*, Anno XVIII (2000) # 71: 85–96.

Inglis, Sarah Elizabeth. "Danza de la Muerte: Greek Arms Dealing in the Spanish Civil War 1936–1939." Thesis. (Department of History, Faculty of Arts and Social Science, Simon Fraser University, Burnaby, BC, Canada, 2014).

Jung, Dieter. "Der Einsatz der deutschen Handelsshiffahrt wahrend des Spanienkrieges 1936–1939." *Marine-Rundschau* (Mai 1979), Jahgang Heft 5: 322–29.

Kabaciński, Dawid. "Wojsko Polskie wobec wojny domowej w Hiszpanii: wybrane zagadnienia Przegląd." *Historyczno-Wojskowy* 14 (65)/3 (245) (2013): 31–56.

Kitroeff, Alexander. "The Greek Seamen's Movement 1940–1944." *Journal of the Hellenic Diaspora* Vol 7 #3–4 (1980): 73–97.

Lammers, Donald N. "The Nyon Arrangements of 1937: A success sui generis." *Albion: A Quarterly Journal Concerned with British Studies*, Volume 3, No 4 (Winter 1971): 163–76.

Liverpool Journal of Commerce and Shipping Telegraph.

Mattesini, Francesco. "Il blocco navale italiano nella Guerra di Spagna (ottobre 1936–marzo 1939). Parte prima: Comme si giunse alla prima campagna sottomarina e ai bombardamenti navali di Barcellon e di Valencia." *Bollettino d'Archivo dell'Ufficio Storico della Marina Militar* (September 1997): 7–168.

Mattesini, Francesco. "Il blocco navale italiano nella Guerra di Spagna (ottobre 1936–marzo 1939). Parte seconda: Le operazioni navali dell'estate 1937, e l'attivita della Regia Aeronautica contro I porti della Spagna repubblicana." *Bollettino d'Archivo dell'Ufficio Storico della Marina Militar* (December 1997): 39–170.

Mills, William C. "The Nyon Conference: Neville Chamberlain, Anthony Eden, and the Appeasement of Italy in 1937." *The International History Review* Volume 15 (1993), #1: 1–22.

Monakov, M., and Y. Ribalkin. "Los marinos de la flota soviéta y la asistencia a la España republicana (1936–1939)." *Revista de Historia Naval* Ano XI (1993) #41: 61–77.

Moreno de Alborán y de Reyna, Fernando and Salvador. "El Hunimiento del Komsomol." *Revista de Historia Naval* Vol XIX (2001), #74: 97–99.

Münching, L. L. von. "Een herinnering aan veertig jaar geleden: De Nederlandse zeemacht tijdens de Spaanse Burgeroorlog (1936–1939)." *Marineblad* (1976): 342–55.

O'Donnell Torroba, César. "Las Pérdidas de Buques Mercantes Republicanos Causadas por Hidroaviones de la Legión Cóndor Durante la Guerra Civil Española (1936–1939)." *Revista de Historia Naval* XI (1993) #43: 55–84.

Osborne, Peter A. "A Memoir." *The Chough*, magazine of the HMS Hood Association, Part 1 (Spring 2021): 6–9.

Osborne, Peter A. "A Memoir." *The Chough*, magazine of the HMS Hood Association, Part 2 (Summer 2021): 21–26.

Osborne, Peter A. "A Memoir." *The Chough*, magazine of the HMS Hood Association, Part 3 (Winter 2021): 11–15.

Padelford, Norman J. "The International Non-Intervention Agreement and the Spanish Civil War." *The American Journal of International Law* Vol 31, #4 (October 1937): 578–603.

Peñalva Acedo, Jorge. "El combate de Cabo de Palos (6 de marzo de 1938). El hundimiento del crucero Baleares." *Revista de Historia Naval* XXXVI (2018) #59: 101–14.

Press Bureau, Spanish Embassy, London. "List of Ships Interfered with, attacked or sunk During the War in Spain. July 1936–June 1938." (Spanish Embassy, London, 1938).

Puchol Franco, Miguel S., and Manuel Rodríguez Aguilar. "El hundimiento del vapor *Eleni* en la Guerra civil Española." *Revista de Historia Naval* Ano XXXI (2013) #120: 67–85.

Richardson, R. Dan. "The Development of Airpower Concepts and Air Combat Techniques in the Spanish Civil War." *Air Power Historian*, Vol 40, No 1 (Spring 1993): 13–21.

Roskill, S. W. "Naval Policy Between the Wars. International Commission for Maritime History, British Committee." Lecture at National Maritime Museum, Greenwich (April 20, 1977).

Salerno, Reynolds M. "The French Navy and the Appeasement of Italy, 1937–1939." *The English Historical Review*, Vol CXII, No 445 (February 1997): 66–104.

Salgado, Augusto. "Portugal and the Spanish Civil War at Sea 1936–1939." *The Mariner's Mirror*. Volume 107 #1 (January 2021): 54–69.

Scott, R. J. "Limerick Steam: A history of the Limerick Steamship Co 1893–1970, Part I." *Ship's Monthly* (March–May 1982): 28–30.

Tanner, Stephen William. "German Naval Intervention in the Spanish Civil War as Reflected by the German Records, 1936–1939." Thesis. (Faculty of the College of Arts and Sciences of The American University, 1976).

De Toro, Augusto. "L'intervento navale tedesco nella guerra civile spagnola (1936–1939): Parte I: L'organizzazione e l'invio degli aiuti via mare." *Revista Italiana Difesa* (November 1987): 74–87.

De Toro, Augusto. "L'intervento navale tedesco nella guerra civile spagnola (1936–1939): Parte II: L'attivita della Kriegsmarine." *Revista Italiana Difesa* (April 1988: 80–94.

De la Vega, Julio. "Operation Ursula." U-boat website, uboat.net/articles/index.html?article=59.

Viscasillas, Jaime Antón. "Centenario del Arma Submarina (1915–2015). Fundamentos históricos y juridicos sobre su origen y creación." *Revista de Historia Naval* XXXII (2014) #137: 43–67.

Young, Lieutenant Commander M. H. C. "Aircraft Attacks or Gunfire against Warships." *Journal of the Royal United Services Institution* Volume 81, #522 (May 1936): 340–46.

Archives

Armee de l'Air, Vincennes, France.

2B79/1-Étude sur l'offensive menée en 1938 par les forces aériennes nationalistes contre les portes Gouvernemental.

2B78 Dossier 1 Annex III Chart of attacks on Barcelona September 4–October 21, 1938.

Guildhall Library, London.

Newall Dunn Cuttings Folder, Bill Meir.

UK National Archives, Kew, Richmond, London.

ADM 116/3512 Proceedings of the 3rd, 4th, 5th and 6th Destroyer Flotillas during the Spanish Civil War.

ADM 116/3514 Proceedings of HM Ships (A–G) in Spanish Waters during the Spanish Civil War 1937.

ADM116/3519 Reports of proceedings in HM ships. Ships G–H.

ADM 116/3520 Reports of proceedings in HM ships. Ships H–V.

ADM 116/3521 Damage to HMS Hunter.

ADM 116/3522. The Nyon Agreement. Measures to protect British shipping in the Mediterranean. Volume 1.

ADM116/3525 Nyon Agreement. Telegrams relating to the Nyon Conference. Volume 4.

ADM116/3532 Nyon Arrangements – Air Attacks on Merchant Shipping. Volume 11 (Sept 37–March 39).

ADM116/3533 Nyon Agreement zones.

ADM 116/3534 Spanish Civil War. Attacks by Government and Insurgent Aircraft on HMS Blanche, HMS Royal Oak, HMS Gypsy, HMS Havock, HMS Gallant, HMS Fearless and HMS Hardy; Submarine attack on HMS Havock. Report, Rear Admiral Destroyers September 4, 1937 on Attack upon HMS Havock on August 31.

ADM116/3678 Proceedings of HM ships in Spanish waters.

ADM116/3892 Proceedings of HM ships in Spanish waters.

ADM116/3896 Diplomatic and evacuation of refugees and prisoner exchanges.

ADM116/3917 Activities of Italian and unknown submarines.

ADM 116/4084. Spanish Civil War Miscellaneous papers about incidents involving British ships and vessels.

ADM 116/4084 Spanish Civil War Miscellaneous Papers.

ADM 196/122/23 Service Records Hillgarth, Alan Hugh.

CAB 23/88/5 Minutes of Cabinet meeting April 19 1937.

FO 371/21352 Foreign Office: Political department, General Correspondence. Political: Western. Spain. Spanish Civil War 1937.

FO 371/22641 Foreign Office: Political department, General Correspondence. Political: Western. Spain. Spanish Civil War 1938.

FO 371/20533 Foreign Office: Political department, General Correspondence. Political: Western. Spain. Spanish Civil War 1936.

FO 371/21351 Foreign Office: Political department, General Correspondence. Political: Western. Spain. Spanish Civil War 1937.

HW 18 Decrypts of Italian Navy Enigma messages.

HW 21/1 Intelligence Reports of Foreign Air Forces. April 3–December 14 1936.

HW 21/2 Intelligence Reports of Foreign Air Forces. December 15 1936–July 14 1937.

HW 21/3 Intelligence Reports of Foreign Air Forces. July 15–November 26 1937

HW 21/4 Intelligence Reports of Foreign Air Forces. November 29 1937–March 17 1938.

HW 21/5 Intelligence Reports of Foreign Air Forces. March 18–July 8 1938.

HW 21/6 Intelligence Reports of Foreign Air Forces. July 9–October 20 1938.

HW 21/7 Intelligence Reports of Foreign Air Forces. October 21 1938–January 10, 1939.

Warwick University, Warwick Digital Collections, Archives of the Trades Union Congress.

Spanish Seamen in British Ports (General File) 1939–1942 (292/946/25a).

Spanish Seamen in British Ports (General File) 1939–1940 (292/946/25b).

Websites

Aberdeen Ships: Vendaval. www.aberdeenships.com/single.asp?inde=101430.

Activities of the Basque Auxiliary Navy (1936–37). www.marinavasca.eu/en/actividades.php?o=5.

Aeronavale, l'almanache année 1937. https://aeronavale.org/lhistoire-de-laeronautique-navale/lalmanach/annee-1937.

Aleksandr Rozin. www.alerozin.narod.ru. "Soviet sailors in the Spanish Civil War" www.alerozin.narod.ru/SovietSpain.htm. "Supply of weapons to the Spanish Republic" (Снабжение Испанской Республики оружием 1936–1939гг.) www.alerozin.narod.ru/SpainSupply36v39.htm.

Andrey Nelogov Soviet Merchant Marine. Civil War in Spain 1936–1939. www.shipsnostalgia.com/guides/Soviet_Merchant_Marine._Civil_War_in_Spain-1936–1939.

Anonymous, Soviet shipping in the Spanish Civil War. Research Program on the U.S.S.R., No 59, New York, 1954. HathiTrust Digital Library. https://onlinebooks.library.upenn.edu/webbing/book/lookupid?key=ha004243441.

Axis Biographical Research, Michael D. Miller et al., Kriegsmarine, Gareth Collins and Michael Miller. https://geocities.restorivland.org/~orion47/WEHRMACHT/KRIEGSMARINE/Generaladmirals/

CARLS_ROLF.html. Luftwaffe, Gareth Collins and Michael Miller. https://geocities.restorivland. org/~orion 47/WEHRMACHT/LUFTWAFFE/Generalleutnant/HARLINGHAUSEN-MARTIN. Html.

Axis History Forum. forum.axishistory.com.

Betrán, Concepción & Michael Huberman, Against the Grain: Spanish Trade Policy in the Interwar Years. Published online by Cambridge University Press. https://doi.org/10.1017/S0022050721000474.

British Merchant Navy. www.merchantnavy.net.

Cherini, La Marina Mercantile 1818–1975. www.cherini.eu/cherini/Mercantile/presentazione.htm.

Christos' Military and Intelligence Corner. chris-intel-corner.blogspot.com/2012/08/italian-codebreakers-of-wwii.html#:~:text=The%20Navy%27s%20codebreakers%20were%2.

SS *Douglas*. https://en.wikipedia.org/wiki/SS_Douglas_(1907).

Feldgrau. Pre 1939 U-boat missions? Entries from May 31, 2020, to December 29, 2022. www. feldgrau.net/forum/viewtopic.php?t=15448.

Foreign Ships Sunk: Spanish Civil War and the Seafarers and Dockers. Spanishsky.dk/resources/ foreign-ships-sunk/.

Forside-Sjohistorie. www.sjøhistorie.no/no.

Fullana, Jeroni F. and Eduardo Connolly and Daniel Coti, "El crucero 'Baleares,'" Lleonard Muntaner Editor SL, Palma, 2001. http://web.archive.org/web/2011091201330/http://crucerobaleares.es/ capitulos_crucero_baleares.php.

Greek Shipping Miracle. https://greekshippingmiracle.org/en/history/from-a-crisis-to-a-war-1930–1939/.

HMS Hood Association. www.hmshood.org.uk/index/php.

Lloyd's Register of Ships Online. https://hec.lrfoundation.org.uk/archive-library/Lloyds-register-of-ships-online.

Lonsdale, Sarah, "The blockade-running British women at the forefront of Basque evacuations." https://uk.news.yahoo.com/blockade-running-british-women-forefront-of basque-evacuations. com (May 22, 2017).

Luftwaffe Officer Career Summaries, Henry L. deZeng IV and Douglas G. Stanley. www.ww2.dk/ lwoffz.html.

Miles Forum, La Guerra Civile Spagnola: La Marina Mercantile nella Guerra di Spagna, l'importanza della logistica, March 16, 2010, by Lancia Novara 5. https://miles.forumcommunity. net/?t=36185402.

Moreno, Rafael, "Historia del intento de secuestro del submarino republicano C2 en Francia. August 4 2018." www.defensa.com/ayer-noticia/historia-intento-secuestro-submarino-republicano-c2-francia.

Museum of Wales website, William James Tatem, 1st Baron Glanely 1868–1942. https://museum.wales/ articles/1100/William-James-Tatem-1st-Baron-Glanely-1868–1942/#:~:text=William%20James% 20Tatem%2C%201st%20Baron%.

Naviera Aznar-Auñamendi Eusko Entziklopedia. https://aunamendi.eusko-ikaskuntza.eus/en/ Naviera-aznar/ar-79084.

Poggiaroni Giulio, Naval Intelligence Operations of the Servizio Informazioni Segrete. https:// commandosupremo.com/servizio-informazioni-segrete/.

La "Red Espinosa" de espionaje en la Guerra Civil Española by Jorge Benavent. www.monografias. com/trabajos99/red-espinosa-espionaje-guerra-civil-espanola/.

Revista de historia naval-Dialnet. https://dialnet.unirioja.es/servlet/revista?codigo=1182.

Royal Navy Organisation and Ship Deployment, Inter-War Years 1919–1939, by Dr Graham Watson. www.naval-history.net/xGW-RNOrganisation1919–39.htm.

Royal Navy Casualties, Killed and Died, 1936–1937 – Patriot Files. Casualty Lists of the Royal Navy and Dominion Navies, Armistice 1918–August 1939. www.Patriotfiles.com/archive/navalhistory/ xDKCas 1936–1939.htm.

Santafé, Antonio, Palma de Mallorca, plaza estratégica durante la Guerra Civil Española. www.lacruelaguerra.com/articulos/palma-de-mallorca-plaza-estratégica-durante-la-guerra-civil-española.

The Ships List, Fleets. www.theshiplist.com.

The Stanbrook Story and the Spanish Civil War. https://viewfromlavila.com/2018/03/28/the-stanbrook-story-the-unlikely-british-heroes-of-alicante.

Soviet Empire, Spanish Republican Navy during the Civil War. www.soviet-empire.com.viewtopic.php?t=47726.

Soviet fleet. http://vadimvswar.narod.ru/ALL_OUT/BrizOut/tvindx.htm.

Spanish Civil War and the Seafarers and Dockers, France Navigation. Spanishsky.dk/France-navigation. This entry based upon Rien Dijkstra. De Spaanse Hemel Spreidt zijn Sterren (Brave New Books, 2018).

Stichting Maritiem-Historische Databank. www.marhisdata.nl.

Strelbitskiy, K. B. Spain in 1936–1939 Years. Civil War at Sea. Loss ships belligerents and neutral states. http://vadimvswar.narod.ru/ALL_OUT/BrizOut/tvindx.htm.

Strübin_Charles-ausland-SwissShips. www.test.swiss-ships.ch/reeder/ch-emigrants/struebin/chas-struebin-ausland.html.

trafina_history_e. www.test.swiss-ships.ch/reeder/ch-reeder-history's/trafina/trafina-e-company-history.html.

Tyne & Wear Archives and Museums: Danger and adventure for Tyne and Wear ships' crews in the Spanish Civil War. https://blog.twmuseums.org.uk/danger-and-adventure-for tyne-and-wear-ships-crews-in-the-spanish-civil-war/.

U-boat. Sections: The U-boats, The Men, Italian Submarines in World War Two, The U-boat War in World War One (WWI), Allied Commanders. www.u-boat.net and www.u-boat.net/fates/losses/cause.htm.

Wells, Jerry A. United States Ships Participating in the Spanish Civil War (1936–1939). www.spanishphilatelic society.com/2019/04/22/united-states-ships-participating-in-the-Spanish-civil-war-1936–1939/.

Werner, Matts. The truth about the Allegro Affair. https://mattswerner.blogg.se/2010/February/seppl-a-stage-ahead-of-politics-allegroa.html.

Index

General Index

Abyssinia Crisis, 10, 12, 13, 31, 55, 123, 124, 125
Admirals' Conference, 61, 70
Admiralty, 9, 12, 17, 20, 21, 31, 32, 48, 64, 66, 85, 86, 89, 90, 91, 93, 99, 101, 107, 119, 121, 122, 123, 125–27, 133, 135, 139, 159, 164, 171, 172, 181
Aegean Sea, 45, 112, 116, 118, 120, 123, 125, 126
Aero-Marine Engines, 73
Aircraft
    Cant Z.501 Gull, 74, 75, 127, 128, 139, 159
    Cant Z.506 Heron, 159
    Dewoitine fighters, 141
    Dornier Whale 65, 74, 137, 159
    Fairey IIIF, 125
    Gourdou-Leseurre GL-32, 95
    Hawker Nimrod, 125
    Hawker Osprey, 125
    Heinkel He 111, 129, 141, 153, 170
    Heinkel He 59 Boot, 74, 75, 128, 129, 135–38, 158, 159, 171, 174
    Heinkel He 60, 74
    Junkers 87 Stukas, 170, 171
    Junkers Ju 52, 7, 8
    Potez 25, 76
    Savoia-Marchetti S.62, 65, 74
    Savoia-Marchetti S.79, Hawk 74, 75, 138–41, 150, 152, 153, 156, 170
    Savoia-Marchetti S.81 Bat, 7, 10, 74, 75, 114, 127–29, 135, 138, 140, 141, 152, 170
    Short Singapore, 125
    Supermarine Scapa, 125
    Tupolev SB Katie, 44, 46, 65, 66, 129, 141, 150, 159, 172
    Vickers Walrus, 108

Air Forces
    8th Fast Bomber Wing (Balearic Falcons), 139, 152, 170, 171, 173, 174, 178
    12th Bomber Group, 65, 66
    12th Fast Bomber Wing (Green Mice), 139
    27th Fast Bomber Group, 139
    28th Fast Bomber Group, 138
    71st Group, 65, 66
    225th Land Bomber Group "Balearic Bats," 127
    Condor Legion, 38, 39, 74, 105, 107, 129, 135, 136, 141, 153, 156, 170, 177
    Dragons of Death, 10
    K/88, 105
    Legionary Air Force, 40, 76, 152
    Majorca Air Forces, commander of, 74
    Nationalist Air Force, 74, 154
    Naval Support Detachment, 65
    Republican Air Force, 65, 67
    Royal Air Force (RAF), 12, 125
Air lines
    Air France, 136
    Ala Littoria, 10
Air Ministry, 126
Alboran Sea, 50, 176
Alexandria, 118, 168
Algeciras Bay, 5, 7
Algeciras, 8, 23
Algiers, 34, 44, 56, 75, 113, 114, 125, 127–29, 136, 141, 146, 176
Alicante, 19, 42, 44, 46, 48, 52, 54, 62, 74, 87, 91, 92, 94, 133, 156, 159, 175, 176, 177, 181, 185
Almeria, 59, 63, 64, 68, 72, 74, 75, 131, 158, 162, 174
American Civil War, 164
American Expeditionary Force (AEF), 99
Ankara, 111, 117, 125

Anschluss Crisis, 150, 168
Antwerp, 41, 43, 49, 54, 57, 82, 86, 91, 92, 105, 107, 133, 136, 151, 156, 158, 159
Archimede-class submarines, 133
Army of Africa, 4, 8
Arzeu, 125, 127
Athens, 164, 166
Aviles, 78, 83, 102, 107, 108

Balearic Islands, 1, 9, 23, 31, 32, 34, 35, 65, 66, 70, 71, 122, 131, 135, 136, 139, 140, 144, 146, 152, 163, 168, 172
Baltic Exchange, 27, 53
Baltic Merchant Fleet, 146
Banks
    Bilbao, 99
    Eurobank, 44
    Gosbank, 44
    Narodny, 52
Barcelona, 4, 14–16, 20, 22, 25, 30, 31, 39, 40, 47, 54, 59, 62–64, 70, 72, 73, 75, 94, 117, 125, 128–30, 132, 135–41, 143, 146, 151–54, 158–60, 162, 163, 168, 170–72, 176, 178
Basel, 53, 184
Battles
    Atlantic, 2, 181
    Cape Matapan, 183
    Ebro, 152, 167
    Jutland, 13, 68
    Trafalgar, 182
    Waterloo, 13
Bay of Biscay, 38, 73, 77, 82, 100, 108
Bayonne, 82–84, 91, 92, 100, 101, 106, 107, 109
Bergen, 42, 170
Berlin, 18, 21, 38, 56, 57, 64, 68, 82, 161, 163
Bilbao, 4, 22, 23, 27, 43, 48, 49, 52, 77–100, 108, 109, 130, 171
Billmeir Award Scheme, 54
Bizerta, 115, 125, 126, 173, 174
Black Sea Merchant Fleet, 45, 121, 126, 146
Black Sea, 25, 119, 126, 128, 129, 144, 151, 165
Board of Trade, 21, 27, 48, 88, 89, 90, 91, 92, 100, 103
Bône, 115, 144
Bordeaux, 43, 48, 56, 78, 85, 90, 92, 96, 98, 101, 104–7, 145

Bosphorus, 45, 111, 113, 120, 123
Bougie (Béjaïa), 66, 125
Brest, 56, 83, 104, 105, 109
British Chamber of Shipping, 92
British merchant marine, 25–28
British-American Tobacco Company, 97
Burgos, 19, 100, 116, 132, 157, 164–66, 168, 173, 175
Burriana, 118, 134, 139

Cabinet, 31, 32, 71, 86, 88, 89, 90, 122, 123
Cadiz, 2, 4, 6, 17, 18, 37, 38, 41, 42, 61, 69, 74, 129, 131, 137, 142, 147, 177
Cagliari, 70
Cantabrian Sea, 8, 77, 89, 90, 102, 107
Canarias-class cruisers, 2, 5, 36, 67, 70
Canary Islands, 1, 4, 31, 34, 48
Capes
    Attia, 66
    Béar, 141
    Begur, 63
    Bon, 112–14
    Busto, 34
    Cherchell, 129
    Creus, 63, 64, 133, 158, 176
    Garde, 130
    Gata, 34
    Huertas, 66
    Machichaco (Cape Matxitxako), 82, 84
    Matapan, 70
    Nao, 118
    Ogoño, 82
    Oropesa, 34, 118
    Palos, 149
    Quejo, 131
    Rosa, 130
    Sant'Antonio, 65, 133, 134, 159, 174
    Sebastion, 64
    Tenez, 65
    Tinosa, 134
    Tordera, 62
    Tres Forces, 10
    Vidio, 103
Cardiff, 27, 30, 54, 100, 114, 162, 169
Casablanca, 20, 136, 168, 176
Castellon, 34, 65, 118, 134, 149, 166, 174
Castle-class vessels, 79
Castro Urdiales, 87, 95, 96

Ceres-class vessels, 12
Charles Strubin & Company, 53, 108
Ceuta, 8, 18, 23, 50, 61, 72, 128, 129, 131, 146, 147, 165, 167, 177
Cartagena, 4–6, 23, 42, 44, 46, 59, 63, 68, 72–74, 87, 106, 107, 111, 115, 118, 129, 133, 134, 136, 150, 153, 173, 174, 182
Chemical weapons
    Mustard gas, 41, 46
    Phosgene, 41
Chestfield Golf Club, 54
Churruca-class vessel, 119
Committees
    Cabinet Committee on the Protection of British Shipping, 97
    Chiefs-of-Staff Committee, 180
    Committee for Imperial Defence, 31
    Committee of Imperial Defense, 168
Confédération Générale de Travail (CGT), 96
Constanta, 113, 118, 120, 128
Coronation Naval Review, 94
Corsica, 129, 146
Corunna, 34, 38, 39, 79, 83, 86, 87, 103
Corpo Truppe Volontarie (CTV), 10, 40, 71, 138, 168, 177
Confederación Nacional de Trabajo (CNT), 22, 48
Counties Steamship Management, 54
The Cowl (La Cagoule), 56, 108
Cromer, 169, 170
Cruise to the North, 8

Dardanelles, 45, 117
Defence Requirements Committee, 11
Deutschland-class armored ships, 1
Directive 318, 76, 141
Dodecanese Islands, 45, 57, 117, 181

Electric Boat shipyard, 2
English Channel, The, 24, 33, 38, 77, 143, 183
Enigma, 55
España-class battleships, 1, 2

Favignana, 70, 112
El Ferrol, 4–6, 38, 40, 63, 71, 78, 79, 82, 84, 85, 103, 107, 182
Flushing (Vlissingen), 99
Foreign Legions

French, 173, 182
    Spanish, 10
Foreign Ministries
    French, 104
    German, 69, 111, 150
    Greek, 164, 165
    Nationalist, 160, 165
Foreign Office, 9, 13, 20, 21, 70, 86, 89, 100, 103, 112, 116, 127, 144, 155, 169, 172, 175
Formentera, 9, 10, 137
French Army, 55, 151
French Communist Party, 43, 175
French Navy Ministry, 64–66, 85, 102, 168

La Galite, 127
Gandia, 158, 175, 176
Gdynia/Danzig, 43, 48, 86, 107, 114, 143, 158, 164
General Corps (Cuerpo General), 3, 5
Generalidad, 9
Genoa, 15, 18, 19, 50, 51, 57, 63, 158
Gibraltar, 7, 8, 15, 17, 19, 20, 23, 24, 33, 53, 59, 64, 65, 67, 69, 75, 87, 103, 112, 115, 119, 125, 134, 140, 143, 145, 146, 150, 163, 167, 175, 176
Gijon, 4, 34, 77, 78, 79, 80, 92, 96, 97, 102, 103, 104, 105, 106, 107, 108, 131
Glasgow, 75, 185
Greek Merchant Marine, 28–31
Greek Merchant Shipping Secretariat, 164, 165
Greek Powder and Cartridge Company (Pyrkal), 47
Greek Seamen's Union (*Naftergatiki Enosi Elladas*-NEE), 30
Greek Ship-owners Association (EEE), 29, 165, 166
Grimsby 139, 158,
Grimsey, Latham & Co, 53

Hamburg, 37, 48, 82, 127, 177
Hispano-Marroquí de Transportes (Hisma), 72
Holland-type submarines, 2
Hong Kong, 101, 163
Hotel Cristina, Seville, 55
Huelva, 24, 39, 41, 47, 57, 100, 167

Ibiza, 9, 10, 67, 137, 172, 174
Ingenieurskaantor von Scheepsbouw (IvS), 2

International Board for Non-Intervention, 32
International Brigades, 42, 62
International Brigades' Memorial Trust, 185
Intelligence Organizations
    Abwehr, 38, 56
    Branch B (Beta), 55
    Communications, Cipher and Photography
        Section, Nationalist Naval Staff, 55
    German Naval Intelligence, 170
    Government Code & Cypher School
        (GC&CS), 55
    GRU (*Glavnoye Razvedyvatel'noye
        Upravleniye*), 44
    MI5, 82
    Nationalist Military Information and Police
        Service (SIPM), 55, 169
    Naval Intelligence Division (NID), 55, 116,
        117
    Navy Secret Intelligence Service (SISRM), 55
    NKVD (*Narodny Komissariat Vnutrennikh
        Del*), 43–46, 82, 146
    Observation Service (B-Dienst), 55
    Red Cross (Crociera Ruiz), 56
    Servizio Informazioni Militari (SIM), 38,
        55, 56, 108
International Red Cross, 97
International Union of Seamen and Harbor
    Workers, 56
Irish Free State/Ireland, 21
Irun, 56, 77
Istanbul, 56, 117, 121, 143
Italian Navy Ministry, 57, 112–14, 116
Italian State Railroads, 40, 41

J. A. Billmeir and Company, 53, 184
John Brown shipyard, 2
Júpiter-class minelayers, 2, 5

K-Boats/Black Beetles/X-Lighters, 2, 9, 10

La Goulette, 83, 129
La Maddallena, 57, 60, 71, 133
Lambert Bros, 165
Lampedusa, 112, 113
La Pallice, 85, 92, 96–99, 106, 109
Larache, 7, 8
Las Palmas, 65, 179
La Spezia, 23, 62, 67, 115, 131

League of Nations, 68, 121, 123, 163
Legislation
    Merchant Shipping (Carriage of Munitions
        to Spain) Act of 1936, 19, 163
    Merchant Shipping (Wireless Telegraphy)
        Act 1919, 26
    Neutrality Act 1937, 48
Le Havre, 56, 104, 105, 157, 167
Leningrad, 82, 83, 105, 169
Les Sables d'Olonne, 99
Lisbon, 4, 15, 18, 33, 35, 36
Livorno, 119, 121
Lloyds of London, 27, 161, 165
London, 11, 14, 21, 27, 29, 31, 52–55, 64,
    69, 70, 88, 89, 91, 96, 105, 109, 111, 121,
    123, 126, 131, 142, 150, 157, 158, 161,
    162, 164, 168, 172, 175
L'Oréal, 56
Los Alcazares air base, 67
Los Llanos air base, 173

Madeira, 33
Madrid, 5, 17, 18, 21, 44, 46, 49, 77, 78, 86,
    138, 176, 184
Majorca (Mallorca), 4, 9, 10, 18, 46, 56–58,
    61, 62, 66, 71, 74, 75, 115, 122, 124, 125,
    127, 129, 131, 134, 135, 139, 141, 142,
    146, 150, 152, 154, 159, 162, 164, 172,
    173, 177, 178, 184
Malaga, 6–8, 15, 16, 47, 59, 71, 72, 74, 167
Malta Channels, 112
Mar Cantábrico Incident, 84–85
Malta, 19, 46, 55, 60, 64, 113, 125, 145, 162,
    182
Marseilles, 15, 16, 24, 29, 33, 35, 47, 49,
    54–56, 59, 62–64, 66, 70, 108, 115, 117,
    128–31, 136, 137, 139, 145, 146, 151,
    156–60, 164, 165, 171–73, 176, 182
Max Hölz-class merchant ships, 46
Melilla, 4, 17, 23, 34, 39, 40, 50
    German, 39, 63, 64, 72
    Italian, 71, 72
    Soviet, 73
    Type 40K, 73
Memorial to The Blockade Runners to Spain,
    185
Mers-el-Kebir, 143, 173, 183
Mersey-class vessels, 79

Messina, 113, 115
Mexican Army, 42
Minorca, 4, 5, 34, 70, 122, 129, 136, 158, 159, 172
Mirabello-class destroyers, 167
Moscow, 43, 44, 46, 49, 51, 68, 72, 121, 123, 146, 151
Motor Torpedo Boats (MTB)
Mulberry Harbors, 158
Munich Crisis, 135, 167, 169
Murmansk, 45, 108, 145
Musel, 78, 97, 102, 105, 107

Naples, 41, 119, 168, 169, 177
Narvik, 22, 169
National Defence Permanent Committee (CPDN), 144, 181
National Union of Rail, Maritime and Transport Workers, 185
National Union of Seamen, 108, 170
Nationalist Army, 109
Nationalist Higher Naval Council, 131
Naval crew committees (Comités de Buque), 6
Naval Patrol Scheme, 33, 34, 35, 39, 60, 61, 64, 66, 68, 69, 71, 96, 127
Navarino Bay (Pylos Bay), 162
Navigatori-class destroyers, 167
Navies
    Basque Auxiliary Navy, 78, 79
    French Navy, 16, 35, 100, 102, 139, 141, 143, 150, 168, 183
        Admiral Commanding the Special French Deployment in the Mediterranean (Alsud), 16, 31, 126, 130
        1st/Mediterranean Fleet, 31, 163, 168, 183
        2nd/Atlantic Fleet, 31, 34, 96, 163
        2nd Destroyer Flotilla, 96
        2nd Light Squadron, 98
        DSM, 168, 183
    German Navy 13, 15, 34, 35, 37, 38, 55, 62, 150
        2nd U-boat Flotilla, 68
        Commander of Naval Force in Spain, 60
        Navy High Command (OKM), 15, 38, 60, 67, 68, 82, 112, 137, 167
        Reconnaissance Force, 34, 60

Ship Transport Department, 37
Submarine Commander, 60
Italian Navy, 11, 34, 39, 41, 62, 70, 71, 121, 126, 132, 167, 177, 178, 183
    1st Fleet, 60, 174, 183
    2nd Fleet, 71, 126, 169, 183
    4th Squadron, 113
    1st Submarine Squadron, 115, 118
    3rd Submarine Squadron, 113, 118
    4th Submarine Squadron, 115, 117, 118
    6th Naval Division, 132, 167, 168
    Sicilian Naval Command, 57, 112, 173
    Submarine Command, 59, 113, 115, 120
    Training Command, 113, 173
Mexican, 42
    Nationalist Navy, 16, 20, 23, 34, 55, 71, 72, 86, 95, 99, 105, 114, 121, 129, 132, 141, 142, 146, 165, 166, 170, 175
    Africa Naval Command, 72
    Cruiser Division, 132, 149
    Head of Blockade Forces in the Mediterranean, 132
    Ribadeo Flotilla, 83
    Strait Flotilla, 18, 50
    Republican Navy, 2, 16, 17, 42, 59, 70–72, 74, 86, 101, 104, 109, 130, 141, 166, 167, 173
    Republican Commander, Cantabrian Naval Forces, 78
    Heavy Squadron, 5
    Submarine Flotilla, 5
Royal Spanish Navy, 1
Royal Navy, 10, 11, 12, 13, 20, 21, 27, 30, 32, 35, 55, 65, 77, 78, 85, 87, 88, 90, 91, 93, 95–97, 101, 102, 116, 121, 122, 132, 134, 141, 143, 150, 158, 161–64, 168, 172, 175, 181
    Battlecruiser Squadron, 89, 142
    Home/Atlantic Fleet, 11, 13, 14, 34, 125, 127
    Eastern Fleet, 182
    Mediterranean Fleet, 11, 12, 14, 34, 64, 122, 125, 142, 162
    Flag Officer Western Germany, 183
    1st Battle Squadron, 155
    2nd Battle Squadron, 94
    1st Cruiser Squadron, 142, 182

2nd Cruiser Squadron, 107
2nd Destroyer Flotilla, 119
4th Destroyer Flotilla, 89, 93
5th Destroyer Flotilla, 85
6th Destroyer Flotilla, 93
1st Minesweeping Squadron, 64
Force H, 182
Royal Netherlands Navy, 19, 33
East India Fleet, 33
Soviet Navy, 50–51
Black Sea Fleet, 50, 73, 123, 173
Pacific Fleet, 72
Turkish Navy, 117
U.S. Navy, 11, 15, 60, 88, 154, 182
Spanish Service Squadron, 15
Squadron 40 (T)/European Squadron
D, 15
Nazaret Beach, 156
Neederlandsche Bevrachtingskantoor Van Driel,
46, 55
New York, 84, 137, 184
Newcastle-upon-Tyne, 21, 83, 91, 98, 155
Non-Intervention Agreement, 69
Non-Intervention Committee (NIC) and
Observers, 32–35, 47, 50, 61, 66–68, 83,
86, 87, 92, 104, 105, 113, 127–29, 134,
136, 137, 155, 156, 157, 161, 163, 164,
169, 172, 176
North Sea Office, 63, 69
North Sea, 143, 169, 170, 181
Novorossisk, 117, 143
Nyon Conference, 123–24, 126, 127
Nyon, 120, 123

Odero-Terni-Orlando (OTO) shipyard, 121
Odessa, 24, 44, 62, 114, 117, 130, 143–45
Official Management of the Merchant Marine
(GOMBE), 144
Officina Commercial España, 52
Oil companies
Royal Dutch Shell, 49
Standard Oil of New Jersey (Esso), 49, 114
Standard Oil of New York or Socony
(Mobil), 49
Texas Company (Texaco), 48, 49, 185
Olympics, 14
Operations
Oporto, 42, 77

Oran, 23, 54, 56, 64, 68, 69, 75, 125, 128,
129, 135, 143, 146, 157–59, 165, 168, 174,
175
Operations
Kh, 44, 46, 145
Magic Fire, 37
Mincemeat, 184
Neptune, 153
Rügen Winter Exercise, 37
Sealion, 183
Torch, 183
Ursula, 60, 68
Oslo, 42, 57, 131, 159

Palamos, 62, 64, 146, 154, 158
Palazzo Venezia, 58, 61
Palermo, 33, 127
Palma de Majorca (Palma de Mallorca), 9, 10,
23, 40–42, 66, 67, 70, 74, 75, 114, 115,
118, 128, 130, 132, 135–37, 139, 141, 142,
146, 147, 149, 154, 166–68, 172, 174, 175
Palos Incident, 82–83
Pantelleria, 112, 113
Paris, 11, 13, 14, 31, 44, 54, 55, 58, 69, 96,
98, 99, 104, 107, 111, 121, 126, 130, 142,
150, 151, 158, 161, 164, 173
Pasajes de San Pedro (Pasajes also Pasaia), 24,
79, 83, 84, 92, 109
Pauillac, 96, 98, 101, 102
Penarth County Grammar School (now
Stanwell School), 93
People's Olympiad, 14
Perla-class submarines, 133
Piraeus, 47, 51, 158
Plan V, 168
Polish Army, 90
Polish Shipping Agency, 43
Politburo, 44, 49
Pollensa (Pollencia) Bay, 10, 62, 70, 74, 75,
137, 159
Port Arthur, Texas, 48, 49, 146
Port de la Selva, 172
Port Mahon, 4–6, 70, 123, 159, 172
Port Natal, 63
Port Said, 114, 126, 129
Port Sudan, 75
Port-de-Bou, 158, 160
Porte-la-Nouvelle, 155, 158, 171

Porthcawl, 53
Porto Cristo, 9, 10
Portsmouth, 90
Portugalete (also Portugaldeta), 78, 81, 84, 99
Port-Vendres, 35, 62–64, 76, 129, 130, 136, 141, 146, 171, 176
Poti, 50, 143
Pseudo lines, 30, 84, 95, 102, 103, 122, 142
Puerto Rosas, 30, 75, 129, 176
Puerto Soller, 119, 133, 134, 141

Q-ships, 155, 171

Red Sea, 12
Regions-class liners, 40, 169, 177
Rethymnis & Kulukundis, 165
Rhineland Occupation, 14
Ribadeo (Rivadeo), 79, 107
Ribadesella, 78, 106
Rif War, 2, 173
rivers
    Adour, 83
    Ebro, 149, 152, 155, 156
    Elbe, 177
    Guadalquivir, 18
    Humber, 169
    Nervion, 78, 81, 84, 86, 89, 94, 95, 98, 99
    Verdon, 98
Rőhstoffe und Waren Einkaufgesellschaft (ROWAK), 100
Rome, 11, 14, 20, 21, 50, 56–62, 64, 68, 70, 71, 74, 75, 112, 116, 120, 121, 123, 124, 126, 133, 137, 139, 140, 150, 152, 154, 161–63, 167, 168, 170, 173, 181
Rotterdam, 41, 43, 46, 49, 52, 55, 82
Royal United Services Institution, 12

sabotage, 55, 56, 109, 160
Sagunto, 137, 138
Salamanca, 33, 59, 63, 72, 74, 90, 107, 116, 132, 154
San Fernando Naval College, 69
Santander, 4, 49, 61, 77, 78, 81, 82, 83, 84, 85, 86, 87, 89, 95, 96, 97, 99, 100, 101, 102, 103, 104, 105, 169
Santona Agreement, 53, 104
Santona, 87, 99, 101, 104
Sardinia, 41, 55, 57, 115, 127

Sauro-class destroyers, 167
Scapa Flow, 108
Sea Observation scheme, 33
Sea of Marmara, 45
SEPEWE (Syndykat Eksportu Przemysłu Wojennego), 42, 43, 46, 47, 164
Sète, 29, 62, 117, 131, 135
Seville, 4, 18, 23, 38, 41, 42, 48, 55, 127
shipping lines
    Abbey, 52, 160, 163
    African and Continental, 54, 157
    Alpha, 156
    Angel Sons, 163
    Angel, Dalling and Company, 53
    Arlon, 54
    Atlantic and Mediterranean Trading Company, 54
    Baron, 21, 24
    Barry, 156
    Bland, 7, 21, 24
    Bramhall, 48, 138
    Bright Navigation, 163
    CAMPSA (Compañia Arrendataria del Monopolio de Petróleos), 25, 48, 49, 157
    Canadian Pacific Railway Company, 26
    Cape, 103
    Cia Maritima del Nervion, 84
    CN Mixte (CNM), 66, 127
    CN Paquet (CNP), 15, 136
    CN Sota y Aznar, 52, 80
    Compañia Transatlántica Española (CTE), 9, 25, 42, 96
    Consett, 95
    Constant (South Wales), 21, 100
    Continental Transit Company, 54
    D. Alexander, 24
    Davaris, 47
    Deppe, 24
    Deutsche-Ŏstafrika Linie (DOAL), 18, 35, 37, 40
    Dillwyn, 54, 92
    Elder Dempster, 84
    Euskalduna, 22
    Fearnley & Eger, 49
    Finchley Steamship Company, 30, 135
    France-Navigation, 31, 43, 46, 53–55, 95, 98, 100, 104, 105, 135, 145, 146, 163, 164, 166, 175, 177

Fred Olsen, 24
Garibaldi (S.A. Cooperativa de Navigazione Garibaldi), 23
Good Hope, 92
Gothic, 163
Guardian, 21
Halford Constant, 53
Hamburg-Bremer Afrika, 37
Hansa, 37
Hansagesellschaft Aschpurwis & Veltjens, 40
Hans Storaas, 42
Hellenic Tramp, 49
Highbury, 30
Inchaustegui, 43
Inter-Levant, 158
J. Hansen, 49
J. Lauritzen, 128, 158
Kenfig Pool, 53
Koninklijke Nederlandse Stoomboot-Maatschappij (KNSM), 24
Leif Hoegh, 49
Limerick, 21, 134, 171
Llewellyn, 21
London, Midland and Scottish Railway Company (LMS), 82
Ludwig Mowinckel, 24, 49
MacAndrews, 21, 24, 135
Maclay and MacIntyre, 48
Majorca, 37
Mid-Atlantic, 25, 52, 53, 108, 157, 161, 169, 171
Murrell, 46
Nailsea, 21
Nantucket Chief Steamship Company, 146
National Bulk Carriers, 154
Naviera Amaya, 108
Naviera Aznar, 80
Neptun, 9, 15, 37
Newbegin, 53, 75, 155
Noemjulia, 129
Nord-Deutscher Lloyd (NDL), 38
Oldenburg-Portugiesische Dampfschiffes Rhederei (OPDR), 7, 18, 37, 63, 82
Oldenburg-Portugiesische Dampsfschiffs (OPD), 100
P. Aldecoa, 46
Pallas, 156
Panama, 113

P & O, 7, 130
Phoenix Shipping Company, 108
Pinillos, 23
Prospero, 30
R. Gardella shipping line, 130
Ramos, 22
Ravelston, 24
Rederi A/S line, 181
SAN Adriatica, 40
SAN Italia, 40, 41
SAN Lloyd Triestino, 40, 41
Schiaffino, 43
Scotia Corporation, 54
Sheaf, 21, 54
Sloman, 23, 37, 39, 40
Socdeco, 87
Società Italia Flotte Reuniti (SFIR), 15
Società Italia Flotte Reuniti (SFIR), 15, 40
Società Italiana Petroliere d'Oriente, 66
Societé Belge des Enterprises Commerciales, 54
Societé de Navigation Côtière, 176
Societé Jean Miloas, 55
Société Naval de l'Ouest, 176
Springwell Shipping Company, 20
Standard Transportation Company, 117
Stanhope, 20, 53, 158, 166, 181, 184
Stone & Rolfe, 24
Thames, 30
Thameside Shipping, 30, 54, 136
Tirrenia, 40
Townsend Brothers, 157
Tripovich Servizi Marittimi Mediterraneo (TSMM), 15
Union Castle, 63
Union, 30
Velasco, 23
Verano, 134
Veronica, 53, 91, 93
W. A. Souter, 54
W. Dickinson, 24
W. H. McEwen, 53
Westcliffe, 20, 30, 87, 157
White Star, 26
Wilhelmsen, 159
Ybarra, 111
Sicilian Channel, 50, 70, 112, 113, 115, 116, 165, 166, 173, 184

Sicily, 45, 55, 70, 112, 115
Simancas Barracks, 77
Sociedad Espanola de Construccion Naval (SECN), 2, 63
Son Sant Joan airfield, 70
Sonar, 68, 70, 119, 149, 150
    Type 119, 133
    Type 124, 119
Southampton Master Mariners Club, 12
Southampton, 97, 98
Spain's gold reserves, 44, 151
Spanish merchant marine, 21–25
Special Ships, 37, 38, 39, 40, 82, 167, 168, 174
Special Staff W, 37
St Louis, Rhôna (Port-Saint-Louis-du-Rhôn), 131, 156
St Nazaire, 65, 109
State Department, 84
St-Jean-de-Luz, 15, 78, 88, 90, 91, 92, 93, 94, 95, 104
straits
    Gibraltar, 4, 6–8, 17–21, 60–62, 74, 79, 84, 106, 121, 131, 132, 143, 146, 150, 159, 164, 164–68
    Messina, 115
    Sicily, 57
Strength Through Joy (KdF), 38, 177
Suez Canal, 63
Sunderland, 91, 96, 169
Sydney, 182

Tangier, 6, 7, 16, 71, 159, 167
Taranto, 115, 117, 168
Tarragona, 59, 136, 138, 139, 157, 158, 171
Tenerife, 23, 48
Teruel, 139, 146
Third Carlist War, 17, 31
Topazio-class submarines, 57
treaties and diplomatic agreements
    Anglo-German Naval Agreement 1936, 13, 31, 35, 124
    Anti-Comintern Pact 1937, 143
    Declaration of London (1909), 17
    Declaration of Paris (1856), 17
    Easter Agreement 1938, 161
    Gentlemen's Agreement 1937, 70
    Montreux Convention 1936, 45
    Munich Agreement 1938, 167, 168

Non-Intervention Agreement 1936, 41, 46, 86, 127, 131, 150, 164
Nyon Agreement 1937, 125, 126, 127, 134, 142, 168
Protocol on Submarine Warfare 1936, 58
Treaty of London, 1930, 11, 124
Treaty of Versailles, 1919, 7, 13, 14
Washington Naval Treaty 1922, 11, 17
Trieste, 40, 159
Tripoli, 55, 155
Tunis, 114, 115, 129, 177
Turbine-class destroyers, 167
Tyneside, 24, 54, 80, 84
Type II-class submarines, 61
Type VIIA/VIIC-class submarines, 2, 60, 61, 68
Toulon, 16, 17
Tyrrhenian Sea, 124, 126, 139

United Merchant Marine Officers' Association, 181
Ushant (Ouessant), 38, 83

Valencia, 4, 46, 47, 54, 59, 62, 65–69, 71, 75, 76, 80, 83, 85, 86, 99, 101, 113, 114, 118, 119, 127, 128, 130, 132–34, 136–38, 140, 145–47, 149, 151–53, 155–57, 159–61, 163, 168, 171, 172, 174–76, 178
Vallcarca, 154
V & W-class destroyers, 12
Velasco-class destroyers, 131
Vera Cruz, 35, 47, 84, 164
Verdon, 99, 104, 105
Victory Convoy, 8
Vigo, 35, 38, 48, 87, 177
Vinaroz, 149, 166

Waldorf Astoria Hotel, 184
Wall Street, 181
Washington, D.C., 146, 182
West Hartlepool, 46, 155
Westbrook estate, 54
Whitby, 27
Wilhelmshaven, 60, 61
Wollweber League, 56
Worshipful Company of Shipwrights, 54

Zara-class cruisers, 17
Zeebrugge Raid, 13

Index of Personalities

Aguirre y Lecube, José Antonio, 85
Alafuzov, Commodore Vladimir, 73
Alba and Berwick, Duke of Jacobo Fitz-James Stuart y Falcó, 109
Aldama, José Ignacio, 52
Allard, Paul (Giulio Ceretti), 43, 98
Andrews, Captain Joseph, 87
Angel, Claude, 48, 53, 54, 71, 163
Angioi, Colonel Paolo, 55, 56
Arbona Pasto, Sub-Lieutenant Antonio, 61
Argüelles, Captain Manuel, 169
Argyropoulos, Admiral, 47, 165
Aschpurwis, Henry, 23, 37, 40
Atatürk, Kemal, 126
Attlee, Major Clement, 162
Aylen, Captain Clarence, 63
Azaña y Díaz, President Manuel, 4
Aznar Zavala, José Luis, 80

Backhouse, Admiral Sir Roger (later Lord), 13, 87, 89, 97, 106, 122, 150, 181, 182
Balaguer, Captain Rodriguez, 111
Baldwin, Sir Stanley, 12, 32
Barberot, Captain, 16
Barnett, David, 30, 54
Barone, Admiral Pietro Borghesse, 113
Basset, Marcel, 59
Bastarrache, Captain Felix, 99
Bastarreche Díez de Bulnes, Rear Admiral Francisco, 70, 72, 118, 132, 135, 136, 142
Basterrechea Zaldívar, Francisco, 86
Bayo y Giróud, Captain Alberto, 9
Bernasconi, General Mario, 76, 140, 141, 154
Bernotti, Admiral Romeo, 71, 126
Berti, General Mario, 138, 168
Bertrán y Missitu, Major José, 56
Bigliardi. Commander Candido, 120
Billmeir, Jack, 30, 47, 48, 53, 54, 82, 94, 105, 106, 144, 162, 163, 171, 172, 175, 178, 174, 181, 184
Binney, Admiral Hugh, 155
Blackmore, Captain, 169
Blake, Admiral Sir Geoffrey, 89, 90, 93, 94, 182
Blanco Gárcia, Lieutenant Antonio, 55
Blogg, Henry, 169
Blomberg, Field Marshal Werner von, 58, 59, 74
Blum, President Leon, 31, 65, 98, 100, 149, 160

Bobadilla y Ragel, Lieutenant Commander Rafael Fernández de, 62, 182
Bodosakis-Athanasiadis, Prodromos, 47
Boehm, Rear Admiral Hermann, 34, 60, 61, 183
Bogdenko, Lieutenant Commander Valentin, 72
Bonaccorsi, Major Arconovaldo (Conte Aldo Rossi), 10, 70
Bond, James, 9
Borghese, Senior Lieutenant Junio Valerio, 119, 133, 184
Bowers, Claude G., 16
Boyd, Captain Dennis, 119
Brass, Sir William, 162
Buiza Fernández-Palacios, Admiral Miguel, 5, 129, 130, 167, 173, 174, 182
Burbidge, Edward Leader, 52
Burmitsov, Lieutenant Commander Ivan, 86, 104, 107

Calderón y López-Bago, Lieutenant Commander Manuel, 80
Calvert, Admiral Thomas, 107
Canaris, Admiral Wilhelm, 38, 56, 58, 170
Capone, Lieutenant Commander Teodorico, 113, 114
Cárdenas del Río, Lázaro, 42
Carls, Rear Admiral Rolf, 7, 8, 9, 15, 18, 32, 77, 82, 83, 183
Casado López, General Segismundo, 173, 175, 176
Casey, Frank, 185
Caslon, Commander Clifford, 86, 87, 90, 182
Castro Arizcun, Admiral Luis de, 6, 72, 78, 80, 88
Catepodis, John (Ioannis Katopodis), 30,
Cavagnari, Admiral Domenico, 57, 58, 114, 120, 131, 183
Cerrina Feroni, Lieutenant Commander Giulio, 113
Cervera Valderrama, Admiral Juan, 6, 19, 20, 56, 61, 63, 69, 70, 72, 74, 76, 89, 129, 132, 134, 135, 137, 139, 142, 150, 166, 174, 179, 182
Cervera y Topete, Admiral Pascual, 1
Chamberlain, Neville, 12, 112, 121, 123, 161, 162, 167, 168, 170, 175

Chatfield, Admiral Sir Ernle, 12, 13, 14, 31, 97, 106, 123, 124, 150, 182
Chautemps, Camille, 126
Chilton, Sir Henry, 19, 88, 90
Churchill, Winston, 9, 13, 54, 121, 124
Ciano, Count Galeazzo, 38, 56, 58, 112, 119, 123, 126, 131, 150, 153, 154, 161, 162, 167, 169
Ciliax, Admiral Otto, 68, 166, 183
Ciurlo, Commander Ernesto, 115
Conrad, Joseph, 27
Cossintine, Captain Harry, 103
Costa e Silva, Mr, 104
Cottaropoulos, P. G., 31, 55, 146, 155, 158
Courage, Commander Rafe, 119, 182
Criscuolo, Senior Lieutenant Alfredo, 133, 184
Crone, Captain Arnold, 140
Cunliffe-Owen, Sir Hugo, 97
Cunningham, Admiral John, 122
Cunningham, Admiral Sir Andrew Browne, 9, 34, 125, 142, 150, 162, 182
Cuse, Robert, 84

Daladier, Édouard, 31, 143, 160, 167, 168
Danckwerts, Captain Victor, 93
Darlan, Admiral François, 31, 65, 122, 143, 144, 151, 168, 181, 183
De Gaulle, General Charles, 183
Decoux, Admiral Jean, 31
Delbos, Yvon, 65, 96, 105, 122, 123, 125, 126
Denning, Lieutenant Commander Norman, 116
Dewey, Commodore George, 1
Diakos, Ioannis, 47
Dick, Captain Charles, 94
Dickson, Captain Archibald, 175, 181, 185
Dimitrov, Captain Gregorious, 118
Docker, Beatrice, 93
Docker, William, 93
Dönitz, Captain Karl, 60, 183
Douhet, General Guilio, 140, 154
Drago, Lieutenant Colonel Carlo, 137, 141
Drake, Mrs Eloise, 77, 78
Drew, Captain Thomas, 66
Ducoux, Admiral Jean, 13
Duff Cooper, Alfred, 122, 134
Dulm, Vice Admiral Maarten van, 32
Dupuy, Captain Georges, 104
Durand-Veil, Admiral Georges, 13, 31, 32, 65

Dutilleul, Émile, 98

Eden, Anthony, 13, 21, 32, 86, 88, 90, 112, 121, 122–25, 134
Egia y Untzueta, Joaquín de, 81
Elia, Captain G., 63
Elizabeth I, Queen, 3
Emanuele, Colonel Santo, 56
Emiliani, Lieutenant Commander Domenico, 117
Epiphaniades, T. N., 30
Eshov, Nikolai, 44
Espinosa Rodríguez, Lieutenant Commander Manuel, 56
Esteban Hernandez, Sub-Lieutenant Carlos, 5
Esteva, Admiral Jean-Pierre, 126, 168, 183
Everset, Captain, 136

Fairfield, Admiral Arthur P., 15, 88
Falangola, Admiral Mario, 7
Faldella, Lieutenant Colonel Emilio, 50, 57
Ferrando Talayero, Midshipman José Luis, 109
Ferretti, Admiral Giovanni, 57, 61, 69
Field, Admiral Sir Frederick, 11
Fischel, Admiral Hermann von, 61, 67, 68, 183
Fisher, Admiral Sir William, 12
Fleet, Captain Frederick, 155
Fleming, Ian, 9
Foley, Sir Julian, 48, 54
Formiguera, Manuel Carrsco, 85
Franco y Bahamonde, General Francisco, 2–4, 18, 20, 38, 50, 58, 65, 70, 72, 76, 86, 87, 100, 111, 112, 120, 129, 132, 134, 138, 140–42, 149, 150, 154, 157, 161, 162, 166–68, 170, 171, 174, 176, 181, 184, 185
Franco y Bahamonde, Lieutenant Colonel Ramón, 2, 74, 135, 139, 140, 141, 159, 160–62
Franco y Bahamonde, Nicolás, 112, 131
Freiwald, Senior Lieutenant Kurt, 60, 183
Fromont, Francine, 43
Fuentes López, Admiral Valentín, 78, 85, 93, 101, 107, 130, 167

Galán Rodríguez, Colonel Francisco, 173
Gamboa, Marino de, 52
Gamelin, General Maurice, 151
García Conde, Pedro, 111, 131
García del Valle, Captain Joaquín, 5

García, Francisco, 22
Garino, Lieutenant Commander Silvio, 118
Gasnier-Duparc, Alphonse, 14, 31, 66, 98
Génova Torruella, Lieutenant Commander
    Arturo, 58, 62
Gensoul, Admiral Marcel-Bruno, 16, 31, 183
Giamberardino, Admiral Oscar di, 60
Glanely of St Fagans, Baron William Tatem, 102
Godden, Mr Abingdon, 175
Godfrey, Captain John, 126
Godfroy, Admiral Réné-Émil, 98
Goering, Hermann, 37, 39, 40, 41, 58, 74,
    177, 183
Gomá Orduña, Major José, 139
Grandi, Count Dino, 112, 162
Graves, Robert, 9
Gridley, Captain Charles V, 1
Grosse, Lieutenant Harald, 60, 61, 183

Halifax, Earl of Edgar Wood, 123, 134, 159
Harlinghausen, Captain Martin, 137, 141, 156,
    158,
Hassel, Ulrich von, 112
Hemming, Francis, 33, 164
Henderson, Sir Neville, 123
Hey, Lieutenant Commander Hellmuth, 60
Hidalgo de Cisneros y López de Montenegro,
    General Ignacio, 67
Hillgarth, Lieutenant Commander Alan, 9, 10,
    119, 136, 172, 173, 184
Hilton, Captain Thomas, 154
Hintze, Captain, 163
Hitler, Adolf, 13, 15, 32, 37–39, 67, 68, 150
Ho Chi Minh, 163
Hoare, Sir Samuel, 13, 32, 88, 90, 93, 181, 184
Hogarth, Samuel Crawford, 21
Huret, E., 176

Iachino, Rear Admiral Angelo, 61, 173, 183
Indaren, Captain Rafael, 130

Jackson, Robert, 155
Jakobson, Evald John, 53
James, Vice Admiral Sir William, 14, 31
Jensen, John, 54
Jensen, Jürgen, 150
Jones, Captain D. E., 157
Jones, Captain David John "Potato," 91, 92,
    102, 181

Jones, Captain John "Ham and Egg," 91, 92
Jones, Captain Owen "Corn Cob," 91, 93, 102
Jones, Captain Reginald, 102

Kaminsky, Captain D. F., 117
Katopodi, Spyros, 43
Kennedy-Purvis, Vice Admiral Charles, 142,
    182
Kermode, Captain W. R., 157
Kielland, Captain Gabriel, 42
Kindelán y Duany, General Alfredo, 74, 76,
    135, 137–39, 154, 140, 141, 160, 161, 162
King, Admiral Ernest J., 182
Kingston, Robert, 157
Klumper, Lieutenant Werner, 74
Klünder, Captain Günther, 136, 137
Kokotos, Georgios, 164
Kugel, Alfred, 128
Kuznetsov, Captain Nikolai, 66, 72, 73

Laborde, Admiral Count Jean de, 96, 98
Lackey, Admiral Henry E., 16
Lais, Admiral Alberto, 167
Lange, Commander Werner, 56, 60, 112
Langevin, Paul, 98
Langlois, Captain Jules, 176
Largo Caballero, Francisco, 44, 73
Lasheras Mercadal, Lieutenant Jesús, 109
Lauro, Lieutenant Commander Rafaelo, 67
Laval, Pierre, 13
Lee, Laurence "Laurie," 14
Legnani, Admiral Antonio, 59, 184
León, Francois, 54
Lindau, Rear-Admiral Eugen, 37
Litvinov, Maksim, 51, 123
Llewellyn, Captain L. J., 155, 162
Llopis Ferrándiz, Rodolfo, 175
Lloyd George, David, 162
Longobardo, Lieutenant Commander Primo,
    59, 184
Louis XIV, King, 90
Ludwig, Daniel K., 154, 185
Lusena, Lieutenant Commander Sergio, 117,
    133, 134

Mackensen, Hans-Georg, 167
Maisky, Ivan, 50
Manca, Senior Lieutenant Beppino, 117
Manceratini, General Giuseppe, 152, 172

Mant, Captain Henry, 155
March Ordinas, Juan, 10
Margottini, Commander Carlo, 10, 184
Maria Teresa, Queen, 90
Maroni, Rear Admiral Paolo, 167
Marschall, Rear Admiral Wilhelm, 16, 137, 177, 183
Mavroleon, G. M., 47
Mavroleon, Georgios, 30
McEwen, Thomas, 53, 93
McGrigor, Captain Rhoderick, 89
McKinnon, Admiral Lachlan, 105, 107
McReynolds, Samuel D., 84
Meir y del Rio, Admiral Miguel de, 4, 6
Mellina, Lieutenant Commander Giusseppe, 115, 118
Metaxas, Ioannis, 30, 47, 165
Meyer-Döhner, Commander Kurt, 69
Mezentsev, Captain Grigory, 50, 51
Miaja Menant, General José, 176
Milch, General Erhard, 37
Milonas, Jean, 158
Moccagatta, Lieutenant Commander Vittorio, 59, 184
Mola y Vidal, General Emilio, 3, 4, 39, 77, 86, 88
Monreal y Pilón, Lieutenant Commander Federico, 130
Monte, Commander Mario de, 55
Montgomery, James, 155
Monti, General Adriano, 152, 154
Montojo y Pasarón, Admiral Patricio, 1
Moreno Fernández, Admiral Francisco, 3, 4, 50, 61, 64, 84, 85, 94, 130, 132, 134, 136, 137, 139, 142, 146, 161, 166, 173, 174, 182
Moreno Fernández, Commander Salvador, 4, 77, 78, 87, 90, 94, 97, 98, 101, 102, 105, 107, 182
Moriondo, Admiral Marenco, 132, 167
Mouget, Admiral Georges, 31
Muirhead-Gould, Commander Gerard, 172, 173, 182
Muselier, Rear Admiral Émile, 31, 183
Mussabaun, Máximo José Kahn, 47
Mussolini, Benito, 10, 11, 13, 15, 17, 38, 40, 41, 57, 58, 62, 71, 112, 116, 120, 126, 131, 132, 134, 138, 150, 152–54, 161, 162, 166, 168

Mussolini, Sergeant Bruno, 138

Navarro Capdevila, Commander Fernando, 6, 7
Negrín López, Juan, 44, 73, 167, 173, 175
Neurath, Baron Konstantin von 15, 123
Newbegin, Edward, 53, 163
Noel-Baker, Philip, 163

O'Duffy, General Eion, 40
Odend'hal, Rear Admiral Jean-Ernest, 98
Ollive, Admiral Emmanuel, 31
Ordóñez Mapelli, Lieutenant Commander Melchor, 134
Orlov, Admiral Vladimir, 51
Osorio y Gallardo, Angel, 151

Pacchiarotti, Captain Ernesto, 113, 114
Paladini, Rear Admiral Riccardo, 112–15, 184
Pandelis, Basil (Vassilios), 30
Papadakis, A. G., 164
Pariani, General Alberto, 56
Pascua Martínez, Marcelino, 146
Pérez Pérez, Lieutenant Commander Horacio, 130
Perrière, Senior Lieutenant Arnauld de la, 2, 26
Perth, Earl of Eric Drummond, 161, 162
Pétain, Marshal Philippe, 173
Pflug-Hartnung, Horst von, 170
Phillips, Captain Tom, 122
Picker, Charles, 73
Pini, Admiral Vladimiro, 60, 114, 126, 169, 184
Pittman, Key D., 84
Pneumaticos, Michael, 29
Pope, Alfred, 93, 101, 102, 171
Pound, Admiral Sir Alfred Dudley Pickman Rogers, 13, 20, 117, 122, 125–27, 134, 142, 143, 150, 162, 164, 168, 182, 183
Prado Mendizábal, Lieutenant Commander Pedro, 6, 167
Prance, Captain Gwilym, 93, 94
Pridham, Captain Arthur, 94
Prieto Tuero, Indalecío, 68, 72, 85, 86, 107, 167
Primo de Rivera y Orbaneja, General Miguel, 2, 6
Pritt, Dennis, 163
Proskurov, Captain Ivan, 66, 67
Pursey, Commander Harry, 88, 104

Quevedo, Luis Araquistáin, 43

Raeder, Admiral Erich, 15, 32, 37, 58, 59, 63, 67, 68, 136, 183
Ramos, Roberto, 22
Ramsey, Rear Admiral Charles, 94, 95, 97, 100, 101, 102, 143
Ravel, Maurice, 90
Reefe, Sub-Lieutenant Hans, 128
Regalado, Commander Francisco, 112
Ribbentrop, Joachim von, 68, 69
Riccardi, Admiral Arturo, 162, 174
Ricci, Senior Lieutenant Mario, 133
Richard, Admiral Alfred, 31, 130
Richards, Captain William, 172
Richthofen, Major General Wolfram von, 170
Rieber, Captain Thorkill, 48, 184
Riggs, Ted, 27
Rindyuk, Captain A. A., 114, 118
Roatta, General Mario, 38, 40, 55, 57, 74
Roberts, Captain Edward, 139, 140
Roberts, Captain John, 145
Roberts, Captain William, 91, 93, 101, 104
Roberts, Florence, 93, 105
Robinson, Captain Frederick, 96
Rohde, Matthias, 37
Roosevelt, Franklin D., 48
Ruiz de Atauri, Rear Admiral Manuel, 6, 8, 72
Runciman, Viscount Walter, 21, 88, 90, 93, 96, 100, 103
Rusca, Lieutenant Commander Virginio, 114
Russell, Captain Thomas, 95

Salas González, Vice Admiral Francisco Javier de, 3, 6
Salazar, António de Oliveira, 35
Sampson, Admiral William T., 1
Sanjurjo Sacanell, General José, 2–4
Sartorius y Díaz de Mendoza, Lieutenant Colonel Fernando Count of San Luis San Luis, 159, 172
Saville, Rupert, 77, 78
Schenk, Captain Otto, 68
Schley, Commodore Winfield S., 1
Scott, Captain Stanley, 163
Scott, David, 91
Scurfield, Commander Bryan, 64, 183
Serrano Súñer, Ramón, 16

Simili, Admiral Edoardo, 62
Simopoulos, Charalambos, 164, 165
Simpson, Captain James, 159
Skavronskaya, Maria, 73
Slavin, Lieutenant Commander Semyon, 111
Slutski, Abram, 44
Smirnov-Svetlovsky, Admiral Petr, 123
Solieri, Captain, 128
Somerville, Admiral James, 9, 10, 28, 118, 119, 122, 139, 142, 166, 182, 183
Sota y Aburto, Luis Ramón de la, 80, 96, 97
Sota y Llano, Ramón de la, 80
Spence, Captain S. L., 163
Sperrle, Major General Hugo, 38
Stabolgi, Baron David Kenworthy, 103
Stalin, Josef, 44, 46, 146, 172
Stears, Captain R. H., 102
Still, Captain A. H., 91, 93, 94
Street, Richard, 106
Strubin, Charles (Karl-Ernst Strübin), 53, 54, 55, 108, 158, 184
Sturdee, Captain Sir Lionel, 100, 101
Suances Jáudenes, Lieutenant Commander Pablo, 62, 134, 182

Taft, Captain Hiram, 154, 181
Tait, Captain William, 122
Theophylatos, G., 55, 146
Thompson, Captain, 158
Thorez, Maurice, 43
Till, Gordon, 30, 54
Tripiccione, Colonel Donato, 55
Troncoso Sagredo, Major Julían, 56, 90, 91, 94, 108, 109

Ubieta y González del Campillo, Admiral Luis González de, 48, 130, 149, 172, 182
Ungría Jiménez, Colonel José, 56
Uribarri Barrutell, Captain Manuel, 9
Uritskii, Semen, 44

Valle, General Giuseppe, 139, 141, 167
Vanderbilt, Frederick William, 96
Vassilakis, Captain Nicolas, 164
Vassiliov, J. N., 30, 115
Vaughan, Walter, 91
Velardi, Brigadier General Vicenzo, 40, 74, 75, 76, 137–40, 152, 154, 160, 161

Veltjens, Colonel Josef, 39, 40, 77, 177, 183
Veniselos, M. K., 158
Verano, Captain Adolphus, 134
Verano, Mrs Laura, 134
Verdiá Jolí, Admiral Remigio, 5, 61
Victor Emmanuel III, King, 169
Vierna Belando, Admiral Manuel de, 129, 149
Vintiades, Emmanuele, 50
Voroshilov, Marshal Kilment, 44, 146, 172

Walton, W. G., 30, 129
Warlimont, Lieutenant Colonel Walter, 57, 63
Wedgewood Benn, William, 162
Wellington, Duke of Arthur Wellesley, 90
Whitford, Lieutenant Commander Q. P., 12
Wilberg, Lieutenant General Helmuth, 37
Williams, Captain John, 164
Windsor-Clive, Earl of Plymouth Ivor, 86
Wollweber, Ernst, 56

Young, Lieutenant Commander M. H. C., 12

Zarpellon, Lieutenant Commander Giuseppe, 5
Zermeno Araico, Captain Manuel, 16, 42

Index of Ships

Warships and Naval Auxiliaries

Argentina
Veinticinco (25) de Mayo, 16, 74

France
Aisne, 107
Albatros, 146
Alcyon, 34
Arras, 102
Bourrasque, 107
Chevalier Paul, 141, 146
Commandant Teste, 31, 125, 168
Dupleix, 125
Duquesne, 16
Émile Bertin, 96
Epervier, 137
Gerfaut, 130
Indomptable, 155
Intrépide, 34
l'Audacieux, 99
L'Épinal, 100
La Cordeliere, 141

La Palme, 146
La Pomone, 20
La Poursuivante, 141
le Fantasque, 98, 103, 135
Le Tonnant, 16
Maestrale, 10, 71
Maillé-Brezé, 65
Malin, 105
Marseillaise, 16
Milan, 136, 141
Orage, 100
Ouragan, 105, 107
Sciroco, 71, 159
Somme, 96, 98, 105
Suippe, 141
Tartu, 141
Tempete, 7
Thétis, 76
Typhon, 105
Vauquelin, 130
Vauquois, 105

Germany
Admiral Graf Spee, 82, 177
Admiral Scheer, 18, 67, 68, 150, 167, 177
Deutschland, 9, 18, 67, 167
Köln, 18, 35, 81
Königsberg, 82, 83
Leipzig, 68
Leopard, 7, 18, 67
Strassburg/Taranto, 131, 150, 166
U-33, 60
U-34, 60
U-35, 61

Great Britain
Arethusa, 64
Barham, 125
Basilisk, 8, 133, 137
Blanche, 14, 86, 91
Boadicea, 101
Boreas, 150
Brazen, 71, 87, 89, 92
Brilliant, 86
Bulldog, 99, 101
Comet, 78
Cyclops, 125
Delhi, 141
Despatch, 125

Devonshire, 172, 175
Escapade, 101, 103
Faulkner, 96
Fearless, 105, 106
Firedrake, 93, 94, 136
Foresight, 106
Fortune, 64
Foxhound, 79, 105
Fury, 95
Galatea, 9, 119, 143, 176
Gallant, 66
Glorious 125
Grenville, 9
Greyhound, 9, 143
Havock, 119, 120, 121, 182
Hereward, 119
Hero, 9, 158
Hood, 27, 90, 93, 94, 125, 142, 143, 182
Hostile, 172
Hotspur, 119
Hunter, 64, 183
Hyperion, 163
Impulsive, 174
Intrepid, 174
Keith, 105
Kempenfelt, 102, 150
Maine, 14, 176
Malaya, 125
Nubian, 175
Prestol, 86
Prince of Wales, 96
Repulse, 96, 125, 126
Resolution, 94, 100, 105, 106
Revenge, 12
Royal Oak, 27, 65, 90, 94–97, 100–3, 108, 182
Shropshire, 71, 90, 122, 159
Southampton, 107, 108
Sussex, 175
Vanoc, 30
War Bahadur, 7
Warspite, 126
Wild Swan, 7
Woolwich, 125

Italy
Adriatico/Lago, 67, 112, 126
Alberico Da Barbiano, 126
Aquila/Ceuta, 131
Aquileia, 42

Archimedes/General Sanjurjo/C-3, 62, 132, 134
Armando Diaz, 113
Alessandro Poerio/Teruel, 131
Antonio Sciesa, 58
Barletta/Rio, 66, 67, 112, 115, 126
Berillo, 118, 119
Bolzano, 67
Ciro Menotti, 59
Conti di Cavour, 162, 174, 177
Diaspro, 115, 118
Emanuele Filiberto Duca d'Aosta, 71, 177
Emanuele Pessagno, 167
Enrico Tazzoli, 59, 118
Eugenio di Savoia, 7, 71
Evangelista Torricelli/General Mola/C-5, 58, 62, 135
Falco/Melilla, 131
Fiume, 174
Freccia, 113
Galileo Ferraris/General Sanjurjo III/L-2/C-3, 59, 117, 133, 134
Galileo Galilei/General Mola III/L-1, 133
Giovanni da Procida, 37, 118, 131
Giovanni delle Bande Nere, 126, 173
Giulio Cesare, 162, 174, 177
Giussepe Finzi, 118
Goriza, 17, 174, 177
Gradisca, 42
Guglielmo Pepe/Huesca, 131
Helouan, 41
Iride/Gonzales Lopez/L-3, 118–20, 133
Jalea, 59, 118
Jantina, 118
Lanzerotto Malocello, 9, 10
Luigi Cardona, 113
Luigi de Savoia Duca degli Abruzzi, 168
Luigi Settembrini, 117
Malachite, 118
Malocello, 40
Naiade, 57
Nicolo Zeno, 75
Nodriza, 99
Onice/Aguilar Tablada/L-4, 133
Orsa, 172
Ostro, 113, 114, 115
Pancaldo, 114
Pier Capponi, 117
Pietro Calvi, 118

Pola, 174
Quatro, 167
Raimondo Montecuccoli, 71
Saetta, 113
Santorre Santarosa, 113, 115
Strale, 113
Taranto, 131, 150, 166
Topazio, 57
Trieste, 169
Turbine, 114, 115
Usodimare, 172
Zara, 174

Mexico
Durango, 16

Netherlands
Hertsog Hendrik, 19
Java, 19
Johann Mautits van Nassau, 19

Portugal
Alfonso de Albuquerque, 35
Dao, 35

Spain
Aguilar Tablada/L-4/Onice, 133
Alfonso XIII/Espana, 2, 3
Almirante Cervera, 5, 6, 8, 71, 77, 78, 79, 85,
    87, 91, 94, 95, 97, 98, 101, 102, 105, 107,
    130, 141, 147, 166
Almirante Valdés, 8
Antonio Cánovas del Castillo, 130
Baleares, 4, 66, 71, 103, 104, 129, 131, 149,
    150, 166
Bizkaya, 82, 104
B-5, 58
B-6, 78
C-3, 61
C-2, 78, 104, 109, 166, 173
C-4, 85, 104, 109, 166
C-5, 73, 80
C-6, 85, 86, 104, 107
Canarias, 4, 8, 20, 50, 56, 61, 70, 71, 75, 84,
    85, 113, 122, 128, 129, 130, 131, 150, 174
Ceuta/Aquila, 131
Churruca, 8, 118
Císcar, 85, 86, 96, 97, 99, 104, 105, 107, 166,
    173
Ciudad de Alicante, 169

Ciudad de Mahon, 25
Ciudad de Palma, 85, 99, 101, 105
Ciudad de Valencia/Nadir, 169, 170
Dédalo, 2
Donostia, 80, 85, 109
D-5, 99
D-6, 99
Eduardo Dato, 130
Espana, 78, 85, 89, 90, 94, 95
E-1/Gür, 2, 60
Galerna, 87, 94, 96
General Mola I/Evangelista Torricelli, 58, 62,
    135
General Mola III/L-1/Galileo Galilei, 133
General Sanjurjo III/L-2/C-3/Galileo Ferraris, 59,
    117, 133, 134
General Sanjurjo/C-3/Archimede, 62, 132, 134
Gipuzkoa, 84, 104, 109
Gonzales Lopez/L-3/Iride, 118–20, 133
Huesca/Guglielmo Pepe, 131
Iparreko-Izarra, 105
Jaime I (auxiliary cruiser), 115
Jaime I (battleship), 4, 5, 7–9, 64, 66, 68,
    72–74, 78
José Luis Díez, 78, 84–86, 99, 104, 109, 167
Júpiter, 63, 65, 84, 95, 102, 105, 107
Lazaga, 64
Lazaro, 147
Lepanto, 8, 149, 150
Libertad, 4, 5, 8, 18, 67, 73, 129, 149, 150,
    173
Mallorca, 115, 143
Mar Cantábrico, 174
Mar Negro, 174, 175
Melilla/Falco, 131
Méndez Núñez, 5, 58, 67, 72, 73, 129, 149,
    173
Miguel de Cervantes, 4, 58, 166, 173
Nabarra, 85
Républica/Navarra, 1, 131, 166
Puchol, 147
Teruel/Alessandro Poerio, 131
T-3, 107
Velasco, 78, 80, 83, 95, 137
Vulcano, 63, 65, 105, 106, 146

Soviet Union
Tashkent, 121

Turkey
Hamidiye, 117

United States
Cayuga, 15
Hatfield, 88
Kane, 67, 80, 104
Manley, 65
Olympia, 1
Quincy, 15

Merchant Ships

A. Andriev, 81
Abbarra/Genovera, 87
African Explorer, 154, 174
African Mariner, 143, 171
African Trader, 100, 103, 105, 106, 175
Aizkarai-Mendi/Blanca, 23
Alcira, 137
Aldecoa, 46, 114, 129, 137
Alfonso Perez/Cantabria, 169, 170
Alice Marie, 98
Alix/Malaga, 131
Allegro/Balboa, 39, 40
Alresford, 170
Andra, 87
Andutz Mendi, 62
Aniene/Ebro, 23, 40, 71, 140, 152, 172
Antonio de Satrústegui, 129
Antonio Matutes, 178
Aragon, 82
Araitz-Mendi, 80
Araya Mendi, 75
Argentina, 25, 171
Arichachu/Tivoli, 24, 109
Arlon/Valetta, 103, 135, 156
Armuru, 117
Arnabal-Mendi, 23
Arriluce/Arriluze, 79
Artois, 176
Atlantic Guide, 176
August Schultze, 63
Aurora y Maruja, 104
Aurora, 174
Axpe-Mendi, 99
Azteca/Sebastián/Itxas-Alde, 81
Backworth, 27, 95, 97, 103
Badalona, 48

Balboa/Allegro, 39, 40
Barcino, 171
Barletta, 171
Bartoroy, 56
Belle Hirondelle, 65, 179
Bellwyn, 174
Beny/Jaron/Vena, 43, 164
Berlin, 38
Blackhill, 83
Blagoev, 46, 117
Blanca/Aizkarai-Mendi, 23
Bobie, 30, 53, 103, 104, 107
Boccaccio, 56
Bodil, 158
Bodon, 99
Bramden, 53, 106, 138, 163
Bramhall, 20, 48, 53
Bramhill, 105, 139
Brinkburn, 96, 91
Brisbane, 157
British Commodore, 114
British Corporal, 127
Burlington/Nausicaa, 115, 158
Cabo Creux/Kardin, 75, 156
Cabo de Palos, 62
Cabo Prior, 79
Cabo Quintres, 170
Cabo Roche, 23
Cabo San Agustin, 111, 115, 145
Cabo Santo Tomé, 73, 111, 130
Cabo Villano/Contra, 23
Cabo Villano/Contra, 23
Cala Esperanza/Cala Engosaura, 65
Cala Mayor, 67
Calabria, 169
Campas, 48
Campeador, 113
Campeche, 44
Campero, 62, 75
Campoamor, 79, 109
Candleston Castle, 102
Cantabria/Alfonso Perez, 169, 170
Cap Falcon, 84
Cap Ferrat, 47
Caper, 30, 103
Capo Vital/St Winifred, 156
Carimare, 96, 98
Carpio, 118

Carrier, 83
Cassidaigne, 135
Castillo de Olite/Postishev, 174
Castillo de Soller, 172
Castillo Mombeltrán/Hellinikon Vounos, 165, 156
Castillo Penafiel/Smidovich, 83, 86, 174
Celtic Star, 144
CENS, 107
Cervantes, 135
Château Margaux, 96, 98
Château Palmer, 96, 98
Chella, 15
Cheluskinets, 146
Chepo, 35
Chicherin, 44
Chitral, 7
City of Wellington, 113
Ciudad de Barcelona, 62, 179
Ciudad de Cadiz, 117
Ciutat de Reus, 132
Claus Böge, 57
Clonlara, 134
Colon, 40
Comandante Dorise, 137
Compostela, 50
Conde de Abasalo, 113
Conde de Figuera, 83
Conde de Zubiria, 83
Consett, 95
Conte de Savoia, 128
Contra/Cabo Villano, 23
Coquetdale, 86, 91
Corfu, 130
Dalmatic, 178
Darro, 46, 115
Delfin, 59, 74
Dellwyn, 158, 163
Dimitrov, 117
Djebel Amour, 127
Djebel Antar, 66
Djenne, 15
Dniester, 8
Douglas, 82
Dover Abbey/Yorkbrook, 39, 54, 84, 107, 109, 140, 156, 171
Ebro/Aniene, 23, 40, 71, 140, 152, 172
Edith, 18, 128, 158

El Djem, 155
El Mansour, 76, 135, 141, 146
El Montecillo, 23
El Saturnino, 167
Elanchove, 80
Elcano, 106
Eleni, 158
Elise, 4
Emilio Morandi, 10, 40
Endymion, 134, 135
English Tanker, 49, 157
Espana 3, 6
Etrib, 20
Etruria, 159
Ettore, 135
Euphorbia, 143, 154
Europa, 181
Farnham, 155, 156
Fernando Poo, 25
Foynes, 171
François, 131
Galdames, 84, 85
Gardelaki, 131, 146, 164
Garonne, 49
Garoufalia, 165
Genovera/Abbarra, 87
Genthills, 100
Geo. W. McKnight, 113, 114
Gibel Dris, 7
Girgenti, 37, 39, 77
Gobeo, 79
Gordonia, 101, 102
Gothic, 163
Greatend, 75, 79, 155
Greathead, 79
Guarija, 137
Guernica, 170
Guilvinec, 145
Gulnes, 42, 179
Habana, 96–98, 111
Hamsterley, 91, 93, 94, 96, 97, 138
Hannah, 133
Harpa, 129
Hellinikon Vounos/Castillo Mombeltrán, 165, 156
Hermes/Nephaligeretis/Suzy/Ionanna/Melitios
Hilda Moller, 105, 106
Hillfern, 42, 48, 53, 71, 80, 100, 106

Hordena, 86
Iciar, 46
Ilford/Iossifoglu, 49
Indra, 24
Iolkos/Woodford, 49, 118, 119, 121, 122
Ionanna/Hermes/Suzy/Nephaligeretis/Melitios
Ionia/Romford, 18, 49, 128, 130
Iossifoglu/Ilford, 49
Isleno, 23
Itxas-Alde/Azteca/Sebastián, 81
Itxas-Ondo, 97
J. J.Sister, 129
Jaime II, 129
Jalisco/Yolande, 16, 42, 81, 130, 171
Janu, 146
Jaron/Beny/Vena, 43, 164
Jata Mendi, 79
Jean Weems, 136
Jenny, 95, 102
Jona, 129
Joyce Llewellyn/Seabank Spray, 53, 99, 139
Juan Sebastion Elcano, 25
Juss, 146
K. Ktistakis, 127
Kamerun, 18, 35, 37
Kardin/Cabo Creux, 75, 156
Katina, 47
Kenfig Pool/Seabank, 53, 100, 102, 104, 105
Kiev, 118, 119
Kim, 44
Kimon/Leonia/Ariston, 47
Knitsley, 95, 96
Komsomol, 44, 46, 49, 60, 166
Konstan, 80
Koutoubia, 8, 129
Kuban, 44
Kurland, 80
La Corse, 136
Lahneck, 18, 37
Lake Champlain, 26
Lake Geneva, 134
Lake Hallwil, 154
Lake Lugano, 158
Laris/Katina II/Shepo/Chepu, 75
Latymer, 100
Le Tre Marie, 10
Legazpi, 75
Lena, 81

Lézardrieux, 136, 146, 175
Liberté, 101
Liguria, 169
Linhaug, 46
Llandovery Castle, 63, 64
Loukia, 64
Loulis, 176
Lucky, 140, 159
Macgregor, 21, 91, 93, 94, 97, 102
Madda, 75
Magallanes, 42
Magdalena, 83
Mar Bianca, 75
Mar Cantábrico, 9, 84, 85
Mar Caribe, 66
Mar Caspio, 83
Mar Negro, 115
Margam Abbey, 160
Margaret-Rose, 105
Margari/Redstone, 108
Mari/Houstone, 108
María Amelia, 83, 109
Maria Thérésa Le Borgne, 64
Marie Llewellyn/Kellwyn, 54, 91, 102, 156
Marion Moller, 101, 103
Marionga, 159
Mariopi, 71
Marques de Comillas, 9, 10
Marrakech, 100
Marta Junquera, 83
Marvia, 54, 98, 103, 136
Mary Tere, 108
Maryad, 156, 160
Marzo, 108
Max Hölz, 166
Meknes, 96
Melitios Venezianos/Hermes/Suzy/Ionanna/
Melitios Venezianos, 30, 37, 47, 82, 98
Memas, 66
Menin Ridge, 20
Mina Piquera, 70
Miocene, 49, 171
Miriam, 120
Mirupanu, 30, 103
Molton, 102
Mongioia, 127
Montesquieu, 96
Muneric, 163

Nagos, 86, 146, 165
Nantucket Chief, 146
Naukratoussa/Stanmore, 47
Nausicaa/Burlington, 115, 158
Navarinon/Stancliffe/Lena 31, 55, 158
Navarra, 59
Neath Abbey, 52, 135, 160, 163
Neoptolemos/Stancroft, 30, 47, 154, 163
Nephaligeretis/Hermes/Suzy/Ionanna/Melitios
Nephaligeretis/Stancourt, 30, 37, 47, 82, 98
Neva, 43, 44
Nevona, 66
Noemjulia, 128
Nuria Ramos, 23
Nyassa, 39
Oakgrove, 95, 97
Olavus, 94
Ottinge, 42
Oued-Mellah, 136
Palos, 82, 83
Paramé, 115
Partridge Hill, 143
Pattersonian, 169
Pegasus, 117
Pellice, 7
Perros-Guirec, 98, 100
Petite Terre, 107
Piemonte, 169, 177
Pilton, 102
Plavnik, 128
Ploubazlanec, 98, 100, 103, 105, 106, 145, 177
Pluto, 82
Poli, 50, 51
Polyfloisvios/Stanbroke, 47
Pomaron, 146
Postishev/Castillo de Olite, 174
Prada, 137, 146
Prekla/Stanleigh, 30
Principessa Giovanna, 15
Ramón Alonso Ramos, 22
Reina, 107, 108
Republic, 26
Río Miera, 169, 170
Rita Garcia, 22
Robert Ley, 177
Roche Rouge, 92
Romford/Ionia, 18, 49, 128, 130
Rona, 82

Saga, 71
Saint Prosper, 176
Sama, 107
Santurce/Widstone, 108
Sarastone, 91, 102
Sardegna, 169, 177
Sarkani, 19
Saustan, 49, 62
Schors, 131
Seabank Spray/Joyce Llewellyn, 53, 99, 139
Seabank/Kenfig Pool, 53, 100, 102, 104, 105
Sebastián Martin, 118
Sebastián/Azteca/Itxas-Alde, 81
Securitas, 158
Sergo Ordzonikidze, 44
Seven Seas Spray, 53, 91, 93, 101, 104, 109, 171
Sevilla, 7
Sheaf Spear, 31
Shetland, 137, 138
Sicilia, 15, 71
Signe, 71
Sil, 6
Silvia Tripcovich, 15
Smidovich/Castillo Penafiel, 83, 86, 174
Solitaire, 48
Soton, 82
Soussien, 19
Springwear, 20
St Louis, 38
St Quentin, 75
St Winifred/Capo Vita, 156
Stanbridge, 105, 106
Stanbroke/Polyfloisvios, 47
Stanbrook, 30, 93, 144, 154, 175, 181
Stanburgh, 160, 179
Stanbury, 155
Stancliffe/Navarinon/Lena, 31, 55, 158
Stancor, 175
Stancourt/Nephaligeretis/Hermes/Suzy/Ionanna, 140, 156, 171
Stancroft/Neoptolemos, 30, 47, 154, 163
Stangate, 174
Stangrove, 106, 107, 172
Stanholm, 20
Stanhope, 155, 162, 175
Stanleigh/Prekla, 30
Stanmore, 30, 31, 54, 105, 106

Stanmount, 145
Stanray, 106, 108
Stanwell, 138, 157, 158, 162
Stanwold, 106
Stanwood, 105, 106
Staryi Bolshevik, 44
Sud, 107
Sunion, 143, 157
Surreybrook, 100
Suzy/ Hermes/ Nephaligeretis/ Ionanna/ Melitios
Sydney, 131
Sylvia/ Silvia, 43, 82
Syryanin, 146
Tevere, 71
Theophile Gautier, 117
Theresa L. M. Russ, 176
Thorpebay, 170
Thorpehall, 20, 30, 87–90, 92, 97, 99, 106, 157
Thorpehaven, 157
Thorpeness, 139, 155, 157
Thurston, 46, 98, 155
Tiflis, 48
Timiryiazev, 46, 114, 118
Tirranna, 159
Titanic, 26
Torras Ybages, 160
Tramontana/ Arichachu, 24, 109
Trégastel, 98, 100, 101
Tripcovich, 40
Tsepo, 129
Tsurupa, 146
Tuskar Rock, 102
Ulumus, 179
Uruguay, 25, 171

Urundi, 40
Usamoro, 18
Usaramo, 35, 37
Valentín Ruiz Senén, 109
Valetta/ Arlon, 103, 135, 156
Varlaam Avanesov, 117
Venal Beny/ Jaron, 43, 164
Venezianos/ Stancourt, 30, 37, 47
Venezianos/ Stancourt, 30, 37, 47, 82, 98
Verbormilla, 30
Vicente de Roda, 154
Victoria, 165
Volgoles, 44
Waldi, 4
Widstone/ Santurce, 108
Wigbert 35
Wisconsin, 154, 181
Woodford/ Iolkos, 49, 118, 119, 121, 122
Yolande/ Jalisco, 16, 42, 81, 130, 171
Yorkbrook/ Dover Abbey, 39, 54, 84, 107, 109,
    140, 156, 171
Zorroza, 62

Other Vessels

Authorpe, 156
Belyakov, 146
Blue Shadow, 77
Chasseur 91, 136
Chkalov, 146
Citta di Milano, 7
Goizeko-Izarra/ Warrior/ Warrior II, 96, 97, 98
H. F. Bailey, 169
Hercule, 114
Margaret Rose, 158